# TANK MEN

# TANK MEN

**Robert Kershaw**

HODDER &
STOUGHTON

First published in Great Britain in 2008 by Hodder & Stoughton
An Hachette Livre UK Company

1

A CIP catalogue record for this title is available from the British Library

Hardback ISBN 978 0 340 92347 4

Typeset in Bembo by Hewer Text UK Ltd, Edinburgh

Printed and bound by Mackays of Chatham, Chatham

Hodder & Stoughton policy is to use papers that are natural, renewable and recyclable
products and made from wood grown in sustainable forests. The logging and
manufacturing processes are expected to conform to the environmental regulations of
the country of origin.

Hodder & Stoughton Ltd
338 Euston Road
London NW1 3BH

www.hodder.co.uk

To my wife Lynn and three sons Christian, Alexander & Michael

# CONTENTS

# CONTENTS

# DRAMATIS PERSONAE

## ALLIES

## British and Commonwealth

**Eric Allsop**. Lt. 8 RTR. Born 1918. Fought through the desert into Italy and discerned a growing professionalism that was impatient with previous cavalry 'donkey-walloper' philosophies. You had to be good in order to survive.

**Peter Balfour**. Lt. 3$^{rd}$ Bn Royal Scots. Charted increasing professionalism among tank men in Normandy to survive and get the war quickly finished. He disliked the SS and was seriously wounded shortly before the end of the war.

**James Carson**. Lt. Welsh Guards. He had a fond regard for his crew, who taught him everything and discovered the tank turret was a 'social leveller'. He disliked Germans, particularly the SS who executed one of his crews, and fought from Normandy through NW Europe to Germany.

**Jack Clegg**. Corporal. 1$^{st}$ Fife and Forfar Yeomanry. Jack Clegg need not have gone to the war because he had a safe appointment as a gunnery instructor in the UK. He decided to serve overseas and arrived in time for the NW Europe campaign. He was killed three months before the end of the war.

**Bill Close**. Pte to Sqn Comd. 3 RTR. Born 1914. Joined in 1933 and fought at Calais, Greece, the Desert and North Africa, Normandy and NW Europe. He was commissioned and ended the war as squadron commander. His remarkable experience encompasses the span of this book.

**Robert Crisp**. Capt. 3 RTR. A newly promoted Captain, he had played test cricket for South Africa. He served in Greece where he developed sceptical and frank views about the technical performance of British tanks. 'Strategists wanted to make a tank which was as much a horse as possible', he declared.

**Keith Douglas**. Lt. Nottinghamshire Sherwood Rangers Yeomanry. Born 1920. He was one of the finest soldier-poets to emerge from the Second World War. His book *Alamein to Zem-Zem* offered an evocative picture of the Desert War after Alamein. He was killed within days of landing after D-Day.

**Stephen Dyson**. Tpr. 107 Regt RAC. A twin, who joined a Churchill tank regiment with his brother Tom and fought through Normandy to Germany. His brother survived.

**Henry de la Falaise**. Lt. 7/12 Lancers. His experience with an armoured car rearguard typified the chaos and confusion that characterised the British withdrawal to Dunkirk along roads totally dominated by the Luftwaffe in 1940.

**AF Flatow**. Maj. 45 RTR. Squadron Commander/ Regt 2IC. The TA tank officer whose regiment suffered such casualties at Alamein that it was broken up.

**Bert Foord**. Tank Designer. Born 1912. Bert Foord's unique perspective on British tank design from his apprenticeship in the 1930s to participation in the Sherman Firefly programme exposes the UK 'cottage industry' approach to tank design during the Second World War. He likened the process to 'jogging along', in stark contrast to US mass production.

**Ian Hamilton.** Lt. 22$^{nd}$ Dragoons. Born 1922. Hamilton was a flail-tank troop commander who landed at Normandy and fought his way through NW Europe into Germany. He lost his last tank crew two days before the end of the war.

**Stuart Hamilton.** Mr. 8 RTR. Fought the Desert and Italian campaigns and vividly described the stages of deterioration leading to combat fatigue.

**Patrick Hennessey.** Cpl. 13/18 Royal Hussars. Trooper in the first swimming Duplex Drive (DD) tanks to land on D-Day and subsequently fought through NW Europe with Shermans to Germany.

**Stuart Hills.** Lt. Nottinghamshire Sherwood Rangers Yeomanry. Born 1924. Ex-Tonbridge schoolboy and friend of Keith Douglas, who landed at D-Day with DD tanks and was one of the few troop commanders to survive a war in which thirty-fiveof their officers were killed.

**Cyril Joly.** Lt-Maj. 3 RTR. Sqn 2IC and later Bde Major. Arrived in Egypt in 1940 and later wrote an impressive literary account of his experiences.

**David Ling.** Capt/Maj. 44 RTR. Squadron Commander. Born 1915. He joined with an engineering background having served an apprenticeship with Rover cars before the war. His brother serving in the RAF was killed on Christmas Eve 1940. He was discharged with a full disability pension in 1943 and joined a Benedictine Monastery in 1964.

**John Mallard.** Lt-Capt. 44 RTR. Born 1918. A pre-war TA officer who served throughout the Desert campaign and witnessed first-hand the painful blending process of TA to regular army.

**Bernard Montgomery.** Gen later Field Marshal. Commander of the Eighth Army after August 1942 and architect of the decisive Desert victory at El Alamein in November 1942. His complacent belief that the Sherman 75mm 'would suffice' after their introduction condemned British tank men to confronting superior panzers in Normandy and NW Europe with inferior tanks.

**Richard O'Connor**. Lt Gen. Commanded the Western Desert Force during Wavell's victorious desert offensive in 1940. He was captured by Rommel's forces early in 1941.

**Bert Rendell**. Sgt. 1 RTR. Born 1912. He was an old regular who joined in 1934 and was in Egypt when the war broke out. Frank and direct, he was an effective soldier and born survivor.

**Peter Roach**. Radio Operator. 1 RTR. Born 1913. He spent two years with the merchant navy before joining the army and was old enough to develop an irreverent attitude towards military life. 'As civilians we took from the army what we needed and ignored the bull', he said.

**Paul Rollins**. Tpr. 40 RTR. Born 1919. He joined in 1938 and fought the Desert campaign and Italy. He had a low opinion of US performance at Kasserine.

**Jack Rollinson**. Tank driver. 3 RTR. Born 1918. He had been a pony driver in the local pit at Worksop Nottinghamshire and graduated to driving cranes. He escaped the dole queue when he was called up in 1940 and fought at Calais. He suspected the army had a low opinion of drivers.

**Michael Trasenster**. Lt. 4/7 RDG. Born 1923. Landed on D-Day with DD Tanks and was one of the few original tank commanders in Normandy to complete the NW Europe campaign and finish the war in Germany. He was able to identify the steady deterioration leading to combat fatigue. He realised Sherman inadequacies could be overcome if wit and cunning were employed.

**Peter Vaux**. Lt. 4 RTR and staff officer (Int), fought at Arras in 1940 and was badly wounded in the desert.

**Jake Wardrop**. 5 RTR. Born 1918. Very much a 'soldier's soldier' he was keen on outdoor pursuits, scouting and swimming with a love of all things mechanical. His father was an engineer. He joined in 1937 and see-sawed from trooper to sergeant and back again. He was highly respected as a motivated and professional soldier. He was killed in action during the last days of the war.

**Peter Watson.** Cpl. 2 RTR. Born 1918. Joined in 1939 starting as a driver/operator and graduated to tank commander. He served in France 1940, then Egypt 1941 and later the Far East. He was slightly sceptical about officers. After the war he worked in local government.

**Archibald Wavell..** General. CinC Middle East at Cairo during the victorious offensive against the Italian Army in 1940, commanded the less successful *Brevity* and *Battleaxe* until relieved of his desert command and sent to India.

**Andrew Wilson**. Lt. 141 Regt RAC. Churchill 'Crocodile' flame-thrower troop commander, who could not understand why the Germans would execute flame-thrower crew POWs in Normandy. He fought through NW Europe to Germany.

**Alan Wollaston**. Sgt/Sgt Maj. 3 RTR. Born 1917. Wollaston came from a long line of serving regular soldiers and virtually all the male members of his family were in the army. He experienced two evacuations prior to arrival in the Western Desert, at Dunkirk and Greece.

## American

**Belton Cooper**. Capt Ordinance Officer 3$^{rd}$ US Armoured Div. Cooper experienced at first-hand the inability of Sherman crews to confront heavier German panzers in Normandy and Germany. His tank recovery experience was an audit of the human and technical consequences of the Allied decision to pit mass production of inferior tank types against superior German quality.

**J. Ted Hartman**. Tank driver 11<sup>th</sup> US Armoured Division. He arrived in Europe as a 'rookie' tank driver in time for the Battle of the Bulge and fought his way through to Germany rising eventually to tank commander.

## Russian

**Vladimir Alexeev**. Lt. T–34 tank commander 5<sup>th</sup> Guards Tank Army. Fought in the battles around Stalingrad and Kursk and participated in the final assault on Germany. He was a committed Communist Party member, who sustained himself by his philosophy 'you only live once'.

**Anatoly Kozlov**. Lt. 5<sup>th</sup> Guards Tank Army. Born 1922. Fought in the Stalingrad battles and Kursk and was part of the drive into Germany. He appreciated the extent to which fear of Commissars influenced tank crew bonding at the front and the decisive impact of Lend–Lease vehicles on Soviet tank army mobility.

### AXIS POWERS

## German

**Ludwig Bauer**. Lt. Pz Regt 33. Born 1920. He served in the same regiment during a remarkable span stretching from the invasion of Russia to Kursk, through Normandy and NW Europe to Germany. He used up his proverbial nine lives by being knocked out nine times, losing friends each time, the last friendly fire, ironically. He was badly burned and awarded the Knight's Cross.

**Hans Becker**. Feldwebel.12<sup>th</sup> Pz Div. Exchanged his chauffeur's uniform for black panzer prior to the occupation of Czechoslovakia. He fought in Poland and was captured in Russia.

**Winrich Behr**. Aufkl Abt 3. Armd Recce. A confident panzer commander who claimed 'English tanks were no good against our panzers'.

**Otto Carius.** Lt. Pz Abt 502. Born 1922. He progressed from being a Czech 38t crewman to a Tiger company commander and Jagdtiger unit, serving in Russia and NW Europe. Highly experienced and a Knight's Cross holder, he had a low opinion of American tank capability and was bitter at losing the war.

**Karl Drescher.** NCO. Aufkl Abt 116. Experienced the cynicism that afflicted the panzer troops vainly trying to stem the Allied advance while all around civilians were insistent on surrender.

**Hermann Eckardt.** Feldwebel. Pz Regt 8. Born 1920. A remarkable experience, he fought the entire Desert campaign with the Afrika Korps, escaped Tunis in 1943 and served the remainder of the war in a Stürmgeshutz (SP) battalion during fighting withdrawals from Russia through Poland to Germany. He was awarded the Knight's Cross and was wounded defending the last river obstacle before Berlin.

**Karl Fuchs.** Feldwebel. 7$^{th}$ Pz Div. Born 1917. His unique trooper's experience as Schütze (tank gunner) to Feldwebel (Sergeant) commander of a light Czech 38t tank is typical of the idealistic fervour of the early days of the Panzerwaffe. He was killed outside Moscow in 1941 before the disillusionment of defeat.

**Heinz Guderian.** General. Panzer Army Commander and Inspector General Panzer Troops. Born 1888. Guderian was the 'father' of the panzer arm and proved his capabilities as a Corps and Army commander during the French and Russian Blitzkriegs of 1941–2. He was dismissed after the first Soviet winter counter-offensive but reinstated as Inspector-General Armoured Troops in 1943.

**Kurt Hoehne.** Lt. Dr. Luftwaffe 88mm Flak Comd. Studied tropical medicine at Tübingen University, achieving a doctorate, and was then drafted into the Luftwaffe. He volunteered for the paratroopers and exchanged his place as an Afrika Korps doctor to be an 88mm Flak gun commander.

**Hans von Luck**. Lt – Oberst. 7th and 21$^{st}$ Pz Div. Born 1911. He came from a Prussian military family but disliked 'drilling'. He was disappointed to be sent to a motorised unit on joining, preferring cavalry, but enjoyed fast cars. His view of the British was that 'we understood each other'. He had fought in Poland, France and Russia, and found his initial euphoria tempered by sober judgement. By Normandy he was acutely aware of the scale of Allied material superiority.

**Kurt Meyer**. Tpr - Oberführer. 1$^{st}$ SS and 12$^{th}$ SS Panzer Division. A committed Nazi who fought in Poland, France, Russia and Normandy, eventually appointed commander of the Hitlerjugend Division in Normandy. He was indicted for war crimes following the Malmedy massacre during the battle of the Bulge.

**Erwin Rommel** Lt Gen. later Feldmarschal. Appointed Commander of the Afrika Korps after distinguishing himself as Commander of the 7$^{th}$ Panzer Division, one of the first units to reach the French Channel Coast during the 1940 Blitzkrieg.

**Joachim Schorm**. Lt. Pz Regt 5. A panzer company commander who was shut up in action inside his panzer for twenty-four hours.

**Wilhelm Wessel**. Lt. War artist. Produced a book of fascinating watercolours portraying everyday life in the Afrika Korps.

## Italian

**Coglitore** Lt. 12$^{th}$ Italian Bersaglieri, witnessed 'how much the human body can be mutilated' in action.

**Paolo Colacicchi**. Italian 10$^{th}$ Army, experienced Wavell's first desert offensive.

# INTRODUCTION

IRAQI DESERT 28 FEB 1991

My first view of an exploding tank stunned me. It was February 1991 – the first Gulf War.

The battlefield belonged to us, and as I had read in many Second World War accounts, we systematically 'cracked' open the abandoned Iraqi tanks to make them totally unusable. The flash and smoke of the explosion, then the reverberating 'crump', preceded the pressure wave. A turret flipped forward from the hull to stand momentarily on end, its protruding gun barrel holding it up like a giant pogo stick before toppling over. Flames roared skyward eighty feet as if from an inverted rocket launcher. A moment later the upturned turret also ignited to whoosh and splutter as propellant from shells stacked inside spewed fire. Howling projectiles flew in all directions and the air above and around was full of careering, whistling scrap metal. We were pinned down for twenty minutes.

This was war in the desert. I had read about it during my tedious years of service in Germany, but never believed I would be experiencing this.

Throughout the first Gulf War I kept an operational diary. It was a real discipline, illuminating subsequent historical research. I recognised the ring of truth reading other people's diaries. My experiences were nothing like those described by the soldier poet Keith Douglas in *Alamein to Zem Zem,* when every day might conceivably have been his last. It was never like that in the Gulf in 1991, but from then on I found I could recognise snippets of authenticity in first-hand accounts, diaries and interviews that I read from other campaigns.

With its stunning contrasts of colour and mood there is a perception that the vast remote desert in some way nullifies the impact of war. As one Second World War Italian veteran soldier observed, there are no homes and few civilian bystanders in the way. Yet the veneer of civilisation remains perilously thin. American engineer tanks ahead of us bulldozed Iraqi anti-tank gunners beneath their trenches when they continued firing, which was reported as over-reactive distasteful behaviour to the twenty-four-hour TV watchers back home. Likewise a British tank commander was admonished by his indignant crew in 1941 when he ordered reverse tracks collapse trenches on Afrika Korps anti-tank gunners. Having experienced the visceral horror of an anti-tank strike, he took no chances.

Firing at tank crews bailing out of crippled tanks occurred haphazardly during the Gulf War. Overwhelming range superiority conferred a realisation that hammering on turrets with machine-gun fire – like rapping on a door – provided sufficient invitation for the hopelessly outclassed Iraqi tank crews to vacate before the killer round arrived. But not all hard-pressed tank crews can afford to be chivalrous in fast-moving engagements. In the North African campaign British and panzer crews routinely machine-gunned survivors when it was a risk to allow technically competent adversaries to fight another day. Anything that prolonged conflict delayed going home. Civilised behaviour can swiftly be corrupted. As one desert commander put it to us in the Gulf War, there is a fine dividing line between innocently removing articles of military value such as binoculars from the fallen, and robbing the dead.

The spectacle of war is often mentioned in this book. Panoramic desert scenery with the dust of massive armoured columns on the move reducing the sun to the dust of an indistinct moon, produces indelible images. Smouldering black tank hulks, oxidised as though they had been there for hundreds of years rather than hours, looked like Second World War desert battlefield photographs. Huge columns of smoke contrasted sharply with the royal-blue skies and produced a cinematic vista, marred only by tangled wreckage and pitiful bodies sprawled in the way.

It is exceptionally difficult to recreate the stench of war but most veteran accounts allude to it at some stage. The smell is physical in its pungency and promotes a feeling of corruption that ultimately depresses. Sixty years after landing at D-Day my father confided that he still felt nausea at the smell of diesel – it had been floating amid bodies washing up on the beach. Since the Gulf War I have had a problem with the aroma of spoilt meat, an obnoxious cloying odour that I never seemed to wash out of my desert uniforms.

By 28 February 1991 we were 200 miles into Iraq, perched on the edge of a smoking pocket of wrecked Iraqi armour. After four intense days the sky was a subdued grey with a grease-stained mist at ground level. There was relief in that one could measure the future. I flew in a helicopter with Lieutenant General Franks, the commander of the VII US Corps, on a peremptory end-of-war reconnaissance, and we touched down amid a group of Abrams tanks in the dirty dun-coloured desert. The sky, stained by the smoke from burning oil wells, was an unearthly orange, Martian hue.

An experienced tank man, the General walked over to speak with the crews. They were covered in carbon smut from their chemical suits, which were starting to come apart in the heat. Faces were grimy from turret combat, accentuating white wrinkle lines and crows' feet around the eyes. The General was strangely affected by his talk with the tank men. He had visibly aged during the past four days of directing combat, striving to preserve life while smashing Iraqi armour. My diary reminded me of the incident: '. . . chat with the tank crewmen made the General somewhat emotional'. The whole scene had a poignancy to it, neatly framed with black smoke languidly rising from a burning vehicle in the background.

Tank crews are not unlike aircrews in that both roles have to do with the impact of machines on human beings. However, within minutes aircrew rotate from deckchair to mind-numbing combat, then return to sleep in their beds. Tank men live with physical privation and the mental stress of pending combat. Technology has a vital role, as does the survival prospects of both, in speed of reaction and crew cohesion. The people in this book endured an enclosed, suffocating, noisy metal box, fearful of being struck and burned alive by an enemy they could not see. Dominated by mechanical considerations, their earthy environment set these soldiers apart from the rest.

They are the Tank Men.

# 1

## GENESIS

### 'MOTHER' TANK

In the middle of September 1916 the Western Front on the Somme exuded menace. Beneath the smoke and dust that hovered by day and the crackling cacophony of sounds and flashes at night, there existed a devastated landscape that opposing armies were unable to cross. On the British Army's blackest day here 57,470 men perished. Thirty-two of its 129 fighting battalions lost more than 500 men each. The Somme encapsulated the stalemate of two lost years. Casualties rose to 90,000 at the end of the first month and reached 1.2 million by November. Soldiers gathering in the assembly areas prior to the next flurry of activity instinctively appreciated that they would not live long.

Two months after the start of the battle the weather remained very warm. One soldier recalled being in the wagon lines of the logistic and assembly area before going up the line. There were 'quite a few of us', he remembered, and 'somebody came along and said, "The war's finished." "Oh?" was the response. "Just go down about half a mile and look in the field there and you'll see." He wouldn't tell us why. Anyway we went down and there was quite a crowd there and there were tanks, things we had never seen or heard of.'

They were viewing a metal monolith that defied description. Infantryman Ernest Ford, aged twenty, saw what looked like 'armour-plated cars with caterpillar tracks, "Tanks", as we later discovered.' Robbie Burns, a 7th Cameron Highlander enduring shell fire in his trench, 'heard this brrrr' and thought, 'What on earth is that noise? It got louder and louder.' He and his men clambered up on to the parapet, as did the Germans opposite, and watched it go by with five or six soldiers crowded behind, sheltering with fixed bayonets. 'We didn't

5

know what they were for, perhaps for taking down barbed wire, we thought.' Twenty-year-old Norman Dillon's battalion of the 14th Northumberland Fusiliers was awaiting the call forward to attack the village of Flers. 'It was a stinking night,' he recalled, with shell fire including gas whooshing overhead, when, in front of him and his sergeant, 'a queer object crawled over the mud and there it was. The first tank in action.'

H.G. Wells had written a science-fiction account about *The Land Ironclads* which appeared in the *Strand* magazine in England in 1903. *The Time Machine* in 1895 and *The Invisible Man* in 1897 had already established him as the master of the science-fiction genre. He described fighting machines 80–100 feet long with portholes through which semi-automatic rifles were fired. There were no big guns or machine-guns, and despite the invention of the spark ignition engine by Gottlieb Daimler in 1885, Wells's ten-foot-diameter wheels protected by a steel skirt were driven by steam. These lozenge-shaped metal fighting boxes that now trundled across trenches on the Western Front had tracks revolving around a hull with skeletal anti-grenade cages festooned on top. Revolving turrets affixed to sponsons on its flanks made them look like land battleships. Bert Chaney, of the 7th London Territorial Battalion, called them 'mechanical monsters such as we had never seen before'. 'Big Willie' had evolved from a drawing-board concept to standing in the foundry yard inside ten weeks. It was now in action at Flers on 15 September 1916.

Tank driver Archie Richards's description of this action was more surreal than Wells's earlier fictional account. 'It was a hot September that year, and the stink – oh – the smell was terrible, terrible,' he recalled when interviewed in the 1990s. 'Arms and legs were sticking out of the trenches, and rotting bodies.' They had been obliged to cover ground strewn with the long-dead corpses of troops from failed Canadian, Australian and Colonial attacks, the grisly signature of deadlocked tactics. 'We had to go over the old trenches, and bodies and everything else.' The tanks' tracks ploughed up the stench which even permeated the suffocating reek of hot oil and burned cordite in the crew compartment. 'I expected war to be dreadful, but I was seeing it in the raw,' he observed.

The Germans had no idea what was happening. Leutnant Otto

Schulz's company of Westphalian infantry was billeted in a school near the village of Marval on the day of the attack. 'We had heard rumours about a new Allied weapon, and our intelligence had sent us notes about a vehicle which they believed was being built in certain French factories.' Schulz, a tall, spare and correct officer, fastidious about his appearance, chose not to share this knowledge with the ordinary soldiers. In hierarchical and class-divided European armies in the early twentieth century such detail was not readily discussed. The company was alerted and sent towards Flers to contain the emerging tense situation. 'But when we saw the first real tank it was like nothing we had ever imagined,' he remarked.

'Big metal things they were, with two sets of caterpillar wheels that went right round the body' was Bert Chaney's description of them. They appeared to be a two-edged sword. Three tanks were advancing through the 7th London TA Battalion's positions. They had straddled the British trenches, 'crushing the sides of our own trench out of shape with their machine-guns swivelling around and firing like mad.' Their commanding officer furiously rained blows on the side of one of them with his staff cane, trying to get them to stop. Nobody knew what they were, except that they were British. 'There was a bulge on each side with the door in the bulging part,' observed Chaney, 'and machine-guns on swivels poked out from either side.' The roar of the engines and exhaust smoke belching out of the top made it resemble a beached whale. So far as Chaney could see 'a petrol engine of massive proportions occupied practically all the inside space'. It advanced, 'frightening the Jerries out of their wits and making them scuttle like frightened rabbits', Chaney remembered.

Leutnant Otto Schulz's first view of his surreal assailants was of a single tank perched helpless in the open. Observation through binoculars revealed a track torn off by shell fire. Two of his platoons of Westphalian infantry were ordered forward to approach and grenade the thing, but constant and accurate machine-gun fire kept them beyond throwing range.

One German machine-gunner flailing the metal boxes with metallic drumfire said, 'We got nothing from the tanks but sparks.' This was disconcerting, as hitherto the machine-gun had been the queen of no man's land. Some of the tanks were by this time grotesquely festooned with shrouds of ripped up barbed wire, normally impervious to artillery fire, adding to their awe-inspiring appearance. They appeared to tear it up with abandon, a task previously resolved at considerable expense in preparatory effort and lives. 'One stared as if one had lost the power of one's limbs,' a Bavarian prisoner of war was recorded saying. 'The big monsters approached us slowly, hobbling, rolling, rocking but always advancing.' Otto Schulz, having appreciated how totally ineffective his infantry were against these machines, heard there had been a breakthrough at Flers. 'Someone shouted, "The Devil is coming!"' said the Bavarian prisoner of war, 'and the word passed along the line.'

'Panic spread like an electric current,' reported another German infantryman, describing his first encounter with a tank, 'passing from man to man along the trench.' Some fought while others fled. 'As the churning tracks reared overhead, the bravest men clambered above ground to launch suicidal counter-attacks, hurling grenades on to the tanks' roofs or shooting and stabbing at any vision slits within reach.' Like Schulz's futile infantry attacks, 'they were shot down or crushed, while others threw up their hands in terrified surrender or bolted down the communication trenches towards the second line.'

Drivers had understandable inhibitions about running over dead bodies. Second Lieutenant Vic Huffam's tank *Dolly* actually drove down the main street of Flers, which was reduced to an 'absolute shambles'. The road 'was just a mass of bodies and brickwork'. They stopped the tank occasionally and Huffam tried to clear a way through the corpses, but was frequently driven back inside by the intensity of artillery fire. Eventually, he admitted, 'I had to give up', and he told his driver Archer to get on with it. 'He was pretty sickened when I gave the order to advance over these bodies, but there was not much else we could do.' Eighty years after the event Archie Richards, who was driving another tank, admitted: 'You couldn't pick your way through. If they fell in your way, you had to go over them. We never deviated the tanks for anything except targets.'

Onlookers viewing the machines for the first time thought they were invincible. No fighting machine until now had ever demonstrated sufficient mobility to cross no-man's-land, engage the enemy on its terms while offering the crew protection against machine-gun bullets and the worst effects of artillery fire. Fifty tanks participated in the battle of Flers-Courcelette on 15 September 1916, but their effectiveness balance sheet was mixed. Only thirty-two reached the start line, of which thirty got moving. Nine pushed ahead of the infantry and caused considerable loss to the enemy; nine fell behind but did good work clearing up. During the day five were ditched and nine broke down because of mechanical problems. Just twenty or barely 40 per cent of the force actually closed with the enemy and engaged in combat.

What the figures fail to convey is the enormous emotional and moral impact of a weapon system that appeared able to overcome the impasse of no-man's-land. Allied press headlines trumpeted the event, proclaiming 'diplodocus triumphant!', a great 'jabberwock with eyes of flame' and 'land Dreadnoughts' had inflicted crushing blows on the enemy. Few adjectives gave justice to the bizarre event. One correspondent articulating the swampy wasteland of the Western Front wrote about 'blind creatures emerging from the primeval slime'. Archie Richards stopped his tank astride a German trench with guns laid on each side. 'They had never seen anything like the tank before,' he recalled, 'and when they saw we were armed with small guns and machine-guns, they gave up straight away.' Some of the German machine-gunners could be seen silhouetted against the sky with guns on their shoulders, 'going like hell back to their lines'.

Infantrymen on both sides regarded the new machines with awed bewilderment. What were they? Bert Chaney watched with the 7th London TA Battalion as four men emerged from one of the machines marooned on a tree stump. With the battle raging around they got out, 'stretching themselves, scratching their heads, then slowly and deliberately walked around their vehicle inspecting it from every angle and appeared to hold a conference among themselves.' They exuded an air of clinical detachment, totally alien to infantrymen immersed in the physical squalor of trench life. The new type of soldiers, tank men, then demonstrated an ingrained habit they could all identify with. 'After standing around for a few minutes, looking somewhat lost, they calmly took out from the inside of the tank a primus stove and, using the side of the tank as a cover from enemy fire, sat down on the ground and made themselves some tea.' They were human after all. But what manner of men were they? Where did they come from? Bert Chaney could see that 'the battle was over as far as they were concerned.'

The genesis of these machines was the stalemate that had existed on the Western Front since the first battle of Ypres in 1914. German advances were stopped but Allied advances stalled also. Miles of opposing trenches, festooned with barbed-wire barricades and dominated by machine-guns and artillery, stretched from Nieuport on the Belgian coast to Switzerland. Horrific casualties demonstrated the total superiority of defence over offence. A Royal Engineer officer, Lieutenant-Colonel Ernest Swinton, submitted a paper to General Headquarters (GHQ) on 1 June 1915 advocating the employment of 'Armoured Machine Gun Destroyers to overcome the impasse'. These would utilise 'petrol tractors on the caterpillar principle', and be 'armoured with hardened steel plates proof against German steel-cored, armour-piercing and reversed bullets, and armed with – say – two Maxims and a 2-pounder gun'. The intent was to directly engage opposing enemy machine-guns on advantageous terms. Present technology could partly achieve some of the stated remit.

The spark ignition engine had developed to the extent that more than 100 horsepower (hp) was achievable within a relatively compact power plant. Caterpillar tracks were already being used commercially, notably by the Holt's firm in the USA which was producing agricultural tractors. A version mounted on caterpillar tracks was already employed in France by the Royal Artillery as a heavy gun tractor. Armoured cars were used by both sides but were unsuited to the muddy trench conditions on the Western Front. A convincing working model with agreed specifications was now needed to move forward. Lieutenant-Colonel Maurice Hankey, the influential Secretary to the Committee of Imperial Defence, shared Swinton's speculative view that the trench stalemate might be overcome by the possible military use of Holt's caterpillar tractor. They submitted a joint paper to the War Office on Boxing Day 1914, which elicited a short cryptic note. 'If the writer of this paper would descend from the realms of fancy to the region of hard fact,' it stated, 'a great deal of valuable time and labour would be saved.'

However, the paper came to the attention of Winston Churchill, the First Sea Lord at the Admiralty, who saw the merit of Swinton's ideas, and diverted necessary funds to pay for the development. A Landships Committee was formed.

By June 1915 a specification emerged for a machine armed with two machine-guns and a quick-firing light gun, crewed by ten men, capable of crossing broken country and barbed wire. A top speed of not less than four miles per hour on flat ground with a sharp turn and reverse capability was needed. The machine had to climb five-foot earth parapets and traverse eight-foot gaps. In short, it had to negotiate trenches under fire and operate out to a radius of twenty miles. William Foster's of Lincoln was awarded the development contract on 24 July.

Component parts were identified and gathered. Power was provided by an existing Daimler 105hp engine, barely sufficient to propel the mass of armour required but already in production. Armour plate and machine-guns were available, and the Navy offered sufficient 6-pounder guns and ammunition to cover the light-gun requirement. Two conundrums remained: the shape of the metal box to house the components and where to find a caterpillar track able to support the emerging weight and endure the wear and tear the 'Landships' would subject them to.

Within three weeks of receiving the development order work on a prototype began and a tracked metal box called *Little Willie* was produced. Mechanical genius Major Walter Wilson solved *Little Willie*'s problems: insufficient track, top-heaviness and minimal ground clearance.

Ernest Swinton, after viewing a full size mock-up of the practical manifestation of Wilson's sketch, wrote:

> Although an engineer it took me some minutes to size the thing up at close range. Its most striking features were its curious rhomboidal, or lozenge, shape, its upturned nose, and the fact that its caterpillar tracks were led right around the hull, instead of being entirely below it . . . I felt that I saw in front of me – though only in wood – the actual embodiment of my ideas and the fulfilment of my expectation.

The long tracks meant that the unwieldy-looking vehicle would be able to climb and span broad trenches. Its height meant the abandonment of any idea of a rotating turret. Instead guns would be mounted in 'sponsons', or turrets, welded on to the sides of the hull. Even the incipient track weakness was overcome by the production of new lightweight pressed-steel plate. This mock-up, *Mother,* would become *Big Willie,* a viable fighting vehicle. *Mother* ran for the first time on 16 January 1916.

So secret was this project that Tritton's workers were not awarded the War Badges proving they were engaged in work of national importance, leading to some being sent 'white feathers', a symbol of cowardice issued by over-zealous patriotic women. A practical demonstration was arranged under conditions of great secrecy at the Duke of Salisbury's estate at Hatfield Park on 2 February. Of the vehicle's name, Swinton later wrote: 'We rejected in turn – container – receptacle – reservoir – cistern. The monosyllable Tank appealed to us as being likely to catch on and be remembered.'

Those attending the trial included Kitchener, the Secretary of State for War, Lloyd George, the Minister for Munitions, and Reginald McKenna, the Chancellor of the Exchequer – the men in power who would influence the finance, production and manning for the new weapon system.

Dense clouds of exhaust smoke belched from *Big Willie* as four of the crew swung the huge handle to start the Daimler engine. Lloyd George subsequently wrote: 'I can recall the feeling of delighted amazement with which I saw for the first time the ungainly monster plough through thick entanglements, wallow through deep mud and heave its huge bulk over parapets and across trenches. At last, I thought, we have the answer to the German machine-guns and wire.'

Swinton was writing the foundations for tactical doctrine within weeks. Despite some reservations the 'Tank' was to be in action eight months later on the Somme. An initial order was placed for forty machines and then 100. Crews to man these secret machines had now to be recruited and trained.

Just before the outbreak of war Victor Huffam, a young British engineer, had come home on six months' leave from Australia. His 'devil may care' temperament inspired him to volunteer as soon as war was declared, and he joined the Norfolk Regiment as an officer. He recalled that early in 1916 he was shown a 'Strictly Secret and Confidential' War Office Order which read:

Volunteers are required for an exceedingly dangerous and hazardous duty of a secret nature. Officers who have been awarded decorations for bravery, and are experienced in the handling of men, and with an engineering background, should have their names submitted to this office.

Huffam wasted no time applying. Recruits had to be technically minded but could not for reasons of secrecy be told why. In company with 300 other like-minded lieutenants and volunteers from units all over the British Isles, Huffam attended a meeting at Wellington Barracks in London. They were addressed by Swinton, 'who warned us that we had volunteered for a very dangerous mission and said if any man had any doubts he was to step back one pace'. Nobody moved. In May Huffam reported to Bisley and was issued with a crossed-machine-guns badge 'and found myself a Lieutenant in the Heavy Section of the Machine Gun Corps (HSMGC). This provided no clue whatsoever as to our real unit!'

New recruits were chosen from a limited pool of manpower with motoring or technical backgrounds. In England in the early twentieth century motor cars were still the preserve of the sporting and wealthy. Edward Wakefield remembered 'the War Office advertised that they were forming a special branch of the fighting service to be known as the Motor Machine Gun Corps. I liked the word "motor" because I had a motor cycle.'

Siberia Farm near Bisley Camp was chosen as the birthplace of the Tank detachment in February 1916 because it lay alongside the depot and training school of the Motor Machine Gun Service, which offered a ready-made and partly trained nucleus of officers and men with some form of motor experience. Even the motor trade was called upon to assist. Mr Geoffrey Smith, the editor of *The Motor Cycle* periodical, attracted many well-qualified tradesmen. Yet, as Edward Wakefield recalled, their knowledge of soldiering was zero. 'The sergeants – all regulars – had got to turn us from being a civilian into a wartime soldier, and it was difficult.' Haig, the Western Front GOC, wanted to include tanks in the forthcoming Somme offensive. 'And the time was not in their favour,' Wakefield remembered. 'They wanted us in France where the war was.'

Still secrecy prevailed. Vic Huffam thought 'the veil was soon lifted a little when we saw stuck on a sandy ridge, a sponson with machine-guns'. This was the turret-like container fixed to the side of the tanks. 'All officers and some 300 men underwent a machine-gun course,' he remembered, 'but no one was shown a tank.'

In June 1916 the Heavy Section moved to Lord Iveagh's estate at Elveden, near Thetford. After Huffam and the others had marched the seven miles from the rail station to Canada Farm Camp, they 'were surprised to see soldiers from the Hampshire Regiment, cavalry and Indian units stationed on the perimeter surrounding the farmhouse and buildings'. They had been incarcerated. Inside there was a railway siding where for the first time they were introduced to *Little Mother*. 'Our first tank – a real tank to train on, and a reminder,' Huffam thought, 'of what "hazardous duty" could mean.' Significantly the inhabitants had been moved out of the area.

The first tank men were thrown into battle at Flers-Courcelette within three months of arriving at Canada Farm. Doctrine was rudimentary because fighting machines were unprecedented. Swinton was not considering anything beyond the simple concept of punching a hole in the German lines to assist the infantry. Penetration ought to be achievable up to the opposing artillery zone, but nobody was looking at exploitation beyond – that was the cavalry's business. Crews made do with skimpy knowledge. 'I and my crew,' wrote one tank commander, 'did not have a tank of our own the whole time we were in England. Ours went wrong the day it arrived.' He catalogued a series of shortfalls he and his men had to overcome. 'We had no reconnaissance or map reading . . . no practices or lectures on the compass . . . we had no signalling . . . and no practice in considering orders.' The 30-ton machines were grossly under-powered and unsophisticated, breaking down frequently as drivers – tense with anxiety – made errors. On the way to the front the crews found themselves pressured by outlandish security measures and called upon to give wasteful and mechanically wearing demonstrations to curious commanders. Like most soldiers in warfare, they were exhausted before they even reached the start line. As they passed through the wagon lines behind the Somme the fatigued infantry, thinned by losses and tempered by cynicism, viewed them certainly with bewilderment, but also hope.

Despite the mixed results of their first employment the public at home was thrilled. Moving-picture shows were crammed with crowds seeking to see the first 'Tanks' movie film. For the same reason that spellbound satellite-TV audiences watched minute-by-minute reports of precision-guided-missile strikes during the first Gulf War in the 1990s, people in 1916 were fascinated by the new technology of war. This sense of wonderment encouraged recruits to join tank units. 'They certainly impressed me,' declared Sam Lytle, who had joined the Liverpool Scottish infantry in 1914 and viewed them at Flers. 'Of course, I was only a lad at the time' – he had lied about his age on enlistment – 'but to see those damned great things, snorting and rolling their way through the mud, machine-guns sticking out everywhere and all firing at once – no wonder Jerry ran! I'd have run if they'd been on the other side.' He volunteered to transfer in early 1917.

General Sir Douglas Haig demanded 1,000 new tanks and in the set up on 8 October 1916 a new Tank Corps HQ to develop tanks in France. Heading the new Corps was Brigadier Hugh Elles, aided by his new chief staff officer Major J.F.C. Fuller, a sceptical and intelligent infantryman. Fuller set about collecting, synthesising and disseminating every scrap of information about tanks and how best to employ them. During the winter of 1917 tactical notes were published and technical direction was issued to crews and the newly founded workshop organisation.

Despite all the enthusiasm, tanks were employed piecemeal and unimaginatively over the wrong ground at the battles of Arras, Bullecourt, Messines and Passchendaele. 'It was unfortunate that the decision to send the tanks rested with officers in high places,' complained Sergeant J.C. Allnatt, a tank driver at Messiness in the Ypres salient. 'If these officers had been to see the salient, and if they had had the brains of a child, they surely would never have committed the tank crews to practically certain death. Every member of the Tank Corps, even those of the lowest rank, knew that they should not be there.'

The Mark I *Mother* prototype, with its 'female' machine-gun version designed to protect the 'male' 6-pounder variant, was rapidly upgraded to a Mark IV. By April 1917 these were arriving in considerable numbers at the front. Although underpowered by the same 105hp engine, its frontal armour was increased from 10mm to 12mm, rendering it impervious to German armour-piercing bullets. A previous German official report had read, 'comparatively easy prey for the artillery, who detailed special guns to deal with it'. They had not yet, however, faced a massed tank attack.

This occurred at dawn on 20 November 1917, when the full strength of the British Tank Corps, 476 tanks, drove at the Hindenburg Line along a six-mile front at Cambrai under cover of a surprise artillery bombardment by 1,003 guns. Waves of tanks emerging spectre-like from the mist and smoke of that November morning terrified the leading German formations. 'Without exaggeration,' wrote a German officer viewing the ensuing flight, 'some of the infantry seemed to be off their heads with fright.' Special barbed-wire grapnel tanks were in front, clearing the way for the second wave. Progress was amazingly rapid for officers and men used to measuring progress in yards. A huge breach almost six miles wide and up to 4,000 yards deep was torn in the line. It cost 4,000 British casualties, but over 4,200 German prisoners were taken with 100 guns. 'An advance of over five miles in one day! Not bad, you know,' declared Private Alan Bacon, 'considering that a similar penetration at the Third Battle of Ypres took three *months* to accomplish and cost tens of thousands of lives.' Ten days later a short sharp gas-and-smoke bombardment heralded a German in- fantry counter-attack employing the new *Sturm,* or storm, tactics and restored the line. Fifty British tanks were marooned on the wrong side of the line, providing the Germans with a free nucleus of tank equipments, if they chose to use them.

## THE VIEW THROUGH THE CHAIN-MAIL MASK

Close confinement of officers and men within tanks, like the effect of stunning casualties on infantry battalions, was beginning to erode the traditional class divide between officers and other ranks. 'I think it's true to say we were a band of brothers – real enthusiasts,' stated Captain Donald Richardson, the commander of *Fray Bentos* with F Battalion. The Tank Corps was a new and distinctive arm that would develop its own unique characteristics. 'The old infantry view about talking shop in the mess just went overboard in the Tank Corps of those days,' Richardson recalled. 'We sat around until all hours at night talking about carburettors and magnetos, 6-pounders and the relative merits of the Hotchkiss and Lewis machine-guns.'

Tank crewmen were distinguishable by their unorthodox clothing. Most were issued with the upturned soup-plate helmet, but it was painted light blue and they wore a leather jerkin over their uniform. Faces were partially veiled by chain-mail, not dissimilar in appearance to an African witch-doctor mask, or 'crusader chain-mail masks' according to Private Eric Potten. Alfred Simpson, serving with the heavy section of the Machine Gun Corps, described it as 'made of dark leather and shaped to the contours of the upper half of the human face. There are two slits for the eyes and a curtain of chain-mail hangs down from the nose line.' Its function was to shield the face against the 'flaking' effect of tiny metal splinters that violently spun off the inner hull when it was struck by bullets on the outer armour. These inflicted small but uncomfortable and infection-prone wounds to exposed flesh. Simpson and other crew members viewed each other through these grotesque and restrictive veils, which echoed the confined conditions inside the tanks.

The Mark I measured 31 feet long by 18 feet 8 inches wide and 8 feet high. At the rear was a 'tail,' or pair of metal wheels, connected to an axle to assist steering. The fighting compartment housed a giant, 6-cylinder Daimler engine roaring at 1,000rpm, completely exposed to make it easy for the crew to lubricate the moving parts. The downside of the arrangement was the lack of protection from heat and fumes, and the need, when tired or distracted in battle, to dodge dangerous moving parts while on the move. Eight men were packed into the remaining space. Two, the commander and gearsman, were at the front; four were loading and firing the Lewis guns and 6-pounders at the sides, and there were two brakesmen at the rear. A pipe from the exhaust manifold carried the smoke through a hole in the roof. Crews leaned a can of water against this pipe to make tea. This virtual oven, however, meant that temperatures commonly reached 125 degrees Fahrenheit. 'Heat in the fighting compartment became unbearable after a short while,' recalled Alf Simpson, 'and it was not uncommon for some crews to end a day's fighting in vest and pants.'

Tank design had thus far concentrated exclusively on the machine's fight capabilities. Scant thought had been applied to the man inside. All he would see was a violently pitching landscape framed through a letterbox-size opening. Other crew members were only dimly discernible in the dark, hazy interior.

In battle the din of the roaring engine and rattling tracks, concussive cracks from the 6-pounder firing and the insane chatter of Lewis guns was amplified by the hermetically sealed metal interior. Intelligible communication with other crew members was difficult. Engine heat combined with petrol, oil and cordite fumes assailed the senses. Commanders could do little to assist gunners to find and engage targets and had to concentrate on driving the tank by hand signals to the man changing the gears and the two men at each track to the rear who 'braked' to change direction.

Crews developed various signals to drive and steer the tank. Alf Simpson remembered that when the driver wanted to change gear he banged on the transmission to attract the attention of the gearsman and held up one finger for first and two for second gear. 'Two fingers pointed down meant engage neutral.' William Francis, with the 5th Battalion, recalled that his driver would 'get hold of a spanner and tap the side of the tank' to indicate whether he wanted to go left or right. 'I think one tap was for him to turn right and two taps was turn left.'

Doing this in the din of battle was physically and mentally taxing. Sudden unexpected drumfire on hulls transformed anxieties to naked fear. 'Talk about noise,' declared Albert Driver, driver of the tank *Early Bird* at Cambrai, 'the sound of bullets on our plating was like fifty hailstorms on one corrugated iron shed.' With the fumes and 'if the guns were going as well' remembered Eric Potten with the 6th Battalion, 'you were completely done for a little while when you got out again.' Physical release combined with emotional relief at surviving another day, as Private Archie Richards vividly recalled:

> As soon as we were out of action, we could open the tank traps. Oh, you would never believe the relief. You took long breaths of fresh air, you gulped it in. There was freedom – freedom all round. Freedom of limbs, freedom of arms, freedom of breath, freedom of mind.

Fatigue was accentuated by the constant and severe buffeting crews endured inside their machines when moving. 'The engine was quite powerful and vibrated the machine somewhat,' remembered Richards, 'But it was the movement that was worse, up and down, this way and that. I had a job sometimes to set on my target to shoot. I'd just get set and ready to fire, and bang, the tank would lurch somewhere, throw me right off'.

Obstacle crossing was particularly trying. Bumping across the fascine-filled trenches of the Hindenberg Line was an imprecise act. 'Could we ever get over?' one tank commander recalled thinking, tense at the memory of disasters seen during pre-assault training.

> Anyhow, down we dropped and up, up, up — no one thought of the balance point — until at last we crashed down upon the other side, splitting open my section commander's head, and petrol cans, oil cans and ammunition boxes scattered all over the place.

Proponents of the tank showed propaganda pieces like *The King Visits a Tankadrome* in which an awesome image was shown of a tank surmounting a huge concrete ammunition bunker shaped like a rock boulder. Lieutenant Alan Scrutton was present during filming:

> It came up with a great deal of noise, appeared on the flat top, balanced for a second on the crown of the descent and as it dropped, inch by inch, it suddenly lost all grip and shot to the bottom, burying its nose several feet in the mud of the field below, just in front of His Majesty.

Those in charge of the demonstration winced. The silent film cheerfully displayed the next frame showing 'His Majesty's concern about the lads inside'. 'We all stood holding our breath,' Scrutton remembered, 'wondering if anyone inside was still alive, when, to our amazement, after a short pause, the tank went slowly on its way and came to an even keel alongside the King.' 'The Lads Inside', the film continued, showing them cheerfully climbing out. 'Out hopped Haseler, the commander,' recalled Scrutton, 'with a grin all over his face, made light of it and was congratulated by the King.' He was followed by 'two other men looking very shaken'. They were wearing dress uniform and looked sheepish and deferential. The film shows the King being led away, having 'no idea', as Scrutton pointed out, 'that the remainder of the crew were still inside the tank unconscious!'

New tank crews had to deal with claustrophobia from the very start, not aided by the limited and constantly undulating vision offered by the vision slits. Lloyd George, cushioned in the comfortable surrounds of Hatfield Park during the first practical demonstration, observed. 'To enter, it was necessary to stoop under the sponson, insert the head and trunk and finally pull up the feet; to leave one lowered the feet until they touched the ground and then folded the body downwards until the head was clear.' He would also note that this was a demonstration, conducted in a civilised and relaxed manner: 'On Lord Salisbury's golf course it cost a number of bruises; in action, with the machine on fire, it took great good fortune to emerge at all.' The perceptive Lloyd George identified the unease shared by all tank crews in battle – about how to get out in the event of disaster. 'The last resort was a small manhole in the roof' – but, he noticed, 'it would have admitted only a very undersized man in great desperation.'

The tank was designed to overcome the stalemate imposed by machine-gun, wire and artillery and restore mobility to operations on the Western Front. The German General Staff was confident in the ability of their infantry and artillery to deal with the new threat. An arms race of tank against gun began and tank men would have to cope with the emotional consequences of winning or losing. There was no debate about which had the lead at this point. Artillery guns were having devastating effects on the early tanks.

Marooned tanks always attracted the attention of German artillery batteries. 'The tank staggers and a blinding flash comes through the half-closed driving port,' recalled Captain Donald Richardson, whose tank *Fray Bentos* was subjected to several days of bombardment during the Third Battle of Ypres. 'An explosion, louder than the rest, lights up the whole interior of the tank and sends a fusillade of rattles against the hull.' With another tank burning fiercely nearby, 'a blinding detonation staggers the tank and a piece of white hot metal flies between Hill and Trew', two of his crew. Then, after their tank had been rocked by bangs and the concussive impacts of near misses:

A large, jagged splinter came violently through the gun port and took Arthurs full in the face, tearing through his lower jaw and burying itself in his chest. He fell without a sound and the slant of the tank pitched him into the engine, his body slithering on to the floor, and leaving a smear of blood on the engine cover.

Of the 378 mass of tanks attacking Cambrai 179 were lost on the first day, thirty-nine of these knocked out by the German 213 Field Artillery Regiment, whose enterprising commander had specifically trained his gunners to engage moving targets over open sights.

Alfred Simpson recalled that it was a 'gruesome task' salvaging the hulks, 'particularly where the tanks had been burned out'. 'We would get the sponson door open,' explained Simpson:

'And there would be several pairs of legs standing there. Just legs. Nothing on top of them. Perhaps the fire had been more intense from the waist height or something; I don't know what the reason was but it was the same in every tank. Just legs . . .'

## CREW ERGONOMICS AND TANK VERSUS TANK

When Haig placed his first order for 100 tanks at the beginning of 1916, the French had placed a firm order for a French variant with the manufacturer Schneider for 400. Both sides were blissfully ignorant of their parallel developments of tanks, or *chars d'assault,* as the French called them. The French 'Swinton' leading the effort in 1915 was artillery Colonel Jean Estienne. As in Britain, existing technology was utilised to produce a tracked form of armoured car, then a wire-cutting vehicle, until it coalesced into a tracked vehicle not dissimilar to Tritton's *Little Willie* prototype. Without realising they were six months behind British development, the French took a short cut by accepting the armoured box on short tracks and placed the substantial order without exhaustive trench-crossing trials. Two variants emerged: the Schneider, with a 75mm gun and two Hotchkiss machine-guns, and the French Army design department's St Chamond tank, which had a better 75mm and four machine-guns. Seventeen millimetres of armour

made them impervious to small-arms fire. The dramatic appearance of
the British tank caused the French some chagrin, because the Germans
widened their trenches to eight feet to cope with the 'terror weapons',
which did not greatly impede the British but did the French. French
tanks did not appear in substantial numbers until 1917, by which time
the Germans had adapted their artillery to dealing with moving targets
over open sights.

While Cambrai demonstrated the potential for massed tank assaults,
it stretched the new Tank Corps to its human and material limits. Some
47 per cent of the 378 fighting tanks were lost on the first day and on
the second day casualties, exhaustion and mechanical wear and tear
prevented a replication of the effort and success of the first assault. As a
consequence the battle descended into a Herculean infantry and
artillery slogging match.

Despite heavy losses of Allied tanks in the summer and autumn of
1917, both the British and French tank forces improved in quantity
and quality. By November the British took delivery of nearly 1,000
Mark IVs, with 450 ready for action. The French had some 500
Schneiders and St Chamonds. Owing to the haste with which the
tank had been developed, mechanical unreliability blighted performance, as did also bad ergonomics and the scratch-trained crews
drafted in to man the rapidly expanding tank formations. French tank
driver Winston Roche recalled the confinement and 'terrible' sensa-
tions living in and fighting his machine. 'You are practically sitting on
the engine, and the noise of the engine and gun concussions outside
the tank – it's like being in a maelstrom of noise, racket and
discomfort.' Echoing the British tank crews, Roche continued,
'You're just tickled pink to get the damn thing back to where
you can park it and get out!'

Technology started to change the shape of the tank towards the end
of the war. As heavier types were improved, smaller and more
numerous tank types appeared. William Tritton made a proposal for
a 'Chaser' tank as early as December 1916 and during 1917 the first 14-
ton Medium A or *Whippet* tanks were developed. They were the first
recognisably modern-looking tank, driven by one man, with low-
profile tracks to keep the weight down and separate the engine and
transmission from the crew in the back. With a speed of over 8mph

they were twice as fast as the Mark IV, but had a fixed turret with four swivelling machine-guns.

The comparative failure of the early French Schneiders and St Chamonds led Estienne to campaign for the introduction of the Renault FT. This was designed as a cheap, easily produced machine-gun carrier of only 6 tons to provide direct fire support for the infantry in the assault. Nicknamed the 'Mosquito', it could be deployed by being off-loaded from a truck. 'Infantry loved them,' declared Winston Roche. Despite being light 'it gave you a feeling you were invincible because you could hear the bullets hitting the sides'. 'If they had an especially tough machine-gun nest that was going to take a lot of lives,' Roche declared, 'you could run right on up to it just like you were thumbing your nose at it.' It went safely through the wire, enabling them to 'go right up to it and shoot right in there and clean them out'. With its fully revolving turret and raised superstructure on tracks, and its engine at the rear, this two-man tank could be built cheaply and in very large numbers. Production ran at seventy-five per week in the middle of 1918, and 3,000 were produced by the time of the Armistice. Its outline was recognisably modern and represented a step nearer the day when defences might be overwhelmed by masses of tanks.

Finally the Germans recognised that Allied tank developments might have to be matched. The Russian collapse after the October Revolution meant that offensive operations would be required if the forces released from the East were to swing the balance in the West before the Americans arrived. A wooden mock-up was produced in January 1917 for the A7V and 100 were ordered. Only twenty were ever made. They made their debut in the Ludendorff Spring Offensive in 1918, fighting alongside reconfigured British tanks captured earlier at Cambrai. Simply a large armoured box crewed by eighteen men on top of a Holt-type chassis, the tank's tortoise-like hull overlapped the tracks, giving it an ungainly, top-heavy appearance and impeding mobility. Armed with a 57mm gun and six machine-guns, it was powered by two Daimler 100hp engines, which at 8mph gave it twice the speed of British tanks.

Sam Lytle served two years in the infantry before transferring to a tank battalion. On 24 April 1918 he recalled 'Jerry had put down a lot of mustard gas on the Bois d'Aquenne where our tanks were lying. So we thought we had better get up there and do what we could about casualties.' The Germans had launched an attack against the Villers-Brettonaux position spearheaded by four infantry divisions and thirteen of their own tanks. Their presence meant that for the first time tanks might face each other. What would the impact of machine against machine be on men? A heavy bombardment of high explosive and gas shells preceded the advance.

When Lytle arrived he remembered what a 'dreadful place that wood was. Full of dead and dying birds, and the gas hung heavy about in the trees and bushes.' Tank crews already in situ had been caught out, they had masks 'but either they weren't very effective, or some of them hadn't put them on properly, because we found several tank chaps suffering badly from the effects of the gas.' Tank crews were vulnerable to gas as it could linger within the vehicles. Until now, tanks on both sides had focused on combating static infantry machine-gun and artillery emplacements. Moving targets traversing undulating ground were a new experience. Lytle was startled by a warning from the infantry in the woods. 'Look out! Jerry tanks about!' he heard someone shout. 'Then I saw one of them,' he recalled. 'Looked just like an iron tortoise with the armour plating hanging down around the tracks like a skirt almost touching the ground.'

German A7V tanks had led the infantry through the early-morning gas-laden mist and smoke toward the Bois d'Aquenne and the villages of Villers-Bretonneux and Cachy. 'The mist aided the penetration of the line,' recalled Leutnant Ernst Volckheim, a panzer commander, 'and the English were totally surprised at the appearance of tanks.' Officers had laboriously surveyed the ground in motor vehicles prior to the advance, even taking their tank drivers with them. Their 'heavy field kitchens', as the A7Vs were ostentatiously labelled, had been brought up from the rear by train and unloaded in darkness at night. 'Morale was high because for the first time we were driving into the enemy,' recalled Volckheim.

Thus far the German advance had proved unstoppable. 'Panic reigned everywhere among the enemy,' Volckheim observed, 'who was seeing this new dangerous German weapon for the first time.' The mist was thick, with visibility down to 30–40 metres. They soon outdistanced the infantry and trundled forward alone. 'Everything that could be discerned as enemy on the attack line was annihilated,' Volckheim stated. Prisoners of war were marshalled together by the tanks and sent back as the mist began to clear. To his left Oberleutnant Steinhard's group of four panzers 'suddenly saw three English tanks, which he immediately engaged with his main armament'.

Second Lieutenant Frank Mitchell's crew in their Mark IV were suffering badly from the effects of gas, their eyes puffed up and smarting, exposed patches of skin sore and inflamed. 'A great thrill ran through us all,' Mitchell later wrote. As he looked through a loophole:

There, some three hundred yards away, a round squat-looking monster was advancing; behind it came waves of infantry, and further away to the left and right crawled two more of these armed tortoises.

So we had met our rivals at last! For the first time in history tank was encountering tank!

This was a chance encounter. Nobody had envisaged or designed for tanks fighting tanks. What followed was a strange version of 'blind man's buff'. Ranging shots barked out as the tanks zig-zagged toward each other, driving around trenches and obstacles..

'Above the roar of our engine sounded the staccato rat-tat-tat-tat of machine-guns,' wrote Mitchell, as 'another furious jet of bullets sprayed our steel side, the splinters clanging against the engine cover. The Jerry tank had treated us to a broadside of armour-piercing bullets.' The tanks manoeuvred for favourable positions and fired ranging shots over a period of half an hour before a panzer commanded by Leutnant Biltz struck first one then the other of the British female tanks, who withdrew. Having been holed they were vulnerable to machine-gun fire. The powerful German machines moved at 8mph, twice the pace of the slower Mark IV, enabling faster drives to superior firing positions or cover. Mitchell's position was precarious. His rear Lewis gunner was wounded by an AP bullet that penetrated the plate, while his 6-pounder gunner, working single-handed, was aiming with his left eye as his right had been swollen by the gas. Both sides instinctively sought sheltered dips in the ground. Meanwhile:

The roar of our engine, the nerve-racking noise of our machine-guns blazing at the Boche infantry and the thunderous boom of the 6-pounders, all bottled up in that narrow space, filled our ears with tumult, while the fumes of petrol and cordite half stifled us.

Seven Whippet Medium tanks, expecting to deal with the infantry reported around Villers-Bretonneux, blundered into the advancing panzer *Gruppe*. 'Another German fighting vehicle saw seven light tanks coming and succeeded in hitting three, while the others quickly sought cover', Leutnant Volckheim observed with satisfaction. This engagement was so rapid that Captain Price, the Whippet leader, retreated and reported that his detachment had been hit by a field gun. He had not spotted the tanks.

This tank meeting engagement, like so many that would follow it as time went on, was confusing and unpredictable. The primary difference was the slow-motion pace at which the fighting was conducted. 'Our own infantry,' Mitchell remarked, 'were standing in their trenches watching the duel with tense interest, like spectators in the pit of a theatre.' He realised he was never going to hit a moving target while he was 'going up and down like a ship in a heavy sea'.

I took a risk and stopped the tank for a moment. The pause was justified; a well-aimed shot hit the enemy's turret, bringing him to a standstill. Another roar and yet another puff at the front of the tank denoted a second hit! Peering with swollen eyes through his narrow slit, the gunner shouted words of triumph that were drowned by the noise of the engine. Then once more he aimed with great deliberation and hit the third time.

Volckheim claimed that the German vehicle was 'able to retire under its own power'. Mitchell was convinced he 'had knocked the monster out!' and proceeded to shoot up the fleeing crew with machine-guns as they emerged. Difficulties in confirming the impact of hits was to characterise future tank warfare. Reports from this confusing engagement are not clear. Mitchell was left in possession of the field, but Volckheim concluded, 'the Germans had demonstrated their superiority over the British tanks'. Machine had been pitted against machine, and this would have implications.

The impact on both sides was considerable. While the German conviction about the need for tanks to support offensive operations was strengthened, they also identified the need to halt in order to accurately engage targets, a practice that was to pay dividends in future conflicts. HQ British Tank Corps saw the need to mount an anti-tank weapon on all tanks and develop practice techniques for shooting accurately on the move; probably a false deduction. It was decided that as many of the female tanks as possible should have a 6-pounder affixed. In essence, this chance encounter was, in the absence of any other experience, to provide some inspiration for future armoured fighting techniques, particularly among the avant-garde of tank developers. It was, however, eclipsed by the final momentous push against Germany and the approaching inevitability of an Armistice.

'August 8th was the black day of the German Army in the history of this war,' declared General Erich von Ludendorf as the Allied armies advanced on Amiens. Even with improved Mark V and other tank types, the Tank Corps had difficulty, as at Cambrai, sustaining tank operations at the same pace and intensity as the infantry and artillery battle. On the first day 430 tanks were engaged, which reduced to 155 the following day, eighty-five the next and only thirty-eight on the fourth. This steep decline in effectiveness had more to do with mechanical breakdown, crew sickness and exhaustion than enemy action. Unsprung tracks produced bruising, bone-shaking rides in which the men were pitched around hot engines while enduring stressful noise levels. Tank designers had neglected the human dimension in their designs and the cumulative impact of this neglect was only now becoming apparent.

Tanks were a break-*through*, not a break-*out* weapon, and could barely keep up with the infantry and artillery. One survey conducted in August 1918 assessed that with good weather and ground, sound engine condition and average-intensity fighting, 'crew can be counted on for twelve hours in action after leaving the line of deployment'. Bad conditions, though could substantially reduce this. The report revealed a typical example:

In the action of the 23 August some crews were physically ill after two hours fighting. These tanks had done a bit of running and it had been impossible to overhaul the engines. Consequently the exhaust had warped and joints became loose, and the tank was full of petrol fumes. Three men were sent to hospital, one of them in critical condition.

In the spring following the Armistice four tanks took part in a ceremonial march over the Hohenzollern Bridge, crossing the River Rhine into Cologne. It was the precursor to the occupation of Germany. Four years earlier only German infantry and artillery had crossed moving west and tanks had been the stuff of science fiction. Technology had moved at breakneck speed in three short years. It remained to be seen whether the new technology had outstripped human capacity in crew ergonomic terms to keep up.

# 2

## NEW TANK MEN

### NEW MACHINES

'Thank God we can now get back to some real soldiering!' declared an 'old-school officer' to J.F.C. Fuller, the chief staff officer of the fledgeling Tank Corps on the day the Armistice was signed. The French and British armies resumed peacetime soldiering with a lifestyle centred on the cavalry regiment. At a time when technology, accelerated by wartime developments, was changing the world, professional soldiers would have to make do with existing equipments and reduced budgets. Cheap motor cars poured from the factories, outnumbering the horse and carriage that characterised the pre-war generation. Production of Henry Ford's Model T rose to 24 million in 1924.

At war's end the Tank Corps comprised of over twenty battalions, but within months it was reduced to four. 'The tank proper was a freak,' declared Major General Sir Lewis Jackson, the Director of Trench Warfare and Supplies at the Ministry of Munitions, to an audience at the Royal United Services Institute on 17 December 1919. 'The circumstances which called it into existence were exceptional and not likely to recur. If they do they can be dealt with by other means.'

Politicians saw tanks as an unnecessary expense in peacetime. The Americans had simply bought two-man French light Renault tanks on arrival in France. Four Medium C Whippet tanks rumbled past the Cenotaph during the impressive victory parade of 1919, but there was controversy surrounding the formal adoption of tanks as an established British service arm for five years after the war. Royal approval was finally granted for a tank corps of initially four battalions on 18 October 1923.

There was no threat in Europe and armies had to compete for scant resources. Defeated Germany was forbidden to manufacture tanks, aircraft or battleships, under the punishing protocols of the Treaty of Versailles that followed the Armistice.

Britain and France led the way with the formal establishment of a tank corps, but there was little agreement over what tanks were for. Walking-pace tank advances had given the Germans time to bring up reserves and re-form the front. In four days of fighting the Tank Corps lost 72 per cent of its tanks. Neither was the French or American experience appreciably better. The French lost 367 and the Americans seventy tanks on the Argonne-Champagne front at a cost of 40 per cent of their crews. Clearly the tank was not a war-winning wonder weapon.

Tanks were not employed according to the advice of their proponents. Swinton saw his idea of a mass surprise attack with minimum artillery preparation compromised at Flers. It had been devised as a stalemate-busting, maybe war-winning option, a huge tank 'raid' to constrain the Germans into tying up huge defence resources. Instead it developed into a full-scale offensive that was compromised by unrealistic objectives and poor planning.

Disagreement among tank experts themselves provided ammunition for detractors. Fuller imagined attacking the opposing HQs, the 'brain', of commanding generals to make the enemy front line collapse. His 'Plan 1919', though was thwarted by the German request for an Armistice.

Captain B.H. Liddell-Hart was another British thinker seeking to resolve the deadlock of trench warfare. His solution was that there was always an unexpected place or way to hit the enemy, an 'indirect approach'. Liddell-Hart proposed that an advance would break open the front and flow into the interior, spreading disaster through the chain of military command right up to the enemy's government level. By the late 1920s, Britain was leading the way in tank technological development and created an 'Experimental Force' to test its theories.

Britain had developed the Vickers Medium Tank Mark I by 1921. This was recognisably modern with a sprung suspension and revolving 3-pounder (47mm) gun turret and six machine-guns. The high-velocity, flat-trajectory gun indicated that tank-to-tank combat was envisaged. Its fighting compartment and general layout, and particularly its 150-mile radius and mechanical reliability, put it far ahead of any other fighting vehicle at the time.

The Experimental Mechanical Force was established on Salisbury Plain in 1927. Combined within it were tankettes, armoured cars, Vickers Medium tanks, an infantry battalion mounted in half-tracked vehicles with machine-gun carriers and six-wheeled trucks, engineers, and an artillery regiment with some 18-pounder guns. This innovatory approach symbolised Britain's reputation in the early 1930s as a world leader in the training and tactical handling of mechanised formations. At the same time it was a demonstration of naked political ambition by the fledgeling RTC (Royal Tank Corps) to achieve influence in a future British mechanised army. Its inception was steered by Colonel George Lindsay RTC, who like Fuller saw the force as a miniature prototype for a tank force with few supporting arms and services. The Director of Staff Duties (DSD) army view, by contrast, was to test the practicality of an all-arms mechanised division.

In a series of exercises pitting the new experimental force against superior cavalry and infantry formations, the armoured element, despite creative result 'fixing' by supervising umpires, invariably won. Key to these exercise victories, conducted during large manoeuvres on Salisbury Plain, was radio-transmission control. Direct voice radio dynamically accelerated the reaction and movement timings of the armoured force. Command tanks were fitted with crystal-controlled radio sets which were easier to tune to one another and light years ahead of previous Morse telegraphic traffic. 'The large-scale manoeuvres in co-operation with the infantry lasted often for several weeks,' remembered one tank driver, 'and during that time the participants were on almost continuous duty.' He thoroughly enjoyed the high tempo of such exercises: driving a tank, 'when one becomes used to it,' he enthused, 'can at times be wonderfully exhilarating'. Thundering over undulating ground,

> The quick rush down the slopes, the roaring up the stiff little hills, swaying, bucking, leaping, bouncing over furrowed fields with the engine shrieking like a demon and the rush of air on one's face – these are pleasant memories which remain fresh in the mind, still bringing a thrill and a sort of nostalgia for the dead days.

Fuller and Liddell-Hart's views were idealistic because they paid scant attention to the basic crew-ergonomics of manning these vehicles. The protection and mobility afforded by armoured vehicles meant the crew 'could become a true fighter of weapons by ceasing to be a human pack mule,' declared Fuller.

So captivated was he by the potential for war fighting that he believed conscript armies would be replaced by a 'New Model Army' built around tank capabilities. Liddell-Hart, by now the principal media spokesman for tanks and a contributor to the *Daily Telegraph*, believed, like Fuller, that tanks could therefore replace infantry. He was completely opposed to including an infantry battalion, even a battalion of machine-gun specialised troops, in Lindsay's original concept for setting up the Experimental Mechanised Force. This was the idealistic backdrop to the manoeuvres conducted on Salisbury Plain in the early 1930s.

Tank men actually engaged in these manoeuvres viewed progress from a different perspective. 'Where we were going, what time it would end, none of us knew except the leaders,' commented a tank driver:

> We followed blindly. I used to wonder what would happen if this was actual warfare and the staff cars bombed to bits. None of the tank crews would know what to do - whether to retreat, proceed or hide up. In war time, if the same sorry procedure were adopted, there must inevitably be extreme confusion and enormous casualties.

Poor communications bedevilled the experiment. It was difficult to make a motley collection of fifteen different vehicle types within the total 280 work. Crucially, technology had changed, but not attitudes. 'In no-man's-land everything possible went wrong,' recalled the tank driver on exercise. Headquarters tanks received orders by wireless from staff officers and then 'made frightful blunders when re-transmitting by flags to the Whippets and Mediums not possessing wirelesses. The net result was 'indescribable confusion' resulting from contradictory signals.

> Halt and advance? How can we do both? Oh wash that out! I should think so! Left incline? That's better. Oh but it isn't, we'll land in a

river! What? Wash that out too? Then where the devil . . . ? Oh! Right incline! Now we know . . .

What now? Halt? But surely, we can't halt here? We're in sight of the enemy guns. They're not fifty yards away, and firing at us like blazes . . . we're being blown to bits.

This wry reportage of radio traffic inside the turret ended with tactical defeat. 'Still . . . obey orders. It's only manoeuvres. Thank Heaven!' he cryptically comments.

At the end of the 1928 training season the Armoured Force was effectively closed down, although an experimental tank brigade was established in 1931. This left the traditional 'old guard' in the ascendant in the tank-versus-horse debate as the best advocates for change were dispersed and sent to other jobs. There were genuine concerns at the direction of the debate. General Sir Archibald Montgomery-Massingberd, the General Officer Commanding (GOC) Southern Command, believed the mechanised force 'although invaluable for experimental purposes . . . was definitely affecting adversely the Cavalry and Infantry'. The infantry wanted heavy tanks that advanced at walking pace, of course under infantry command. The extremists, led by Fuller and Liddell-Hart, wanted armies composed of tanks with virtually no supporting arms whatsoever. Perceptive observers saw the importance of versatility, giving selected elements of the whole army a degree of mobile cross-country capability. 'What was wanted was to use the newest weapons to improve the mobility and firepower of the old formations,' declared Montgomery-Massingberd, who viewed the experiment in his command with some suspicion. 'What I wanted in brief was evolution and not revolution.'

Even as the Experimental Mechanised Force was being put through its paces in England, groups of official-looking men formed up on the railway platform at Berlin in Germany to catch the Eastern Express. Every year at precisely the same time, groups of the same size took the same train from Bahnhof Berlin-Zoo dressed in civilian clothing, remarked Oberleutnant Klaus Müller, who accompanied one of the parties: 'They travelled with numbered suitcases of the same size and colour. This always brought wry grins to the faces of the station officials and porters who smilingly wished them a pleasant journey and 'good-bye for now'.'

German panzer soldiers attending clandestine courses in Russia were an open secret by 1932, to those who sent them on their way.

The German panzer arm or Panzerwaffe had forty-five tanks divided into nine *Abteilungen* (troops) at the end of the war in 1918. Between 1920 and 1926 the first post-war Commander in Chief, Generaloberst Hans von Seekt, turned the Reichswehr (the small remaining profes-sional German Army) into a virtual cadre organisation to retain the key elements needed for future expansion. Under the eyes of the Inter-national Allied Control Commission he started to rebuild the German Army with particular attention paid to technical excellence. A secret agreement was made with the Soviet Union in 1922 to train German panzer and Luftwaffe personnel in Russia in exchange for assistance to Soviet heavy industry. Von Seekt, astutely aware of the vulnerability of Germany after the occupation forces left in 1925, considered various options to defend a weakened Germany against possible intervention from east or west. A 'people's war' of resistance was regarded as dishonourable by the Reichswehr, who opted for a counter-manoeuvre strategy to meet any of many threats. Crucial to this was the development of motorised forces for mobile defence.

Heinz Guderian, a thirty-four-year-old *Hauptmann* (captain), was the future creator of the German panzer arm. In 1922 he was selected for a staff job with the new Inspectorate of Transport Troops. He was well aware of the potential of the new radios, having served with a heavy-wireless station among other appointments during the First World War. Uninspired at first by his new job, 'I therefore initially looked for precedents from which I might learn about the experiments that had been made with armoured vehicles,' he later wrote. He was assisted in this by Ernst Volckheim, who had witnessed the only tank-on-tank engagement of the war at Villers-Brettoneux. Volkheim was 'collating information concerning the very limited use of German armoured vehicles', Guderian recalled, 'and the incomparably greater employ-ment of enemy tank forces during the war'. As the English and French had more experience, he found that 'it was principally the books and articles of the Englishmen, Fuller, Liddell-Hart and Martel, that excited my interest and gave me food for thought'. Guderian, an eminently practical staff officer, learned from rather than adopted their theories. 'Deeply impressed by these ideas I tried to develop them in a sense practical for our own army', which was much worse off than the British. The Treaty of Versailles obliged the Reichswehr to circumvent traditional norms and develop creative solutions that by necessity precluded them from Allied development paths.

In March 1927 contracts for the design and production of two experimental tanks under the code-name 'Army vehicle 20' were awarded to each of three firms: Daimler-Benz, Krupp and Rheinmetall. Six 'big tractors' (*Grosstraktor*), with a 75mm gun in a revolving turret, were built in secrecy by Rheinmetall and delivered to the clandestine testing ground set up at Kazan in 1929 in the Soviet Union. They were followed by four six-ton 'light tractors', or *Leichttracktor*, armed with a 37mm gun. A 'small tractor', or *Kleintracktor*, was produced by Krupp, armed only with machine-guns. Shortcuts were taken by buying and adapting the existing British Carden-Lloyd chassis; thus the British contributed to the development of the Panzer Mark I light tank.

Klaus Müller, who attended one of the secret courses recalled Guderian visiting in 1932 to test-drive some of the experimental vehicles. Technical tests were made on the tracks and running gear. Important decisions were made at Kazan regarding shooting training, the optimum design of crew fighting compartments, and optics. Russian students attended some of the courses, Russian tanks were driven and stilted social events conducted. No badges of rank were worn. 'Despite beer and a lot of vodka,' Müller recalled, 'nobody got drunk and the discipline was good.' Both sides were on their guard. Russian shooting training was found to be too cavalier for the Germans, with their penchant for close supervision and organisation. 'When the bangs go off, everyone gets out of the way,' explained the Russian interpreter to Müller. 'They all know there is a shooting range here.' A Russian course member, ignoring instructions to fire high, emptied 1,000 rounds of machine-gun ammunition into a neighbouring factory, injuring one of the workers. 'What became of him was unknown,' Müller wryly recalled.

In 1933 the relationship with the Russians deteriorated. Russians were not allowed to attend future courses and the programme was closed down. All the installations were painstakingly dismantled and course administrative personnel transported under escort to Leningrad for passage back to the Reich. A new Chancellor had been appointed in Germany, Adolf Hitler.

Hitler, who had fought as an infantryman in the First World War, was receptive to innovative ideas. As the National Socialist party organisation was brought into close association with the armed forces, discreet military training was offered for future Luftwaffe pilots and drivers. During a visit to the Kummersdorf army ordnance testing ground, accompanied by Guderian, Hitler saw the potential of panzers for the first time. 'That's what I need. That's what I want to have,' he said. By October 1935 Guderian, now a forty-seven-year-old colonel, was Chief of Staff to the newly created Panzerwaffe. He set out to deliver.

Subterfuge was continued. Hitler directed in 1934 that the army was to be rebuilt in secrecy. In the autumn of 1934 an organisational chart for a *Versuchs,* or Experimental, Panzer Division 1934/35 was distributed to the Army Staff for comment. Tank theorists in all other armies were nonconformists in a hostile world. Guderian, however, was bringing ideas to fruition that were widely acceptable to the men around him.

The tank-versus-horse debate and its importance relative to infantry did not occur in the German Army as with the Allies. Tanks were another tool in the box of military options. Guderian conducted exhaustive historical studies, observed English exercises and incorporated recent panzer practice and was convinced 'that tanks can only realise their maximum potential if the other weapons, to which it is always reliant on help, in terms of speed and cross-country mobility, can be brought together as the same denominator'. Major Walther Nehring, Guderian's assistant, recalled him explaining: 'The tanks in this group of combined weapons plays the first violin, the others must follow the tune.' The Germans, denied the open advantages conferred on the Allies by Versailles, had arrived at their own solution to the tank employment conundrum.

The Allies and the Germans were shaping their thoughts on how to fight the tank (as tank men refer to their calling). They were academic and theoretical proposals untested in combat. Technical innovation in the recent history of modern warfare tended to promote the primacy of defence over offence; since the American Civil War infantry had been going below ground level in trenches to survive. Now a weapons system had arrived that might restore mobility – if human problems could be limited or eradicated. An intrinsic interrelationship between man and machine started to emerge in the years leading up to 1939. Thus far, tank development had subordinated crew comfort and combat sustainability to weapon superiority.

There was no historical precedent how to fight tanks. The nearest parallel to *Big Willie*'s laborious progress across no-man's-land in 1916 was the ancient war elephant, used by Alexander the Great in 3BCE and Hannibal two centuries before Christ. They were normally employed for shock effect and were fast and strong.

However, elephants were easily stopped by five and could be stampeded into their own lines. Like gas in the First World War, they did not discriminate between friend and foe unless conditions were right. The elephant, like the First World War tank, possessed limitations and advantages in equal measure.

By the early 1930s designers were producing tanks that could run at speeds of between 20 and 28mph. The last time a war machine achieved such mobility was the ancient chariot. Tank design was a compromise between three fundamentals: mobility, meaning the suspension and running gear; protection in terms of the thickness of armour and shape of the hull; and firepower. Design improvements in one sphere inevitably cause problems in another. The war chariot had similar design conundrums, whereby technical advantages or disadvantages affected the crews' chances of survival.

Like tank mobility, the technology of the chariot was complex for its time. They were built by technicians to achieve bent-wood construction and required extensive logistic support. The driver, like tank drivers, required technical expertise to keep his vehicle running and was therefore a peculiar warrior type – a technical specialist.

To achieve the same degree of cross-country mobility for tanks in the 1930s, sprung suspensions were developed. Mechanical unreliability and the lack of springs had contributed greatly to the pronounced crew fatigue that inhibited tank unit performances in 1918.

To fight a chariot effectively with a crew of two or three required good teamwork. The Trojan warrior Asius, for example, in a mêlée described by Homer, went 'on foot in front of his chariot, which the driver kept so close to him that his shoulders were fanned all the time by the horse's breath'. Tank drivers need to instinctively predict where their commanders would wish them to best position the tank to shoot or seek cover.

Tank protection and firepower of course differed significantly from that of the chariot. Tank men fought from within the confines of a metal box with nothing like the 360-degree vision of the charioteer. Anticipating the grisly impact of an anti-armour projectile within the dimly lit, claustrophobic confines of tanks was completely outside the charioteer's experience. There were parallels regarding mobility. The ability to read ground, mechanical skills, teamwork, and the imperative to think and react quickly, were all characteristics shared by the charioteer and the tank man.

In chariot warfare, drivers needed technical expertise. The machines, to be used *en masse* had to be husbanded within specialised military formations that taught the crews how to control their machines and maintain and repair them. Where would the particular type of men required to serve tanks come from in the twentieth century?

## NEW MEN

Training and selecting tank men was an unknown art and different nations employed different approaches.

Although many British tank recruits had some technical skill, the overwhelming majority were compelled to join by unemployment. 'It was a very, very difficult time,' remembered Bill Close, who joined in 1933. 'In the thirties the slump was very, very difficult and in a small country town there was no hope for a lad like me, and I decided that the army was a good thing.' Another private enlisted in the Tank Corps after being unemployed for three months claimed, 'There was nothing else for me to do. 'In the northern town where I lived half the normal adult population was out of work.' Having seen 'so much real poverty among them', he resolved 'that I could never have faced a life similar to theirs. So I joined the army.' They did not all seek to become tank crews. 'I thought joining the army would be a bit of a "lark",' wrote the northerner. Bill Close had fancied the 11th Hussars, 'the fashionable regiment', but it was over-subscribed. Cavalry appealed, as 'the idea of horses intrigued me somewhat, but the recruiting sergeant said, "Sorry, son, no vacancies, why don't you join the Tank Corps?" And so I said "OK".'

'By the time I decided to take the King's shilling, I was following a well-trodden family path,' declared Alan Wollastan, who joined in 1937 shortly after his twentieth birthday. 'It was inevitable,' he said, 'particularly in view of the economic conditions in the 1930s, when a military career was a better option than civilian life.' He was to join the 3rd Royal Tank Regiment (RTR). Jake Wardrop joined at nineteen, unable to settle in a nine-to-five job. Having inherited a love of mechanical things from his father it was natural, according to those who knew him, that he should join the Royal Tank Corps. Fred Goddard was asked to assemble a spring-type washing peg, initially hidden by a cloth, under time pressure. 'I was informed after,' he later wrote, 'that many who had taken the same test had not been able to assemble the same peg.' Harry Webb from Birmingham recalled that on arrival at the recruiting office, 'I was given an aptitude test which consisted of stripping a bicycle bell and reassembling it', after which 'I had to swear allegiance to the King.'

Fred Goddard had a 'love for engines', but the air force was out of the question owing to his poor education. At the army recruiting office he was sensitive about his lack of education certificates and the poor state of his teeth. With typical army pragmatism the recruiting sergeant, having identified his mechanical bias, suggested that 'as I was only five feet four inches tall, I would fit into a tank very well' – and they would sort out his teeth. He was in.

Paul Rollins was attracted in 1937 by a Sunday newspaper which showed a picture of a tank on manoeuvres on Salisbury Plain. He saw 'the tank crew standing outside in their black uniforms and black beret, and I thought I'd like to join that'. Not long afterwards he passed his driving test, aged seventeen, and joined up. 'I put a year on my age, otherwise you had to go into boy's service and that wasn't very nice, was it? You had to be in by ten o'clock – oh no.'

Technology and guns or the schoolboy's daydream of 'derring-do' in an age of futuristic warfare was another attraction. Michael Halstead, who was to join the Queen's Bays cavalry regiment at the beginning of the war, 'was thrilled by the idea of naval warfare and great guns in traversing turrets'. Tanks provided an attainable version of this as his father was in the army. 'I saw my first tank, a derelict First World War Mark IV or V, when I was with Papa on Salisbury Plain, aged six,' he later wrote. 'I was fascinated, and never forgot the moment.' Tom Heald had seen three tanks at school and realised his eyes would probably be too poor for the air force. 'I immediately came to the conclusion that if I could not join the RAF, tanks were for me.' Likewise Trooper Bright 'wanted to be a fighter pilot but I did not have the education to qualify for one', so he opted for 'the next best thing', he became a tank driver.

The German experience was not unlike the British, except that conscription occurred earlier after the Reichswehr was assimilated by the Wehrmacht in May 1935. The attraction of the Reichswehr had been three square meals a day and a roof over one's head during the worst of the unemployment period, and like other governmental uniformed jobs – the police or Post Office – it was a job for life with a pension at the end of it. Like the Royal Tank Corps, the Panzerwaffe tended to attract those with technical interests because it at least provided some mechanical training in the absence of anything else.

Patriotism played a role to an extent difficult to comprehend today. The British believed in their Empire. Much of the school atlas was coloured red and it was viewed as a force for good. National Socialism extolled the virtues of the Fatherland, the *Volk,* above all else.

Hans Becker, a chauffeur, recalled 'the fever of patriotism which was raging throughout Germany' in the spring of 1937. With little inducement to remain a civilian he felt 'my drab uniform could easily be exchanged for a more glamorous one'. Having done this, he found himself 'a chauffeur again, but instead of an ordinary car I was now driving a Krupp's armoured one'. Karl Fuchs, a twenty-two-year-old teacher, was conscripted in 1939 and after a number of tests and psychological examinations was assigned as a tank gunner. 'Next week we'll be able to climb into our tanks for the first time,' he wrote in his diary. 'Tanks are really awesome!' Hermann Eckardt, from a farming background in Lindach Swabia, joined the panzer arm because he was 'fascinated by technology and anything new'. Initially Otto Carius had wanted to be a musician, but 'then I changed my mind and began to take a fancy to mechanical engineering'. He was conscripted into an infantry training battalion but considered unsuitable because of his size. The 'little runt' also volunteered for the panzer arm. Carius suspected the 'old man' commanding his unit 'was probably happy to get rid of this half-pint'. Henry Metelmann had been a locksmith and was chosen to be a driver. 'My heart was bursting with pride,' he later wrote.

> What greater honour could there be than having become a German panzer driver! It gave me a superb feeling to watch the powerful panzers roll in front of me, realising to the onlookers by the roadside my panzer was as impressive as all the others.

Unknown to the west, the Soviet Union was forming the world's largest and most diversified tank army. The socialist revolution brought disapproval and technological restrictions, so the Russians, like the Germans, were steered into new ideas. Unlike the British and French they did not need to overcome the opinions of entrenched and conservative cavalry officers. By 1928 Stalin had emerged from internal party feuds to succeed Lenin. The USSR's industrialisation accelerated through successive Five Year Plans between 1928 and 1937, providing a bedrock for an expansion of Soviet military ambitions, and Stalin sought to create the world's most modern and powerful army. Mechanisation of the Workers and Peasants Red Army (RKKA) would create a powerful tank army entirely unfettered by past tradition and 'bourgeois' concepts of conventional warfare. From a standing start at the time of secret co-operation with the Germans at Kazan, by 1932 the RKKA had more tanks than the world's most powerful army, the French. Tanks were divided into several categories for specific tasks: light *tanketta*, amphibious *plavainschchiva* and medium *sredni* tanks. The most numerous were 'fast' *bystrochodya* and heavy tank series. By 1938 the Red Army had an estimated 9,000 tanks, of which the majority were T-26s, BT-5s and BT-7 models. These were thinly armoured and generally weak in armament, but new and quite revolutionary design concepts were being considered and there was original thinking about 'Deep Battle' deployments alongside air support. This abrupt expansion required a huge investment of manpower and training for the new tank crews.

'Guys, let's become tank men! It's so prestigious!' recalled Soviet Lieutenant Nikolai Zheleznov, a tank platoon commander. 'You ride, and the whole country lies before you! You're on an iron horse!' Propaganda extolled the invincibility of the Red Army, and Russians were patriotic in the early heady days of the new regime. Soldiers were very popular in the USSR in the 1930s. People believed the Red Army, which had secured the Revolution, would defeat its foes with 'little bloodshed, on the enemy's own soil'. Dashing Red cavalrymen were replaced in the teenage psyche by fighter pilots in high-speed monoplanes and tank men in impressive armoured vehicles. Young men could improve their education and learn a profession in the army. 'Each one of us was dreaming of service in the army,' recalled tank commander Lieutenant Aleksandr Burtsev, who observed the local village kudos that army service attracted. 'They would leave as simple village boys and come back as educated, cultured, learned men in perfect uniforms and tall boots, physically strong.' Not only did they symbolise the might of the young popular Soviet state, they were well paid, 'they understood equipment and could lead people in work'. Burtzev remembered that 'a whole village would gather to welcome returning serving men'.

'Why did I become a tank man? I saw myself as a warrior of the future,' recalled tank commander Lieutenant Aleksandr Bodnar. It was recognised that the inevitable coming war with the bourgeoisie would be conducted with machines. To pilot a fighter aircraft or fire a tank's main gun was an adolescent's dream. Bodnar, like many of his contemporaries, was encouraged by his father to volunteer and secure the arm of his choice.

Officers were more numerous in the Red Army, which had a less developed NCO corps and was 'classless' compared with European armies. Junior officers were employed in appointments traditionally viewed as appropriate to NCOs in the English, French and German armies. A Soviet professional tank officer's course in the 1930s lasted two years. Every type of tank used by the Red Army would be studied and practically handled, including driving, shooting and armour tactics. Aleksandr Bodnar recalled, 'We had practical classes and studied the hardware in great detail. The M-17 engine is very complicated, but we knew it to the last bolt.' He could carry out the tasks of any crew member, right down to vehicle maintenance, and could strip and assemble the main gun and machine-guns. Training was on a scale completely unknown in Europe.

A financial crisis rocked the British Army at the beginning of the 1930s as Ramsay McDonald's short-lived Labour government disintegrated in 1931. The new National Governments imposed drastic cuts; the army's budget estimate was cut from £40m to £36.5m. By contrast, Adolf Hitler's accession to power was followed by a vigorous rearmament programme in Germany which would not be matched by the British.

Germany reintroduced conscription in March 1935 and the Wehrmacht replaced the Reichswehr. The vehicle-driving commands were renamed panzer regiments, and the formation of three new panzer divisions was announced. An eight-vehicle wide phalanx of Panzer Mark Is shrouded in blue-grey exhaust haze thundered across the parade ground at the Nuremberg Nazi Party Rally, or *Reichsparteitag,* a symbolic demonstration that deception was over. The first conscripted recruits to populate the new panzer divisions arrived in October. There would be no more practising with dummy tanks mounted on bicycles. As Heinz Guderian recalled, 'Schoolchildren, accustomed to stick their pencils through the canvas walls of our dummies in order to have a look inside, were disappointed.' Likewise, he went on, 'The infantrymen who usually defended themselves against our "tanks" with sticks and stones on exercise now found themselves ruled out of action by the despised panzers.' The Russians, Germans and British prepared themselves in entirely different ways. This was particularly evident in the future preparation of the new tank crews.

When eighteen-year-old Harry Webb arrived at Wool station for Bovington Camp and a career with the Royal Tank Corps, 'the station was completely blacked out; all I could hear was a porter shouting out, "Wool, this is Wool".' Along with one or two other young men he eventually managed to find a soldier who was the duty driver. They were 'dumped outside some old 1914-18 wooden huts'. In time a sergeant appeared, apologising for the insufficient bedding and saying that 'we would have to manage the best we could till the morning'. This was not an auspicious start. 'At this stage it was nearly midnight and I was having serious thoughts about having volunteered.'

To Herbert Webster, too, the reception at Wool station seemed a little ad hoc. This time there were twenty or thirty other youths getting off and obviously heading for the Training Regiment at Bovington. Some trucks arrived, and he was relieved 'to avoid what might otherwise have been a very straggly "march" from Wool to Boving-ton'. Fred Goddard had been wondering throughout his train journey 'if I had really done the right thing as twelve years was a terrible long time, but now there was no turning back'. Nobody was initially at the station to meet him, but eventually he was picked up by someone in uniform who confided, 'I'll tell you, old friend, you can take my advice and get over to the other platform and catch the next train back.' Not a promising start.

Few of these recruits were complimentary about the living quarters they found on arrival. 'Our accommodation had to be seen to be believed,' declared a new subaltern arriving between the wars. 'We were housed in a collection of huts known as Siberia. They were neither draftproof nor rainproof.' The Mess, he discovered, was a series of interlocking huts, and 'the only way to sleep in comfort was to hoist an umbrella or waterproof sheet above the bed'. Another recruit arriving one June night recalled his introduction to the Tank Corps as being 'a seven-mile walk in the dark, and being sworn at by an NCO at the end of it'. After being directed to the recruits' hut 'I think I walked past it several times unable to believe it was the place where I would have to live. It was a one-storey, tar-painted wooden building that looked as much unlike a dwelling place as a mouse-trap.'

Bill Close remembered 'that life was very raw and very difficult. Food, particularly, was terrible.' Another recruit, after hiking from the station, recalled, 'There was breakfast all right, but instead of eggs there were a few portions of canned tomatoes which gave off a sickly smell.' Army life was not meant to be like this.

All this was in marked contrast to the arrival of the first German recruits arriving to join Panzer Regiment 5 in October 1935 at Cambrai Barracks Wunsdorf. The huge, airy, three-storey accommo-dation blocks with spacious cellars were now boasted showers and facilities far superior to their British and French counterparts. These buildings still provide the modern German Army, the Bundeswehr, and NATO troops with accommodation today.

The new intake were met at the railway station and preceded by a military band which marched them into the new barracks, resplendent with picture-postcard green bunting, garlands and banners bedecked with prominent red swastikas. These young men were made to feel they were part of a momentous beginning. Green sports fields were flanked by spacious garages and hangars containing factory-new panzer Mark I tanks. Two of these flanked the introductory speaking podium. Even the original prototype *Grosstracktors* from Kazan had been erected impressively on a ramp at the barrack gate. The new accommodation and their reception visually demonstrated the new regime's future vision and resolve. Newly arrived German tank crew apprentices felt there was a plan – and they were part of it.

The British and German systems recruited regionally. British cavalry regiments dating back to the militia and Napoleonic wars took their manpower from specific local areas. Bert Rendell, from the Wilton and Bournemouth area, joined the RTR because it was based nearby at Bovington. 'I don't think I would have joined any other unit,' he said. Robin Boyes, a Northamptonshire farmer, joined the Northants Yeomanry as a trooper. 'I knew all the chaps and I was at school with a lot of them, also at agricultural college, and I had generally socialised with many of them in the county where I was born.'

German panzer divisions were based on a *Wehrkreis,* or military district, equating to a large English county. The formations founded in 1935 included Saxons and Thuringians in the 1st Panzer Division, Austrians in the 2nd and Prussians in the 3rd (Berlin) Division. Others were added before the outbreak of war: Bavarians in the 4th, Silesians and Sudetenlanders in the 5th and Westphalians in the 6th Divisions, and later there were more. Tank gunner Karl Fuchs's initial posting was to Panzer Regiment 36 based at Schweinfurt; his home town was Rosstal, south-west of Nuremberg in northern Bavaria. 'Most of the guys are from Nuremberg and the surrounding villages,' he wrote home, cataloguing a number of names that he knew his father, a serving soldier, would know. Fuchs was patriotic, and serving with his mates provided a comforting homely solidarity. 'As you can imagine,' he told his father, 'we emptied a couple of bottles while we were celebrating meeting each other. This just goes to show that the people of Rosstal are everywhere.' He emphasised how 'our group is really a terrific fighting unit and we all stick together'. Ludwig Bauer, serving with Panzer Regiment 33 throughout the war, was particularly proud of the Austrian antecedents of the Prinz Eugen regiment and very knowledgeable about its history.

'The first day was a blur,' recalled Trooper Herbert Webster, 'spent getting to know each other, registering for this or that at various offices in the camp' and 'being kitted out with various items of uniform'. All too often the bureaucratic machinery would creak and khakis would not fit. While Webster's were a reasonable match, 'some of the fellows looked clownish in trousers too short or too long etc.,' he recalled. Long queues formed outside the regimental tailor's office, all part of the initiation into a strange and, to many, uncomfortable existence.

Part of the seemingly dehumanising process was a short 'army haircut'. Michael Pope, who came from a privileged 'fox hunting' background to join the Royal Horse Guards, was taken aback at the Regimental Sergeant Major's opinion of his bushy hair, which he referred to as 'rat-catching attire'. He roared: 'To the barber's shop at the double for a short back and sides, you dozy-looking pouf, then down into the town for a good strong woman to make a man of you.' Army entry could be likened to a cold shower compared to the soft life that preceded it.

Nothing prepared the men for the homesickness, lack of privacy and earthy vulgarity characterising their new existence. 'Barrack life was pretty awful in those days, no privacy and rotten food,' was how Bill Close recalled his early days. 'The squad occupied two connected huts and its members spent much of their time fighting each other; I was glad I was fairly athletic and useful with my fists'. The contrast between home life, no matter how poor, and barrack life was sharp. 'There was no excuse for not showering even when the water pipes were frozen,' recalled Fred Goddard during his first two weeks of recruit instruction. 'We had to break the ice on the water tubs outside to shave and wash.'

A barrack room would consist of a line of stark metal-frame beds with simple straw mattresses on each side of the room. Each man's 'bed space' was the small area around the mattress bordering the next in line. Military equipment and a few personal possessions were in a box at the foot of the

bed or in a rudimentary metal or wooden locker alongside. Homesickness
was rife in such Spartan surroundings. One recruit described how:

> The sense of desolation would often bring us near to tears. Every-
> thing is bare, hard, rough and uncouth in the extreme. One is
> compelled to undress in a room full of people and exhibit one's body
> to the common gaze and comment. There is not the slightest atom of
> privacy or comfort; not the faintest thing resembling a home which
> can help one adapt oneself to a new life among strangers of all types.

Recruits had little choice other than to conform to their much changed
environment. 'The vulgarity of the life, to which one later becomes
accustomed, was evident right from the first day,' the same recruit
commented. Herbert Webster recalled the shock of being rudely
awakened on the first morning by the sergeant rattling his stick along
the radiators and chanting, 'Hands off cocks – pull on your socks.'

Eventually, eighteen-year-old Paul Rollins realised there was a point
to this perceived misery. His verdict on his squad training sergeants:
'They were very nice people, very strict as you can imagine, but they
were decent people.' He came to terms with his new life and began to
appreciate the professional training he was receiving. 'I never at any
time wanted to get out,' he recalled. 'Funnily enough, I enjoyed it.'
Humour and fellowship soon began to thaw out the cold shock of
immersion into army life.

Personal accounts attest to this 'bonding' process that occurred on
tribal regimental and traditional lines in British barracks. Trooper Bill
Close thought the discipline 'was very good, and, in fact, it did me a lot
of good'. He enjoyed the social life, and being 'lucky enough to be a
fairly good athlete' was able to attract the attention required, as in all
armies, to get promoted. 'Just before the war I was promoted to
sergeant,' Close revealed, 'which was very unusual with five years
service.'

If the British experience was 'bonding', the German process could
more appropriately be described as 'welding'. Germans bonded, as
National Socialist propaganda proclaimed, like 'Krupp steel'. Wehrmacht training was exacting. Nazi ideology encouraged the subjugation
of the individual to the *Volk,* or group. German recruits, by virtue of

National Labour Service, or *Reichsarbeitdienst,* and their time with the
Hitler Youth, or *Hitlerjugend,* were more familiar with military life on
joining. As Henry Metelmann pointed out, 'In the Hitler Youth we
had already received considerable elementary military training, which
meant the army was able to train us more speedily.' He became a tank
driver, claiming 'when we were finally let loose on the panzers, we
knew what it was all about'. Karl Fuchs, working in a National Labour
Service camp, wrote to his parents that he had 'turned into a real work-
soldier dressed in grey'. The Hitler Youth promoted a community of
boys with regular tests of strength and endurance. Aggression was
encouraged alongside vocational skills such as motor engineering,
which benefited the motorised forces, and gliding for the Luftwaffe.
'In the Hitler Youth they taught us to be tough,' recalled Johannes
Köppen. 'What did Hitler say a German boy must be? Swift as a
greyhound, tough as leather and hard as Krupp steel.'

Major Walther Nehring, Guderian's staff assistant, recognised early
on that the new Panzerwaffe needed to be recruited from fit and tough
young men to form the core of an elite arm. He pointed to the
claustrophobic fighting conditions, the dehabilitating effect of noise
from the engine, gun and tracks, the heavy responsibility of being
completely dependent on each other, the need to master radio to
communicate with other tanks, the practical discomfort of buffeting
tank rides, and the tension from machine-gun fire and artillery splinters
striking tank hulls. He concluded: 'Only quality men and fighters can
be used here – and they will be needed!'

Basic training in the Wehrmacht was hard and applied with draco-
nian discipline. Its peculiar application, like British practice, had
developed through generations of NCOs in the Kaiser's Imperial Army
and Reichswehr. 'Don't stick your neck out – and never volunteer!'
was the old soldier's maxim. Recruits were broken rather than bonded.
'Everywhere there was a certain regimentation,' recalled Roland
Kiemig from his days in the Hitler Youth. 'You didn't just walk
around uselessly, you marched.' All tank crew were put through the
same fast-paced basic infantry training described by Kiemig:

> They kept us on the run, they harassed us, made us run, made us lie
> down, drove us and tormented us. We didn't realise at the time that

the purpose was to break us, to make us lose our will so we'd follow orders without asking – is this right or wrong?

Soldiers were run around in circles, frog-jumped, hopped and sprinted up and down on whistle blasts. 'Whenever I see a man in uniform now,' wrote panzer crewman Hans Becker, 'I picture him lying on his face waiting for permission to take his nose out of the mud.' Götz Hrt-Reger, later to serve in an armoured-car unit, was philosophical about the excesses: 'That's a totally normal training in how to be a social being,' he explained. Henry Metelmann remembered a 'tough and methodical' training programme that often drove them to the point of exhaustion. 'Our officers and sergeants made no secret of their aim to mentally and physically break us in order to remake us in their image in the Prussian tradition.' Ludwig Bauer was mercilessly chased about during training. Recruits were ordered by their NCOs to clamber in and out, over, and then under their tanks twenty times on a whistle blast. His course was 'hard', but he accepted it as perfectly normal and was convinced that it later saved his life. There was a gritty realism and urgency in the German training model that was absent from the firm but fair approach of the British. Bauer remembered his training as 'extreme and intensive'; he had to master every weapon type: 50mm and 75mm main armament and machine-guns; and all weapons 'had to be operated blind-folded'. Panzer crew not up to this exacting training were transferred to the infantry.

'From Reveille to Lights Out we never had a moment's peace,' wrote a young British recruit, 'during those first few weeks when we were still struggling to adapt ourselves to an entirely new life.' The wake-up call for a typical day would be 0630 hours. Breakfast would follow a wash in cold water, competing all the time with too many people using too few basins in Spartan conditions in basic wooden-hutted camps. Breakfast was a hurried affair eaten after a long wait in the queue. 'As I remember,' recalled R.W. Munns in the early 1930s, 'it was a piece of bacon with a fried egg, which had a kind of plastic skin over it, with two pieces of bread, a mug of tea and a pat of margarine.' The next step was to make up beds, clean the bed space and prepare the hut for inspection. All activity was conducted at an urgent tempo, loudly encouraged by NCO instructors. After a parade at 0730 hours the majority of men would begin a morning's training. 'Fatigues', or administrative tasks, would be delegated to the luckless. Soldiers learned very quickly never to volunteer or attract attention to themselves. Nevertheless Munns admitted, 'I found the training programme exhilarating for a young fit man with the energy to cope with all that it entailed, and despite our constant hunger we were really very fit.' Each day was a planned and full one. Evenings were spent preparing for the following day's parades and lectures, cleaning equipment, boots and rifles. At 2130 hours each evening all recruits stood by their beds as the Orderly Sergeant checked that all were present, and lights out was ordered at 2215 hours, 'followed by the grunts, groans and snores of the recruits until reveille next morning at 0630'.

'Once we had got beyond the gawky-new-soldier stage,' explained Herbert Webster, 'we were allowed to leave camp in our leisure time and explore the rest of Bovington.' The second half of the six-month training period became 'fractionally' more relaxed. While driving wheeled or tracked vehicles out of camp 'we were able to make a call at a "caff" and feel, to some extent civilised again'. Harry Webb was told, 'You have to earn a black beret and tank badge, my lad', which he gained after a passing-out parade that signified the end of basic training. 'Then we settled down to six weeks' driving and maintenance, six weeks' gunnery and six weeks' wireless courses.' He passed out as a driver mechanic. Life, especially for the previously unemployed, got better. There was a small income, food and a roof over their heads. There were also other more intangible benefits, gradually appreciated by all. 'I had been brought up in a city,' recalled a recruit in the early 1930s, 'and I found it pleasing to be in this setting instead of being surrounded by terraced houses, warehouses, docks and hordes of traffic.' The Tank Corps depot at Bovington was surrounded by 'moorland stretching as far as the eye could see', as well as farmland and woodland. 'I came to have a great affection for the area and spent many hours tramping over the moors and woodlands', an affection shared almost universally by all who served in the Tank Corps. Another benefit derived from shared hardships during training was the bonding effect this had. 'The comradeship enjoyed, from the embryo days of Bovington to the last days of demobilisation,' recalled Herbert Webster,

'is something which cannot be described to those who didn't themselves experience it.'

All this activity was directed to preparation for war. German
conscription preceded the British by four years. This meant five major
intakes, numbered in thousands compared with the later British
hundreds, prior to the declaration of war. Unlike the British, German
training programmes were directed toward an agreed overall aim, to
create a combined-arms mechanised force. Despite conclusions offered
by the Experimental Force of the late 1920s and early '30s, the British
had yet to produce a unified General Staff acceptance of the way ahead
for future tank warfare. German planners had identified an agreed goal.
Surviving copies of Panzer Regiment 5's training programmes in 1938
would be comprehensible to any armoured unit today. There were
barrack-type training activities conducted in the mornings, and practical shooting and other manoeuvres on local training areas in the
afternoons. Technical and signals training featured prominently. An
examination of battalion-level training papers for the same period
reveal a 16-week training scheme to develop all crew roles. A conscripted panzer recruit would complete individual training in a platoon
before participating in a company exercise the first autumn, likely to be
part of a higher formation exercise. Crew training was followed by
potential NCO training the next year. Practical battle training was
conducted throughout. By 1938, evidently, advanced combined-arms
panzer training exercises were being conducted alongside the air force
with motorised participation from the other arms.

The British trained to a more loosely identified configuration
dependent upon the sacrosanct role of the battalion Commanding
Officer. He followed direction but at his own speed and initiative.
Results were variable, depending upon the drive and professionalism of
individual officers and their willingness to adapt to rapidly changing
technical circumstances. A series of financial crises had cost the British
their tank lead by the late 1930s and this impacted on tank development
and training resources. One recruit described gunnery training with
Vickers Medium tanks in the early 1930s. 'There was an element of
danger in teaching young recruits to fire a 3-pounder shell from a
moving tank,' he admitted. Live firing was being conducted on the
move within four sides of a square run. While changing direction

within the square a recruit 'got a little mixed up' and traversed his gun in the wrong direction. 'The gun was now pointing towards the camp,' the witness related, 'and worse still he fired.' Pandemonium ensued as 'the shell screamed over the ranges and into the camp, thudding on to the officer's mess gardens, just as most of the officers were taking morning tea.' The hapless recruit was taken to task and reprimanded. 'There is no record of the comments made by the officers,' the witness wryly remarked.

Preparedness for war was an issue that needed to be faced, and time and money were increasingly short.

# 3

# PREPARING FOR WAR

## DESIGNER'S WAR

On 2 September 1936 small groups of fit-looking young men, dressed in civilian clothes and carrying duplicate cardboard cases, boarded buses in Berlin and departed at intervals for Stettin on the Baltic Sea coast. Each man was provided with passports and given 350 *Reichsmarks* to cover expenses and the cost of civilian clothes. Like expectant tourists they animatedly chatted about their trip. On arrival they boarded the steamships *Passages* and *Girgenti*. Peering inside dimly lit cargo bays they checked and re-checked the lashings on the forty-one Panzer Mark Is lining the hold. There were also twenty 20mm anti-tank guns, vehicles and workshop equipment filling the space. The ships nosed their way out into the Baltic and set course for Cadiz in Spain. On board were 180 panzer soldiers and technicians of the *Gruppe Imker* (Beekeeper) and *Gruppe Drohne* (Drone). These were cover names for Oberstleutnant Josef Ritter von Thoma's tank training companies, dispatched to support Franco's Nationalist cause in the Spanish Civil War. Panzer crews were accustomed to working in clandestine conditions. Their existence had only been admitted eleven months before.

A few weeks after the newly established Panzer Regiment 6 occupied its modern barracks at Neuruppin, near Panzer Regiment 5 at Wünsdorf, an order was posted in both units asking for some unmarried officers and 160 trainers and panzer crew to volunteer for a special mission. It would involve overseas service and require those selected to leave the Wehrmacht. One of the men prepared to exchange a black panzer uniform for the khaki and leather jackets of Franco's men was Leutnant Hans Hannibal von Mörner. He came from a distinguished line of soldiers, but his Jewish ancestry required him to quit the Wehrmacht because of the recently instituted Nuremberg racial laws. It was felt that racial restrictions might not be so rigidly applied if he was seen to be honourably serving his country in a combat zone.

Released from the stultifying confines of garrison life in Germany, volunteers could raise their professional profile and gain valuable active service experience. Von Thoma quickly recognised that 'Spain would serve as the European Aldershot.' Soon German instructors were training the first Nationalist tank battalion: the Regimento de Infantaria Argel commanded by Major José Pujales Carrasco.

Ten days after the German freighters arrived, the first Russian ship, *Komsomol,* tied up and unloaded fifteen T-26 tanks at Seville. The USSR supported the republican side with 731 tanks and 1,000 aircraft. The German 'Condor Legion' – as the contingent was called – fielded 600 aircraft and 200 tanks. The Italians intervened on the Fascist side with 75,000 troops (compared to 16,000 German), 660 aircraft and 150 tanks.

Russian T-26 and T-28 tanks proved an unpleasant shock to their German and Italian rivals whom they outclassed in firepower and armour. On 29 October, shortly after the arrival of the *Drohne* and *Imker* groups, Italian two-man Ansaldo 'tankettes' were badly mauled in a mass attack by T-26s led by Captain Paul 'Greisser' Arman. Eleven were knocked out at no cost to the Russian tanks. In January 1937 the head of the Soviet tank brigade in Spain, General Dimitri Pavlov, blunted Nationalist advances on Madrid employing mass tank attacks. As each side sized up the other's potential, the Italians found they could thwart the Russian T-26 with 27mm anti-tank guns and powerful anti-tank mines. German 37mm guns could also punch through the Soviet armour. Lessons were being learned.

Von Thoma quickly realised that the Panzer Mark I was insufficiently armoured and lacked an effective gun to combat the Soviet variants. 'I offered a reward of 500 pesetas for every one that was captured, as I was only too glad to convert them to my own use,' he later recalled. Four companies were formed from these captured vehicles of which 'the Moors [Moroccan Nationalist soldiers] bagged quite a lot'. There was rarely sufficient co-ordination between tanks, artillery and air support. Tanks often outran supporting infantry or other arms and were then picked off. Solutions were often arrived at by chance. Tank crews realised that if they fired hull down, only turrets were exposed to predatory anti-tank fire. To halt was to invite a strike, which tended to galvanise movement, even when firing. Von Thoma's men realised that mixing anti-tank guns with their outclassed Panzer Is compensated for the superior gun of the T-26. Both sides were groping for solutions.

Leutnant Hans Mörner, the Jewish officer who sought to salvage his military career in Spain, is buried just 20km west of Madrid. He was hit by an International Brigade sniper while commanding from the open turret of his Panzer I. Leading with the turret lid open became established German practice during the later world war. Hans Mörner, unable to reinstate his military credentials, became the first officer in Panzer Regiment 6 to be killed in combat.

About 400 panzer personnel benefited from battle in Spain, with up to two hundred serving at any one time. The irony of the battles around Madrid at the end of 1936 was that German panzer crews fought against their own countrymen serving as infantry in the International Brigades.

The Spanish Civil War produced some lively debate among the theorists which was not translated into technical design because of complacency by the radicals or misinterpretation of too few facts. 'General Franco wished to parcel out the tanks among the infantry,' explained von Thoma, 'in the usual way of generals who belong to the old school.' With the benefit of hindsight, he concluded when later interviewed: 'I had to fight this tendency constantly in the endeavour to use the tanks in a concentrated way. The Francoist successes were largely due to this.'

Russian General Pavlov's conclusion was opposite. Based on reports sent from Spain, the Red Army disbanded their large armoured formations and distributed them among infantry units to provide support.

'The three types of tanks that I have viewed in Spain,' wrote Fuller in *The Times* on 8 April 1937, 'Italian, German and Russian are not the product of tactical study, rather merely cheap mass production.' Light tanks, he believed, would be 'like a destroyer in heavy seas' when operating over difficult terrain. The press, unlike the theorists and designers, were interested in the human aspects of tanks. Fuller pointed out that the claustrophobic interiors of such small vehicles were 'like the inside of a mobile coffin' which 'can hardly be good for morale'. Harold Mitchell, a Conservative MP, came across a knocked-out Soviet T-26 while visiting behind Nationalist lines. Russian tanks 'carry a good gun', he noted, but 'can easily be destroyed at close quarters'. He presciently gave a glimpse of future tactics: 'The method of dealing with tanks is for a man to creep up near and hurl a bottle of petrol at the rubber on the caterpillar wheels, followed by a bomb. The fire which follows usually destroys the rubber and immobilises the tank.' Significantly he noticed that 'the heat inside is such that the men are usually forced to come out'.

These journalistic glimpses of the obvious revealed the public's ignorance of the nature and implication of the tank clashes that occurred in Spain. They did, however, heighten the emotional spectre of mass air attacks on cities, which greatly alarmed British pacifist opinion – the slaughter of 1914–18 had not been forgotten. Newsreels of the Madrid and other bombings shown alongside cinema releases depicting fictional aerial bombardment, such as *Things to Come* (1936), raised fears and questions concerning rearmament. Behind the alarming images came an increasingly familiar squat and ugly shape. The outline of the tank began to enter the public psyche as an image exuding future menace.

The French were dismissive of the Wehrmacht's tank training intervention by the Condor Legion. The newspaper *L'Intransigent* wrote on 20 April 1937 that 'the German tanks were a major disappointment, a two-man crew, 50 kilometres per hour, two machine-guns and almost worthless armour'. In 1935 French production lines were producing superbly armoured and armed tanks by comparison to many other nations. By 1939 France was to have the most sophisticated tank fleet in Europe. The 47mm gun on the Char B-1 and Somua, heavy and medium tanks, was the best weapon of its kind anywhere and employed 60mm of armour protection. These tanks were well designed and configured to fight other tanks, with reliable engines and shielded suspensions. But their crew fighting compartment confined one man to the turret, overtaxing the commander/gunner. French designers were paying insufficient attention to the needs of the men who were to fight the machines.

The human factor was not lost on the British and now the Germans, who began to realise by the mid-1930s that there are three jobs in the turret that need to be accomplished simultaneously in combat. The commander has to search for targets and identify threats from all directions. The gunner focuses his attention on peering through a magnifying telescopic sight to hit targets as directed by the commander. The loader has to retrieve ammunition from bins stored around the turret and reload the main gun and service the co-axial machine-gun. When, in place of this trio in the fighting compartment, commanders operated alone in small one-man turrets, they were completely over-phased in combat, especially against opposing tanks or anti-tank guns.

The German General Staff's overview of lessons learned at the end of the war was clinically measured, acknowledging that the better ranges of opposing tank guns caused 'relatively high losses to the crews'. Poor-quality steel in Russian armour-piercing shot degraded their penetration capacity, and 'up to 75 per cent of the base fuses fail to detonate'. Significantly, the Germans also commented on how initial enthusiasm to serve in tanks in Franco's army soon deteriorated once 'the first losses occurred and it became known what the inside of a burned tank looked like'. The Germans began to insert a human dimension into their tank design. What the 415 tankmen in von Thoma's Gruppe learned entered the collective training consciousness of the Wehrmacht's Panzerwaffe. 'Today, in addition to committed tank crews,' wrote the final report, 'captured Russian tanks are manned by pardoned criminals or Spaniards who have been given a choice between a prison sentence and a one-way trip in a tank attack.' Tank fighting imposed unique emotional pressures. Panzer crews benefited mainly from the human experience their tank men derived from active service.

Guderian and his staff officers had long recognised that the comfort and convenience of crews should be taken into account as design criteria. He insisted that the Panzerkampfwagen Mark III should have five-man crews, so that the men were not overworked or obliged to hurry their functional tasks. Moreover, he wanted an improved layout so that all could be seated. The Panzer III and IV designs developed as a team of vehicles. The III, the main battle tank, was equipped with a 37mm armour-piercing gun and two machine-guns. The IV, designed to supplement and support the III, had a larger 75mm gun firing high explosive. Development and production began in the mid-1930s. Torsion bar suspensions gave a more comfortable ride. In relative terms these were luxurious vehicle design concepts, hand-made rather than mass-produced. As a consequence, they came on line slowly and at great unit cost.

Whereas French crewmen felt isolated in their one-man turrets, German crews were placed next to each other. At the front sat the driver, with the radio operator and hull machine-gunner, while in the turret the gunner and loader could look at each other across the gun, with the commander only head and shoulders above them. In battle they could reassure one another with a glance and even lip-read if need be over the clamour of engine and gun. German armoured protection in the new models was superior, using electro-welding instead of bolted joints or rivets. Armour thickness was varied to save weight, and had face-hardened steel attached, to break up uncapped shot before it could penetrate. The Germans were still lightweights in the tank design boxing match, but they were re-designing gloves and fighting techniques to improve their competitive edge.

Meanwhile the British had lost their lead. In 1935 the French assembled the first armoured division, with the Germans rapidly following suit with three. Columns of panzers fired mass machine-gun salutes as they drove past in eight-deep phalanxes in front of the Nuremberg Party Rally crowds. In Paris during the traditional Bastille Day parades 'squadrons of bombers and fighters flew by in close formation. No fewer than 500 aeroplanes, in groups of seven, passed at great speed over the roofs' wrote the *Illustrated London News* correspondent. 'The roar of their engines was succeeded by the tremendous din of the mechanical forces as they went by.' Europe was rearming. 'The procession was completed by about 200 tanks,' claimed the exuberant observer.

The twenty-four-year-old Bert Rendell, stationed with his regiment at Perham Down, Wiltshire, was unimpressed with the fifty-six new Vickers Mark VI light tanks delivered in 1936. It had a three-man crew, and he complained that 'the gunner/operator was useless when we went to where ever, because he could not operate radios and load and fire all at the same time – so you can see the difficulty.' Crews were frustrated at poor design and lack of progress. 'Advancement was nil' on its predecessors, Rendell concluded. 'But these tanks were made by somebody,' he remarked, 'and in 1937 we were being prepared – they knew it but we didn't – there was a war coming, they knew that.' In February 1934 the Chiefs of Staff Meeting of the Defence Requirements Committee asked the government to spend £40m to re-equip the army over a five-year period. Much of this sum should be devoted to preparing a force for a possible continental campaign. Hitler's arrival on the European scene had not gone unnoticed. Neville Chamberlain, the Chancellor of the Exchequer, responded that the government was faced with proposals 'financially impossible to carry out'. The army's proposed allocation of funds was halved, the navy's left untouched and that of the air force significantly increased. Chamberlain felt confident relegating the army to the 'Cinderella of the Services', because the public, with the spectre of 1914–18 still vivid in its memory, would never countenance another British Expeditionary Force (BEF). British aircraft designers were taken more seriously than tank designers. Army training and other resources were earmarked to provide reinforcement cadres for the Empire, not Europe.

Eighteen-year-old Bert Foord, an apprentice attached to the tank design process in 1930, recalled that 'not many people knew anything about tanks'. He had grown up outside Woolwich Arsenal, where his father was the pier master, often shipping out ammunition. It was natural that he should seek a practical apprenticeship, and he 'went into the woodworking line in the patent shop', where he was soon making tank mock-ups. He offers some remarkable insights concerning the shop-floor side of British tank development leading up to the war. It was less than methodical in process terms. He recalled three floors at the Arsenal housing a 'tank drawing office, royal carriage and gun people'. Shortage of money meant research and development was confined solely to two organisations: Vickers and the Department of Design at the Royal Ordnance factories. In essence there were two committees going their separate ways on tank design. Neither had contact with the General Staff, so they knew nothing about the army's needs.

Bert Foord felt 'the top people were not interested'. He recalled that the army officer, normally a major, 'had a little office at the end of the drawing office and would spend all his time there'. Major G.

MacLeod Ross, who occupied this office between 1933 and 1936, commented: 'The number of men capable of developing a tank was minute.' He bemoaned the absence of an interface with the General Staff, who were uneducated regarding mechanical science. 'While some failed to understand, others were so obstinately bigoted that they did not possess the capacity to understand what [the designers] were proposing.' The whole process was stymied by the Cabinet-sponsored 'ten-year rule', which after 1918 had assumed no British involvement in war for ten years. It was followed, he later wrote, by 'the years when ideas were two a penny; when no one had experience to make up his mind as to the possibilities of the weapon with regard to the state of technics'.

Visitors to the Arsenal went to the patent shop first, Foord observed, where he bolted together tank mock-ups with 15mm plywood, equating to the thickness of the steel plates eventually bolted together to produce the prototype. Financial stringency bedevilled progress. 'We were very short of money,' he remembered. Between 1927 and 1936 the annual sum available for tank experimentation varied from £22,500 to £93,750, when the cost of designing and producing a single experimental tank might be as much as £29,000.

They were completely unaware of the tank arms race conducted beyond the workshop floor. Pre-war tensions had a negligible impact, Foord recalled, and they did not get much information from the newspapers that was relevant to their work. 'I remember the Spanish War,' he said, 'but nobody here did anything. Captain Liddell-Hart wrote books on how to use tanks and the only people to take any notice of it was the Germans, they studied it.'

In 1936 Colonel Giffard le Quesne Martel, who had been involved in early British tank development, attended Red Army manoeuvres in Russia with Major-General Archibald Wavell. They were taken aback at the sheer number of tanks on display, on one occasion counting 1,000 tanks during a single march-past. The Soviet BT 'light-medium' tank exhibited a remarkable top road speed of 30mph and could do 20mph with ease cross-country employing a suspension invented by the American designer J.W. Christie. 'Unless we can improve the A9 [Cruiser tank] to a considerable extent,' Martel commented, 'I cannot help feeling dismay at the idea of our building any large number of these tanks which will be inferior to existing Soviet tanks.' On his return Martel was eventually able to procure one of only three Christie prototypes ever built. The US government took a dim view of the export of forbidden war material, so it was smuggled out in crates labelled 'Tractor' and 'Grapefruit'. On its arrival in England there was no existing UK armaments firm that could handle the further development of Cruiser tanks, so a new firm was created: Nuffield Mechanisation.

Tank design was advisory rather than forming part of a cohesive process. No one person had clear responsibility. On 17 October 1936 the Secretary of State for War advised the Cabinet: 'We have insufficient light tanks of modern design . . . We have no medium tanks for service, although new models are undergoing trials. We have a design for an infantry tank but it has not yet passed its trials.'

Technical development was disrupted as projects over-dependent on commercial components – particularly under-powered engines – were shelved. In 1936 the British government took steps to rearm, but eighteen months later the GOC of Eastern Command General Edmund Ironside confided to his diary: 'The paper on rearmament has come in. It is truly the most appalling reading. How we have come to this state is beyond believing'. He recorded a litany of failures: cavalry regiments not yet mechanised, obsolete medium tanks, no Cruiser tanks, no infantry tanks, obsolete armoured cars and no light tanks. 'This is the state of our Army after two years' warning,' he complained. 'No foreign nation would believe it if they were told.'

## MANOEUVRE VERSUS HORSE WAR

The Panzerwaffe now began to benefit from a series of large-scale military manoeuvres that accompanied a succession of pre-war crises leading up to 1939. During the early morning hours of 25 February 1936 the four-month-old Panzer Regiment 5 was called out with other motorised units of the 3rd Panzer Division and loaded on flat-rail cars. The destination was ostensibly a big exercise at Sennelager. Actually they were on stand-by. Ten days later German troops reoccupied the previously demilitarised Rhineland.

In early March 1938 the 2nd Panzer Division was alerted with little prior warning to participate in the *Anschluss,* or German annexation of Austria. Generalleutnant Guderian, who had by now been appointed the commander of the world's first panzer corps, was tasked to lead the spearhead with his old panzer division and the SS Leibstandarte Adolf Hitler Regiment, included for political reasons. Armoured vehicles were prudently decorated rather than camouflaged with greenery, to symbolise a parade rather than military advance. Much was learned in this first operational panzer advance. Thankfully, as Guderian described it 'at every halt the tanks were decked with flowers and food was pressed on the soldiers'. The problem was that halts were all too frequent as armoured breakdowns averaged 20–30 per cent during the 420-mile journey from Würzburg through Passau to Vienna. As Leutnant Helmut Ritgen recalled, the Panzer Mark Is, which formed the bulk of the tanks employed,

> often coughed and spluttered to a halt when rattling along the road. This meant dismounting, opening the access hatches, and trying to start them up again. Changing the spark plugs or operating the fuel pump by hand – at the cost of blackened, burnt and bruised fingers and faces – sometimes got the 'beast' started again with a loud bang; otherwise it was ignominiously taken away by the recovery team.

There were no mobile fuel supplies accompanying the columns and these had to be commandeered from the Mayor at Passau. Violence was even threatened at one military fuel depot not forewarned about the operation. 'For the rest,' Guderian remarked, 'the Austrian petrol stations along our road of advance were requested to keep open' as crews navigated along routes using tourist road maps.

Although Guderian claimed 'we had added nothing to our knowledge of tank warfare', the crews in terms of practical resourcefulness most certainly had. Crucial experience was gained in the 'alerting, moving and supplying of panzer units'. From now on supply services were established within panzer divisions so that between three and five days' supply of fuel, food and ammunition could be carried by the fighting units. Simple operating procedures such as getting vehicles on the road in the correct unit convoy order, and measures instituted to deal with driver fatigue, provided short-cuts toward future operational effectiveness. Carrying essential supplies, their stowage and dealing with road obstacles provided panzer crews with skills that French and British units would later have to assimilate under the pressure of war. Guderian and his subordinates gained the type of pragmatism that could convert previous tactical notions of the panzer advance into strategic ones. Fast and deep penetrations into enemy territory, such as the march of 420 miles by the 2nd Panzer, and 600 miles by the SS Adolf Hitler, were now manifestly achievable. Similar deep incursions into the enemy's rear might collapse an opponent's will to resist.

These practical lessons were applied more successfully during the march into the Sudetenland after the Munich Agreement in October. Although they did not have to fight, thanks to the Führer diplomatic camp, being prepared to fight proved the stiffest training test yet. Czech tanks were the equal of, if not superior to, most German panzers. There was considerable relief 'as we marched past the formidable Czech fortifications, bloody fighting had been avoided,' remarked von Mellenthin. 'Our soldiers received a touching reception in every village' from the Sudeten-Germans, he recalled, and 'were greeted with flags and flowers'. Guderian thought the moves by the 1st Panzer and 13th Motorised Divisions in two night marches over 170 miles in readiness for the invasion 'a fine performance'. In the words of Leutnant Ritgen, 'These few days of the "Flower Campaign" near Pilsen − with its excellent beer! − did wonders for the pride and confidence of the units involved.' A new expression entered the Wehrmacht's vocabulary to describe cheap and heady success: *Blumenkrieg,* or 'Flower War'.

Medals were distributed for the Austrian and Czech 'Flower' campaigns. Since there were very few soldiers with awards, apart from the few Condor Legion personnel who had returned from Spain, panzer driver Hans Becker soon appreciated the advantages. They 'were accepted by the people as great heroes, and I was now able to share a little bit of their glory'. It did not take long for the smart black-uniformed panzer soldiers to catch on to other benefits: 'The effect of these decorations on the girls was magical. They loved to be seen out with an old campaigner, and what did it matter if his pay stretched no further than one evening a week at a local dance-hall or cinema!'

Over the next few months various units of the 3rd Panzer Division were called out again, a five-day march through severe winter conditions to occupy Prague, another triumphant march-past at St Prague's Wenceslas Square, a huge parade in Berlin on 9 June to celebrate the exploits of the Condor Legion and their return from Spain, and the fiftieth birthday parade spectacular held for Hitler in Berlin on 20 April. The Panzerwaffe featured prominently in mass displays of modern motorised fighting power, sweeping past in majestic drive-bys shrouded by blue exhaust smoke. Military attachés from Poland, Switzerland, Russia, France and Great Britain thoughtfully observed the spectacular procession of new weapons and equipments. Six divisions took part in a parade that took four hours to pass the saluting rostrum, 100,000 men – every eighth soldier in the Wehrmacht. One participant, Franz Ingenbrandt, remembered:

We marched along the east-west axis, a parade march in front of the Führer. It was an experience that every participant would never forget – even today. As our regiment marched by, the bands played our marching song, '*Denkste denn, du Berliner Pflanz*'.

The crowd howled its appreciation as the panzer columns rolled by. The taboo of the Versailles Treaty had invested tanks with glamour. Feelings in the diplomatic stands were mixed. Many shared Guderian's conviction, expressed later, that Hitler appeared at the pinnacle of success. 'Would he have the necessary self-control to consolidate it, or would he overreach himself?' Whatever the outcome, 'the situation was highly inflammable'.

As the panzer arm was consolidating and incorporating the wealth of practical knowledge and experience it gained from these large-scale bloodless manoeuvres, the British and French armies were just emerging from a stultifying horse-versus-tank debate. The day of the horse was clearly past, but attitudes did not reflect this. 'The tank will not drive the cavalry from the battlefield,' announced one cavalry journal in 1923, 'it will in future increase its radius of action.' The Wehrmacht did retain cavalry divisions into the early years of the next war, as did

Poland and Russia, because they were another tool in a range of combined-arms military options as well as being appropriate to particular terrain and budget realities.

In Britain it was an all-or-nothing debate between those who wished to retain the 1914 status quo and the new proponents of mechanised warfare. Major-General R.G. Howard-Vyse, the previous Inspector of Cavalry, suggested that 'constant association in peace with that comparatively swift animal, the horse,' had a beneficial effect upon cavalry soldiers, producing 'a quickness of thought and elasticity of outlook which are almost second nature.' These were of course characteristics also sought by modern tank crews. Another old cavalry journal declared, 'There is every possibility of a bullet being invented which would make the tank (with its innate clumsiness as compared with a horseman) as vulnerable, if not more so than a cavalryman.' A clear lesson emerging from the Spanish Civil War was the vulnerability of tanks to anti-tank guns, mines and artillery. The German General Staff adapted to mechanisation in a more focused and integrated way. Discussion preceded a decision that, once taken, was upheld by all service arms, recognising each had a part to play. Change in Britain was transacted reluctantly with an absence of objectivity that followed 'tribal' regimental fault lines. An element of inverted snobbery further characterised the tank-versus-cavalry debate evident still after mechanisation. General Howard-Vyse pointed out:

> It is, I think, common knowledge that the natural enthusiasm for machinery, with which the Tank Corps is doubtless endowed, has tended in the past to lead them to concentrate on this side of their duties, to the comparative neglect of those tactical principles, ignorance of which has always invited, and always will invite, disaster . . . the Tank Corps have no tactical tradition on which to build.

Change, when it came, was too late. The separate units in the British Army formed into one Royal Armoured Corps (RAC) when war was only four months away. The Germans had meanwhile completed four training seasons with complete divisions.

Neither side in the coming conflict had much idea how it would be fought except that air would play an important part. 'One's main difficulty is forming any sort of picture of what these opening stages will be like,' wrote Brigadier Percy Hobart six years before, trying to deduce the possible use of a tank force *early* in a European campaign. 'My own feeling,' he offered, 'is that Air and Gas will play so large a part that concentration of troops or any plans involving deployments à la von Schlieffen will be quite impossible.' The Germans were likewise unclear, but they single-mindedly and energetically pursued developments that, although questionable, were not yet proven wrong. Hans von Luck had been assigned to a cavalry regiment in Silesia in the early 1930s, but was unexpectedly transferred to the 1st Motorised Battalion. 'A bitter disappointment,' he later wrote, because he regarded cavalry as an elite force 'and I loved horses and riding'. 'But we soon realised that the seven motorised battalions in the Reichswehr were to become the nucleus of the later tank force.'

Horse attitudes still permeated the mechanised cavalry units. In 1938 Sergeant Brown, serving with the 10th Hussars, had been taught to drive the light two-man Mark VIB tank. 'Of course,' he remembered 'the saddest thing was losing our horses, except the officers who kept them for their private use, for polo and races.' Fred Goddard experienced the changeover from horses to tanks at the same time. 'I felt sorry for some of the cavalry chaps who came to Bovington to train on tanks.' He observed how long it took for them to get the black dungarees the Tank Corps already wore. 'They had to put up with a lot of remarks from us when mounting the tanks still wearing spurs,' he recalled. Michael Pope, 'addicted to the sport of foxhunting', was adamant even as war began that he would join the Household Cavalry, the last of the mounted units to survive mechanisation. He had lived closely alongside horses since childhood. 'If I was to defend my King and Country,' he declared, 'then it had to be astride a charger, not from a tank, aircraft, ship or on my flat feet.' These structural upheavals taking place immediately before the war inevitably had an impact on general preparedness. Aidan Sprot was to be commissioned into the Royal Scots Greys, still transitioning to armour at the outbreak of war. Of some 500 or 600 soldiers in the regiment 'probably not more than fifty soldiers had ever driven a motor car,' he observed 'and yet they were given these very complicated tanks, with a very complicated engine, with a very complicated gun and a very complicated wireless.'

The term 'donkey walloper', popularly applied to cavalry officers and men, conjured up a caricature image of eccentric riders encouraging reluctant mules into the twentieth-century mechanisation process. Eccentricity was the hallmark, often cultivated, of the cavalry officer compared with his Tank Corps colleague.

Tank Corps officers appeared more focused and intensely preoccupied with their profession, including as many ex-grammar as public school officers in their ranks.

This incongruous juxtaposition of tradition and innovative progress had a corrosive effect on preparation for what was to prove a brutal war. Aidan Sprot explained that when he arrived in the regiment 'they had twenty horses left and two little Mark VIB pre-war English tanks'. Training proved fun and amusing 'because these tanks didn't have any internal communication so we tied strings around the driver's shoulders and steered him like a horse. If we wanted the tank to go right we pulled the right rein.' The German panzers had radios fitted four years before and had been training with them ever since.

A technological consequence of the horse-versus-tank debate was that the financial squeeze delayed the essential mechanisation of the cavalry units, adding to the divisions that already existed in the tank school regarding the proposed way ahead. Cruiser medium tanks had sacrificed armour as a consequence of commercially provided, underpowered engines. To compensate, a heavier armoured tank was ordered to provide support specifically to the infantry. In 1935 the Mark I infantry machine-gun tank was produced; but, powered by only a 70hp Ford V8 engine, it could only manage 8mph. Its 60–65mm of armour was impervious to all known anti-tank guns. The resulting divergence of heavy and light tank development was the beginning of the Infantry and Cruiser tank dichotomy that was to bedevil subsequent unit and formation tank establishments. The Germans, by contrast, were instinctively opting for a mass of equipments designed to operate together, moving at like speed.

The only reserve that the British tank force could call upon in the event of war was the hastily converted TA battalions formed in 1938 and 1939. 'The news coming in was not good,' remembered Fred Goddard. 'We were drawing toward a crisis as in 1938.' Conscription was announced in April 1939 and the first call-up was on 1 July.

Ian Hammerton, a TA trooper with 42 RTR, was called out and immediately subjected to the vagaries of army clothing alongside thousands of others. Issued kit was either 'large, larger, very large or incredibly tiny'. Swapping items over time enabled them to look less like 'Fred Karno's Army'. Instruction *en masse* in these circumstances, such as on VD prevention, bordered on the bizarre. Hammerton recalled a red-faced and clearly embarrassed Medical Officer explaining the intricacies of a seeming mystery. 'I want to talk to you about something,' he began, 'I needn't go into details,' – and he did not. 'That was our lecture on avoiding VD,' declared Hammerton. 'It left me none the wiser as I didn't know what on earth it was all about.'

There was scant time to get the new TA tank battalions ready. 'More recruits were arriving at Bovington,' Goddard recalled, 'and training became more intense.' But the whole ambiance of TA training up to this point had been recreational rather than operational. It offered a pleasant change from work routine with an annual two-week holiday at a training camp, with people who knew each other from their respective local communities, cementing friendships and social ties. John Verney idolised his cavalry squadron commander, whom he thought 'soldierly looking'. He was shocked to appreciate later that he had no military credentials 'unless a permanent state of inebriation at the yearly camp for the past ten years could be called a military qualification'.

Most of the officers were drawn from the professional and landed classes or large company concerns; junior officers were invariably their sons or managerial staff. John Verney had mixed feelings about his fellow cavalry TA officer colleagues. These were 'squires, farmers, land agents and the like, born and bred in the country and sharing a hundred tastes and acquaintances from childhood'. He grew to love them when they went to war, but at this stage 'the effort of pretending to be someone I was not was proving to be a strain'. Eighteen-year-old John Mallard, who served with 44 RTR TA, believed 'the TA at that time was very much a social club'. Verney 'hated the ritualistic dinners and the long hours of horseplay, which by tradition followed them'. One had to be a particular type, as Mallard recalled: 'Officers were taken in if they liked you.'

John Mallard felt that the 1938 conversion of six TA battalions to RTR regiments 'was not very successful'. In fact 'a large proportion was more suitable for digging trenches than training in a tank regiment'. There were few equipments available to train on; they had some trucks 'and a tank hull with no turret for tracked driving'. It took a year for the new equipments to 'dribble through'. Difficulties occurred during the transition; 'all the elderly officers were pushed out' because they could not cope with the transition from infantry to tanks. Some cavalrymen could likewise not cope with mechanisation. Paul Mace recalled one such case in the East Riding Yeomanry. Guy Cunard 'could reel off the name and breeder of almost every winner of all the big races and its lineage'. But 'Give him a tank, and he was terrible, having no idea nor interest in how machinery worked nor anything about it.'

The NCOs were usually the foremen, working in civil life for the officers; and the other ranks, the work-force of the large landowners or commercial organisations in the area. John Mallard commented, 'Our age meant we were flexible enough to be retrained, but many of the soldiers were also not right – elderly officers and NCOs were the ones to go.' In their place came 'large intakes of new chaps'. The conversions he described were a 'massive task' involving a substantial 'weeding out process'.

Instructor-Sergeant Paul Rollins recalled the same unsuitability. 'They were not tank men at all. So what they did was get rid of 300 and they got an intake of another 300.' Major George Wade encapsulated the TA experience on the eve of war. He was the director of Gabriel Wade & English, a large timber firm in Hull, and a squadron commander in the East Riding Yeomanry. When he telephoned his clerk Colin Brown on 25 August 1939 he was talking to his corporal clerk and civilian employee. 'Brown,' he said, 'go at once to Hull Barracks as the balloon is about to go up.' His clerk spent the next four weeks telephoning around, calling out the regiment's men. He even had to buy food and prepare menus locally until the army system could take over.

'If orders of known and tried equipments are not placed we may be caught short of tanks in the near future,' wrote the Deputy CIGS, Lieutenant-General Sir Ronald Adam to Sir Harold Brown, the Director of Munitions production: 'If we do not press ahead with new designs we shall find ourselves with tanks that are quite incapable of coping with German standards and which instead of being assets are death traps'.

Industry was proving incapable of reacting to the surge in rearmament – now urgent, but too late.

> We have ordered, purely as insurance [Adam's report continued], tanks of the type of A9 and we are faced with the fact that although the first of these orders was placed in early August 1937, hardly any of these machines have been delivered up to the last week, some twenty months later.

Even if they were delivered, both the A9 and A10 Cruiser tanks were suspected of being obsolescent for a European war. Recent trials of the German 20mm gun, fitted on the lightest German panzers and some armoured cars, showed that it 'can not only pass through the armour carried on the A13 Mark I [Cruiser tank] but that it can burst effectively after penetration of the armour'. In technical terms it appeared that British tanks were way behind in the tank design arms race. 'We must have known what the Germans were doing,' stated John Mallard, caught up in the transition of an infantry Gloucestershire battalion to 44 RTC, 'but we did not grasp the nettle. We did with air, but not with tanks.'

During the summer of 1939 Guderian was preparing for large-scale motorised autumn manoeuvres. At the end of August he was summoned to a conference and told to change his plans; his XIX Corps was going to form part of the invasion of Poland. The German Panzerwaffe 1st Light Division received about 130 Czech Skoda 35(t) tanks, a reliable offspring development from the Vickers 6-ton tank. The Allies were to pay for the diplomatic sell-out of Czechoslovakia. It was superior to the Panzer I and II mainstays of the German tank force. German radios were fitted and all Mark Is and some Panzer IIs were discarded from the regiment. Even training without Czech instructors or training manuals, they were firing on the ranges by July. Panzer Battalion 67 in the 3rd Light Division was also issued with Czech tanks. One of its company commanders commented after live firing at the Putlos ranges on the Baltic coast: 'Our tanks were very good cross-

country – but the armour was very weak and the radio fit primitive . . .
The commanders' and gunners' vision when the turrets were closed
down was bad.'

Preparations for the coming operation were hectic. Panzer units
were still training new recruits, re-equipping and reorganizing. When
Guderian was told that war was imminent he knew that only eighty-
seven of the new Mark IIIs and 197 Mark IVs had been delivered.
Tank production was competing with the needs of the growing
*Luftwaffe* (air force) and *Kriegsmarine* (navy). Guderian's views would
not have been dissimilar to those of the British, also acutely aware of
their own limitations. In Panzer Regiment 5, for example, one of the
earliest tank units to be established, there were only 3 Panzer IIIs and
9 Panzer IVs, but 63 Panzer Is and 77 Panzer IIs. The Wehrmacht's
tank strength was 1,026 Panzer Is and 1,151 Panzer II vehicles and
164 Czech tanks. Panzer Is had been ordered as a substitute measure
to provide driver training for the newly established panzer crews.
'Nobody in 1932 could have guessed,' Guderian dolefully wrote later,
'that one day we should have to go into action with this little training
tank.' They were 'the runt of the litter', declared panzer crewman
Otto Carius. The 'Krupp's sports car', as it was christened by its
crews, was driven to war with the same enthusiasm as shown later by
the under-equipped British.

## WAR

The air during the night of 31 August/1 September 1939 was sultry
and heavy on the German-Polish frontier. Across a 1,000km arc
stretching from eastern Prussia south through Pomerania and Silesia to
the recently occupied Czech lands, German soldiers moved into their
assembly areas. The planned configuration was to enable the encirclement of Poland's armies in a great pincer movement due to snap
shut east of Warsaw. Light rain began to fall as momentary exposures
of flashlights exposed shiny wet tank hulls and helmets bobbing about
in the dark. The subdued clatter of mess-tins, equipments and
weapons occasionally broke the stillness of damp, overhanging fir
boughs and dripping trees. The atmosphere was tense. 'People felt

something was up,' wrote Unteroffizier Jendreschik in the 3rd Light Division. 'We were pleased to finally get on with it.' Live ammunition was issued on 23 August in anticipation of action on the 26th, but it was inexplicably cancelled. Rittmeister Freiherrn von Esebeck with *Aufklärungs* (recce) Battalion 3 in one of the northern assembly areas glanced at his watch. It was 4.30 a.m. and he could see the sky lightening to the east. 'A thin mist covers the countryside,' he later wrote, 'it is unlikely that anyone slept during the night. All thoughts were focused on what lies ahead.'

There was no 'hurrah–patriotism', only tension over what the next day might bring. Unteroffizier Rolf Hertenstein, a Mark IV tank gunner with Panzer Regiment 4, recalled the difference between departing for this campaign and the flower-bedecked departures of 1914. 'It wasn't like that for us,' he recalled. 'We weren't really excited, nor did we want a war, because you could be one of the fatalities.' The prevailing view was: get it done. 'Well, there is a war on now. That's what we're here for,' he later wrote resignedly. His mood was echoed by Leutnant Alexander Stahlberg. 'None of the brave mood of 1914, no cheers, no flowers,' he recalled as the local Stettin regiments left the town heading for east Pomerania. 'We stole away in the darkness.'

The false alarm on 25 August had meant that units of the 3rd Light Division who had already closed in on the border had to withdraw 60km backwards. Army Group South headquarters had received the cancellation with jubilation. Oberst (Colonel) Blumentritt recalled the Army Group Commander 'von Rundstedt had some bottles of Tokay fetched from the town of Neisse to celebrate' what was termed a 'happy release'. On the 31 August a terse new order reinstated the invasion go-ahead for 0445 hours on 1 September.

'Not much is known about Poland,' reflected von Esebeck, constantly checking his watch. The Führer's proclamation announcing war was read out and they were briefed on their anticipated route. After the repeated changes of orders, 'The tension for all of us is at breaking-point. Will we be sent into action at all?' he wondered. 'Will the Poles put up a fight?' Six panzer divisions, four recently mechanised light divisions of ex-cavalry and four motorised infantry divisions were to spearhead a concentric attack from two German armies. Twenty-seven infantry divisions and one cavalry brigade would follow the spearheads.

They were attacking a Polish force of similar size with thirty infantry divisions, eleven cavalry and two motorised brigades.

Only one of Poland's envisaged four mechanised brigades (OMS) was ready for action. Nine armoured battalions were deployed in company units of only about thirteen vehicles each, supporting infantry divisions or cavalry brigades. There were about 130 TP light tanks with a 37mm gun and 440 TK series Tankettes with a 20mm cannon. Poland had not been able to afford an ambitious modernisation programme, and in 1936 France had agreed to lend armoured vehicles and provide a loan to pay for them, but only fifty-three Renault FT tanks with 37mm guns had been delivered. There were armoured cars with the reconnaissance squadrons of cavalry brigades. The Poles would indeed fight, but they were as ignorant about the Germans as the invaders were about them. About 3,200 German panzers were to attack 600 Polish tanks.

Eight days before, Hitler's diplomatic coup of signing a last-minute non-aggression pact with Russia had shocked the western powers and appeared to make a war inevitable. Germany could assault Poland with no fear of a Russian response. It was, nevertheless, a campaign of some complexity as General Franz Halder, the German Army Chief of Staff, was alarmed by reports of Russian troop movements also. 'It could not be ruled out that the Russians will move, once we have had our first successes,' he wrote in his diary.

At 0445 hours a thick ground mist permeated the forward German positions on the frontier. In the north only 30 per cent of Luftflotte 1's aircraft could start up, and only 80 per cent of Luftflotte 4, striking from the south, was flying as the first artillery salvos of the Second World War grumbled along the length of the Polish frontier. It was an inauspicious start. Nevertheless, the panzer units began to grope their way into the mist. 'Engines growl into life to our right and left,' recalled Oberleutnant Rudolf Behr, commanding a heavy panzer Mark IV platoon, 'and from further back there is a whining and clattering of the smaller combat vehicles.' The panzers moved forward along the dusty, sandy tracks bordering Poland to a series of new realities.

Officers and crews had absolutely no experience of combat. Mass movements of tanks in action led purely by radio had never happened before. A new dimension, air power, was sweeping over their heads. Never before had the combined employment of armour and air been tried out on such a scale. A large-scale exercise had been planned for the Grafenwöhr training area in north-east Bavaria for the 21–25 August, designed to test tactical support for the army by Stuka dive bomber and bomber units. It was curtailed for the real thing.

Oberleutnant Lossen, advancing into the Danzig Corridor in the early-morning light with Panzer Regiment 6, could see 'burning villages and towns light up the horizon all around like torches'. As the sun rose it burned off the mist and bathed the emerging combat zones with the radiant sunshine of a glorious hot early-September day. Von Esebeck, moving ahead with the armoured reconnaissance, remarked to his crews, 'From 0445 hours, we will be using live ammunition. No quarter given from now on.'

This was no exercise; the Panzerwaffe tank men were to receive their baptism of fire well before their future western opponents. Its impact would further differentiate them from other tank men.

# 4

## A DIFFERENT WAR

### BAPTISM OF FIRE

At 11.15 a.m. on Sunday 3 September 1939 the Prime Minister Neville Chamberlain's echoing and occasionally crackly voice announced to millions huddled around wireless sets in sitting-rooms throughout England: 'I am speaking to you from the Cabinet room at 10 Downing Street.' He explained the British Ambassador's final note had been delivered to Germany:

> Stating that unless we heard from them at 11 o'clock that they were prepared at once to withdraw their troops from Poland, a state of war would exist between us.

Not everyone was listening. Trooper Dai Mitchell, serving in the 5th Battalion of the Royal Tank Regiment, was still in bed. 'Sunday morning and we had been on the tiles all night!' He had been woken up with a mug of tea after a typical soldier's Saturday night out and was enduring the hangover. The momentous events unfolding had not been paramount in his mind. 'I remember little about the build-up to war that summer,' he recalled.

'I have to tell you now that no such undertaking has been received,' Chamberlain announced, 'and that consequently this country is at war with Germany.' The Prime Minister expressed disappointment at the failure of his peace overtures and declared that Britain and France had resolved 'to go to the aid of Poland'. Chamberlain concluded with the statement: 'I am certain that right will prevail.'

Mitchell had not really been paying attention. 'Somebody switched on the radio and that dear old fogey Neville Chamberlain was quacking away,' he remembered. 'Then the penny dropped, a state of war existed between Great Britain and Germany. Life would never be the same again.' It was not. His battalion moved into a tented camp at Windmill Hill. They remained there for two months while a newly formed training regiment occupied their peacetime quarters. Nobody thought of Poland, it was too far away.

'Like the majority of young people, I think my reaction when war had broken out in 1939 was not one of fear, but rather one of exhilaration,' declared Herbert Webster, who volunteered for the Royal Armoured Corps. 'Life in future might be more demanding, it might be more dangerous; one thing was certain – life would be different and exciting!' For many of the serving regulars and TA the announcement set off a familiar rhythm of 'hurry up and wait'. At the end of August as the crisis culminated, Trooper T.A. Bright in the 7th (TA) Leeds Rifles RTR, newly converted to armour, was playing football when his brother came shouting that a telegram had arrived. He was to report to Carlton Barracks immediately that night. One or two others had already got there when he arrived, and more came singly or in small groups. They were issued with blankets and palliases (straw mattresses) and slept on the barracks floor. 'War was declared on 3 September,' he remembered, 'we expected to be in it straight away but it was to be a long time before that happened.' They relocated to a nearby school. 'It was early times and there was nothing done.' Squads were formed, kit was issued, and they were given some drill and lectures and got bored. Bright was charged for fighting and confined to barracks for three days. As it was a local unit, everybody knew each other. 'The Orderly Sergeant happened to be courting a girl from the next street to where I lived,' Bright remembered,' and he thought he would do a good turn by letting my mother know that I would not be going home for three days.' Discipline in the Territorial Army was of a different order from that experienced by most regulars. 'Unfortunately when he called I answered the door and that put the cat among the pigeons.'

Seventeen-year-old Ian Hammerton had joined 42 RTR, a Terri-torial unit, two months before. Glancing through the window of Martin's Bank in King William Street in the City, he saw a newspaper billboard proclaiming, 'Territorials Called Up'. 'A strange atmosphere was apparent everywhere,' as I went home on the train, 'he recalled.' There was a knock on the door that night announcing the arrival of his call-up papers. On 2 September he set off for Clapham Junction with a small case of belongings, 'leaving behind an apprehensive father and mother who had seen it all before'.

Peter Balfour, who was later to join a Scots Guards tank battalion, was in his final term at Eton on the outbreak of war. 'My whole time at Eton was latterly very much overshadowed by the fact that war was clearly coming,' he remembered. At the time of the Munich Crisis he and his fellow pupils sandbagged the dining room to make a bomb-proof shelter. The oldest boys had been allowed to go to Hendon to await Chamberlain's return from Munich, 'and we saw him come out of the aeroplane waving the piece of paper in his hand'. His father felt 'nothing very much was happening' and that as he had a few months to go before he was old enough to join the army, he might as well go to France to learn French. He should be perfectly safe.

Tank designer Bert Foord was on holiday at Barry, in South Wales, when war broke out. Air-raid sirens were echoing through the city as he drove back through London. 'Mum and Dad were sitting in a brick-built air-raid shelter at the bottom of the garden with the neighbours.' Foord noticed that his father looked slightly incongruous – 'he had his tin hat on'. Design work had in no way accelerated as war approached. 'We were less motivated by competition, rather we were working it out for ourselves,' he recalled. The so-called 'Old Gang' of designers who had created the First World War tanks was drafted in to help. There was some reorganisation, but essentially the tank construction system Foord describes is a cottage industry rather than production-line process. The draughtsmen at Woolwich Arsenal were moved from flats to Wood Lee, a large house with grounds between Egham and Staines. The stables were converted into an experimental workshop. There were no tank plants. Dispersed English plants worked on small contracts their own way, with small production runs of a large variety of models and little central direction.

Michael Halstead, whose fitness was temporarily downgraded, was assisting the Oxford University Officers Training Corps (OUOTC) as a trainer, having joined in 1938. He remembered Major-General

Swinton, one of the tank founding fathers, giving a restricted lecture to the staff on the history of the tank. 'Most interesting and secret,' he wrote in his diary after the event. 'If I had known how far Britain was behind Germany in tank development I might have opted for the Royal Artillery unit of the OUOTC.'

'It was with mixed feelings that I sat on the platform bench,' remembered eighteen-year-old James Palmer, called up for the Tank Regiment. 'Dad and Muriel had come along with me, and both looked terribly upset.' The expectation that they would be 'home before Christmas' was an expectation his father had shared in 1914, barely a generation before. At the moment of departure 'Dad was very emotional and upset. I know he was thinking of another such occasion, twenty years ago, when he had stepped on such a train', and that had been to fight the war to end all wars. Palmer 'felt both excitement and anxiety, and was really at a loss as to what was happening. I knew that I would not like being in the army, yet I felt a little pleased at being one of the first to go.'

Ernest Hamilton, due to join the 15/19 Hussars, recalled: 'My dad said to me, "You're a bloody fool".' His father had been wounded and gassed in the First World War, and 'early in my army career I realised he was right'. It was harder for mothers to say farewell to their sons. Hamilton's mother said goodbye to three of them, his eldest brother leaving for the navy two days after he departed. At the time 'My mother hadn't shown any emotion,' Hamilton remembered, 'but after the war she told me that it was months before she would go into my bedroom.' James Palmer's mother, had passed away, and he was seen off by his girlfriend Muriel, who clung to him in tears. His father had to turn away as she kissed him. 'It was all so dramatic,' Palmer recalled, 'and a lump in my throat prevented me from saying much.' But he could still emotionally identify with those around him who did have mothers to say goodbye to. 'I remember a woman crying as she spoke to a young lad about my age who was waiting to board the train, and I thought that my mam would have been doing the same thing if she had been there.'

As the train set off for Warminster, Palmer noticed other young men sitting in the compartment. 'They just sat looking out of the window and I did the same, but I think our thoughts must have been exactly the same. We didn't feel like talking and were all busy with our own thoughts.' Eventually he spoke to one of them and realised he was going to the Tank Corps at Warminster. Once the unit name was mentioned, other men, who had previously been quiet, perked up because they were also going. 'It was good not to be alone, and fags were soon passed round' as contemplative reflection was overtaken by barrack-room camaraderie. That first night was filled, Palmer recalled, with boisterous chattering and jokes as the recruits quickly adapted to their new environment.

The outbreak of war signified the end of a particular era for many of the young officers who had joined or were now impelled to do so. Aidan Sprot, who had been thoroughly bored with life as a banker in London, enjoyed the social side. 'In those days,' he recalled, 'there were a lot of deb dances and I luckily got in that circle.' 'We had come to terms with girls, it seems,' wrote Michael Halstead, much enjoying his first year at Oxford. 'By 1940 my diary is laconic but full of girls' names, and the titles of history books to read; and also popular tunes.' By war's end public-school officers were to comment on the high toll of friends they lost during these years. All this was to come and was swallowed up in patriotic notions of duty and a convincing belief that the cause for which they would fight was indeed just. John Mallard had been in the TA since 1936, when he joined aged eighteen, and was very much involved in the weeding-out process of converting infantry to tank men. 'I have always felt that I was very fortunate to have had these four years between school and the outbreak of war,' he later wrote. While working with a provincial bank in Bristol, he had enjoyed the TA and a full social life. 'I was able to grow up and enjoy life in pleasant surroundings and with a lot of friends.' Many young men were drafted into the army through the accident of birth just as they had reached this stage in their lives. 'Later on in the war I met a number of young men who went straight from school and into the army and had no time to enjoy themselves – and so many of them were killed.'

The difference between the distant war experienced by the Panzerwaffe and new tank crews forming up in England could not have been more pronounced. By 3 September the outcome of the Polish campaign was compromised by the decision of the two primary western powers to declare war on Germany. In the north the German Fourth Army and III Corps were slicing into the Polish Corridor and sealing off

Danzig while the Third Army was driving south from East Prussia. Coming up from the south the attacking Eighth and Tenth Armies began the first moves to create a gigantic pincer that would eventually coalesce around Warsaw and the River Bug, while the Fourteenth Army moved against Krakow. Luftwaffe attacks had achieved virtual air superiority, yet the apparent ease of momentum belied the intensity and savagery of the fighting on the ground.

In England Fred Goddard had completed his tank training at 58 Regiment at Bovington when war was declared. 'I remember thinking I had done the right thing after all' after hesitating whether to join. 'Now we were at war and I was fully trained.' Trooper Bright thought the practice of 'Standing-to' on alert each night around the TA Halls and drill centres 'was a right farce'. An orderly was dispatched around the pubs and barracks to ensure all were present before 'Stand-by' was sounded – the signal to occupy defence positions. 'Everyone would rush into the school from various places through the back railings while the guard was at the front gate.' In essence the men were being sorted out into future organisations, drawing equipments and guarding the local Church Fenton aero-drome near York. Roll-call was answered at the climax of this Keystone Cops charade and 'five minutes after we were dismissed the place was empty', Bright recalled. 'Everyone dashed back to their pints at the pub just round the corner from the school.' It was not like this for German tank men in Poland. Their baptism of fire was an entirely different formative experience.

'I had a funny feeling when we first attacked,' recalled Rolf Hertenstein, advancing with Panzer Regiment 4, 'there would be no flowers thrown to us in Poland – it was serious this time.' After a tense wait the panzer crews moved beyond the frontier and dis-covered their first war phenomenon, an apparently empty battlefield. 'The battlefield looked deserted,' observed SS Captain Kurt Meyer; 'however, innumerable soldiers were advancing toward the enemy.' They rarely saw the enemy, only evidence he had been there. Von Esebeck, advancing with his reconnaissance battalion, passed the first casualty at the Polish customs house, being attended by a medical orderly.

The soldier looks at us, eyes wide with astonishment. He is badly wounded and says nothing. It is as much as he can do to wave a hand, wishing us well as we push on with our long journey, in which he will take no further part.

It was a stark reminder that they were not on an exercise manoeuvre, and the first indication that they were nearing the combat zone.

Once the sound of intermittent shots mingling with chattering machine-gun fire is discerned above the dull thudding impacts of artillery fire, tension returns again. Tank commanders snatch a last look at the terrain to memorise it before heads duck down into turrets and hatches and covers are closed. 'Looking out through the narrow slits of my turret, I see the tanks of my platoon travelling to right and left of me,' observed Oberleutnant Rudolf Behr, commanding a platoon of heavy Mark IV panzers. 'Everything looks dead. But he has got to be there; in the scrubland, behind the hills, in the farmsteads among the clump of trees.' Leading tanks are often unable to pick out the enemy until he opens fire. 'Then suddenly my crew and I hear a hard clanging blow that reverberates faintly through the whole tank. We've been hit by an anti-tank gun!' Fortunately for Behr it was track damage, and the crew could dismount and fix it. Not everyone was so fortunate.

Part of the crucible that is active-service experience is the initial shock of being 'blooded'. SS Captain Kurt Meyer recalled the whiplash sound of a Polish anti-tank gun cracking out across an 'eerie silence', bringing one and then rapidly another armoured car to a smoking halt. Anti-tank guns were normally part of a combat team, supported by infantry machine-gunners, who would attempt to engage the crews as they tried to get out. Meyer watched as round after round penetrated the vehicles. Nobody could reach the panzers because of the storm of crackling machine-gun fire preventing the crews from bailing out. 'Each time a round penetrated the armoured car's interior the shrieks of our mortally wounded comrades grew louder.' Some attempted to clamber out but were cut to pieces by machine-gun fire. 'The moans in the vehicle grew weaker,' observed Meyer, pinned down himself. 'Spellbound, I watched blood dripping from the fissures in the first vehicle. I was paralysed. I had not yet seen a live Polish soldier, but my comrades were already lying dead, right in front of me.'

On the opening day of the campaign Panzer Regiment 7 in the Third Army, supporting an infantry attack on fortifications north of Mlawa, became snagged in a barricade constructed from railway tracks. The obstacle had not been identified from air photographs. Several panzers stranded on the barricade were picked off by artillery and anti-tank guns, and more vehicles were lost driving along the barrier to find a gap. In war, unlike on manoeuvres, inexperience was punished. 'The attack was a disaster,' reported the Panzer Division Kempf to Third Army Headquarters. 'Terrible losses of panzers, number unknown. An attack here is hopeless.' Panzer Regiment 7 lost seventy-two tanks at Mlawa from its complement of 164 and had to withdraw, leaving the infantry attack pinned down at the barricade. Elsewhere the panzer impetus steadily built up momentum, aided by the crippling impact Luftwaffe air support was having on Polish mobilisation.

Fighting the battle from the claustrophobic and dimly lit confines of a metal hull and directing it from a small turret with restricted vision had been trained for, but the intensity of the real thing was unexpected. Cross-country mobility was creating a blur of fast-moving actions and events, outpacing the infantry, who often fell behind. Battle was executed through radio, which meant leadership by voice only.

Speed of reaction and the need to combine all turret and crew skills in unison to fight or defend the tank were paramount. Only combat truly tests this capability. Panzer gunner Rolf Hertenstein with Panzer Regiment 4 recalled dealing with the main enemy, opposing anti-tank guns. 'It was now a question of who would hit the other first.' A flash of gunfire was the only signature. On the road to Lemburg a shell cracked past, through the space between his tank and a Mark III only four to five feet away. Fog and smoke obscured the route ahead. His tank commander ordered him to fire but he could not see anything. 'I had the turret straight ahead at twelve o'clock, but as I turned it a little to the left, I saw another gun flash.' Again a round swooshed past and he immediately responded. Then it was quiet. Carefully they rumbled forward to investigate. 'On the side of the road there was a Polish 37mm anti-tank gun surrounded by its dead crew. The gunner had just been putting the next shell into the gun, and that round might have been the end of us.'

Dialogue in the fighting compartments of tanks became a mixture of shouted commands and radio traffic. Rudolf Behr, in the advance with his Mark IV panzer platoon, spotted Polish infantry ahead. 'That's a real gift for us!' he pointed out. 'I yell out the direction and range to my gunner' – who is sitting to his left – 'and then bawl to my loader' – on his right – 'what type of shell to load. I order my driver through the intercom' – because he is sitting beyond shouting distance, forward and right in the hull – 'Forward, faster close in on the enemy!' He must then direct the rest of the platoon by radio. 'To our left, ten o'clock, single tree, enemy infantry – destroy!' Sitting left and forward with the driver was the radio operator, who dealt with routine radio traffic. In this instance he would engage the enemy with the hull-mounted machine-gun. Behr meanwhile engaged the dense groups of infantry with high explosive, directing the gunner alongside. 'I observe the effect: fabulous!' As they disperse they are further scattered by machine-gun fire. By this time the tiny turret and fighting compartment has become a cacophony of sound, fumes and emotional tension.

> The loader is sweating. He can hardly keep up with the gunner's rate of fire. Smoke pours out of the breech and blackens our sweating faces. Our shirts stick to our bodies. Altogether, the noise of our engine, the racket of our gun and machine-gun, the heat, the fumes, and the inevitable battlefield excitement . . . produce an atmosphere known only to the tank man, one he is used to.

The importance of individual technical skills became increasingly apparent to panzer crews on this campaign. Behr explained that his driver, in addition to maintaining his vehicle:

> Has to steer the heavy tank, and change gear quickly and frequently; keep a steady eye on the instruments; with my help find his way through the terrain; manoeuvre the tank into the right firing position to give the gunner the best line of fire; and, in addition, help me to identify targets.

Every crew member had to engage in such seamless co-operation to fight the machine effectively. Behr assessed each man 'must utterly devote himself to operating the equipment entrusted to him, and carry out the procedures acquired in rigorous training'. The cumulative impact of these demands and the faster tempo of battle underlined again the lessons of 1918: the technical and physical difficulties of maintaining tanks in combat for prolonged periods of time.

'Eight days in action without a break,' declared *Aufklärung* (recce) commander Oberleutnant von Bünau, 'day and night, night and day on reconnaissance.' Exhaustion was taking its toll. These men had to be constantly scouting the ground in advance of the panzer spearheads. 'The men are tired, drivers cannot keep their eyes open, our faces are covered in grime, and in the hot September weather we are constantly tormented by thirst.' In three days the 3rd Panzer Division with Panzer Regiment 5 drove 380km after being re-routed to form the huge pincer movement calculated to end on the River Bug at Brest-Litovsk. Panzer Regiment 35, the first to reach Warsaw with the 4th Panzer Division, completed a 400km approach march over 'unbelievably bad' roads. Panzer crewmen were beginning to master the intricacies of these long and punishing road marches which involved skirmishes and meeting engagements en route. Cutting the Danzig Corridor, investing Warsaw and now approaching the Bug, the panzers – aided by the Luftwaffe – had tied down the Polish armies sufficiently tightly to facilitate their destruction by follow-on infantry divisions.

Von Esebeck, with *Aufklärungs* Battalion 3, recalled roadside orders from General Guderian for the coming advance. Asked to pass his map, von Esebeck handed it over, folded as normal into a day's march square for ease of consultation in the confined turret, but Guderian said, 'No, no – unfold the whole map'. Pointing to the edge of the map spread on the ground, Guderian indicated the Bug River bridge he wanted. 'I cannot believe my ears,' the young recce commander recalled, 'a hundred kilometres as the crow flies!' They had to drive through the night, often in first or second gear because the road was 'in reality a sandy channel'. Vehicle commanders could only follow the blacked-out mass of the vehicle just ahead, and eye strain was exacerbated by gritty dust and indistinct vision through smeary goggles. 'The driver of our command tank asks me to take over from him for a while,' because rotating crew positions was the only way to keep going. 'His arms hang like logs at his sides,' von Esebeck noticed, 'he cannot raise them any more.' They eventually secured their distant objective, but 'even for a short spell I find driving the tank difficult,' he remarked.

Poland provided the panzer crews with their first baptism of fire well before the British and French could gather like experience. Communication norms in the 1930s – when people did most of their journeys on foot or bicycle, few had cars and even fewer had ever flown – placed Poland virtually at the other side of the world. Going to war over Poland would not result in immediate assistance; it was too far. British and French tank crews began to focus on the coming war with Germany, not how to help the Poles. This resulted in a degree of complacency; nobody envisaged the immediate dispatch of an expeditionary force. Meanwhile the Germans tasted the bitter realities of conflict, the first brutal instruction that would give them some advantage over the uninitiated British and French.

The first lesson was the abrupt and shocking transition from peace to conflict. One soldier recalled that at the beginning 'We were hauled out of our beds at one o'clock and then it was – line up! A proclamation from the Führer!' They were given the reason for the invasion and why they were fighting and then: 'Na – Ja – four hours later and we were in Poland.' Oberstleutnant Friedrich von Mellenthin, serving on the III Corps staff, believed the Polish campaign was 'of considerable value in "blooding" our troops and teaching them the difference between peacetime manoeuvres and real war with live ammunition'. During the first night of the campaign Oberleutnant Lossen with Panzer Regiment 6 appreciated 'that most of us young soldiers begin to grasp what war is really about'. Their tanks had laagered in a 'somewhat uncomfortable exposed and uncertain position' for the night.

The groaning of wounded Polish soldiers fills the darkness around. Somewhere in this darkness lurks an enemy whose intentions are unknown to us, but who in his desperation seems capable of anything. Locked in the sheds of burning farms, the cattle bellow helplessly. German artillery shells howl overhead. Here we lie with our senses alert and tense, waiting for the hours to come.

Peacetime norms were immediately invalidated by the grim realities of the combat zone. Prior to hostilities Panzer Regiment 5 had lined up all its tanks at the Gross Born exercise area and painted white recognition crosses on all sides of the turrets. Crews quickly perceived that they simply provided excellent aiming points for Polish anti-tank guns. They were gradually blacked out or smeared over as the campaign progressed by veterans more intent on surviving than conforming to parade-ground practice. The new insignia in time became a black cross with a thin white outline.

Nervousness at the outset of the campaign was another characteristic the Germans identified. Nervous German soldiers were convinced they were being fired at by civilian 'sharpshooters' throughout the campaign, but this was rarely true. 'I learned how "jumpy" even a well-trained unit can be under war conditions,' explained von Mellenthin. He recalled the example of a Luftwaffe general circling over his corps battle headquarters in a Fiesler-Storch prior to a liaison touch-down. 'Everyone let fly with whatever he could grab' while the air-liaison officer 'ran about trying to stop the fusillade and shouting to the excited soldiery that this was a German command plane'. The air-force general was responsible for the close air support provided to the corps and 'failed to appreciate the joke'.

One thing that exercises had not prepared anyone for was the obvious fact that war is conducted amid the civilian population. This dawned on even the most insensitive crew members as they sped past village after burning village. Whole communities were reduced to skeletal blackened chimney stacks surrounded by flattened and smouldering debris. Unteroffizier Pries, with Panzer Regiment 6, recalled a surprise visit by Adolf Hitler accompanied by Guderian, who was driving the panzer advance along the Tuchel-Schwetz road in the Polish Corridor to the River Vistula.

> The bodies of dead Poles lay piled up among a chaotic litter of baggage wagons, motor vehicles and numerous guns, whose teams of horses lay dead in their harnesses. Heaps of munitions lay next to countless hurriedly discarded rifles, bayonets, gas masks and all kinds of other equipment. It was a sombre, doom-laden sight.

Observing the smashed artillery regiment, Hitler asked Guderian: 'Our dive-bombers did that?' 'No,' Guderian responded 'our panzers!' Hitler was plainly astonished.

Shocking though the military carnage was, all identified with the civilian population's dire circumstances; they were an uncomfortable reminder of domestic norms back home. Kurt Meyer, with the SS Leibstandarte, recalled Polish refugees mixed up in a Polish military column wiped out on 10 September on the Oltarzew road near Warsaw. 'There was no longer any difference between soldier and civilian,' he observed. 'Modern weapons destroyed them all.' Caught up amid dead and wounded horses hanging in their harnesses were women and children who had been 'blown apart in the fury of war. Whimpering children clung to their dead mothers or mothers to their children.' Poles and Germans alike attempted to disentangle the mess. 'Not a shot was heard,' he remarked, 'the war had been suspended.' The refugees were exceedingly bitter at having been caught in the fire-fight while fleeing Posen. Meyer surveyed the indescribable scene: 'I did not see a single German soldier smiling on the "death road" at Oltarzew. The horror had marked them all. The September sun shone brightly on the blood-covered road and changed the destruction into a flytrap.'

After the initial shock and surprise, soldiers tended to mentally disassociate themselves from such scenes, an emotional defence mechanism. Atrocities were committed by both sides against civilian populations. Respect for norms was subordinated to military necessity. Von Esebeck's reconnaissance unit soon resorted to minimalist house-clearing methods to clear Polish resistance.

> It does not take our men long to develop an excellent technique; one shell aimed low at the corner of the house, one above it in the middle of the building, and one into the roof. That's enough to bring the whole Polish construction clattering down.

What was learned in the villages was duplicated at Warsaw. Panzers were unsuited for urban fighting. Enveloping dust, machine-gun fire spitting out of cellar apertures and grenades tossed from upper storeys and basements soon separated the insufficient numbers of supporting infantry from the tanks. Vulnerable Panzer Is and IIs were picked off by concealed anti-tank guns. The regimental diary described how, running beneath tank fire, 'Brave Poles threw prepared explosive charges against tracks, which tore off a wheel.' Turrets became snagged against falling walls and could not traverse.

The tank of Oberleutnant Claas, commander of the lead company, was hit by a concealed anti-tank gun. He ordered his reluctant driver to continue, and it was set on fire by the next strike. Both he and his radio operator clambered out but were severely wounded. Oberleutnant Morganroth, commanding the 8th Company, was similarly knocked out. Within minutes of climbing into another panzer he was killed by another strike. Two platoons of tanks charged into a woodland park, but only three panzers came back. The attack was repulsed and the panzers pulled back to an assembly area, where it was discovered that only fifty-seven tanks were running from the 120 that had started that morning. There were eight dead and fifteen wounded accounted for, but some thirty panzers were still missing. Warsaw could not be taken by tanks alone.

## LANCE AGAINST TANK

It was inevitable that at some stage in this war the new way of mechanised fighting would be pitted against the old. Lieutenant M. Kamil Dziewanski, a platoon commander with the Suwalki Polish Cavalry Brigade, remembers how his unit had to improvise in order to deal with German panzers. They employed the tactics of 'pursuit, ambush and ruse'. He described how 'we would creep up under tanks to wreck the treads with hand grenades, or approach and throw what the Finns later called "Molotov cocktails".' The brigade possessed a number of small anti-tank guns, often horse-drawn, with which the brigade claimed thirty-one armoured vehicles. The ferocity of the Polish cavalry, which was only fleetingly seen in the extensive wood-land, was legendary. SS Captain Kurt Meyer's unit was surprised by Polish cavalry galloping out of a smoke-screen. They were not stopped by small-arms fire. 'It was only when the motor-cycle platoon opened fire and brought down some horses that the fierce cavalry troop galloped back into the fog.' Lieutenant Dziewanowski described these hit-and-run tactics. 'By night we lost ourselves in woods and marched over the trackless ground to harass the enemy's armoured columns.' It made little difference, except in the absence of panzers or air support.

'We saw a long serpent of troops winding its way lazily through a cloud of dust,' recalled the Polish cavalry platoon commander. It was on 9 September during operations in the vicinity of Warsaw. A German infantry battalion lay stretched before them on the line of march. The command 'Trot march!' rang out, Dziewanowski recalled. 'The enemy had not yet seen us, and the rising sun promised a clear day.' It was in effect the swan-song of the Polish Suwalki cavalry brigade – and that of the horse in war. The mass of cavalry emerged from cover, stretched out in attack formation on the open field. As they trotted forward, heavy machine-guns still hidden in the woods began to flail the German infantry, caught completely unawares in a three-deep marching formation in column. 'Draw sabres, gallop, march!' rang out the command, while on the road 'the Germans were becoming a frantic mob'. Bedlam reigned, and 'there were shouts, confused orders and chance shots' as some Germans tried to make a stand in the roadside ditch while others sought cover from the hail of machine-gun fire behind wagons.

'Within a few seconds,' Dziewanowski recounted, 'we reached the highway, sabres and lances working fiercely.' The impetus of the charge swept across the road and cut down those attempting to escape, while shots from the thickets bordering the road continued to thump into the mass of humanity mingling on it. 'We were out of breath and dog-tired, but elated by the dreamed-of victory,' said Dziewanowski. Large groups of Germans began to surrender. Panic had marred the accuracy of German return fire, and only three cavalry were dead, although thirty to forty horses were lost. 'But this victory was only temporary,' Dziewanowski admitted; 'as the days passed, we were forced back.'

Accounts by surviving cavalrymen suggest that they were deployed as dismounted anti-tank hunting groups. The horse conferred mobility and could carry or tow some of the ordnance or weapons required. It is quite possible that panzers and cavalry clashed in unexpected engagements. General Guderian claimed that just such an action occurred during the 3rd Panzer Division advance on the River Vistula. The wooded nature of the terrain makes such an action feasible, but perhaps not as Guderian asserts. 'The Polish Pomorska Cavalry Brigade,' he claimed, 'in ignorance of the nature of our tanks, had charged them with swords and lances and had suffered tremendous losses.' Hans Joachim Bruno, a young NCO in a horse-artillery unit, said that, based on his experience, he would consider such an action as conceivable.

We experienced our first surprise from the Polish cavalry on the fifth day of the war. They were already labelled special, and we were doubly convinced as these Polish cavalry attacked German units and heavy weapons. One could describe it as heroic courage. They saw what was rolling at them and despite that attacked. We depressed our barrels and fired with the infantry and heavy weapons next to us. It was a full attack, they rode to smash into us – or tried to – as if they were on an exercise. They were blown all over the place while galloping right up into the fire of our heavy and light artillery pieces.

Oberleutnant W. Reibel advanced with his tanks from the south with Hoeppner's XVI Corps. As his panzer company moved into its night-time laager, burning villages bathed the horizon 'in a red glow'. There was a cry: 'Polish cavalry approaching on the left!' They seized their weapons. 'But it was only a false alarm,' he observed. 'Herds of riderless horses were searching for human beings.' As the horses snickered, neighed and shuffled about in the red twilight given off from the flaming houses, the scene suggested to the quietly watching panzer crews that the era of the horse in war was over.

Although the size of the Polish army was impressive, they were never able to bring their numerical strength into action. Concentrated Stuka dive-bomber and low-level air attacks preceding the German spearheads broke Polish resistance. The burning villages constantly referred to in veteran accounts were invariably set on fire by air strikes before the panzers even got there. It was not that the Polish air force was totally destroyed on the ground in the first few days. Indeed bombers continued to make determined attacks on German forces up to 16 September, and Polish aircraft and flak shot down more than seventy German bombers, whose defensive armament was found wanting. But, inferior in numbers and design, the Polish air force was unable to contest Luftwaffe air supremacy. With total control of the skies, Stuka dive-bombers replaced or supplemented the artillery that the panzers often outran, heralding a new tank mobility that the original proponents of tank warfare could only dream of. Oberleutnant Lossen, with Panzer Regiment 6, recalled speaking to wounded Polish prisoners who were totally 'demoralised' and confirmed that 'next to German planes it is the tanks that have caused them the most distress'.

Polish armies and, especially, their reinforcements, ammunition and supplies, were battered before they could even reach the front line. Mobilisation was stymied. Formations that did manage to move achieved scant progress and soon found their supply system breaking down. 'We had no chance of getting a train to where we wanted to go,' declared twenty-seven-year-old Polish engineer Leonard Witold Jastrzebski. He was desperately seeking to join his unit and hitched a ride on a military train carrying equipment to the tank units. They constantly had to disembark from the train, which was frequently halted 'under regular bombardment from German planes'. He recalled someone coming along the track after the train halted again at sunset on 17 September. 'Don't wait around,' he was advised, 'don't wait, the Bolsheviks have entered the country. Boy, that was a shock – I can never forget that.'

By this time General von Bock's Army Group North and Rundstedt's Army Group South had penetrated deep into Poland. German pincers had encircled Polish armies to the west and north-west of Warsaw. Third Army's I Corps had invested the city from the east. As the outer wings of both army groups launched even wider eastern envelopments towards Bialystok and Brest from the north and Lvov to the south, the Russians crossed the border. Despite two more weeks of fighting, this signified the end of the campaign. All that was left was the capital and the need to snuff out scattered Polish pockets.

'Oh, that was the end!' declared Jastrzebski. 'We had no chance. Two armies attacking from both sides. How could we Poles survive?' The Poles had massed their strength against the Germans in the west and denuded the eastern frontier to do so. Andrzej Boguslawski was a twenty-year-old student serving with the 1st Polish Lancers. A year at university was terminated by the war. He bitterly recalled the Soviet attack 'like an unexpected knife in the back'. His unit fought Red tanks on horseback, employing the same hit-and-run attacks employed against the Germans. Boguslawski claimed they destroyed twenty-two Red tanks. 'I saw many of them! It was the most successful operation on the eastern front' but alas, it did not last long. By about 25 September his unit was forced to flee across the Lithuanian border.

The Russians brushed aside the token resistance at the frontier and advanced over 60km on the first day. Soviet tank Lieutenant Georg Antonov recalled that the inability of their logistics to keep pace caused more problems than the Polish army. The decision to dilute tank divisions and spread them across the infantry after the Spanish Civil War had a widely deleterious effect. 'There were no fuel dumps, and many tanks, tractors and other vehicles could not move on account of lack of fuel,' Antonov complained, 'and had to stop on roads and in fields.' It was virtually a repeat of the German breakdowns, stemming from inexperience, during the occupation of Austria. 'Two echelons were spread over hundreds of kilometres,' Antonov claimed. It was an unimpressive performance. 'The appearance of our soldiers was bad, particularly those who came in from the reserve.' Indiscriminate firing on their own troops and incidents on the demarcation line with the Germans did not go unnoticed; the Wehrmacht to their own conclusions regarding Soviet military preparedness.

On 22 September the 3rd Panzer Division conducted a joint victory parade with the Russians through Brest-Litovsk. 'The Soviets made a right poor impression,' remarked Dr Hans Bielenberg, a regimental orderly officer, who took part in the motorised drive-past. 'The vehicles, above all the tanks, were – I must say – a collection of oily junk.'

This procession of worn-out vehicles, including panzers badly in need of overhaul, signified the end of the manoeuvre phase of the Polish war. The 3rd Panzer Division moved into eastern Prussia, while the XIX Motorised Corps commanded by General Guderian was dispersed, with only its staff headquarters remaining. Warsaw was besieged and scattered Polish resistance fought on until the final surrender on 5 October.

Panzer driver Hans Becker admitted the Polish campaign 'did not turn out to be a picnic like the previous ones. Despite its briefness – it lasted only eighteen days [for the panzer units] – the fighting proved hard.' The Panzerwaffe lost 236 complete wrecks. This left many crews feeling vulnerable, having observed technical shortcomings. The few Mark IIIs and IVs with their big guns had to be 'carried' by the smaller machine-gun variants and this cost avoidable casualties. 'The quality of our material left much to be desired,' was the feeling of Oberstleutnant von Mellenthin. 'I came through unscathed,' commented Hans Becker, 'but was very glad when this severe blitzkrieg was over.' Many did not.

Panzer Regiment 5, equipped mainly with light panzers, lost thirty-eight crew, killed because of their weak protection. The average age was twenty-four.

German tank crews had learned a lot. Guderian's XIX Motorised Corps with Army Group North had handled both panzer divisions and two light divisions as a single entity. Army Group South had split its armour among the various armies and corps. This was at least a step in the direction of a tank army. Guderian was clear about the need for combined action by tanks, artillery and infantry within the panzer divisions and the requirement to work closely with air support. Crews could now multi-task among themselves, map-read across featureless and strange terrain and quickly form marching columns, and were well versed and practised in the use of standard operating procedures. Experience had taught them first hand about the Clausewitzian 'frictions of war', all those physical impediments – terrain and logistics, emotional and physical – that got in the way of achieving complete results. The  panzers were inferior to those of most European armies, but new and more powerful ones were being assembled.

The crews had been severely tested. 'While it lasted,' Becker later wrote, 'we led gipsy lives with no thought of washing: even one's friends became unrecognisable behind their beards; and in the final battles, when the war reached a climax of fury, there was barely time to eat what little we needed to keep up our strength.' They were veterans, and not the same men as four weeks ago. 'Real glory had touched us at last, but as we rested at Posen licking our wounds we were thoughtful rather than exuberant,' he confided.

## THE WEST – 'NO WALK-OVER'

'This was no war of occupation, but a war of quick penetration and obliteration,' wrote the American *Time* magazine. 'They called it *Blitzkrieg,* or "lightning war".' *Blitzkrieg* has since become a term synonymous with the modern operational war of manoeuvre. Although the campaign had been impressive to the uninitiated press, however, the professionals were less galvanised. General Franz Halder, the German Chief of Staff, who was obliged to advise Hitler on how to deal with Britain and France, jotted down in his diary: 'Techniques of Polish campaign no recipe for the West. No good against a well-knit army.'

The Polish campaign was not the outcome of any novel strategic or operational planning. German armour was not employed independently on the operational level at the tactical level within a division framework. 'Paying due credit to our panzer forces in Poland,' wrote Generalleutnant Georg von Sodenstern, the Chief of Staff of Army Group A, 'we must nevertheless note that armour has little or no chance of success against such defences [in the West].'

In Poland only a swift campaign end had avoided logistic disaster, because the Wehrmacht and Luftwaffe ran out of ammunition. Most motorised columns lost up to 50 per cent of their vehicles and there were acute shortfalls of trained officers. Panzer driver Hans Becker recalled, 'The news that we were also at war with France and England had been withheld from us until the fighting in Poland had finished.' Others were likewise disturbed. 'It won't be a walk-over, as in Poland,' Leutnant Hans von Luck with the 7th Panzer Division was warned. 'The French and the British are quite different opponents.'

During the 1930s French cavalry were reformed into three *Divisions Légères Mécaniques* (DLMs), or 'light mechanised divisions'. Within them were the best tanks in Europe, more sophisticated than anything the British or Germans could field. The Somua S-35s, Renault R-35s and Hotchkiss H-35s were completely new armoured fighting vehicles, equipped with heavier 45-55mm armour and superior 37mm and 47mm guns. By 1936 the impressive Char-B was appearing, with 60mm of armour and a 75mm and a 47mm gun. Its steering system was superior to that of any other tank. By May 1940 there were 3,400 French tanks in service, of which 2,900 were superior modern types.

Advances in French technology did not go hand in glove with clear thinking. Nearly half the total strength was fragmented into small units of fewer than fifty vehicles under infantry command. The rest were restricted to 'cavalry' roles such as scouting and forming small protective screens ahead of infantry. These role dilemmas had technical consequences. As infantry support did not involve long distances, fuel tanks were small. There was a lack of radio fits and a preponderance of one-man commander/gunner turrets. French tank crews thought themselves an elite and dressed in distinctive leather jerkins with da Vinci-style crash helmets, but their training was as patchy and misdirected as their envisaged role.

British rearmament programmes only slowly produced desperately needed new tanks, due to political delays in agreeing to send a British Expeditionary Force (BEF) to France and indecision over funding. By May 1940 the BEF's principal armoured units were the 1st Army Tank Brigade, with seventy-seven Matilda Is and twenty-three Mark IIs, a few Mark VI light tanks and Bren gun carriers and seven mechanised cavalry regiments. The latter were each equipped with twenty-eight obsolete machine-gun armed Mark VI light tanks and 44 Bren gun carriers. One regiment had thirty-eight Morris armoured cars. All the mechanised regiment fighting vehicles were inferior to all their German counterparts except the light Panzer I. Apart from the few Matildas, the 300 British tanks were therefore completely reliant on French 'heavies' to match the Germans.

If German perception that the French and British would be 'no walk-over' was correct, German planning would have to compensate. Yet among the 157 divisions earmarked for the coming conflict only sixteen were fully motorised. The Wehrmacht, like its Imperial predecessor, remained primarily horse-drawn. It employed 2.7 million horses in the Second World War, almost twice the 1.4 million of the First. The British Army and to a lesser extent the French were more motorised, but still dependent on horse and rail for supplies, and were infantry-orientated in their philosophy. Germany's late start in the development race caused by the Versailles restrictions had resulted in two types of army in the Wehrmacht. Ten panzer and six motorised divisions formed a speedy 10 per cent, while the remaining 90 per cent was horse-powered. Only sixteen elite divisions could therefore prosecute *Blitzkrieg* warfare. So 2,439 panzers would face 3,254 French (and 600 British) tanks. Only two-thirds of German tanks could engage their French counterparts with any realistic chance of success.

War with Britain and France came as a shock to Adolf Hitler. Warnings had been interpreted as bluffs. 'Our enemies are little worms,' Hitler pronounced when he addressed his generals prior to the campaign, 'I saw them at Munich.' Although he had initially been depressed at the Allied declaration of war, Hitler was then so encouraged by the success of the Polish campaign that, ever the gambler, he resolved to strike immediately in the West. Horrified military advisors managed to persuade him to postpone his plans. This tortuous stop-go planning process saw twenty-nine postponements up until 10 May 1940. The Germans original plans was to by-pass the French Maginot Line, sweeping through Holland and Belgium. However, after top-secret German documents outlining their offensive plan were discovered by French military intelligence, the plan was replaced by General von Manstein's radical *Sichelschnitt,* or 'Sickle-Cut' proposal. This called for a feint attack along the lines of the captured plan, with a surprise group including seven panzer divisions breaking out into the French interior to head for the Channel coast. Allied armies drawn into Belgium would be cut off and eliminated.

The revolutionary sickle-cut attack would require equally radical methods; in particular, the employment of the panzer force at the operational level. *Schnelle Truppen*, or speedy mobile units, had to range independently ahead of the infantry. Army Group A, due to attack through the Ardennes, was headed up by Panzer Group Kleist. It would have a fleet of 41,140 vehicles, including 1,222 battle tanks carrying 134,370 men. They would carry their own fuel and ammunition with them. Nothing like this had ever been fielded in the history of warfare.

'Training was now in earnest, most of it being marching and bashing of boots,' recalled Bert Rendell, who had enlisted in 1 RTR five years before. 'Though I found no difficulty in this, I thought it a bit strange that parade-bashing was carried out to this extent in an armoured unit.' Now that war had broken out, 'the mechanics and gunnery that I'd craved for would have been of better use to us.' Roger Blankley, serving with the newly established 48 RTR, remembered the arrival of their first Matilda tank in early 1940. 'We were allowed to look but not touch,' he said, 'mostly it was kept under wraps.' Their first vehicles were a motley collection of what was available, two-man light tanks with Rolls-Royce engines and Carden Lloyd carriers. The latter, small-tracked 'tankettes' with one machine-gun under a canopy, were promptly christened 'ice-cream carts'. As Blankley observed, they were quite fast and useful for training 'but having a habit of suddenly deciding to go their own way whatever the driver did'.

Trooper Bright, experiencing the transition of TA infantry to tank battalion, 'could see that things were flaring up'. He was sent to Aldershot for a course in tanks, while 'others went to gunnery class'. The hard winter of 1939–40 interfered with training. Bright had to abandon his tank on Rigton Moors during a training exercise, and it took five days to dig and tow it out of a frozen snowdrift. Training progressed haphazardly. 'There were a lot of Leeds rifle blokes in the unit at the beginning,' he remembers, 'who would never be mechanically minded soldiers, and they had to be sent to other units.' What was left produced variable standards. He recalled live firing of revolvers at targets from 50 feet then running forward to engage at 30 feet. 'There were bullets flying all over the place,' he said. 'Some of us fired three rounds and then ran forward to fire . . . but some of the lads were still firing their first three rounds from behind us.'

'Gradually we got sorted out,' Bright explained, but tank training was likewise mediocre. 'We went on a training scheme' during tank manoeuvres around Aldershot 'which managed to do a hell of a lot of damage but didn't help much at all,' he recalled. There were near-collisions with civilian motor vehicles at night and 'other tanks going straight through cornfields or whatever on the way'. Novice crews were being taught by instructors who had not experienced war. Training aids were rudimentary. Paul Rollins, a trooper with 1 RTR at this time, confessed 'we actually didn't train on many tanks at all'. They had mock-ups with a gun that looked like a tank 'but it was just a rolling platform'. On top was a .22 air gun, and this 'little pop-gun' was used to simulate firing at a landscape picture target.

'We were supposed to be going to France,' recalled Sergeant Bill Close, who was with 3 RTR. 'We packed and we spent our time wandering around the south of England for nearly four or five months.' He was in the reconnaissance troop, 'roaming around in Daimler scout cars', training as best they could, but 'it was a period of waiting for something to happen'. Corporal Harold Parnaby remembered cross-country manoeuvres on Salisbury Plain before embarking for France with the East Riding Yeomanry, which he dismissed as exercises in 'playing silly buggers'.

By 1940 the BEF was expanded to ten divisions in three corps numbering 237,319 men. They were inserted between the French First and Seventh Armies. Newly arrived tank crews were buoyant. They were doing something outside their normal experience. The East Riding Yeomanry docked at Le Havre at the end of February 1940. While waiting for the arrival of their vehicles there were three or four days for young men from Hull, Driffield, Beverley and other parts of the East Riding to explore their first ever foreign town. International travel in the 1930s was the prerogative of the wealthy; now the war initiated a form of military tourism that the troops of all nations embraced with relish. Part of the experience was exposure to different cultural norms. Corporal H. Moor remembered the showers next to a laundry, unusually run by girls. 'What a shock if you took too long, you had a slap on the backside,' he explained with some relish. 'So we made sure it took a long time to have our showers!'

France was an adventure for the young troopers, heightened by the prospect of war. Everybody sought out the red-light district, although they preferred to hint that it was not themselves but their friends who indulged. 'Come in boys, for a drink' was the invitation extended to Corporal H. Moor and his pals on the Rue de Galleans in Le Havre. 'They did and were served by girls in the nude – not even shoes on – and for a day's pay they were yours. We were scared to death after our upbringing to see such behaviour.' The soldiers gawped and enjoyed the spectacle. 'Come in, boys. This is where your dads came,' implored the girls in the red-light district, recalling the previous generation's like experience. 'By the looks of that lot in there,' Moor wryly observed, 'it must have been they who looked after our dads too!'

Billeted in villages throughout the British sector, the soldiers immersed themselves in the local communities, employing the same ribald warmth and humanity as their fathers had before them. These social links did much to compensate for dull training regimes conducted during the coldest winter for half a century. Henry de la Falaise, a young subaltern with the 12th Lancers, a Morris armoured car regiment, recalled, 'The average winter temperature there was never much above zero, mostly under.' He was grateful to change to a 'warm billet' when this operational spell was finished. With the approach of spring the weather improved and, with it, spirits. Corporal Moor so enjoyed the village where he was billeted that he admitted 'he could live there'. Egg and chips was the favourite and only meal served in the local café.

Some tank road driving was conducted that spring, but very little tank range practice. Nobody was concerned, because during March and April the weather was glorious. A holiday atmosphere reigned. An opinion poll conducted back home by the *Daily Telegraph* found that despite glaring British weaknesses in 1939, the majority of those polled believed the war could be won quickly. If there was ever such a thing as a 'good war', the British tank men were convinced that it had arrived.

*Sitzkrieg,* the laconic German expression for 'Phoney War' (literally, 'sitting war'), came to an end on the evening of Thursday 9 May. The 3rd Panzer Division headquarters at Krefeld near the Ruhr received the code-word 'Danzig' at 2103 hours: 'Immediate readiness to move at 0700 hours 10 May 1940,' it read. Many of the officers and married men were away enjoying their Whitsun break. Motor-cycle dispatch riders began roaming the darkened streets of Krefeld and the surrounding villages, calling out key personnel and pulling others from all the known *Gasthauses* and bars. Call-out exercises such as this conducted immediately prior to the weekend were in no way unusual. Weather permitting, the division had been exercising, shooting and conducting night marches and loading exercises, often preceded by a practice alarm. The night was short, and as the men quickly made their way to barracks or emerged from their accommodation into the cold, grey light of dawn, they noticed swarms of aircraft passing overhead, flying west.

It was no exercise. The division was ready to move at 1000 hours. But they waited and waited until the following day. There were traffic jams on the border. They could not move. This was their prelude to a new form of tank warfare: *Blitzkrieg.*

# 5

## BLITZKRIEG IN FRANCE

### STOP-START WAR

As Trooper 'Butch' Williams drove his Matilda Mark II tank out of Ribeaucourt village in the Somme valley on 10 May, the villagers lined the road to wave goodbye. 'Garlands of flowers were thrown on to the tanks by young maidens,' he recalled, 'who for some reason, had been conspicuous by their absence during our two-week stay in the village.' By the time they reached Douellens rail-head nearby, their troop leader's tank had broken down. 'We didn't see the crew again,' Williams commented, 'until we mustered back in England' after the Dunkirk evacuation. His own tank *Grimsby* had already developed an oil leak in the left-hand engine but was running. As soon as they sighted the British Lion Memorial at Waterloo, in Belgium, they were ordered to withdraw. By this time there was 'oil sloshing about in the hull', the cross-country steering was faulty, and the only way he could change gear was to lever the gear-change rod with a crowbar through the engine cover. For Williams and his crew, the stop-start war had begun.

'The balloon went up while we were sitting in the lounge of the George at Fordingbridge, watching the coots skidding over the surface of the Hampshire Avon,' remembered Sergeant Bill Close. At the time 3 RTR was awaiting the call forward to join the 1st Armoured Division, assembling 'somewhere in France'. A regimental policeman stuck his head through the door of the pub and said, 'All 3 RTR personnel report back to camp immediately.'

Henry de la Falaise was awoken by howling air-raid sirens in Paris. Turning on the radio, he heard 'the agitated commentator broadcast the most important news he has had to deliver since war was declared last September: at daybreak the German armies hurled their might against the Belgian and French defences in a mass frontal attack.' De la Falaise began a chaotic stop–start journey on overcrowded trains to the front. 'It is like fighting your way into the New York subway at a rush hour,' he complained. Passing through Lille to Brussels and then Arras, the train was constantly halted, to await pauses in bombing attacks, before being able to move on.

German airborne units had landed at key points in Holland and Belgium, while Army Group B, which included three of the panzer divisions, advanced to link up with them. Forty Allied divisions reacted as planned and advanced to meet this attack along the line of the River Dyle. As they moved up, the columns of the Panzer Group Kleist were winding their way 170km across the Ardennes region from the German border through Luxembourg, Belgium and France to the River Meuse. Light Belgian and French screening forces were brushed aside.

'We have reached our first-stage objective, the Luxembourg border!' declared Hauptmann Carganico with the 1st Panzer Division. It had been a long, hot drive. Tank drivers had been 'sitting for five hours in this terrific heat behind their gear levers, changing gear – steering uphill and downhill – stopping and starting'. He was sitting in the greatest traffic jam Europe had ever seen.

The gigantic armada of 41,140 vehicles, consisting of 1,222 tanks, 545 tracked and 39,373 wheeled vehicles, had a theoretical length of 1,540km. It took an average of ten hours for a 150km-long panzer division to pass by, and eight and a half for the 130km-long mixed panzer and motorised elements. A motorised infantry corps carried 134,370 men with their supplies. Panzer Division carried 20,000 Pervitin tablets in its baggage, to keep the soldiers awake. By 12 May the convoys were jammed up on the northern march route from the Meuse River 250km back across French, Belgian, Luxembourg and German territory to the River Rhine.

Progress was variable for the crews, who rode outside their panzers to ease cramped conditions as they moved through the wooded Ardennes. It depended on bypassing demolition craters and carefully negotiating narrow bridges and timber trackways laid over soft ground. Periodically the droning traffic noise would be punctuated by gunfire and explosions, coming from skirmishing and demolitions ahead. For most crews the monotony was broken only by the distinctive gleam from red, white and blue striped frontier post barriers or abandoned weapons and equipment littering the road. Panzer *Gefreiter* (corporal) Möllman recalled the lack of sleep: 'Our eyes are burning and stinging. It is as though the eyelids were inflamed.' All the pressure at this stage was on the drivers, 'the silent heroes' within the columns. 'They clench their teeth,' observed Möllman. 'Stay awake at all costs! Roads, roads, roads – always the same. The men at their side talk to them, telling them anything that comes into their heads. Anything to stay awake.'

Allied air cover was nowhere to be seen above the heads of panzer crew, who were feeling acutely vulnerable. 'We were expecting enemy air attacks against such a massive movement of our troops,' admitted Leutnant Alexander Stahlberg, who was with the 2nd Motorised Division, 'but days were to pass before we saw the first French or English aircraft overhead.' Johann Graf von Kielmansegg, carefully monitoring supply resources for the 1st Panzer Division, was well aware of the consequences of discovery.

> Again and again I cast a worried look up at the bright blue sky; my division now presents an ideal attack target because it is not deployed and it is forced to move slowly forward on a single road. But we could not spot a single French reconnaissance aircraft.

A vital prerequisite for *Blitzkrieg* success is domination of the skies. This had formed part of the Panzerwaffe's evolving expertise in Poland and was now experienced by tank crews in the west. Germany mobilised three-quarters of its air potential against only one quarter for the French. The net result was German superiority during the surprise attacks, with 2,589 German pitted against 1,453 Allied aircraft. Two Luftwaffe air fleets bombarded airfields, troop concentrations, fortified field positions and rail junctions. Most important was that they devoted more resources to continuous ground support than the Allies.

De la Falaise complained one week into the battle that the skies were 'dotted' with German aircraft and fighters searching for targets. 'Un-challenged, they fly low, their engines idling.' He indignantly added, 'Some of them insultingly make barrel rolls and loops over our heads.' Repeatedly strafed and bombed, and intimidated by low over-flights, he admitted: 'Everyone is beginning to feel uneasy and even mortified about the unexpected and total absence of British or French planes', while the German pilots 'stunt over our heads as if in a peacetime air show. They have been practically unmolested.' Tank crews soon learned to avoid railway stations and sought to bypass or accelerate along long straight roads.

Much of the impact from hostile air attack was psychological. Charlie Brown, serving with the BEF, declared, 'If anyone said he wasn't frightened when the Stukas [German dive-bombers] were around he was a liar – anybody!' Whenever a Stuka dived down on enemy positions the pilot would switch on a penetrating siren called a 'Jericho trumpet' that howled like a banshee. Attached to bomb fins were 'organ pipes' that produced a shrill whistling noise on release. The combination was fearsome, causing victims to feel they were being personally sought out as the target. 'To be dive-bombed by Stukas was a nerve-shattering experience,' declared John Dixon, a subaltern with the East Riding Yeomanry. 'With their cranked wing shape, they could drop like a stone from the sky, position their bomb accurately and, with the howling mechanism in operation on the dive, those on the ground were forced to scatter in terror.' A great pall of smoke would erupt from the target, 'and the explosions shook the air'.

Above all it was the feeling of utter helplessness that was dominant. 'They'd do acrobatics for about five minutes,' recalled Charlie Brown, as the squadrons set themselves up in free-wheeling moves to attack. 'You're in a ditch if you could find one and you are saying to yourself, "For God's sake drop them and get it over!"' 'The worst part of the BEF,' judged Second lieutenant V. Gillison, 'was the complete air supremacy of the Germans. We seldom saw any of our planes and that did not help morale.'

The intensity of air attack was magnified by the totally unexpected violence and destruction unleashed with seemingly little preparation. On 13 May, 310 bombers, 200 dive-bombers and 300 fighters flew 1,215 sorties in rolling attacks along a 4km stretch of the Meuse around Sedan – an unprecedented concentration. Even German soldiers felt queasy watching it at work. Hugo Novak, a light anti-aircraft gunner, saw that 'all hell seems to have broken loose', as he looked across the Meuse: 'A sulphurous yellowish-grey wall rises on the other bank; it keeps growing. The enormous air pressure causes glass panes to rattle and crack.' Squadron after squadron of Stukas dived perpendicularly like predatory birds on their quarry. Cumulative impacts of ground-shaking explosions, one following the other, took their toll.

'The gunners stopped shooting and hit the dirt,' remembered French General Edmond Ruby on the other bank, 'the infantrymen dove into the trenches and remained there motionless.' They were totally deafened by the screech of diving aircraft and ear-splitting cracks from explosions. 'Five hours of this nightmare sufficed to shatter their nerves.' The psychological impact of cumulative bombing was the most pronounced tactical surprise inflicted on the Allies and was to influence their reaction to developments throughout the subsequent campaign. First Lieutenant Michard, enduring the bombardment at Sedan with the 55th French Infantry Division, described how:

> Explosions keep crashing all over the place. All you can feel is the nightmare noise of the bombs, whose whistling becomes louder and louder the closer they get. You have the feeling that they are zeroed in precisely on you; you wait with tense muscles. The explosion comes like a relief. But then there is another one, then there are two more and ten more . . . the whistling sounds are superimposed and criss-crossed like a fabric without gaps; the explosions blend in a ceaseless thunder. When the intensity of that sound abates for a moment, you can hear yourself gasping for air. So, here we are, motionless, silent, crouched, hunched over, mouth open so that your ear-drums will not burst.

Michard was bombed into a virtual stupor. 'Twice I had acoustic hallucinations,' he claimed. The inability to move and release adrenalin through violent physical activity added to the sense of claustrophobic frustration. 'You feel as if you want to scream and roar,' he explained. Fear of air attack permeates all Allied veteran accounts, even long after the war.

The difficulty of commanding huge vehicle fleets in order to execute the operational mobility required of *Blitzkrieg* contributed to the stop-start nature of the campaign. Tank crews had to grope their way through unfamiliar terrain to reach key objectives. Poland was a valuable experience, but the scale of this was unprecedented. It had never been attempted across the more urban, populated and developed road network in western Europe. Air power transformed the ability to support greater mobility on one side, while impeding the enemy on the other. Indecision was the third fundamental factor impinging on the stop-start nature of the *Blitzkrieg* campaign. The Germans had started, the Allies were stopped.

'Greatcoats on – greatcoats off!' was the wry response of British soldiers urged to 'hurry up in order to wait' as orders were frequently countermanded in the rapidly developing confusion. The BEF and in particular its armoured regiments reaped the whirlwind of years of government neglect and prevarication prior to last-minute rearmament. The cabinet delayed its decision to dispatch the BEF to the last possible moment. Military thinkers had little idea how a war might be prosecuted in a modern Europe with new weapons in any case. The state of equipments on the ground reflected this. The leadership shown in handling the last-minute effort was also questionable.

Lieutenant John Dixon, with the East Riding Yeomanry, aged twenty-two, remembered being taken out on a TEWT (Tactical Exercise Without Troops) shortly after arriving in France before the start of hostilities. Supervised by a suspect cavalry major, he realised 'even our meagre knowledge managed to get him all confused'. When the 'Blitz' started he was issued with a .38 revolver the day after, 'but with only three rounds available and no lanyard!'

On 13 May he recorded a lot of excitement around the headquarters. Common to all British veteran accounts from this period is how little they knew. 'All were very excited and wanted to know what we were doing,' Dixon wrote, 'but we were under orders not to say anything.' Infatuation with the 'need to know' principle, which blocked any information with even a remote security caveat, proved a real hindrance. Dixon suspected 'we were off', but 'we were told that we were going further forward for advanced training. I actually believed it!' Lieutenant Dixon went to war with the 1st Reconnaissance Brigade in a sector due to be attacked by three panzer divisions with three rounds in his revolver.

As they moved forward, tank crews slept in whatever accommodation was available. Farms were favoured, because barns and outhouses provided shelter and cover from aerial view, and there was room for vehicles to be effectively supported mechanically and logistically. Henry de la Falaise's diary record with the 12th Lancers describes a succession of 'forced' abandoned houses, farmhouses, a château, a café, a brewery, villas, unfurnished rooms and sleeping rough in orchards and fields. Unteroffizier Möllman, with the Panzer Gruppe Kleist, wrote 'we wrap ourselves in blankets and lie down somewhere on the grass or in a field'. Anything was an improvement after driving all day in the cramped confines of a tank. 'We can stretch our legs out properly at last,' he recalled.

Food was taken where found. 'There were no rations available,' declared Matilda tank driver Trooper 'Butch' Williams with 7 RTR, 'we had to live off the land, so I went down to the village to procure a brace of chickens' from among deserted houses. De la Falaise seemed to subsist on chocolate, biscuits, eggs and tinned beef. Williams recalled an unusual meal taken on the move: 'Between the four of us we had a small tin of shrimps and a packet of sweet tea biscuits washed down with champagne.' Trooper W.G. Eldridge, moving up with the 10th Hussars from Cherbourg, was issued with cigarettes, chocolate and one condom. Whatever they ate – and the spasmodic availability of supplies often made for bizarre mixtures – it was never enough.

Both sides complained about the effects of sun and dust on approach marches during the unusually hot weather. 'The glare of the sun on the narrow long straight roads and the fine white dust stirred up by the tanks affected the eyes of many of the drivers and tank commanders,' observed Technical Sergeant Major K. Dunk with the 10th Hussars, it left them 'painfully red and swollen'. Panzer crews would always liberate British protective goggles given the chance, remembered Leutnant Wolf-Max Ostwald. He described the state of his tank crews at the end of the day as 'tired and drained, with red, inflamed eyes'. 'The leader of the reconnaissance troop cools his driver's eyes with a wet handkerchief, although he can hardly keep his own eyes open, and tears are rolling down his blackened, dirt-streaked face.'

Tank movement was increasingly mired in roads congested with refugees 'bringing us face to face,' recalled Matilda driver Trooper Williams, 'with the real unpalatable side of war, this vast tide of human beings, all with that bewildered, dazed expression.' It is estimated there were twelve million people on the roads of northern France at this time, bound for 'goodness knows where'. For Charlie Brown, in the Royal Army Service Corps, 'it was the saddest thing I saw, old people, young people, people of all ages, cripples.' Newsreels show women pushing tiny prams heaped with possessions with massive cloth bundles strapped to their backs labouring along bright, sun-lit roads, with children sharing loads suspended on sticks like stretchers. 'It really hurt us to see the accusing stares,' remembered Williams, 'mostly from the older men who clearly thought we should be back somewhere fighting the Boche, not swanning around.'

Henry de la Falaise recorded in his diary a reconnaissance on the second day of the offensive and finding the road so filled with refugees 'we can hardly move forward'. Time was lost bypassing crowds until there was no recourse but to push through. 'Slowly, carefully, we move on through the flow of fleeing humanity,' he wrote. 'Every now and again they start to run' in panic at another air raid. The Luftwaffe frequently flew the axis of a panzer advance, strafing and machine-gunning roads to clear them of military and civilian vehicles. 'I can hear frantic screams when bombs plaster the road ahead.' There was little that Allied columns seeking contact with the enemy could do when roads were so clogged with their own kind. 'We have to stop,' wrote de la Falaise, 'while this flowing human tide brushes by us, bumping into the armoured car as it stumbles along accompanied by the crash of nearby explosions and the bleating and mooing of the terrified farm beasts.'

German panzer columns pushing towards them were not totally impervious to the impact they had on the civilian population. 'Yes, I found this awful,' admitted Hans Becker, with the 7th Panzer Division.

I thought to myself, what if you had to leave your house and farm and didn't know when you would return, and ended up looking like this. This had an effect on me. *C'est la guerre,* as the French would say. But the sadness was if someone returned later and saw that his house was destroyed. What must this person be thinking? He must be really angry with the Germans!

'Its all right for you, Tankie, you've got a portable air raid shelter,' someone jibed at Trooper Williams driving his Matilda tank. Air attacks stymied movement to and from the front. The BEF, with its light-skinned and obsolete Mark VI tanks in the cavalry regiments supplemented by open Bren gun carriers, was more vulnerable than the French army with its heavy tanks. After a mission 'the heavy bombers usually flew straight back to base,' recalled Williams 'but the fighter-bombers and Stukas seemed to enjoy flying back low over the roads, strafing all and sundry, creating terror.'

The French heavies were to be the first to engage the Germans tank on tank in the first major tank battle in history. It occurred in Belgium, near the Gembloux Gap between the rivers Meuse and Dyle when the 2nd and 3rd French DLMs clashed with the 3rd and 4th Panzer Divisions. On 12 May Lieutenant Robert Le Bel from the 11th Regiment of 3 DLM was observing German armour through field-glasses from his Hotchkiss H-39 tank, parked beneath an apple tree on the outskirts of Jandrain.

I saw an extraordinary show which was played out about three kilometres away: a panzer division shaping itself for battle. The massive gathering of this armoured armada was an unforgettable sight, the more so that it appeared even more terrifying through the glasses. How many were there? It was not possible to tell from so far away but they were numerous and their guns seemed to be potent.

It was a fascinating glimpse of an unprecedented event. Whole divisions of tanks were about to clash on mobile operations. Le Bel further observed:

Some men, probably officers, walked to and fro gesticulating in front of the tanks. They were probably giving last-minute orders to the tank commanders, the head and shoulders of whom I could see between the open two parts of the turret hatches. Suddenly, as if swept away by a magic stick, they all disappeared. No doubt 'H'-hour was approaching. A dust cloud soon appeared on the skyline, disclosing the enemy move.

The stop-start phase was now to develop into a war of movement, advance and pursuit. Le Bel knew that battle was about to be joined. 'I got down into the tank, closed the hatch and peered through the episcopes.'

## CLASH OF ARMOUR

Panzer driver Hans Becker reflected after Poland: 'I had great faith in my own powers of survival. You are much too young to die, I would tell myself; others may fall but not you; you will certainly see your home again.' Panzer crew members possessed an inner confidence not shared by their opponents. This was a factor of training, experience and leadership. Many had experienced war. Trooper Williams with 7 RTR had also noticed that 'by now, all our pre-conceived ideas about going into action, so painstakingly drilled into us on our training schemes at Catterick and Aldershot, were forgotten, and we were acutely aware this was a new type of warfare.'

The German Tactical Panzer Company Training Manual had analysed and taught the fundamentals of tank fighting to a better degree than any comparable Allied offering, and it had been available since March 1939. These fundamentals were applied by the Germans at Gembloux. Winning the fire-fight, concentrating fire on enemy command and signals vehicles and, in particular, firing when stationary and then moving were battle-winning combinations. German crews were taught to keep the sun behind them while manoeuvring into the flanks and rear of enemy tanks. Radio proficiency meant that all this could be put into practice. 'In battle I never reminded myself that this was not an exercise,' maintained Becker, 'that the bullets were real and the other side in dead earnest when they fired them.' He was quietly confident. 'Like the gambler who believes he will win, I believed that I would survive.'

Henry de la Falaise commented on French resolve as the tank crews of 3rd DLM went into battle. 'Their whole attitude,' he later wrote, 'is that they are going to give the Boche a kick in the face that he will remember and which will send him reeling back to his homeland.'

German confidence was shaken when they discovered that shot from their 37mm guns bounced off the superior French armour without having any effect. French tank crews regarded themselves as a mechanised elite. 'They are particularly proud of the new Somua tanks with which their division is equipped,' wrote de la Falaise, 'and its wonderful 47mm anti-tank gun which they say will punch the German panzers so full of holes that they will look like sieves by the time they get through with them.'

'My first target!' exclaimed Sergeant-Major Georges Hillion of the 4th Squadron Cuirassiers. 'I fired and saw the direct hit.' His unit of Hotchkiss H–39s was engaged on the eastern extremity of Crehen. 'The panzer stopped and I saw a brilliant light and smoke pouring out of the tank.' He dispatched another, aware of 'some suspicious knocking on the tank' from incoming machine-gun fire. They were fighting a mixture of tanks and infantry in among trees when 'we received the first strike on the rear of the tank, which immediately stopped'. Corporal Phiz, his driver, was unable to restart the engine, and they were stranded in the open 300 metres in front of the enemy, who immediately concentrated their fire on the stricken vehicle. 'A shell burst through the turret, I was wounded in the face and left arm; blood covered my face and I could not see any more from my left eye'.

German after-action reports noted the slowness of French turret-traversing mechanisms, and that their 'especially sluggish turning' enabled them to be shot up from the side. It was soon apparent that 'the ability to see out of the enemy tanks appears to be poor', whereas the panzer gunners observed and identified targets through an open hatch before ducking down to use the periscope. Inaccurate French gunnery was distracted by zigzag charges by German panzers trying to close and shoot at the sides. The most telling comment was the realisation 'that the French always fought' German regiments 'with only a small number of tanks'. Discoveries about French shortfalls were quickly passed on by radio, but these initial findings came at considerable cost.

Sergeant-Major Hillion fought on as shell after shell crashed into his Hotchkiss tank, its 40mm of armour protection able to soak up much punishment. Blinded in his left eye, he continued to try and fire his machine-gun with his right when 'a powerful shock struck just behind me'. Shooting up the rear of French tanks was often the only recourse for under-gunned panzers. 'I felt a violent pain in the back and a burning sensation on the whole left side of my face'. An anti-tank round entering the crew compartment was often accompanied by a searing flash of kinetic energy produced by its violent passage and metal flakes and scabs flying off the turret sides from the shock of impact.

'The Devil is coming!' exclaimed German soldiers aghast at the sight of the first British tanks crawling over their trench parapets.

The view through this chain-mail mask worn by a British tank crewman encapsulated the pitiless nature of the new type of conflict that pitted machines against men.

The first tank duel was fought at Villers-Brettonaux on 24 April 1918. German tank commander Ernst Volckheim claimed 'the English were totally surprised at the appearance of our tanks.' The battle was conducted like 'blind-man's buff', peering through restricted vision slits.

Bill Close, far left, on exercise with 3 RTR in the 1930s.

Civilian driver on tank trials: 'We just jogged along,' claimed British tank designer Bert Foord.

Panzer I 'Krupps sports cars' take the salute. Nazi parades tended
to display mass rather than substance.

German tank crews participated in massive mobile tank operations directed by radio for the first time.

Crewmen had to endure gruelling feats of physical hardship – exhaustion marks the face of this panzer crew member.

A young British troop commander in 8 RTR after a long day of desert tank fighting.

A British tank driver in the Western Desert.

Harald Kuhn was indignant watching this German newsreel of panzer crew frying eggs on their tank in the scorching desert heat. 'Where did they get the eggs?' he indignantly asked, 'and above all, the fat!'

On arrival German panzer crews were less used to desert conditions, but learned quickly. Here they dubiously regard either lunch or a potential mascot.

The German 88mm flak gun in the ground role was the most potent gun in the desert and worked lethally in tandem with panzers. However, the crew were exposed and vulnerable and could be reached by high explosive shells once the Grant and Sherman tanks were introduced.

A near miss for an Allied tank.

Desert improvisation – a panzer crew shelter made from a tent and packing cases.

Feldwebel Hermann Eckhardt welcomed action as a means of supplementing tedious German rations with British bully-beef.

A Cruiser A9 – note how restricted conditions were for this four-man tank crew.

Crew 'bonding' was of paramount importance to the fighting effectiveness of a tank. A British Grant tank crew snatch a hasty meal on the eve of El Alamein.

'Dense smoke filled the tank' as Hillion continued to fire – 'but I was unable to see if I hit anything'. As further rounds slammed into the tank his situation became untenable. 'I was suffocating,' he recalled. 'I leaned down to take off my scarf to try to wrap it around my face and in front of my mouth, but another violent hit struck the turret.' Determined to continue the fight outside the tank, he began to dismantle the machine-gun, calling to his driver to bring the magazines. By now 'the air inside was unbreathable, I felt I was suffocating, my left eye was closed and I could feel my strength failing'. Disentangling himself as best he could, he was clambering out of the tank, pulling and dragging the machine-gun, when 'another terrific blow suddenly blew my helmet off and I fell down the side of the tank.'

Hillion was jerked back into consciousness by an excruciating pain in his legs. 'I opened my right eye and saw a tank rolling over both my legs; the edge of the track just under my knees'. The panzer commander standing in the turret was scanning the area where Hillion's platoon had been defending. 'Fearing he might fire a mercy shot, I strove to keep quiet.' The panzer moved on to investigate the platoon position amid the hedgerows. Shells suddenly rained down, and the exhausted Sergeant-Major was wounded again by splinters to his left hand and partially covered by clods of earth. He fainted again. When he awoke it was dark. 'My right leg was crushed and did not obey me any more, but the left was responding.' His driver was dead, and his regiment lost twenty-four Hotchkiss tanks that day.

On 16 May a single Char-B attacked a German panzer column in Stonne, south of Sedan, knocking out thirteen panzers and two German anti-tank guns. Later examination of its armour revealed that it was hit 140 times without a single projectile getting through. 'French tanks were not bad, on the contrary,' commented C.C. Christophé, a war reporter embedded with the 2nd Panzer Division. Rolf Hertenstein, a Panzer IV commander with the 2nd Panzer Division, called it 'a huge monster, the biggest tank we had ever seen. The armour looked very thick, and our gun just couldn't penetrate it.' Fortunately for the Germans, the accuracy of the French was compromised by their propensity to fire on the move.

The very design of French tanks, exuding self-sufficiency, encapsulated an individualist French approach to fighting tanks. Whereas panzers operated in light, medium and heavy teams, the Char-B mounted both a 75mm howitzer and a 47mm anti-tank gun, the armament of two German tanks. Crew ergonomics inside the French colossus were questionable. The commander performed as gunner and loader in the one-man turret, supervised the rest of the crew and directed a platoon or squadron of other tanks. The driver was similarly over-taxed. He aimed the fixed 75mm gun, which could only fire ahead, and elevated it with a hand-wheel. To traverse on the commander's orders required him to turn the whole tank on its tracks. Meanwhile the radio operator and loader sitting in the centre could see nothing. An advanced hydrostatic steering differential produced the fine steering required to fire the howitzer but needed servicing by highly specialised teams. These inefficient crew roles slowed engagement times, with the crew struggling to co-ordinate their roles. Because they were infantry support tanks and were not expected to drive far, their range before refuelling was short and posed a handicap.

Tank-on-tank combat against Char-Bs developed into a form of panzer 'bear-baiting', in which under-gunned German tanks hunted in packs or teams to snap at the flanks and rear. In the town of Mortiers on 17 May, six Panzer IIIs from Panzer Regiment 1 had to combine against a single Char-B that rolled past shooting at them, but was impervious to return fire. Three of the panzers eventually manoeuvred themselves 300 metres behind the French tank while it destroyed an armoured car. One panzer fired directly into its rear while the other two peppered the turret with strike after strike until the crew bailed out, faces bleeding from the metal flakes flying off inside, which had been the only effect from the repeated blows. Although 'completely saturated by hits', read the after-action report, 'none of the 75mm, 37mm or 20mm and special rounds was effective in penetrating.' The tank was only brought to a halt when a 37mm round pierced the engine compartment and disabled the engine.

As the fighting in the Gembloux area petered out on 13 May, the Panzer Group Kleist, having emerged from the Ardennes, forced a crossing of the Meuse at Dinant, Montherne and Sedan. When initial French counter-attacks floundered at the bridgeheads, a large-scale attack employing all three DCRs was planned to push them back.

The 3rd French Armoured Division (DLM), which had only formed six weeks before, was failed by its leadership through a succession of cancelled attacks, unnecessary and then countermanded dispersion, and then inaction while it waited defensively on the flank of the German breakthrough. The 1st DLM was lined up for refuelling directly opposite Dinant, where the 7th Panzer Division commanded by General Erwin Rommel was pouring across.

Both French brigades reached these harbour areas extremely short of fuel after a fourteen-hour, 23-mile journey in low gear through roads congested by military and refugee traffic under constant air attack. Several fuel convoys were burned out on the roads, so that the surviving tankers did not arrive until the morning of 15 May. Unlike the Germans with their efficient 'Jerry-can' system that enabled crews to replenish their own dispersed tanks from stockpiled canisters, the French were reliant on lorried tankers with fuel hoses. These had limited cross-country mobility and could only refuel one tank at a time. Rommel's panzer regiment pushed into the stand-by area, catching the 28th Char-B and 25th Hotchkiss-39 tank battalions in the throes of refuelling. Completely unaware of their vulnerable situation, the tanks were waiting in the open, ready for the petrol tankers, and had not thought to position a security screen to the east. The 7th Panzer Division was equipped with Czech 38t tanks, and these had to approach to within 200 metres to fire their 37mm guns effectively into the ventilation grills of the Char-Bs, while Panzer Mark IV tanks burst high explosive shells among the fuel tankers. Sheets of flame enveloped parked tanks, and rolling clouds of oily black smoke marked the progress of this total debacle for the French.

'When you are involved in combat and the banging starts around you to the right and to the left,' explained Hans Becker of the 7th Panzer Division, excitedly gesticulating with both hands, 'then it's as if the human mechanism is switched off.' Panzer Abteilung 66 drove in wedge formation into the refuelling area, panzers firing outward as the approach fanned out into an arrow-head configuration. 'All you can think of is – watch out! That nobody can shoot you. If you don't, the other will shoot, and you are a goner!' It was a simple philosophy of kill or be killed. The French were at a disadvantage and the German panzers mercilessly exploited their opportunity. According to Becker, instinct took over: 'You have no feelings, you only think watch out, your life is in danger – and shoot. These were my feelings until combat was over.'

One French unit of thirty-six heavy tanks was reduced to three. Many crews lacking fuel destroyed their own tanks. The 1st French Armoured Division (1 DLM) began a general retreat, and only seventeen of its original 175 tanks made it back to the French frontier. The French 2nd Division was shattered by the 6th Panzer Division while it was strung out on the move; many of the French tanks surprised at the railway station. By the morning of 16 May it was split in two and scattered. A gap over 40 miles wide was torn in the French defences and the panzer divisions began their drive toward the coast. There was no Allied armour of any consequence able to stop them.

## WHERE ARE THE BRITISH? PURSUIT AND RETREAT

'We still didn't know the real extent of the German breakthrough,' recalled Trooper Williams of 7 RTR, nursing his crippled Matilda tank *Grimsby* westwards. 'We thought the front would stabilise after some initial setbacks, as it did in 1914.'

Their mechanical problems worsened. 'The oil sloshing around in the hull had penetrated the Rackham steering clutches, so I had to use all my strength on the levers' to change gear. Williams was attached to his tank. 'It was hard work nursing *Grimsby* along the road,' he admitted, but 'a labour of love'. He had schemed to be the first driver of a Matilda tank, 'and in a masochistic way I was enjoying the challenge. I wouldn't have left her for all the tea in China or all the chickens in France.' They were constantly assailed by rumours of German breakthroughs, which 'became only too common as the confusion spread throughout the campaign'. They finally caught up with their unit and in conversation with their commanding officer started to appreciate 'that the chain of command had broken down'. The retreat continued westwards. 'In memory, the last three days of the trek have become blurred, possibly through fatigue and lack of food, into an endless journey of 5 to 6mph max, nursing the engine, which was over-heating.'

Most of the French armoured units were crippled. Four panzer spearheads, preceded by XIX Corps led by 'speedy Heinz' Guderian, as his soldiers called him, exploited the conferred freedom of movement and drove hard for the coast. 'They're running and how they run!' wrote the war reporter embedded with the 2nd Panzer Division. Up to 90km were covered each day until they reached the sea near Abbeville on 20 May. Holland surrendered on 15 May and Belgium was teetering on collapse. Allied units trapped in Belgium were finished, and phase one of the German plan appeared complete.

Extracts from Leutnant Hans Steinbrecher's diary give some indication of the pell-mell advance achieved by the 2nd Panzer Division. On 10 May, driving through massive traffic jams in the Ardennes, he wrote of 'a day he would never have thought possible'. Overwhelmed at the sight of the packed armoured units waiting to move up, he felt 'there were only tanks in the world'. Optimism and confidence were heightened by the wonderful weather and the pace of the advance, which gave little opportunity to pen thoughts. 'We drove the whole day,' he recorded on 11 May; 'if that continues, we will soon find ourselves in England.' They were watching out for the British and 'burning to catch them up'. By the 13 May he was more reflective, sobered by the sights and sounds of combat: 'A huge tank battle lies behind us, tank on tank. It was simply dreadful. What people have to endure!' The campaign was now clearly under way. On 14 May: 'We all have the feeling that a frightful battle is going to break out at some time ahead of us.' The following day he reports: 'Finally the English! We have avenged Cambrai [the First World War British victory]. We were let loose like hunting dogs on the British, I accounted for three tanks alone.' His final diary entry notes: 'Heavy enemy units have been reported to the south-west – whether that's correct?' The question remained unanswered. Hans Steinbrecher's panzer was knocked out in a French ambush, and he was killed by machine-gun fire on bailing out.

Common to British tank crew accounts of the retreat to the coast were exhaustion, heartfelt sympathy for the plight of the French refugees they encountered on the roads, and a growing sense of humiliation at the prospect of defeat. Fatigue dulled their senses. Henry de la Falaise recalled the image of his troop Sergeant Ditton 'fast asleep, all crumpled up in a heap at the bottom of the [Morris armoured] car and wedged somehow between all the paraphernalia which clutters it, his head on an ammunition case'. During a meal halt another of the young troop commanders 'is so done in that he can't keep his eyes open; his head keeps falling on the table'. He finally went to sleep with his face in the eggs. Even when air raids shook them out of their stupor the following morning, 'young Andrew is still asleep in the same position, his face smeared with egg yolk'. Events began to be calculated on the basis of when they last had some sleep. Frequent halts often resulted in unpleasant surprises: a driver, jogged awake, would find that his tank was alone and abandoned on a deserted road, the others having moved on. Veterans recall grabbing perhaps two hours of sleep a day during the retreat.

'My principal memories of that journey are of the heat and dust, and of the thousands of refugees,' recalled David Erskine, who was with the 1st Armoured Division staff, 'their faces set in dogged sadness.' Although it was strictly forbidden, he gave petrol to an old man driving an ancient Renault, who had his old wife, daughter, two granddaughters and a totally overloaded vehicle bulging beneath the weight of household belongings. 'One look at that pathetic family was enough for me. I poured about a gallon into his tank.' He then crank-started the old car and sent him on his way. 'I remember the waves, curiously sad,' he reflected, 'of his family to this day.'

Trooper Williams gave lifts to civilians on his Matilda tank for a variety of reasons. He felt sorry for one young lady who asked him to give her sick mother a ride. 'I persuaded Sergeant Marsden to agree because the girl bore an astonishing resemblance to my fiancée back home in Marlow. Marlow seemed a million miles away, in fact a different world from this chaotic, fear-stricken land.' Tanks are dangerous and awkward vehicles for the uninitiated to mount. Williams indicated with sign language that the young woman should beware the hot spots at the rear of the vehicle, but she badly burned her hand. 'However, she did not complain but sat stoically with her mother on the beer crate behind the turret, just thankful to rest their legs.' When they caught up again with their unit they got a cheery thumbs up from their squadron commander, Major Parkes, who was delighted to see they had kept up. Immersed in the seriousness of their military predicament, he had not noticed the passengers at the back, then 'his face changed to a sort of puce colour and he shouted, "Get those people off the bloody tank!" '

The plight of the civilians personalised the conflict in the minds of the tank crews speeding by in retreat. All at once the war was very close and very personal. It emphasised the urgency of defeating the Germans and visibly demonstrated that they had not done so. Shame and humiliation at likely defeat began to permeate their psyche. Lieutenant Henry de la Falaise has an enduring memory of an eleven-year-old girl coming into the kitchen of his squadron headquarters on the Belgian border. 'She has immense dark eyes, thick curly black hair and her skimpy pink dress is crumpled and soiled. She holds an infant in her arms and she begs for a little milk for the baby, her brother.'

De la Falaise wanted to sleep, but there was something appealing about the young girl, her right shoe split open, her feet swollen and sore after walking forty miles from Brussels. She was looking after sick parents, German Jews who had fled the Nazis, resting in the nearby barn. 'She seems to feel that if she can get her family across the border they will be safe for ever.' She had thirty miles to go, and was pathetically convinced the Allied troops will stop the Germans, at least so that she could get her family across. A kindly woman who owned the farm bathed her feet while de la Falaise's cooks made sandwiches for her and the family. She asked the soldiers whether it was safe to lie down and rest for a few hours. 'Because you see, she adds, I am very tired, and my feet are very sore'. Later she thanked them 'with exquisite politeness and with the dignity of a queen', and they watched her solemnly stepping out into the dark night clutching her baby brother.

De la Falaise found it very moving. 'I suddenly feel ashamed of my weariness,' he confessed. The following morning there was further skirmishing in rearguard actions against the pursuing Germans and more air raids. Presently they were retreating towards the billowing clouds of smoke, tinged with flashes of flame, outlining the city of Tournai. Behind, the panzers were in hot pursuit. Hundreds of refugees had been forced off the roads by the military traffic, and men and women huddled in pitiful groups in the ditches lining the roadside with their belongings piled high on carts beside them. As the Morris armoured cars whined by, de la Falaise recognised with dismay 'the pink dress and tousled black hair of the little Jewish refugee girl from Brussels'. She was among one of the groups. 'At her side is the battered baby carriage, now with a broken wheel. She clutches the baby in her arms, as she stands looking defiantly at the road. Poor kid!' The scene encapsulated the thoughts of the crews dismally surveying the crowds. He felt utterly inadequate and unable to wave because the previous night she had seemed so confident that they would protect her family. 'And here we are,' he bitterly reflected, 'fleeing westward, leaving her behind!'

Major-General le Quesne Martel, the commander of the 50th Division, gave orders at 0800 hours on 21 May for an attack by two mixed columns of tanks, infantry, machine-guns, artillery and anti-tank units against the high ground south-east of Arras. This was to secure breathing-space for a BEF withdrawal. The columns were spearheaded by 7 RTR and 4 RTR had heavy Matilda tanks. The two columns represented therefore the heaviest concentration of armour the BEF possessed. Some seventy-four tanks and two infantry battalions were to be directed into the flank of the 7th Panzer division, streaming unsuspectingly westward up ahead. A further seventy tanks belonging to the 3rd French Mechanised Division were to support their right flank.

The German 7th Panzer Division had enjoyed a series of spectacular advances, shooting up many surprised enemy columns on the French roads. They covered 110 miles in eight days, using tourist maps and filling up at local petrol stations. They abandoned many of their prisoners after running over their surrendered weapons with tank tracks on the road. 'Where are the British, whom we were now crediting with more fighting spirit?' asked the 7th Division's Hauptmann Hans von Luck. 'On the one hand they were tougher than the demoralised French, and on the other they had their backs to the Channel, which separated them from their base on the island.'

British tank crews had now appreciated that the war they had trained for on Salisbury Plain was nothing like what was going on here. Painstaking orders and convoluted procedures did not apply when they were suddenly thrust into the unexpected chaos of modern, fast-moving mobile operations. Trooper Williams recalled, 'We had no map of the area, nor any idea of the objective, neither had we been allowed to net in the radio, but this didn't bother us.' They got on with it. Most tank commanders, lacking any intelligence and denied sufficient time to reconnoitre or marry up with supporting infantry and artillery, were told, 'Start up and follow me!'

'The thing is — and I've thought about this a lot,' reflected Corporal George Andow of 4 RTR. 'Whenever you were training before the war, you always got on the objective, and there was never anything in the training about being suddenly surprised by the amount of armour that was positioned on the objective we were going to.' Experimental training exercises were nothing like the brutal reality that was to follow. 'I think the British Army learned some lessons in France,' surmised Corporal Andow.

'The excitement was enormous at the start,' recalled Sergeant E.V. Strickland of 4 RTR, 'our first real show of strength.' As he set off his tank came to a grinding halt — the usual gear trouble. Trooper Williams remembered having to pick out the line of advance with no directions. The only clue was provided by a company of the Durham Light Infantry, advancing across a ploughed field, bayonets fixed with rifles at the port. Some shells whistled overhead and Williams realised, 'They're ours, this is it!' Whereas 4 RTR kept to the planned direction of advance, the 7 RTR column drifted among elements of the 4th. Nevertheless, the jumble of advancing tanks and infantry plunged into the right flank of the 7th Panzer Division.

'And there suddenly at the top in front of us was a whole stream of German lorries and trucks and half-tracks and motor-cyclists,' observed Peter Vaux, who was in his light Mark VI tank. 'No tanks. And they were as astounded as we were.' They raked the road with fire as the column bore down. Lorries burst into flame and clusters of infantry scattered to avoid the criss-crossing lines of red-hot tracer that left smoke trails behind them. 'I don't know how many Germans we killed and I don't know how many lorries and other vehicles we set on fire — it really was most successful and we really didn't see why we shouldn't go all the way to Berlin at the rate we were going.' Sergeant Strickland arrived at the road to find it packed with German transport of every type. 'Most were burning from the Matilda fire and I proceeded to shoot up the rest.'

This was a classic meeting engagement, each side surprised by the unexpected clash.

Up ahead the German column was mercilessly flailed by tank and machine-gun fire. Second Lieutenant Peter Vaux remembered:

> There was a German motorcyclist just in front of me and he was kicking away at this bike to make it start, and it wouldn't start and there was a vein standing out on his forehead and my gunner was laughing so much he couldn't aim the gun and shoot him.

German soldiers frantically unhitched their anti-tank guns to fire on the Matildas, but the rounds ricocheted off. Spotting a Mark IV panzer coming forward, Vaux was sent back by his colonel to pick up a heavy French tank they had passed to lend support.

The long drawn-out vehicle convoys of *Schutzen* (infantry) Regiment 6 took the brunt of the blow. A terse radio message was sent to Division Headquarters: 'strong enemy tank attack from Arras. Help. Help.' An initial anti-tank block established by *Panzerjäger* (anti-tank) *Abteilung* 42 was rolled over by the tanks. There was panic when a screen manned by the motorised SS Tötenkopf Division was also swept aside. When General Rommel, the 7th Division commander, arrived on the scene speedily directed that every gun, both anti-tank and anti-aircraft, was to open rapid fire immediately. 'All I cared about,' he later wrote, 'was to halt the enemy tanks by heavy gunfire.' Panzer Regiment 25, which was ahead, was ordered to double back and take on the advancing armour in the flanks and rear. The 88mm Flak guns were depressed and levelled at the advancing British tanks.

'We suffered losses because our guns proved too feeble,' stated Leutnant Alexander Stahlberg of the *Panzerjäger* battalion. The 37mm guns came to be contemptuously referred to as 'door-knockers' by their vulnerable crews. The division after-action report complained: 'Our own anti-tank guns do not have a sufficient effect even at close range on the heavy English tanks.' Stahlberg concurred, stating that the gunners 'fired everything they had' but:

The projectiles rebounded off the slanting surfaces. To produce any effect we had to hit the turret ring of the tank or its heavy tracks, which were vulnerable. Hitting a turret ring jammed the turret, destroying a track sent the tank revolving round itself.

This was only discovered by trial and error in the bloody chaos of battle. Rommel stopped the thrust at Arras, not with other tanks, but with heavy artillery and air. 88mm Flak guns could penetrate the Matildas' 60-80mm of armour, and by nightfall nearly 300 Stuka attacks had been flown.

When Peter Vaux returned to the valley, having been unable to get French support, he found that the German heavy tank had disappeared. Down in the valley floor there were over twenty tanks, both A and B squadrons of 4 RTR, and he recognised the CO's tank by its distinguishing pennant. He could not reach him on the radio. Eventually the Adjutant came on air and said, 'Come over and join me.' There was a lot of firing coming from the wood and crest lines either side ahead. It was heavy field gun fire. Bemused by the lack of activity among the squadrons, he discovered why as he drove by:

I thought it very odd that they weren't moving and they weren't shooting, and then I noticed that there was something even odder about them – because their guns were pointing at all angles; a lot of them had their turret hatches open and some of the crews were half in and half out of the tanks, lying wounded and dead – and I realised then, suddenly, with a shock, that all these twenty tanks had been knocked out.

The guns had done their grisly work. Crawling through the grass all around were the wounded and survivors, distinguishable by their bobbing black berets. He had served with this battalion before the outbreak of war and:

There were all those tanks that I knew so well – the familiar names –*Dreadnought, Dauntless, Demon, Devil*; there were the faces of these men with whom I had played games, swum, lived with for years – lying there dead; and there were the tanks – useless –

very few of them burning but most of them smashed up in one way or another.

This was the end of the battalion as he knew it: the best crews, officers and tanks.

'Butch' Williams was still fighting his war with *Grimsby,* their dud engine having kept them out of the main battle. Finally they emerged on the edge of the field. Two Matildas at the side of the road had obviously been knocked out. 'They looked so desolate with no sign of the crews who had brought them so far and into action.' A German armoured car smouldered nearby with the door flung half open. Williams and his crew were experiencing the interminably empty battlefield. 'We hadn't seen a living soul for miles, even the Luftwaffe apparently taking the afternoon off so as not to disturb the tranquillity of this warm sunny day in rural France.' They did engage a single tank, which was dispatched, as well as pinning down German infantry in a village. Prisoners were marched by, and then they were ordered to rally with the survivors. They did not realise it, but the attack had floundered in concentrated gunfire. Both of the tank battalion commanding officers were dead, including their own. As it became dark, 'over in the distance towards Arras, we could see gun flashes and machine-gun tracers slowly arcing over the landscape'. *Grimsby* was at last handed over to the mechanics.

The tank action at Arras on 21 May was a searing episode for both sides and it transformed the operational situation. Rommel, convinced at first that he had been attacked by hundreds of tanks, halted his advance for twenty-four hours, believing further attacks to be imminent. Guderian's arrival at the coast near Abbeville looked more vulnerable than when he had first established the bridgehead. The Arras fighting raised fears among the more senior generals that the panzer divisions might conceivably be cut off from the following infantry divisions, who were making epic forced marches to close up. There was some relief at Hitler's 'halt order' on 24 May, when the panzer divisions were ordered out of the line to refit for the next stage of the campaign, the break-in to the French interior under *Fall Rot,* or Case Red, that followed *Fall Gelb,* or Case Yellow, the initial attack. Guderian protested, but the ruling was not rescinded for two days, by which time Operation Dynamo, the BEF evacuation from France through Dunkirk, was about to start.

Boulogne and Calais were quickly reinforced during the pause in operations after Arras. At the same time Allied forces attempted to eliminate the German bridgeheads that had been established on the south bank of the River Somme near Abbeville. Reinforcements arrived from the British 1st Armoured Division, but much of its artillery, infantry and some armour were hastily dispatched to Boulogne and Calais. Its unit integrity was fragmented even before it began its first battle. Their experience offers a useful insight into the nature of a typical tank action in France at this penultimate stage of the French *Blitzkrieg* campaign.

# 6

# TANK ACTION FRANCE

## ARRIVING

'We thought we were going to the BEF,' surmised Sergeant Bill Close of 3 RTR. 'Instead of that we were entrained and we finished up in Dover as a regiment without our tanks, and we enshipped for Calais – which was a complete surprise.' From the very moment of arrival the reinforcing tank crews and commanders were subjected to the strain of appreciating that events were probably slipping out of control. Major Bill Reeves, a squadron commander, who had been trying to unravel the uncertain course of events prior to the crossing, realised 'our role in Calais was going to be a sticky one and very far from the original one as explained to us the other side of the Channel'. 3 RTR was being thrown into the line as a stopgap measure to shore up the defence of Calais in a vain attempt to stabilise a fast-moving, uncertain situation. The quaysides were burning as they disembarked. German units were approaching the coast but nobody knew where they were. Alan Wollaston remembered that the ship's captain wanted to sail back to England without unloading. 'A captain from our regiment went on board and threatened to shoot the skipper if our tanks were not unloaded.'

It was an inauspicious start, as Reeves confirmed.

> Our tanks were not loaded for an emergency like this but for going to some training area in France; consequently the guns were still in mineral jelly and all had to be cleaned out, oiled, tested and adjusted. The same applied to the wireless sets.

The crews had to squat on the quayside, unfed and tired, cleaning weapons or waiting for equipments to be unloaded while around them the town burned. 'All this was done in an atmosphere of intense hurry, urgency and rumour,' recalled Reeves.

Squadrons were formed *ad hoc* and did not necessarily get their own tanks or even the same crews. It was a 'bit of a mix-up,' declared Alan Wollaston, who was allocated the gunner's seat in a Cruiser tank.

Bill Close confirmed that 'it was a complete shambles when we arrived . . . 'We were not equipped with wireless, so anything had to be verbal.' Radios and spares were languishing in a railway siding in England. This also obliged them to shout rather than converse in the noisy confines of the vehicles or copy the First World War practice of lip-reading. It encapsulated the whole tenor of the desperate battle they were to fight, impeded by changed decisions and inadequate equip-ments. Within hours Close bumped into a German column and four of his five cars were wiped out. 'I was the only car able to escape,' he said, and there was no way, short of driving back, that he could let his commanding officer know.

The rest of the 1st British Armoured Division, of which 3 RTR should have been part, was unloading at Cherbourg on 21 May. Captain Lord George Scott, a squadron second-in-command, de-scribed the chaotic arrival. Some of the new tanks had to wait to have their guns fitted at the quayside because they had arrived on a separate transport. Once they had loaded the train the French engine drivers went on strike and refused to move them. An elderly engine was substituted, with an equally elderly driver, and the train became stuck half-way up the first hill. Another was found to shunt it over the top. It took them forty-eight hours to reach their objective, a few miles south of the Somme. Within days they were in action. There was no time for preparation, in-country orientation or field training.

The very nature of this force was 'expeditionary'. Clearly the British crews were dependent upon host nation support and liaison. Little beyond polite professional exchanges had been achieved with the French in the absence of urgency during the 'Phoney War', and by the time there was a crisis it was too late. Lieutenant-Colonel Keller, commanding 3 RTR at Calais, remembered: 'I had asked for a French Liaison Officer but was not issued with one despite the town being full of French soldiers, transport and refugees.' There was some contact at the human level, but little was achieved in terms of close armoured co-operation.

'One of the impressions which will always stand out in my memory,' admitted Major Bill Reeves, 'was the terrific weight of equipment which we carried in those early stages of the war.' Unlike the Germans, who had benefited from bloodless occupations and were well into their second campaign, the British were not configured to fight in the same practical terms.

> The heat was terrific and I was weighted down with both my pack and haversack on my back, a second haversack at my side, a gas mask at the alert on my chest and gas cape rolled on top of my pack on my shoulder. In addition to all this of course was weapon, ammunition, compass, binoculars and map cases.

It did not all fit into the tank, and the crews were reluctant to ditch equipment which they had signed for and would have to pay for if lost. 'The idea of a crew fighting in a tank in all this regalia was of course ludicrous,' Reeves stated, 'but we did not learn the lesson till a considerable time later. . . . Nobody seemed to know where our lorries were,' Reeves ruefully recalled; the tanks were disorganised and needed refuelling. Maintenance had to be carried out and the troops were subsisting on hard rations 'Morale would have risen enormously if a hot brew of tea could have been served out,' admitted Reeves. 'This would have been done automatically later in the war, but we lacked initiative and experience in the early stages.'

The prevailing disorganised atmosphere bred order and counter-order Lieutenant Colonel Keller, commanding 3 RTR at Calais, complained: 'A great deal of valuable time was wasted owing to my not knowing who or what Brigadier Nicholson [his commander] was and why I had come under his orders and what I was supposed to be doing.' His tanks were never properly deployed, because 'I was being used as an "I" [infantry supporting Matilda] battalion and was therefore impervious to anti-tank guns', which was certainly not the case with Cruiser tanks. A decision was taken to evacuate Calais; it was just as soon countermanded. Keller was ordered to destroy his tanks, then 'half-way through received another message from the Brigadier telling me to stop. By this time it was too late.' The impact on the crews, especially when ordered to conduct a last-ditch defence of Calais, can only be imagined.

All this was compounded by the lack of information. Fires at Boulogne were illuminating the night skies to the south-west, and sounds of heavy explosions to the south and south-east indicated the enemy was rapidly approaching. 'During this time we heard very little news of the general situation,' recalled Bill Reeves, 'and in fact we probably knew far less about the war than our people sitting at home.' Snippets of news were picked up from the BBC, supplemented by rumour. Even before going into action Trooper W.F. Eldridge of the 10th Hussars, who were moving up by train, conversed with troops going in the opposite direction. 'We began to hear of troops being lifted off the beaches some place further up the coast.' They did not hear about Dunkirk until much later.

Pinned down by practical problems, contradictory orders and uneasy at the pace of worrying developments, the newly arrived tank crews prepared for action. Bill Reeves, impatient to set off from Calais with his Cruiser tanks, noticed the shrill singing of countless nightingales during a lull. To his surprise, 'every bush seemed to hold one,' he recalled, 'likely waiting to cross the Channel on their spring migration'. It was one of those incongruous moments in war that endure. 'I could not help thinking how completely isolated and unaffected these birds were by the mass madness of the human species, and how much better organised was the realm of nature compared to our wretched so-called civilisation.'

They would soon be joining the war.


## CROSSING THE START LINE

'Monday 27 May 1940 was to dawn misty, still and warm on the Somme Front,' recalled Sergeant Ron Huggins; another fine summer's day. There was to be an attack. 'Our information was that Jerry had a bridgehead over the Somme in the region of the village of Huppy, south of Abbeville,' remembered Sergeant Barry Ross, a Cruiser gunner in the 10th Hussars. 'The object was to chase him over the Somme with the help of the Queen's Bays and 9th Lancers.' Huggins, aware of the task, appreciated 'it was good campaigning weather. We knew it and the Germans knew it.' There was animated discussion among the tank crews on their prospects. 'We were confident and ready to have a go,' said Huggins. 'We had to measure up to our fathers of 1914–1918.'

'Whilst awaiting for the order to start, I wondered if my father felt like me when he was in the leading troop of B Squadron when the Regiment attacked and captured Maichy Le Preux,' reflected Technical Sergeant-Major Dunk. It was not so many miles from Abbeville. This part of the campaign was being fought around the main First World War cemeteries.

Those able to sleep at all only managed to do so fitfully, rolled in blankets next to their Cruiser tanks. 'Stand-to' at dawn meant that gunners and drivers manned tanks while the wireless operators brewed tea and spread margarine and jam on bread or army biscuits. As clouds of steam rose from 'Tommy-cookers', Huggins observed that some men 'made quick visits to their pals in nearby tanks and wished them the best of luck'. Both sides were reflective on the eve or immediate aftermath of battle. Hauptmann von Luck, whose 7th Panzer Division was in the vicinity, was grieving for their dead and severely wounded. 'Predominant, however,' he was later to write, 'was joy that we had survived thus far.' He had already learned the value of stoicism in a kill or be killed environment. 'Learn to endure all things with equanimity,' he advised. There was little point questioning the 'whys and where-fores', one should rather 'build up an immune system of his own against the feelings of fear and sympathy and, probably, to a certain degree, even against matters of ethics, morals and conscience'. In order to operate effectively a soldier had 'to suppress images of horror' and 'distance himself from his neighbour in order to be capable of rational action'. Von Luck was in the middle of his second campaign and had calculated that 'if he manages to do this, his chances of survival increase.'

Huggins and his friends had yet to experience the insights that von Luck pondered, but like so many British soldiers they approached the coming tempest pragmatically, with boisterous activity and active preparatory work. He described how 'thoughts turned to home and loved ones; comfort, warmth and security left behind'. Meanwhile the squadron Sergeant-Major moved around the men, quietly reminding them to fill in the details of their next of kin and the simple Wills page at the rear of their official pay-books. Identity discs had to be worn but no scrap of unit identification taken. Nobody was offended; he was offering the paternal guidance young soldiers craved. Men like the Sergeant-Major represented the tangible part of the permanent regimental fabric to which they belonged. 'No one could know who would still be alive or unwounded in the day's fighting,' Huggins pointed out. They would all have considered their chances; 'such is human tension before battle', he remarked.

Mechanical problems, especially pronounced with the A13 Cruiser tank, made crews feel vulnerable prior to the advance. British veteran tank crew accounts are peppered with references to tank breakdowns and weapon or equipment failures. Sergeant Huggins was concerned because 'my crew found that it had a very defective reverse gear before we left England and I had reported it'. Little was achieved during the chaotic move to Cherbourg and after, and now his driver still struggled to get the tank into reverse gear. The inevitable tease 'that we had the only non-retreating tank in the regiment' was not appreciated.

Tank drivers started engines at the command 'Mount Up!' Zero hour was approaching. 'The Liberty aircraft engines of the A13 Cruisers burst into life with their usual deep-throated roar, vibrating the stillness of the dawn.' As the entire regiment rolled forward, waves of noise washed over the stillness of the quiet dawn and echoed across the front line close by. Promised French artillery support did not materialise. They were not to know that faulty radio communications had meant that their regimental headquarters were unable to receive the attack postponement order.

Across the front line Gefreiter (corporal) Wilhelm Krawzek, manning a 37mm anti-tank gun with Infantry Regiment 25, strained his ears to listen. *Schütze* (gunner) Herbert Brinkforth sat waiting at the telescopic sight, his hand on the firing mechanism. Krawzek began to discern approaching tanks. 'There! They are working their way along, some heavy, some light, all Tommies.' They were driving from cover to cover using bushes and hedges. 'Nerves are practically at breaking-point,' in the words of *Gefreiter* Krawzek, as they realise that this is a substantial advance of up to thirty tanks. Owing to the light calibre of their gun they have no option but to remain concealed and count down the distance to the optimum and rather short engagement range.

An 88mm Flak gun named *Caesar,* manned by Leutnant Klay's battery of Flak *Abteilung* I/64, also sighted on the approaching British. A more fearful contender, the 88mm Flak guns had first proved their worth at Ilza in Poland when, in an emergency in September the previous year, they repulsed a succession of Polish counter-attacks. It had an awesome muzzle velocity of 2,600 feet per second and was increasingly being employed in a fire-brigade role to combat the heavy tanks the panzers could not penetrate. Klay's view was that the attack was appearing a little tentative. 'They approach hesitantly, dart to and fro like grey shadows along the edge of the wood, shudder, come to a halt, and seem not too clear about where to attack.'

'Then it's time,' declares Wilhelm Krawzek. 'Fire at will!' The 37mm shell 'roars out of the muzzle, to bore into the armour of a tank turret'. Machine-guns join in, tracers converging on the approaching tanks. Klay's 88mm gun *Caesar*, having identified the range, opens fire. 'After ten shots, two tanks are in flames, burning fiercely,' Krawzek recalls. 'The penetrative force of our shells is colossal,' Leutnant Klay observes.

> If they achieve a square hit on target, they pierce the monster's armour and send them up in flames. Often, when the impact is too flat, they bounce off like pebbles skimming a pond – over the tank turrets, followed by a shower of sparks.

Observing through his binoculars, Klay believed he had caused chaos among the British tanks, 'and the sight of the burning brutes will not be exactly encouraging for those coming up behind'.

'It all happened so quickly,' declared Trooper James Palmer.

> As we topped the rise, anti-tank guns hit us from the right flank and four tanks were ablaze before they had gone ten yards. The squadron commander was trying frantically to rally the tanks, but engines had stalled, men were struggling to get out of blazing tanks,

and some men were dragging their mates through the mud away from the burning tanks. The casualties that day were twenty killed and twenty-three injured.

'As I looked through my gun sight,' declared Sergeant Barry Ross, 'the rising sun blinded me and no doubt all the other crews suffered the same.' It was not going to be as easy as anticipated. 'What a way to go into your first action – wrong information, blinded by the sun and, worst of all, not knowing who's on the left flank.' Sergeant Major Dunk, who was in the advance guard, saw his troop commander killed as his tank was hit by concealed anti-tank guns. Another 'burst into flames' fifty yards to his left. Deciding to withdraw, his driver violently zigzagged the Cruiser across a field to avoid incoming fire. 'I was terrified in case we threw a track, as these tanks could do when turned at speed.' There was no supporting artillery fire and no French tanks.

## BATTLE AND AFTERMATH

Tank crews on both sides were emotionally attached to their tanks and gave them names. All the tanks in 'D' Squadron in a British unit would be given names beginning with 'D': *Dreadnought, Dauntless, Demon* and *Devil*. They could use these names as pseudo code-names on the wireless net. Similarly, German panzers had names that extolled the heroic, labels designed to promote respect, such as *Griffin, Eagle, Falcon* and *Condor*. A tank hit in battle represented a violent intrusion into the home of a tight community of men who had lived cheek by jowl in intimate proximity for a long time. Crews shared everything: their food, news of their family and women, and a mutual trust in the professional capability of all to serve the weapon system. When tanks burned, so did carefully nurtured relationships.

Rudolf Behr lost three Panzer Mark IVs, with four men dead and three seriously and one lightly wounded, in one painful afternoon in the suburbs of Boulogne. Poland had been nothing like what they had experienced in France, and the real damage was being done, as at Huppy, by concealed anti-tank guns. They were earning a fearsome respect. Behr, feverishly searching the ground forward for likely sites, saw 'a small cloud of dust and smoke breaking out on the tank ahead. That was a hit!' One of his tank commanders struggled out of the turret but then fell across the hull and on to the tarmac road. As he watched the others scrambling out 'a hard metallic blow strikes my tank, and in the crew compartment there is a display of sparks like a fireworks rocket'. Now it was his turn to get out. Below, his driver's head lolled forward with blood running down his face. Fortunately, the gunner had the presence of mind to traverse the turret to one side, enabling them to escape from the side hatch facing away from enemy fire. Behr shouted to his driver but had to leave him behind, believing him probably to be dead. They scrambled to the rear under machine-gun fire. Behr lost drivers, gunners and his radio operator.

These were painful losses. Small white circles were painted over the tanks dark armour plating to commemorate the souls who had lived and died within. Labelled with the date '22.V.40', they were a poignant reminder to new crews that they were sharing spaces with the spirits of those that had preceded them.

*Gefreiter* Krawzek described the predicament of the anti-tank gunner, facing their fully armoured and mobile opponents with only a thin gun shield for protection:

> The projectiles strike the road to the left of us, the hedge to the right of us, the trees above us, the air is filled with crackling, hissing, humming and whistling. Branches fall. The road is pitted. But we bite our lips, as shell after shell flies towards the tanks. [Gunner] Brinkforth fires with icy calm.

For this action Brinkforth became the first private soldier in the Wehrmacht to be decorated with the Knight's Cross. Leutnant Klay's 88mm Flak gun *Caesar* was less fortunate. A succession of explosions straddled the gun position, wounding three members of the crew and knocking out both the half-track tractor and gun. When the gun commander was shot in the head the rest of the crew abandoned the position.

Veterans describe battle in terms of disjointed, shutter-like images which combine with sense-dulling physical blows. 'Suddenly, there were four loud bangs in quick succession, as from a quick-firing gun from within the copse,' Ron Huggins recalled. 'Lieutenant Moorhouse's tank was hit broadside on by all four projectiles and they passed so close across my front that I felt the displacement of air on my face. Immediately his tank went up in a sheet of flame' – the strikes had punctured the long petrol tanks alongside the large engine of the Cruiser. 'At that moment, ammunition also started exploding and I did not think that anybody could have possibly survived in the tank, the brew-up was so violent.' To Huggins's absolute amazement the officer came scrambling out of the turret with blood streaming down his face and jumped aboard his tank. As they began moving off, the driver of the stricken tank, 'Ginger' Hartnell, also got out of the forward driver compartment and ran and grabbed one of the towing eyes to the rear of Huggins's tank. He lacked the strength and time to climb aboard, and they sped off under fire, dragging him behind through the grass on the field.

Leaving the shelter of a disabled tank was rarely a calculated act, because to remain inside was to invite destruction. Veterans often remark on the speed and agility of crew members getting out of damaged tanks, even when disabled and frequently under fire. Not all could. George Cotterill, who was in Huggins's squadron, watched 'Chalkie' Wright, 'a coloured lad', bailing out of his tank and then trying to clamber back inside to traverse the gun that had snagged the driver's hatch door. He was killed by machine-gun fire before he could get inside.

After leaving the protective tank shell, dismounted crews underwent odysseys as they attempted to gain their own lines. Lieutenant-Colonel Keller of 3 RTR was emphatic that 'the revolver does not provide sufficient protection to crews whose tank had been put out of action'. This view, expressed in his subsequent Calais after-action report, was studiously ignored. 'Officers and men have told me,' he emphasised, 'that they felt quite helpless and would all have liked a rifle.' At Huppy on the Abbeville bridgehead, armoured cars were used to try and retrieve knocked-out crews, who had to fight their way out, often against marauding German infantry, and were armed only with side-arms. Many were killed.

Only ten of thirty tanks survived the gauntlet of fire at the 'postponed' regimental tank assault at Huppy on 27 May. Again, as at Arras, there was no supporting infantry. British tank crews were confident enough to engage tank on tank, but the Germans always appeared to have a further mix of tactical assets up their sleeves. Even when they managed to surprise the opposition, Major Bill Reeves had to admit 'it was very impressive to see the reaction of the German column on being attacked. They very quickly dismounted from their vehicles and got their anti-tank guns into action and soon shells were whizzing past our ears.' The British Armoured Corps paid for the false lessons implanted by its tank-purist thinkers and philosophers, Fuller and Liddell-Hart. They had trained 'tank heavy', feeling that mobile infantry, anti-tank support and artillery would play a limited role. German doctrine had honed the outcome into a combined-arms concept, agreed and trained for, which two campaigns' worth of experience honed to a formidable capability.

Inexperience and lack of preparation were reflected in the comparatively high number of friendly fire incidents. 'Blue on blue' casualties stemmed largely from the appalling standards of armoured fighting vehicle recognition shown by both sides. As Lieutenant-Colonel Keller of 3 RTR pointed out, 'German tanks in appearance are similar to ours and, with the confusion existing near Calais, we had to delay opening fire on one or two occasions to make quite certain which side the tanks belonged to.' Dick Howe, commanding a two-tank patrol south-east of Calais, admitted he had 'run the gauntlet both ways, having received 18-pounder fire from the Germans and anti-tank and machine-gun fire from our own troops – an unhealthy trip!'

German tank recognition was equally bad. Retreating British tanks often joined unsuspecting German units or drove unmolested through them. Lieutenant Peter Wiliams of 3 RTR recalled on such an occasion 'some of the German troops waved to us and we returned the compliment'.

By the beginning of June the Dunkirk evacuation was successfully completed. Attacks on the Abbeville bridgehead were also conducted by the 2nd and 5th French (partially mechanised) cavalry divisions. The 1st British Armoured Division lost 110 of its 257 tanks and was finally evacuated from Cherbourg on 18 June, the day before the port was surrendered. Nearly all its equipment was lost. French armoured units including a rebuilt 2nd Reserve Curasair Division continued attacks on the Somme River until 4 June. The losses incurred finished them as effective fighting units.

*Fall Rot* (Case Red), the second phase of the French campaign, began the next day. There were no combat-worthy French armoured units able to oppose the German advance. The 2nd, 3rd, and 4th DCRs had only 150 tanks left between them, and the newly constituted 7th DLM was down to 174 armoured vehicles. A series of fierce small-scale actions fought until 16 June only temporarily delayed the inevitable result and France surrendered on 22 June.

By the third week in June most of the BEF was back in England. Crews ruefully reflected on their experience. Tank-on-tank fighting had been limited. Most of the burden was borne by the French heavies. Arras was a brief high point, but it was against soft-skinned vehicles strung out on the flanks of an already advancing panzer division. Much of the firing had been on the move by machine-gun tanks hosing down lorries and hastily deployed crew-served anti-tank guns with automatic fire. There had been no integral infantry or artillery support of consequence, and it had been quickly outrun. Machine-gun effectiveness requires the spread of rounds on target that firing on the move provides. Precision shooting with the main armament against other tanks was another matter. German combat experience confirmed for a second time the value of engaging accurately from the halt and then moving. The British had yet to assimilate this knowledge.

'Tank heavy' tactics, developed on Salisbury Plain during the experiments of the 1930s, proved ineffective against German combined arms, especially panzer and anti-tank gun mix. The British light but radio co-ordinated flank attack at Arras achieved results far out of proportion to loosely directed but heavier and more powerful French tank attacks. Radio fits were inferior to the German and often jolted off air during cross-country movement. Inexperience combined with a decade of government neglect stymied the British effort. The Germans discovered the British to be as brave as the French and far more aggressive, perhaps to the point of recklessness. They acknowledged the crews were of a tough breed but believed they were badly led. The British had also fielded a tank design against which, for the moment, no panzer could compete. The Mark II Matilda was regarded as formidable and emphasised the need for the Germans to follow up the lesson derived from Poland by up-gunning and increasing armour protection. Captured equipments were taken away for painstaking evaluation.

The legacy of defeat was a bitter pill for British tank crews to swallow. Bill Close of 3 RTR made it back to England. 'I felt very, very disappointed,' he subsequently admitted. 'In fact, I didn't know the fate of a lot of my comrades, and I understood when I got back eventually to Dover that only about a quarter of the regiment had managed to get back.' The unit as he had known it in peacetime had virtually ceased to exist. 'We'd gone to war on a Tuesday night a regular battalion with fifty tanks, and by Saturday we had lost all our vehicles – tracked and wheeled – and nearly half our strength'.

Lieutenant John Dixon met his panzer opposition with just three revolver rounds and did not make it back. His Bren gun carrier, abruptly required to dodge a carrier in front hit by anti-tank fire, careered into a ditch. As it tumbled his revolver, without its issue lanyard, fell from his holster – although the parsimonious three rounds 'wouldn't have been able to put up much of a defence in any case'. His unit had fought a confusing war of movement through seven rearguard actions. 'When we left Cassel,' conducting a fighting retreat, he recalled, 'I had no idea that there was an evacuation going on.' In one of those inescapable ironies of war 'it made one even angrier to think that if we, instead of the Fife and Forfars, had pushed off earlier we might have got back.' He was taken prisoner shortly after seven o'clock on the morning of 30 May 1940.

Bill Close got some leave and went back to Fordingbridge, the place where his war had started when the military policeman had called him out of the pub to barracks. He felt dispirited and guilty to have returned when so many in his unit had not:

> Most wives were still there. They knew little of where we had been or what we'd been doing. Girls whose husbands were missing kept asking questions we couldn't answer, scrutinising our faces to see if we were concealing anything from them.

'To be taken prisoner is not a pleasant experience,' John Dixon remembered. 'It was especially unpleasant for me because I was so completely unprepared for it. Not only had the thought of being taken prisoner never entered my mind, in all my training it had never been mentioned.' Fatigue soon dwarfed these considerations when they were force-marched through a June heat wave into captivity in Germany. The first thing the Germans did was shave off his dark wavy hair, of which he was inordinately proud, to produce a demeaning identity photograph for his concentration camp captors. 'It was only later,' he bitterly recalled, 'that the feeling of humiliation and disgrace began to take hold.'

They had lost. John Dixon was not repatriated to England until 8 May 1945. His war had lasted thirty days.

# 7

## WESTERN DESERT SEE-SAW

### 'FOX KILLED IN THE OPEN'

British tank crewman Sam Bradshaw viewed the new theatre of operations after Mussolini's declaration of war on 10 June 1940. British troops were still being strafed and bombed by the Luftwaffe as they escaped across the English Channel – but nothing could be further removed than this from the European landscape: 'It was barren, it was just limitless,' he said, 'there was nothing to be seen at all – just distance.' Before him stretched the expanse of the Western Desert in present-day Libya.

Bradshaw's unit, the 6th Royal Tank Regiment, had been part of the 'Mobile Force', a scratch unit of armoured fighting vehicles assembled at Mersa Matruh in the late 1930s, 190 miles west of Alexandria. Its role was to watch over the large Italian garrison at Cyrenaica, a further hundred miles west, a deterrent posture at a time of international tension. Sarcastically labelled 'Immobile Force', it was slowly expanded as tensions grew in Europe and renamed Mobile Division Egypt after the Munich Crisis in 1938. The division's dynamic first commander, Major-General Percy Hobart, had applied fierce training to transform the force into the most formidable unit in North Africa. 'The best-trained division I have ever seen,' remarked General O'Connor, shortly to lead it into action. But it was far less fearsome by European standards and compared poorly with the lethal German Panzer Divisions that had just been unloosed in the West.

'You had to have been in the desert in those days to realise how badly we were equipped,' commented Bradshaw. 'I mean the first tank I went into action with was built in 1926.' His unit would soon see combat and would have to fight with what it had. French capitulation on 22 June had released all the 250,000 Italian troops in North Africa for operations against Egypt. Almost no British tanks had been recovered from France in 1940, leaving only 200 light tanks and fifty heavier infantry tanks to defend the British mainland. While Germany would seek to capitalise on its campaign lessons by further improving the thickness of its armour and guns, the British were denied the luxury. A pressing need to cover home defence gaps through existing production lines prevented design improvements. Bradshaw might well view the coming conflict in the Western Desert with trepidation. 'I don't know whether they had taken my tank out of the Imperial War Museum,' he remarked dryly, 'but you know, the vehicles, the British tanks were not of the best.' He was even less sanguine about their technical potential: 'The tracks broke, the engines broke down, the oil was insufficient, the guns were pea-shooters – they were rubbish actually.'

As the invasion threat to the British mainland loomed during the height of the Battle of Britain, the Italians launched a five-division offensive on 13 September.

They were opposed by only ten thousand British troops, who had to withdraw eastwards towards Egypt. Thus began a see-saw conflict during which the Axis and Allies experienced consecutively the elation of offence then the despair of retreat six times before the dominance of North Africa was settled.

Paolo Colacicchi of the Italian Tenth Army also lacked confidence, despite the apparent overwhelming numerical superiority of his army. 'We were certainly not ready to go to war in 1940,' he claimed, 'it was a purely political move by Mussolini, who felt that Hitler was winning too much too quickly and that if he did not make some sort of gesture, take some sort of initiative, he would not be able to sit at the conference table.' Italy had 1,500 tanks on the declaration of war, but the majority were not in the Western Desert and they were outclassed by much of the admittedly primitive British armour. The Italian Tenth Army had about 200 L3 'tankettes', small vehicles that fired only machine-guns. They had fared badly against Russian tanks during the Spanish Civil War, so their crews were not confident. Heavier capability came in the form of medium M11/39 and M23/40 tanks with 37mm and 47mm guns, but they were crewed by units unused to working together with large joint formations.

The desert campaigns were fought across a surface resembling the moon. Tanks and vehicles could make steady going over firm sand and gravel. Large parts of the operations area were level plain; in effect a model sand-table area over which armoured operational concepts could be developed in virtual laboratory conditions. 'It was only in the desert,' claimed the German Commander Erwin Rommel, 'that the principles of armoured warfare, as they were taught in theory before the war, could be fully applied and thoroughly developed.' Undulating steppe-like terrain predominated, interspersed with low mounds and ridges. Maps were virtually featureless.

Walter McIntyre, a British anti-tank gunner, recalled the solitude of the Western Desert, alluding to 'the loneliness, because there was nothing about you, day and night and the next day'. It was 'just one continual . . . like being in prison, but with no walls'. Vehicle access was by broad paths, called 'trighs' or 'pistes', connecting the few sparsely populated settlements and water-holes. Although the coastal zone was a frequently used bivouac area by virtue of its better water supplies, it was fringed by a belt of sand dunes or salt swamps. There was one tarmac road, the Italian-built Via Balba, with its distinctive line of telegraph poles linking towns along the Libyan coastline.

It was the absence of distinctive features and the inhospitable environment that produced the see-saw nature of offensive and counter-offensive. The desert's emptiness reduced an army's ability to sustain prolonged advances over long distances. Sand dunes blocked vehicle access to the south and there were few mountain ranges to funnel movement.

Over everything shone the sun, its 'brilliant hard heat beating on a land, severe and complete', according to tank crewman Peter Roach. Temperatures here were incomprehensible to most Europeans. During the hottest months of June, July and August the midday heat might reach 140 degrees Fahrenheit, plummeting to five degrees at night. Rain fell rarely and only in winter. Sandstorms called 'ghiblis' occurred every four weeks or so throughout the year, reducing visibility to three metres and bringing operations to a standstill. As Peter Roach concluded, 'A man was unnecessary here and seemed to feel it.'

Italian soldiers, coming from their Mediterranean climate and colonial background, were, to a degree, better acclimatised than most. Brushing aside British delaying actions, six of the fourteen Italian divisions advanced with a small armoured group to Sidi Barrani, 60 miles from the Libyan frontier, then inexplicably halted. Tanks and motor vehicles suffered frequent breakdowns, while the infantry, making up the majority of the force, exhausted themselves marching across the lunar landscape. 'Looking back now,' recalls Paolo Colacicchi, 'it seems an extraordinary thing how we moved into Egypt by sending out these enormous columns, not very well protected because we did not have too many tanks, and then each of them settling down in a sort of fortified camp.' Field Marshal Rodolfo Graziani, short of fuel and artillery ammunition, had been pushed unprepared into this offensive. Following exaggerated reports of British reinforcements he opted to secure his line of progress with a string of prepared forts.

Some British reinforcements had arrived in June 1940, and these resulted in an increase of armoured fighting power, including fifty Matilda Mark II heavy tanks. Italian caution had prompted Lieutenant-General O'Connor, commanding the Western Desert Force at Mersa Matruh, and General Wavell, the C–in–C at Cairo, to plan counter-offensives. Small-scale actions during the retreat towards Egypt had revealed just how inferior Italian AFVs were to their British counterparts. Lieutenant David Belchem, who had completed an exchange posting with an Italian armoured unit in 1938, was 'appalled at the age and inadequacy of the equipment with which the Italian units were supposed to prepare for war'.

Italian 37mm guns on the medium M11/39 tank were only effective against British A10s and A13s at point-blank range. Two–pounder Cruiser and Matilda tank guns could penetrate their frontal armour at normal battle ranges. The Italians had nothing to punch through the 65–78mm-thick Matilda heavy infantry tanks. Virtually every British tank had a radio, but not their Italian adversaries. As a consequence Italian tank commanders had to halt and confer with their subordinates if the situation changed – unworkable in the hectic pace of armoured action. 'Mussolini sent men into action utterly ill-equipped, untrained in mobile operations, and often lacking in competent assured leadership,' claimed Lieutenant Belchem. 'How could they be expected to prevail?'

Following months of secret preparations after the September Italian halt, O'Connor attacked at dawn on 9 December. Although his opponent retained a vast front-line numerical superiority of 80,000 troops to the British 30,000, the armoured balance had reversed. Now 275 British tanks opposed about 120 greatly inferior Italian types. Following a stealthy approach total surprise was achieved by the initial British assault on Nibeiwa Camp, as Alf Davies of the 1st Royal Tank Regiment recalls:

> We arrived at a certain spot at about five o'clock in the morning just before it got light, and we were expecting to see Italian tanks or infantry. But instead of that we saw about three hundred men, they all had candles – they were attending Mass. Well, you know, there is no law and we just opened up with machine-guns – and candles, everything went flying elsewhere.

Rarely is surprise so complete. Ethical debates about slaughtering surprised and defenceless enemies in a fast-moving action come with the benefit of hindsight. Davies addressed his doubts later. 'Why did I do that? But you know you have to follow orders, they said open fire – you had to follow orders.' Many of the Italian tank crews were killed before they could even reach their vehicles. General Maletti, the camp commander, was cut down emerging from his dugout. All the Italian front-line armour with the invasion force was destroyed or captured within the five hours of this initial engagement. Italian artillery gun crews fought to the death, firing their 100mm howitzers point blank at attacking Matilda tanks, but succeeded in doing little more than jamming turrets on one or two.

O'Connor's offensive had supplies for only four days when it started, but they kept the momentum going beyond using the booty picked up as fort after fort fell. Italian vehicles were pressed into service and their fuel and water dumps utilised. 'We decided that as they were so far apart they would be unable to support each other,' O'Connor remarked, 'and we moved our troops round to attack them from the rear, the way their rations would come.' By the end of December Sidi Barrani, Sollum and Fort Capuzzo had fallen, and in January 1941 Bardia, Tobruk and Derna capitulated.

Disheartened by his defeats, Marshal Graziani decided to abandon

Cyrenaica and push his retreating columns into Tripolitania, the western part of Libya. A bold decision was made by the British to send elements of the 7th Division across the desert to cut off the Italian columns streaming along the Via Balbia south of Benghazi. This episode epitomised the difference between armoured operations across Europe, with its woods, roads, river lines and centres of population, and those in the new desert 'seascape'. 'More and more,' wrote British war correspondent Alan Moorehead, 'I began to see that desert warfare resembled war at sea.' There were no static positions; men steered by compass, while mixed units of tanks and guns 'made great sweeps across the desert as a battle squadron at sea will vanish over the horizon'. There was no apparent front line and 'one did not occupy the desert any more than one occupied the sea'. It was a question of manoeuvring into those areas offering the best prospect of destroying the enemy. On 4 February General Creagh sent a flying column with infantry, anti-tank guns and armoured cars, but no tanks, to erect a roadblock on the Via Balbia. 'We hunted men, not land,' Moorehead commented, 'as a warship will hunt another warship, and care nothing for the sea on which the action is fought.'

Combe Force reached the coast near Sidi Saleh the following morning and blocked the road with 2,000 men. The 4th Armoured Brigade with only twenty Cruisers and thirty-six light tanks motored as hard as they could to support them.

The Cruiser tank of tank gunner 'Topper' Brown of 2 RTR bumped and lurched its way across the open desert at speeds between 25 and 30 mph. Brown had been 'up the Blue' – the colloquial jargon for the desert – since war had started in September. 'My feelings were ones of complete indifference. I was just utterly fed up, absolutely filthy and badly underfed.' There was little sleep during a night, punctuated by minor skirmishing with Italian stragglers, as well as torrential rain so that 'I was soaked, even wearing my greatcoat'. They arrived at Beda Fomm late on the afternoon of 5 February. The objective was a picture of desert desolation, described by Sergeant Ken Chadwick as 'completely flat, sandy with a little loose scrub, and many empty four-gallon petrol cans blowing about in the wind'. The only distinct feature was a small hill called the 'Pimple', with a ridge and tomb upon it to the north. It was to be a place of slaughter.

Shedding rearguards as it progressed, the Italian column, with much of its armour at the back, was shocked and dismayed to clash with a British force across its road. Immediately the 10th Bersaglieri Regiment in the vanguard blindly launched a series of uncoordinated frontal assaults. Gazing down the Benghazi-Tripoli road, James Palmer with 2 RTR could not believe his eyes. 'The whole of Graziani's army was retreating from Benghazi,' he later related, and 'they were sitting ducks.'

Brown's commander, Second Lieutenant Plough, suddenly said, 'They're here, reverse!' The tank was hull down on a low rise and it was just beginning to get light. Corporal 'Barney' Barnes steadily moved the tank up the slope, presenting the gunner with a field of fire. 'I managed to get into my gunner's seat and the next thing I saw as I looked through my sights was an M13 about thirty yards away, coming straight toward us.' This was point-blank range.

> Without thinking I pulled the trigger of the two-pounder, but as I didn't see any tracer I thought, 'Oh my God, I've missed.' I gave it another one, but just then one of the crew climbed out of the top, so I shot him. Daylight shone through the hole made by my first shot – was I relieved! We were so close that the tracer hadn't time to light up.

Sixty M13/40 medium Italian tanks from the Bambini Armoured Brigade were detached from the rearguard to batter a way through, supported by all available artillery. Likewise more British armoured reinforcements joined the fight at the small hill, 'the Pimple', where Topper Brown's A Squadron of 2 RTR were breaking up assaults. In all some twenty-two Cruiser and forty-five light tanks, well concealed in hull-down positions, were blocking the progress of the Italian columns. Lieutenant Cyril Joly described a similar action, when they had tricked attacking Italian tanks into the handicapped position of shooting at them uphill with the sun in their eyes. Unlike in France, the open Salisbury Plain manoeuvre practices in which aggressive 'naval' warfare tactics were employed did work in the desert. However, British gunnery was still poor. Joly had monitored a number of misses on his radio net talking to his troop commanders. Italian Fiat-made medium

tanks had a good V8 diesel engine, but the hulls were poorly constructed and they were not riveted like their British counterparts. As a
consequence they could be torn apart on impact. Even heavy calibre
machine-gun strikes might pepper the crews riding earlier models with
tiny metal flakes coming off inside the thin armour. Ryan, reported
Joly,

> hit an enemy tank which was turning on the slope before him fairly
> and squarely in the engine, shattering the petrol tanks and starting a
> fire which spread rapidly. Mixed with the flame, clouds of billowing
> black smoke rolled across the desert, blocking my view of the enemy
> entirely. With a dull roar the ammunition then exploded, throwing a
> mass of debris into the air.

Whatever else is going on, the spectacle of violent destruction will
divert the attention of assailants nearby, who become sympathetic
onlookers. Every tank crewman's nightmare is a 'brew', or fire, on
being hit. The M13 is a small tank and its crew of three would have
difficulty extricating themselves from its narrow confines. 'A moment
later,' Joly continued:

> We were horrified to see a figure with face blackened and clothes
> alight stumbling through the smoke. He staggered for some yards,
> then fell and in a frenzy of agony rolled frantically in the hard sand in
> a desperate effort to put out the flames. But to no avail. Gradually his
> flailing arms and legs moved more slowly, until at last, with a
> convulsive heave of his body, he lay still.

Monitoring the radio, Joly heard constant references either to misses or
to hits with no apparent effect. If an armour-piercing round does not
explode the tank, quite often gunners will strike it again and again to
ensure a kill when the damage has already been terminal.

> 'Como Two calling. We have hit this tank three times now, but he
> won't brew. Hello! Wait a moment; there goes the crew – they're
> bailing out. I'll let them go – doesn't seem right to shoot a sitting
> bird. That's one anyway. Off.'

This early in the war, there was a natural empathy for an enemy crewmember enduring the circumstances they all dreaded.

'Topper' Brown's battle at Beda Fomm was interminable. 'Practically all morning we never stopped firing,' he said, 'at wagonloads of infantry or tanks.' He probably knocked out twenty tanks in one day.

He recalled, 'When we pulled back after dark it was sheer relief. My right eye was aching with the strain of looking through the telescope for about 13 hours with hardly a break.'

By 7 February mass Italian surrenders had begun. Ten divisions were destroyed, 130,000 prisoners, 180 medium and 200 light tanks and 845 guns captured. 'Fox killed in the open,' General O'Connor transmitted in clear to Wavell, openly taunting Mussolini with a typical British hunting metaphor on the airwaves. 'The war had started,' declared Italian soldier Enrico Emanuelli, 'and they called it "clean" – because we didn't destroy buildings, didn't kill women and children and, for a while anyway, we didn't have the means or warlike frame of mind which was necessary.'

While 624 British and Indians had been killed and wounded, they had conquered an area the size of England and France between Egypt to the east and, to the west, El Agheila on the border with Tripolitania. Mass surrenders spawned humorous responses to radio enquiries about the number of prisoners being sent back. 'So far as I can see,' reported one, 'there are twenty acres of officers and a hundred acres of men.' Caring for this number of POWs in a desert environment, short of water and shelter, was a severe challenge, especially so for tank crewmen. As Sam Bradshaw of the 6th Royal Tank Regiment pointed out, 'One of the embarrassing and most difficult things for us was we took so many prisoners, thousands and thousands, which as armoured men we can't handle.' He wryly observed, 'You can't take prisoners inside a tank, there is no room.' Only a few can ride on the rear engine deck. He heard one of his squadron commanders appealing on the radio: 'For God's sake send in the infantry, we're surrounded by prisoners!'

Coming at a particularly dark time in Britain's war, victory had been sweet. Churchill had wired Wavell on 16 December 1940 that 'the Army of the Nile has rendered glorious service to the Empire and to our cause . . . James Palmer, closer at hand to the mauling at Beda Fomm, accepted that 'our casualties had been minimal, but to this day I think that the carnage will be forever a scar on the minds of all those tank crews.' The day after the action they were sent to the road to recover repairable Italian tanks amid the sweet stench of burned flesh. It was amazing to see how red oxidised husks of burned-out tanks, fully operational hours before, could look like rust-encrusted hundred-year-old hulks. They observed what – but for the fortunes of war – could have been them. 'Men were hanging half-way out of the tanks with their legs blackened, and these dropped off when we pulled the bodies free. Heaps of gooey black stuff inside the tanks, and these heaps had been men.'

It was better when the raging combustion of ammunition and propellant cremated bodies totally. Seeing half-consumed corpses added to the horror. 'It was a sight that I shall never forget,' he said, 'and I know my soul will be damned for having been a part of it.' Sixteen miles of abandoned tanks, guns and vehicles littered the roadside at Beda Fomm. Swarming all over the debris were Arabs who, Sergeant Ken Chadwick remembered, 'remained throughout the battle; to some troops they sold eggs, and when the action finished the tribe began scavenging amongst the wreckage'. The Italians dug graves by the roadside, and Palmer observed 'tears were trickling down many a face, and both sides were mumbling that they were sorry it had happened'. But it had. Offering cigarettes to the survivors did little to assuage the feelings of guilt. Palmer's conclusion was not dissimilar to that of Wellington surveying the aftermath of Waterloo a little over 125 years before.

> It had been a victory for us – but if that was a victory I didn't want to see any more. I was stunned by the atrocity of war and bloodshed. I had experienced the ultimate degradation of human life.

Five days later General Erwin Rommel flew into Tripoli.

### THE PENDULUM WAR

'Like madmen we jumped around and hugged each other,' said Leutnant Ralph Ringler, assigned to Panzergrenadier Regiment

104, 'we really were going to Africa!' No German soldier prior to the Second World War imagined the possibility of their being involved in any future war beyond Europe. Even a year after the initial deployments it was a source of wonder in the barrack rooms. 'We became a separate caste in the barracks – "The Africans", declared Ringler. 'Our young comrades envied us, the old ones were amused by our enthusiasm – that didn't bother us. Our heaven was full of violins and in Africa there awaited the great adventure.' Like their British counterparts most German soldiers had never been abroad. Now, after two years of war, German soldiers were engaging in a form of pseudo tourism. Tank crews relaxed in the streets of Naples prior to their departure for Libya.

British soldiers, too, made the most of what was really a cruise on their way to Africa. Jake Wardrop, ever the pragmatic soldier, applied his practical organisational skills to purloining ice cream and beer at regular intervals through the ship's steward. 'The weather was lovely and the tan was improving daily,' he declared as they crossed the Equator and neared the Middle East. 'I sat on deck and read a lot and I also dipped in the little pool which we had made – what a life!'

The journey was dangerous, requiring a long Cape of Good Hope detour to avoid marauding U-boats.

Axis troops also shared the peril of maybe not surviving an otherwise exotic journey. Panzer Regiment 5 lost thirteeen medium and heavy tanks to an air raid in Naples harbour before the first panzers even arrived in Tripoli. Leutnant Karl Susenberger, on his way to join the 21st Panzer Division, flew in an impressive formation of thirty-five JU 52 transport planes, that were attacked by the RAF in a storm of tracer fire as they neared the African coast. 'Our fighters and rear gunners took up the fight, but in spite of this the Tommies shot down three JU 52s.' Each aircraft had eighteen passenger soldiers bound for the Afrika Korps. The planes were 'filled with comrades who would never reach Africa', Susenberg declared.

'We knew the Germans had arrived in Tripoli and were arriving with tanks,' said Sam Bradshaw of the 6th Royal Tank Regiment. 'But we did not know in what strength and we didn't know the state of their equipment, because we hadn't fought against the Germans.' Others among the recent change over of British units had. 'One morning I got up and we looked up and a plane went over,' recalled tank crewman Alf Davies of the 1st Royal Tank Regiment. 'The heart sank because there was a dirty great black cross on the plane. Oh – there's the Germans arriving,' he thought. Rommel was not to be opposed by seasoned and victorious troops; these had already been bled off as reinforcements to Greece and the Balkans. The 2nd Armoured and 9th Australian Divisions replaced the 7th Armoured Division. Neither was ready for battle and both were short of equipment.

According to Bradshaw the perception of the Germans by the British tank crews on the ground was 'we knew enough to think they must be pretty good'. After the fall of France the German panzer arm had been euphoric. It had been instrumental in eliminating one European super-power and had badly battered the other, isolating it on the British mainland. Their reputation preceded them. Panzer Regiment 5 was formed from the 3rd Panzer Division that had fought through France and against the British withdrawing to Dunkirk. Their new commanding officer, Generalleutnant Erwin Rommel, had commanded the 7th Panzer Division, one of the spearhead divisions that had reached the Channel coast way ahead of the Wehrmacht's expectations.

Expectations of German prowess were high on both sides. The truth, however, was that the new German troops arriving in Africa were almost entirely unprepared for desert warfare. *Feldwebel* Hermann Eckardt of Panzer Regiment 8 claimed that they were given only eight days to orientate and acclimatise. Bradshaw 'heard stories that the Afrika Korps had been trained especially for desert warfare in massive greenhouses'. He would have been more reassured if he had known the truth.

A special German staff for tropical warfare, the *Sonderstab Tropen*, composed of officers who had fought in the German colonies in the First World War, was set up in Berlin, but commenced work in Libya only as the first German troops arrived. Preparatory work had to be constrained to medical exams, issuing tropical clothing and training for combat in open terrain. This, alongside painting vehicles in desert colours, specialised water supply, hygiene and other particular in-theatre orientations, was all there was time for. In the desert the Germans would fight tanks combined with anti-tank guns. Infantry operated separately as a motorised force. Each of the Afrika Korps divisions, the 15th Panzer, 5th (Light) and later 21st Panzer divisions, was given only one regiment of motorised infantry (instead of the normal two).

'We saw some vehicles moving on the horizon and they were 8-wheeler armoured cars,' Sam Bradshaw recalled. 'The Italians never had 8-wheeler armoured cars, so they must be Germans, and that was the first time we had seen the Germans.' The British were unprepared, not having fully recovered from dealing with the Italians. They had only the old tanks previously left behind for refit by Ordnance in Cairo. Corporal Peter Watson of the 2nd Royal Tank Regiment complained, 'We were still getting our old surviving tanks, done up but still inefficient, under-gunned, under-armoured and completely worn out.' Sergeant Ken Chadwick agreed this view, as 2 RTR was re-equipped with A9s, A10s and A13s, 'all of which were reputed to be in a very poor state of repair'.

Rommel sensed the weakness of the British forces facing them and confirmed by reconnaissance that they were still in a long drawn-out column after fighting the Italians and in a precarious position.

By 31 March, without waiting for the 15th Panzer Division still in transit, Rommel was attacking Mersa Brega. Although penetration was only achieved on a limited front, the British 2nd Armoured Division's support group began to withdraw, and from that moment on the campaign was lost. In two weeks the Afrika Korps clawed back what Wavell had taken two months to achieve – except a besieged Tobruk. Benghazi fell on 3 April, and three days later Generals Neame and O'Connor, the architects of Wavell's victory, were apprehended alongside the road by a German motorcycle patrol. By 13 April the offensive reached Sollum and Capuzzo.

'Rommel was a proper daredevil,' recalled Friedrich Hauber, who was on his staff. 'He was not the sort of general who sat writing at a desk, on the contrary, he wanted to be with his men and said – "Men, I'm here, follow me".' Rommel insisted his newly arrived panzer regiment did what the British had done against the Italians: bypass resistance and go through the desert. This was no mean achievement for men with no idea of the peculiar conditions of Libya, and in total contrast to the way they had conducted operations in Europe only months before. Panzer Regiment 5 motored straight across the desert towards Mechili and Derna, with weaker forces driving along the coast via Msus. Winrich Behr, at the spearhead of the German thrust with *Aufklärungsabteilung* 3, did what he was told. 'We knew that Rommel had played an important role in the French campaign, that he blew his way through there,' so successfully that 'his division was called the Ghost Division.'

Otto Henning, from the same reconnaissance detachment spearheading the panzer dash across the desert, stated, 'We young soldiers had huge respect for Rommel.' At times, however, the cost in men and machines was depressingly high, and a factor of desert inexperience. Hermann Eckardt was sceptical about over-zealous idealistic officers fired up with success in France. Very 'victory conscious', they took unnecessary risks, constantly urging, '*Vorwärts!*' – Forward! Rommel's insistence on repeating ineffective attacks, despite fearful casualties, against the Italian-built and now British-defended fortifications around Tobruk revealed a darker side to his personality.

The impact of this desert dash on the inexperienced Panzer Regiment 5's tanks was equally serious. Its workshop company reported the loss of eighty-three of the 155 tanks that participated, mostly because of breakdowns resulting from high speeds maintained over rough and unsurveyed terrain in order to keep up the tempo of the offensive. 'The average 700 kilometre march distance across the desert had very serious consequences for the panzers,' the report stated. Engines seized up with dust and sand, and shock absorbers, springs and tracks were unable to absorb the punishment. Like the British, the Afrika Korps were at the start point of perennial desert-related mechanical problems. Machines and men were feeling the pressure.

British observations following the French campaign were sparse but unanimous in the need for aggressive tactics to be employed against German armour. The Bartholomew Committee post-campaign report stated that 'an offensive spirit in dealing with tanks should be instilled into all ranks' and anti-tank units within divisions strengthened. 'Now that the Germans can obtain exact details of the powers of penetration of our present weapons it must be assumed that they will increase armour accordingly.' New Panzer Mark IIIs were already arriving in North Africa with additional armour add-ons, and all mounted a new 50mm gun. The Bartholomew Report concluded: 'We should therefore hasten the production of the 6-pounder anti-tank gun.' This new theatre of war was to provide a sand table for armour design development for both sides.

'We were so much better equipped than the English when we came to Africa,' declared Winrich Behr, an officer in *Aufklärungsabteilung* 3. 'English tanks were no good against our panzers, and they were also not equipped to cope with the might of our 88 Flak guns.' Both sides had arrived with equipments designed for battle in Europe, but as Alan Moorehead wrote, 'always the desert set the pace, made the direction and planned the design.' The desert made its own peculiar demands, as the Germans discovered during their first offensive dash across such inhospitable terrain. British vehicles were already 'clapped out' after Wavell's campaign when the Afrika Korps arrived. Many British tanks belonging to the 5th Royal Tank Regiment were using a gallon of oil a mile during the subsequent retreat. In general British crews were not complimentary about their vehicles. Captain Robert Crisp recalled the sixty-odd tanks that 3 RTR had taken to Greece, of which only half a dozen were knocked out by the enemy and the rest discarded. Crisp was a newly promoted captain who had played Test cricket for South Africa. His scepticism about the technical performance of British tanks, which carried some authority on account of his cricket reputation, attracted press comment when he made his frank views known. The abandoned tanks 'were of no help to the enemy; no other army would have contemplated using them,' he declared. These statements can be measured by comparing the primary tank characteristics – firepower, mobility and protection – in the desert context.

In spring 1941 rumours were already circulating back to British crews preparing for action that 'Honeys and Crusaders were no match at all for the Mark IIIs and Mark IVs in equal combat.' Tank driver Jack Rollinson, who had first-hand experience of British A9, A10 and A13 tanks, thought little of them. 'They could knock out a German, but the problem was you never got close enough before he gave you a thorough pasting.' Gunnery appeared to be the primary inadequacy. 'When we did knock out a panzer,' remembered Rollinson, 'it was usually more by good luck than good judgement.' With a 50mm gun shooting a shell twice the weight of British shells, German medium and heavy tanks fired bigger high-explosive and armour-piercing rounds out to longer distances.

Adherence to a short-range tank philosophy of killing enemy armour at 500 yards or so made the British army slow to anticipate the need for a larger tank gun. The consequence was that in 1941 six Cruiser and three Infantry tanks mounted an obsolete gun. As scrapping them would have been an appalling waste of scant resources, production continued into 1943. Its calibre was too small for an effective high-explosive shell. Hermann Eckardt, a tank gunner with Panzer Regiment 8, had enormous respect for the armour on the Matilda tank, but considered that 'the 2-pounder was shit – thank God!'

With the advent of the US M3 Grant tank in May 1942, Allied tanks were at last able to fire a 75mm HE round, which enabled them to emulate previous German tank success by suppressing anti-tank guns at long range. It was a demanding six-man tank to command, with a 'Heath Robinson' construction of a 37mm tank gun turret and hull-mounted 75mm guns, which required different fire commands. Sergeant Fred Dale of 3 RTR recalled: 'The only thing wrong was the height. It was hard to hide behind any ridge without showing the turret. Anyway the crews were overjoyed to be able to fire a large weight shell at the panzer tanks.' One American maintenance sergeant said, 'It looked like a damned cathedral coming down the road.'

The development of the British 6-pounder anti-tank gun advocated by the Bartholomew Report staggered through a frustratingly long development chain established in 1938, but did not deliver until 1942, when the gunnery arms race gathered pace. The Germans began to deliver Panzer Mark IIIs with the improved long-barrelled 50mm gun and additional armour and the Panzer IV with a long-barrelled anti-tank gun. There was little discernable integration on the British side regarding the design of guns and the appropriate size tank to hold them, while German tanks by contrast were able to take significant increases in firepower without radical changes to the suspensions or turrets.

Crucially, there was nothing to match the German 88 Krupp Flak gun, when adapted for the ground role. Even the heavy British Matilda's 78mm of armour was no match. Robert Crisp, commanding a M3 Stuart Honey tank, knew that with the Flak gun's 3,000-yard range, they would be within range of it for 1,800 yards before he could even fire off a shot from his 37mm gun's maximum range of 1,200 yards. 'Eighteen hundred yards, in these circumstances, is a long way.' All British tank crews feared the 88mm.

Despite the introduction of the Grant tank, described as 'super' by tank driver Jake Wardrop, the Germans, who were initially taken aback at its introduction, were still convinced of their innate panzer and gun superiority during their June 1942 offensive towards El Alamein. The Grant in fact spelt the beginning of the end of German anti-tank dominance in the desert. British tanks could suppress them at distance with HE rounds.

Mobility was not just a factor of speed; it was also one of reliability. Both sides laboured under extreme desert conditions. 'Wet' German oil-soaked filters performed poorly compared to British dry ones at the start of the campaign. Engines were steadily improved as new Mark tanks with better power packs were introduced. British crews complained constantly about reliability, as much of the servicing and repairs were conducted by themselves at night. By contrast the specialised German workshop companies serviced their panzers like aircraft. Tank crewmen compared their lot with life in the Royal Air Force. As driver Jack Rollinson explained:

> They fought, went home, ate a prepared hot meal, slept in clean sheets while somebody else serviced and repaired their machines. In comparison, a tank crew drove and fought all day, then in the evening or often long into the night, they serviced and repaired the vehicle, and then refuelled it before thinking about a meal and sleep.

American tanks were universally admired and preferred by British crews. The M3 Stuart, affectionately labelled 'the Honey', 'were great little tanks, fast and reliable,' remembered Jake Wardrop. Captain Crisp recalled that 'drivers gasped in astonishment' when they saw the power unit, 'an aeroplane engine stuck in a tank, with radial cylinders and a fan that looked like a propeller'. Major Cyril Joly thought their only major defect was lack of endurance. 'There was only capacity for enough petrol to cover about 45 miles in battle conditions.' Frequent refuelling could be dangerous and rendered crews vulnerable in battle. But Crisp was delighted it could achieve up to 40mph, 'a comforting thought in the circumstances to know that the German Marks III and IV could manage only twenty or so'.

There were too many British tank types, which created an impediment to mobility. They included light tanks such as the Mark VI, the A9-A10 to A13 range of Cruisers, infantry heavy tanks and inbetweens like the Valentine. Moreover, there were different makes: Vickers Lights, Crusaders, Valentines, Matildas, and then the American variants, the M3 Stuart, Grant and eventually Sherman tanks. More casualties came from breakdowns and from problems with the supply of spares than from enemy action.

German medium and heavy tanks generally had 30mm of frontal protection and 8–10mm of side armour, not that much thicker than later Italian medium tanks, but better constructed and better armed. Despite the vociferous complaints of British crews, their armoured protection was similar if not superior. Some of the Cruiser variants were thin, but protection improved as newer and better Allied tanks were delivered to the front, culminating in the introduction of the Grant with 50mm frontal protection and the Sherman's 76mm of armour. At this stage of the campaign Allied crews achieved better average protection.

Technically the panzers were initially superior but lost ground as the campaign progressed. In tank-on-tank battles the two sides often fought themselves to bloody stalemates. German superiority came from their ability to synergise the fighting power of mixed-combat teams. Technical excellence in radio and mobility supplemented superior leadership and battlefield command skills. German light, medium and heavy panzers were all capable of achieving 25mph and so roamed the desert battlefield at uniform speeds, aiding more precisely focused application of their firepower. British light to medium tanks moved at varying speeds from 36mph down to 15mph and below and did not therefore interact so well tactically in battle. Feldwebel Hermann Eckardt of Panzer Regiment 8 claimed 'the English always had a scattered approach, compared to our unit that was employed *en masse*'. Somehow the Germans always managed to have most of their armour working closely together, whereas the British seemed to be spread about in small groups all over the battlefield.

Despite their relative desert inexperience, the newly arrived panzer regiments of the Afrika Korps immediately grasped the significance of the tank/anti-tank mix. Longer range and higher penetration German anti-tank guns at the beginning of the desert campaigns provided that very superiority British crews ascribed to the panzers. An Afrika Korps report revealed that the combination of tanks and anti-tank guns was the main desert killers. Figures for the 21st Panzer Division told a similar story. George Witheridge, a squadron commander and previous gunnery instructor with the 3rd Royal Tank Regiment, explained the significance behind the toll:

> Psychologically crew members felt they should engage the enemy *tank,* a similar beast, a larger and apparently more dangerous target. They did to their detriment, for the *ground* anti-tank gun was the more effective and being unobserved took its toll of British armour.

Superior guns, more proficiently handled, in a combat mix, by units with better standardised and complementary equipment characteristics, conferred innate superiority. Counting relative numbers of tanks to predict success was clearly meaningless and would account for the disappointment of British tank crews who consistently suffered setbacks despite having more tanks.

German panzers looked different from their English counterparts. During the initial parade ceremony in Tripoli the panzers looked squat and purposeful, uniformity alone suggesting ominous lethality, like the Teutonic knights from the Russian film *Alexander Nevsky,* which was playing in cinemas before the war. Even with modification updates and cluttered with personal effects, panzer stowage appeared tidy. Everything had a clinical function; spare tracks and wheels were fixed to the front of tanks to provide additional protection – a form of spaced armour. Italian tanks had good engines, but looked like primitively bolted together Heath Robinson creations. Panzer crews called the Italian tankettes 'cake-tins'.

English tanks reflected the character of their crews. Stowage appeared chaotic; every British crew had its own idea about the efficacy of positioning and attaching personal effects. The Germans had only three tank types, and their additional self-propelled guns often had the same chassis. This gave an impression of uniform effectiveness. Conversely, the nine to ten British tank types, occasionally with several types in one regiment, reflected British pragmatism. They made the best of what they had.

Variations in uniform further reflect an impression that British tank crews may have been more flexible than their panzer counterparts in adapting to desert ways. The first Afrika Korps crews dressed in smart coarse tunics and shirts, totally unsuited to desert heat which, prompted an inevitable scramble to purloin thinner and more practical Italian uniforms. British tank crews also prized Italian accoutrements, particularly shirts and trousers. The casualness of British desert dress accentuated the amateur 'part-time' attitude of her soldiers, conscripted for the duration of the war and only interested in getting it finished. Nobody wore the grotesque imperial pith helmets that were issued, and Peter Roach remembered that the long shorts, called 'dysentery shorts', with huge turn-ups that covered the knee when let down, were regarded with some hilarity. As ever, the taciturn British soldier produced his own version, more akin to contemporary holiday variants, which improved appearance but not the uniformity. Numerous cartoons by the illustrator Jon emphasised the chaotic nature of English desert dress. Afrika Korps soldiers always gave the impression of a stricter compliance with dress codes, and although they eventually transitioned to shirts and shorts they still appeared more regimented.

Contemporary feature films and documentaries made sixty years after the desert war offer an idealised view of a chivalric contest between the two sides: a 'gentleman's war'. This is broadly accurate, but not wholly. Soldier accounts appear to differ in tone from the more literary and occasionally PR-conscious offerings expressed in officer accounts and interviews. There was not the hatred that featured on the Russian front, but relationships between the desert tank protagonists trying to kill each other could hardly be described as cordial either.

Sergeant Alan Wollaston, aged twenty-four, was a regular who had joined in the late 1930s. Having experienced and survived two catastrophic naval evacuations at Dunkirk and Greece, he had knowledge of the enemy. His assessment of the Afrika Korps was that they were 'very good' and 'very tenacious'. On being asked whether he hated the enemy, he responded 'No' and that his feelings on the whole were 'very neutral really'. The Afrika Korps panzer division pitted against them were 'highly respected as fighters', he believed; 'in fact, I think we were on a par.' Sergeant Bert Rendell, a regular soldier with the 1st Royal Tank Regiment, had a different view after losing several personal friends. His crew fought on after bailing out of their crippled tank rather than accept being taken prisoner. 'They would strip and take everything from you, to get information,' he claimed. Another of Rendell's crew, abandoned and wandering the battlefield, hid in a hole all night fearing 'if they found him and there was nobody around, they would just put the bayonet in'. Rendell concurred: 'We all knew that; they did not bother about taking prisoners.'

The majority view was echoed by Sam Bradshaw, of the 6th Royal Tank Regiment, who described the desert conflict as 'a war without hate – we were professional soldiers doing a tough job, so we built up a mutual respect for each other.'

Afrika Korps soldier Rolf Volker was unambiguous in his view of the British, which was 'exactly the same as they felt about us – we respected them totally'.

Infantry, unsurprisingly, had a more ambivalent attitude and relished the opportunity to take on vulnerable tank crews who had previously menaced them from a position of invincibility. Once fortunes were reversed they exacted their toll. Tank crew had a similar attitude to anti-tank crews. Some panzer 'aces' ascribed greater importance to knocking out guns than other tanks, because they meted out death and injury by stealth. Crews had more empathy with the fears of opposing tank crews they had disabled, because they could more easily identify with their predicament. On one occasion Major David Ling, sitting in the lead tank of a squadron suffering heavy losses from concealed anti-tank guns, reached the limit of tolerance. After enduring twenty-seven hits on his own Matilda, he ordered his troop to run their opponents down. Two guns were crushed while the German crews flattened themselves in their slit trenches. 'I ordered each tank to turn and run along the slit trenches with one track in. I shall always remember my operator loader saying, "You bloody bastard – Sir." Later these actions bedevil you.'

One characteristic of numerous veteran accounts is their reluctance to admit or talk about the primal side of combat. Jack Rollinson's interviewer David Barrett acknowledged, 'I rarely if ever heard any details of the violence that accompanied his adventures.' Many soldiers are modest and reticent about these deeply personal experiences. 'He always covered over these details with throw-away lines such as 'there was a hell of a dust up', and that was all. As Bert Rendell of the 1st Royal Tank Regiment put it, 'War is not an easy thing to try and explain – at times it is not worthy of the human race.'

The astonishing reversal of the second upending of the desert see-saw in the spring of 1941 was only achievable because of the hundreds of miles of indefensible featureless terrain that lay between objectives. Stung by Rommel's dramatic gains, General Wavell, the C-in-C Cairo, counter-attacked during 'Operation Brevity' on 15 May but failed at the Halfaya Pass with heavy British casualties. After reinforcement Wavell launched 'Operation Battleaxe' with a total of almost 400 tanks on 15 June. Superior German tactics, based on the co-ordinated employment of anti-tank guns, resulted in 220 tanks killed, of which eighty-seven were total write-offs, against only twenty panzers destroyed. Wavell was removed to India and replaced by Claude Auchinleck, and General Allan Cunningham was appointed to command a new desert Eighth Army.

After an abortive raid by Rommel, Cunningham launched 'Operation Crusader' on 18 November with 750 tanks, 280 of which were the newly supplied US Stuart tanks, supported by 600 guns. Rommel quickly co-ordinated the resources of his two Panzer divisions and Italian allies to mass and deliver concentrated blows against the dispersed British armoured brigades in a series of bloody battles. At one point two British armoured brigades were reduced from 350 to fifty tanks in just four days. General Cunningham wanted to withdraw but was replaced by General Neil Ritchie. Rommel made a 'dash to the wire' at the Egyptian frontier to cut off the British line of retreat, causing temporary panic in Cairo, but over-reached himself. Ground down to forty German and thirty Italian battle-worthy tanks, he had to retreat westwards once again to his original campaign start point. He had lost 195 panzers.

Yet another astonishing reversal occurred on 21 January 1942, when Rommel launched a counter-offensive supported by a re-supply of the long-promised and upgraded panzer types. Within two weeks the line was pushed 400 miles eastward to the fortified Gazala line covering Tobruk, where it remained for a four-month period of stalemate. Both

159

sides built up their strengths for the next move, which by the end of May meant 637 Axis tanks versus 994 Allied. The Axis still retained the edge in aircraft (1,497 versus 939 Allied), but the Allies were now receiving the M3 Grant, a vastly improved US tank.

Rommel again launched his offensive first, on 26 May, pre-empting Ritchie's own and outflanking the southern end of the Allied line held by the Free French at Bir Hacheim. For a few critical days Rommel was pinned against Allied minefields in the area known as the 'Cauldron', but he managed to break out and sprint for Tobruk, which fell on 21 June. Rommel was rewarded with his Feldmarschal baton, while the frustrated Auchinleck dismissed Ritchie and took over in person. The Allies fell back on Mersa Matruh before continuing their retreat to El Alamein. It was a disaster. No fewer than 138 British tanks were lost by noon during one day on 13 June. At the end of the offensive the British initial total of 850 tanks had sunk to seventy facing 150 Axis tanks.

'We just walked in like a lot of idiots,' admitted tank driver Jake Wardrop, commenting on the Gazala defeats. 'Units were just battering themselves to pieces in a lot of little scraps getting us nowhere.' This was also Churchill's view. Alexander replaced General Auchinleck while Lieutenant-General Bernard Montgomery was appointed the new Commander of the Eighth Army. More British reinforcements poured through Cairo. Major A.F. Flatow of the 45th Royal Tank Regiment was a Territorial Army volunteer who had joined his spare-time unit when it formed up in 1937. The war as he saw it was not going too well. As they passed the prisoner-of-war camp outside Suez 'the prisoners hissed and booed our train, with other actions such as drawing their fingers across their throats and pretending to run away'. Crowds of Egyptians were jeering female military personnel as they boarded trains. He remembered locals buying bunting and flags 'to welcome the Huns as they entered the city'.

The desert see-saw had upended again, with the deepest ever penetration into Egypt by the Germans. Rommel decided to attack from his precarious forward positions before the Allied odds facing him became too great. 'We were completely exhausted,' remembered Rolf Volker of the Afrika Korps:

We didn't have any rest for weeks. We didn't have time to think. When we stopped for one day we would fall asleep sitting in the vehicles. In the week of 26 May onwards when things really got going we got three or four hours' sleep. Every night we were completely exhausted. We had only one thought – let's get to Cairo! Let's go to Alexandria – this is where we really wanted to go!

They were launched on 30 August.

The wounded were taken to hospitals in or around Alexandria and Cairo. Egyptian ladies working in the burns unit of the 9th Scottish General Hospital remembered the stench of burned flesh permeating the ward in hot weather. There was no adequate way of washing these patients. It provided a sinister reminder, if needed, of what was going on at the front.

# 8

# DESERT TANK BATTLE

## REVEILLE AND MOVING OFF

Each day in the Western Desert brought with it the prospect of further monotony or the likelihood of battle. Dealing with fear is a peculiarly individual affair and every soldier handled it his own way. So far as Captain Crisp was concerned, any engagement with the enemy 'would end in our favour, and that if anything terrible were going to happen it would probably happen to other people but not to me'. This was the normal unsettling start to the day for tank soldiers on both sides in the desert.

The night hours would have been spent inside a leaguer or 'harbour' area, with tanks formed into a box-like formation and their guns pointing out providing all-round defence. Vulnerable 'soft-skinned' vehicles would be drawn up in lines inside, ready to depart. There were identified entry and departure points and a security screen. At first light the leaguer became vulnerable to air attack because there was no cover and units would quickly complete their administrative tasks and disperse.

In early 1942 the British War Office identified the physical demands that operations made on men at this time.

Approach march or move in motor transport by night, dawn attack, fighting throughout the day, crisis coming during the second night and/or following day. Leaders have to go at least two nights without sleep, often three or four nights with little or none, and at the end of the period retain the mental alertness necessary for rapid planning. During this period meals *at best* will be confined to one after dusk and one before dawn. Intense periods may be considerably longer in the advance or withdrawal, and will follow each other at short intervals.

162

There have been many studies of fatigue, and most accept that the overall effects are more psychological than physical and result in performance lapses. Disorientation results and mistakes occur. So great was the insidious creep of fatigue from sustained operations during the 1991 Gulf War that it became necessary to fax orders electronically because tired radio operators and commanders could not be trusted to communicate them by voice consistently and accurately.

This then was the backdrop to the mental alertness of tank soldiers awakening at dawn on a normal day of desert operations. Armoured-car driver Victor Overfield called it 'that horrible half-dead feeling we wake with to prepare for three days patrol'. The British War Office stated: 'The men are wakened at about 0500 hours, that is before daylight, get into their tanks, and drive out from harbour to battle or patrol positions, which must be reached by first light.'

Depending on the time of year for first light, or impending activity, only about four hours' sleep was averaged each night and was in any case fitful and often a group affair to share body warmth during cold desert nights. 'Night and morning really lousy cold,' complained Wolfgang Everth of the German 21st Panzer Division. 'Even with three blankets one is frozen like a naked ski instructor.'

Blankets might be wet from rain, the air too close for comfort, or the ground too rocky to settle or too cold. At night tank engine noises attracted concern until they were confirmed friend or foe. Ground vibration from passing vehicles and isolated bursts of distant gunfire would add to the unease, and care was needed to select sleeping positions to avoid being accidentally crushed by tanks. Minds and bodies craving rest were disturbed by repair teams of fitters, who worked close by, hammering and banging on metal. It was likely the prospect of approaching action that fuelled the adrenalin and kept the men going. 'If there had been a battle I would have been alert and wide awake,' admitted Cyril Joly. 'I found it needed a supreme effort to take my share of the duties and to drag my weary limbs about.' Fatigue made even the most mundane tasks difficult.

Leutnant Joachim Schorm's diary account of his activities around Tobruk in April and May 1941 shows a similar measure of exhaustion. He was a company commander with Panzer Regiment 5. Having gone to sleep at 2200 hours the day before, he was up at 0330 hours to participate in a tank and infantry assault on the besieged town. After a day in action, much of it enclosed in his turret, he got his first food next to his tank at 0300 hours the next day. As he described it: 'Twenty-four hours shut up in a panzer with awful pains in my joints and muscular cramp as a result – and what a thirst!'

'The daily formula was nearly always the same,' declared Captain Robert Crisp, 'up at any time between midnight and four o'clock; movement out of the leaguer into battle positions before first light.' There would be a snatched meal, a biscuit with a spoon of marmalade 'before the flap of orders and information'. Radio operator Peter Roach of 1 RTR, then aged twenty-three, described the routine at first light as being 'elemental, ordered, simple and mentally numbing. We rose shortly before the sun, rolled out our bedding and strapped it on the back of the tank, warmed the engine and tuned the radio.' Frequently there was not time for a brew, and 'we stood round shivering in the cool air waiting for the sun to come up over the horizon'.

In itself this ordered existence could be disquieting. Both sides felt depression, especially during periods of inactivity. 'Just lately I've been feeling a bit browned off,' confided Private R.L. Crimp of the 7th Armoured Division to his desert diary. 'There's a sort of psychological complaint some chaps get after long exposure on the Blue called "desert weariness".' A German-compiled report of desert experiences after the campaign referred to the 'fight against mental depression' that afflicted the Afrika Korps at the start. In particular it observed 'an oppressive feeling of loneliness' that 'overcomes everyone more or less frequently in the desert – a feeling that one is cut off from everything that one holds dear'. Apart from leave, battle was the only event that could disperse such gloom. 'Nothing in the landscape to rest or distract the eye,' observed Crimp, 'nothing to hear but roaring truck engines, and nothing to smell but carbon exhaust fumes and the reek of petrol.' It was with such mixed emotions that men went to war. 'It all seems so futile.'

The desert mood reflected the colour of the sky: golden sand when the sky was royal blue, or dirty brown against a sombre grey. Although not actively belligerent, the desert is not entirely benign to humans. It will punish errors but open its secrets to those that treat it with mature consideration. Each of the armies had its own particular attitude to its surroundings. The British adapted with robust pragmatism, often with relish. The Germans had a clinical approach, but the desert is impervious to order. The Italians were slightly distasteful; officers were loath to forego comforts while soldiers never really adapted. These differing attitudes moulded subsequent operations. One either loved or loathed the desert; there was nothing in between.

The prospect of action galvanised spirits and engendered the tense expectancy that focused effort and minds. Soldiers like to be told what is going on. An irritated Peter Roach observed before the battle of El Alamein that 'always it has been do this, do that, and don't think. Now we were considered as of sufficient importance to be briefed. Morale rose another couple of inches.' One tank commander thought 'Operation Crusader' would work well. 'It seemed a pretty good idea to me', and when he told his crewmen 'where we were going deep into enemy territory' they were enthused. For many the prospect of combat was a tangible step towards the end of war and the road home. 'We were all a bit like schoolboys on the last night of term,' the commander admitted. All this preceded the final practical and technical checks before setting off. Combat involved risks, and mechanical breakdowns would add to them. These final checks, like present-day checking of equipment for an extreme sport, would promote uneasiness at what lay ahead. 'My mind' was 'only partly occupied by the inspection,' Captain Cyril Joly of 3RTR admitted. 'Mainly I was thinking of all that a return to battle meant to me – preparing myself to meet the exhaustion and fear'. 'We were ready to advance,' recalled Captain David Ling of the 44th Royal Tank Regiment.

> Yet only ten minutes earlier we were asleep, huddled by the sides of our tanks, fully clothed and with stiff and heavy tarpaulins over us. Now the vapourings of our dreams were replaced by the crude shock of our purpose and speculations of what was to come.

On the German side tanks would form up for an advance in battalions, or 'regiments' in British military terminology. There were about sixty-five panzers in a battalion and some fifty-six tanks in a regiment. Tank crews identified more easily from their personal perspective with the next level down. This was the company of sixteen to twenty panzers commanded by a lieutenant, or the 'sabre squadron' commanded by a British captain or major with sixteen tanks, all directed by radio. Battle groups, or *Kampfgruppen,* were formed and could include motorised anti-tank weapons, infantry, artillery and engineers, the mix depending on the task in hand.

A typical British squadron would set off driving in a wide crescent in open formation, producing a frontage of 4,000 yards and providing observation in clear weather out to a 6,000 to 7,000-yard arc. Armoured cars might precede this formation as the eyes and ears ahead. Regular halts to check navigation or regain visibility from dust obscuration soon placed pressure on commanders and frayed tempers all round.

## FINDING AND LOCATING THE ENEMY

The War Office theatre note blandly observed, 'Battles commonly occur in the early morning or the late afternoon or evening.' But to do this the enemy must first be found and then individual positions precisely located in the desert. This was not easy. Long bone-jarring and uncomfortable drives would result. Great endurance was required from tank crews to avoid actual physical injury caused by the rolling and pitching movements inside hulls on the move, while dust and the heat of the engine mixed with fumes permeated the fighting compart-ment. The worst was when the wind blew from behind, blowing engine heat and clouds of dust raised by the tracks forward and over the tank, 'so that we were enveloped,' remarked one tank commander, 'and found dust getting into our eyes and nose and caking our lips. There was nothing we could do about it.' For radio operators and loaders, unable to see ahead, countering the interminable buffeting was even more irritating. Moving fast across desert terrain at speeds in excess of 20mph made it impossible for drivers to warn everyone to brace in time. Corporal Peter Watson of the 2nd Royal Tank Regiment recalled unexpectedly dropping into a 30-foot deep wadi (a dry watercourse). 'As we hit the bottom I was just putting my head out of the top and I skinned my ears – very painful.' Hours of not being able to relax for fear of injury were combined with the cramps that came from being compressed into confined spaces.

During 'Operation Crusader' the 4th Armoured Brigade centre line covered 1,700 miles, with many tanks recording over 3,000 miles. The cumulative effect on nerves and eyestrain can only be imagined. Each tank commander scanned the horizon, standing in the turret to gain the additional height needed to pick out the tiny silhouettes that meant enemy vehicles. 'We were to get used to the daily "swans" into nothingness after nothingness,' observed Robert Crisp, 'pursuing mirages of enemy conjured up by imagination and fear, mixed-up communications, mistranslated codes and nerve-racked commanders.'

The Germans laboured under the same conditions. When the newly arrived 8th Company of Panzer Regiment 5 was committed to its first operation in March 1941, Unteroffizier Gerhard Klaue's first sight of the 'enemy' during a tense advance to contact was a camel. He mistook it for a vehicle as it rushed wildly at his panzer and alarmed them all before sheering off in a cloud of dust. Hans Peter Quaatz of *Aufklärungsabteilung* 3, an armoured reconnaissance unit, admitted he had 'completely no idea' when he first arrived in North Africa. He recalled his first observations being passed to his veteran company commander.

I said to him, 'Look over there, there is an oasis, there – with the tall trees.'

'No, *Herr Leutnant,*' he replied. 'They are enemy tanks.'

Looking more closely, I saw these tall 'trees' moving about between each other. And he said in his rich Berlin dialect, 'Things here do not always appear as they seem.'

As Major Hans von Luck of the 21st Panzer Division discovered, it was 'often hard to tell whether the shimmering was "something", or a vehicle or merely a camel's thorn bush'.

No one ever seemed to know where the enemy was. Cyril Joly and his crews were irritated by constant references to 'fifty German tanks' they always had to engage despite the large numbers declared destroyed in situation reports. Crews facing ever-burgeoning numbers of enemy tanks declared: 'Hell, they must 'ave a bloody tank breeding ground somewhere.'

The desert landscape to be traversed in order to find the enemy was unlike anything either side had experienced in Europe. Second

Lieutenant Leslie Hill, an anti-tank gunner attached to the North-umberland Hussars Yeomanry, found it very confusing 'because of the lack of geographical features, the heat haze which made bushes look like moving vehicles, the poor performance of magnetic compasses in our metal vehicles, and the inadequacy of the maps we had'. Most navigated by sun during the day and squadron sergeant-majors had to learn to use the sun compass. There were two types of silhouette sought in the desert, those to read maps by and the enemy. Wilhelm Wessel, a war artist attached to the Afrika Korps, said there were so many tracks in the desert 'that any one with a mind to, could create his own'. Constant usage by vehicles widened them haphazardly, changing the configuration of the track network. This created problems, as Wessel explained. 'Those without instinct or enough experience' to trust their own map reading, blindly putting faith in the direction of the piste, tended to 'end up among "Tommy".'

During the move forward to seek action, the crews settled down to their particular routines. 'When operating in the tank,' said radio operator Peter Roach, recalling the cramped confines of his M3 Stuart 'Honey' tank, 'I saw nothing on the move, but incessantly the radio droned on and this became my life.' It was not a job for the claustrophobic. 'I had a bucket seat facing rearwards which gave me a good view of the commander's feet as he sat up in the turret and the gunner Eddy sitting behind the driver.' As the tank bumped and lurched its way across scrub-strewn scree, Roach held on. 'This was my world, hot in the extreme, full of fine blowing dust, noisy, cramped and blind.' He monitored and read events by following the various and recognisable tone of voices he knew, detecting the 'boredom, the fear, the exasperation, the excitement' in all he heard. 'Should we fight,' he said, 'my job was loading the guns, which almost touched my nose when standing up.' Glimpses of battle when they occurred were momentary and rare. Sleep loss affected him more in this static and cramped monitoring position than commanders or drivers, whose tasks were more physical. Mistakes would start to occur as Roach became progressively tireder and it would take longer to transmit information.

Tank commanders as well as their radio operators had to stay alert. Concentrating through the persistent crackling, wheezing, whining and whistling noises that came from the headphones caused headaches that were not improved by the sun's glare. Life and death information came through the radio. As one tank commander put it, 'We courted the vilest and most vehement abuse if, after failing to catch fully any message when it was first transmitted, we had to answer "Say again".'

Many felt the most thankless job belonged to the driver, who was often the last to enjoy any of the rare relaxations that came their way. Tank driver Jack Rollinson of the 3rd Royal Tank Regiment convinced himself that drivers were at the bottom of the crew 'pecking-order' because they never rose beyond the rank of corporal, unless they were driving the command tank, in which case they might reach sergeant. At night, when exhausted crews were asleep, grimy drivers would be seen going over the engines and tracks. In the morning's darkness they were also the first to get their tanks ready for the move. They were kept awake by a feeling of responsibility for their crew and the self-preservation instinct that enabled them to stay on roads and difficult tracks; they might also catnap during frequent halts and pauses. Sitting at the front of the tank, meanwhile, put them first in line to meet any incoming projectiles.

The driver's role was to keep their tanks moving in battle. An immobile tank could mean death for the entire crew. If, as one soldier put it, 'a set of tracks came off and jammed, and if you were in action, you couldn't do anything about it but bail out'. The tank crew had to function as a team; their very survival depended on it. Comradeship with its implicit emotional dependence on each other held them together as the prospect of fighting with the enemy loomed. Sergeant Fred Dale recalled his troop with the 3rd Royal Tank Regiment: 'They were a lovely bunch of lads, always so cheerful. They always worked together. If one crew had finished their maintenance, they would help the other crews finish their maintenance.'

A thin screen of patrolling armoured cars normally preceded the advancing tank squadrons. Victor Overfield, the driver of a Marmon Harrington armoured car, remembered that when approaching likely combat the crew would whistle and sing in turn as 'this always seemed to relieve the excitement that comes before action'. Weapons and radios were checked to confirm they were operable, hatches and shutters closed. Overfield described the mounting tension: 'Five miles, ten miles and nothing yet – what suspense, every minute a living age.'

At this point they were subjected to a vicious air attack by fourteen Messerschmidt 110 fighter-bombers, losing four of their ten patrol cars. Once the activity started he said there were 'no thoughts of fear; there was no time for that'.

If the midday heat could be avoided it was, but frequently there was no escape. The majority of offensives and withdrawals, the pendulum swings of the North African campaign, occurred during the winter and autumn months. But when tactical opportunities beckoned, such as during the German advance on El Alamein after the fall of Tobruk in June 1942, the tanks moved and fought despite blistering temperatures. German *Wochenschau* newsreels – the equivalent of the British *Pathé News* – revelled in showing to cinema audiences back home the effects of extreme heat in this new exotic campaign location. German cinema-goers saw a sweat-encrusted panzer crewmember climbing out of the turret of his tank while his comrades fried an egg on the track guard.

Heat was also a distraction when looking for the enemy. Sergeant-Major Bill Close recalled midday temperatures in excess of 110 degrees, which made life in the tank 'almost unbearable – even the flies dropped dead inside'. Official Afrika Korps reports measured temperatures of up to 45 degrees Centigrade (113°F) inside panzers. Conditions could become unendurable when hatches were closed as protection against artillery fire. Ventilating systems were also shut down during pauses in action, to conserve fuel. 'Nevertheless,' the report opined, 'the German tank crews held out under even these temperatures.' Captain Cyril Joly described how the thick armour plate lining his turret was 'cooked' to the extent that it was 'painful to touch' during a stiflingly hot day with no breeze. 'Inside, where the rest of the crew sat in huddled dejection, the air was thick and stifling, made worse by being flavoured with gun fumes and the smell of hot oil and burned petrol.'

Unless an objective had been specified for a deliberate assault or seen from an ambush, finding the enemy in the desert could be a surprise to both sides. On his initial engagement at Sidi Rezegh, Captain Crisp called his gunner on the radio.

'Cannon. Twelve hundred. You see all those things coming towards you. They're Jerry tanks. Pick out one and stay on it till you knock it out. Get cracking.'

I heard the first shot go off almost immediately, and watched the tracer sail in a long shallow curve. It hit on one of those dark silhouettes, and bounced high into the air.

Precisely locating the enemy to bring effective fire to bear is exceedingly tricky. Bill Close remarked:

> Well, they were usually in a hull-down position. They always seemed to be in a better position than we, and of course when going through the desert they nearly always had the sun at their backs. We were looking into the sun, which again made life very difficult for us.

Until it fired, a dug-in and sandbagged 88mm Flak gun despite its substantial size would not be visible at distance above the heat shimmer. When it did fire, the high muzzle velocity blast stripped off the surrounding surface dust, and suddenly blew it out in a billowing dust signature. This could be the first positive indication that the enemy had been found, offering an average response time of one second at a range of 1,000 metres.

## ADVANCE TO CONTACT

At the point of an armoured advance was the tank 'troop' in British parlance, or *Zug* in German, the lowest tactical denominator. Usually numbering three to four tanks, and sometimes only two, depending on mechanical breakdowns and casualties, it would be commanded by a lieutenant or senior non-commissioned officer (NCO). Experience was variable – influenced by casualty rates, training and the amount of time spent in the combat zone. This was the most basic level at which co-ordinated tactical fire and manoeuvre took place, and leaders strove to keep all their tanks in sight and direct them by radio.

Information regarding the enemy's movements was received from a number of radio sources – reconnaissance or forward artillery observers – who would tune into the same radio frequency. 'On the wireless there were ten tanks here, ten there,' said tank driver Jake Wardrop, 'then someone would report another twenty-five. I was sitting in the seat hoping they were all reporting the same ones.' He explained the normal British response when firing: 'As soon as the fun began, we fanned right out to see what was happening.' Typically, panzer crews were more circumspect and did not disperse to seek their quarry. They stayed behind long-range anti-tank screens to await a favourable opportunity. Adroitly organised within effective all-arms teams, they were deftly handled by commanders who had two successful European campaigns under their belts. They were also skilfully informed by forward reconnaissance and observers using much better radios than the British. When they moved forward it was as part of a *Keil,* or compact wedge formation, designed to thrust home an attack like a spearhead at a selected weak spot in order to lever British resistance apart.

Shooting might open from 88mm Flak guns at the maximum range of 2,000 metres, although hits were rarely scored beyond 1,000. This Krupp-produced artillery piece had been developed in 1931 as an anti-aircraft gun. Having already proved its deadly versatility as an anti-tank gun in Poland and France, it was still manned by air force crews assigned to the Afrika Korps. The two variants produced a remarkable 800 to 1,000 metres per second velocity, firing a projectile more than ten times the weight of the standard British 2-pounder tank gun. The gun was dug in and stabilised by four outriggers, splayed out over rough ground, which lowered the profile and aided concealment. Rapid actions could be conducted from its wheeled carriage. Leutnant Kurt Hoehne, an 88mm gun commander, recalled, 'As soon as a tank became visible, we knocked it out with one or two shots. The tracer trails of our munitions showed us exactly how to correct fire.'

When there was time to calculate ranges and set out markers the 88's accuracy was devastating.

Time on to the target was about a second. Cyril Joly described the sequence of familiar sounds. 'We heard the first crack of the shot passing overhead, followed quickly by the crash of the detonation behind us, and only then the deeper, duller explosion from the gun.' That was a miss, but a hit on an approaching Honey tank was the equivalent of it driving flat out into an immovable object. 'The 88mm armour-piercing entered with a dreadful *bang* through the driver's protection port', said tank gunner R.D. Lawrence. 'It killed Harold Mains, the driver, smashing his head to pulp, then pierced the thin metal basket that formed the floor of the turret, ricocheted against the curved wall of the cupola, and entered John Ferguson, the commander's body.'

Shock and horror dulls the senses, but the primeval urge to survive will generally transcend this.

The nightmare of bailing out now began.

Steve helped me push John out of the turret opening, whereupon machine-gun bullets sprayed the corpse and the tank. The Stuart's engine caught fire. We had to chance the bullets.

The wireless operator was wounded and Lawrence had to heave him up out of the turret. Following a yell that he had made it out and was flat on the sand, 'I went out like a streak.'

Kurt Hoehne had total confidence in the superiority of his weapon system. 'Most of the other guns had only a muzzle velocity of 600 to 800 metres per second,' he affirmed. Moreover, 88mm shells were more sophisticated than most. 'The trigger for the explosion,' he pointed out, 'was a little delayed so that the projectile first pierced the armour with its momentum and then exploded with great force. It could take a whole turret off with one shot.' The British were acutely aware of its potential. 'The word "eighty-eight" was invading the tank crew vocabulary as a symbol of shattering mutilation,' remarked one British tank commander.

Rarely were such duels individual. They were part of a combined-arms fight that the Germans had completely mastered.

In addition to long-range anti-tank fire there was artillery fire to contend with. Near misses could be endured with reasonable safety inside an armoured vehicle, but much superficial damage could occur as well as shaking up of the crew. The fighting power of a tank would often degrade from smashed periscopes and damaged gun mantlets; barrel distortion might occur, and turret bins with rations, water and personal possessions might be blown off.

Artillery caused tank crews to close all hatches and retreat into the interior of the tank. This reduced visibility and with it the capability to use vision to plan ahead or react to sudden situation changes. It slowed the battle down, miring vehicles in dust and mental obfuscation.

'When battened down and using periscopes, tanks soon lose their

sense of direction and tend to play "follow my leader",' remembered
Squadron Commander David Ling. To overcome this he always flew a
large yellow flag to enable his troop commanders to adjust their
formation around him. 'But it had its drawback of making one the
prime target.' As a consequence a high-explosive shell burst on his
turret – 'and I knew no more.'

'I was dead and didn't seem to mind' was Ling's verdict as he
struggled on the edges of consciousness following the impact. 'I knew
now that I was huddled on the floor of my tank, that we were not
moving, that the engine had stopped.' Inside the smoke-blackened
turret he saw the face of Corporal Hill, another crewmember.

> We must have received shocks of equal intensity, for he also was
> beginning to move. I reached him, clutched his arm and groped his
> face; and he returned my grip . . . I asked him if he was all right and
> he was. I did not ask the same of Trooper Bucket, my expert and
> lovable gunner . . . now slumped across his little adjustable seat, he
> sprawled backwards and downwards. His head, split in twain, was
> poised over my chest while his hot blood poured over and through
> me, a black glistening stream from the back of his crushed skull.

He and Hill, trapped in the hull, were entangled, and they had to move
Bucket to evacuate. Fear of fire and the claustrophobic nightmare of
being enmeshed amid the gore of bodies pinning them down inside,
impelled them to get out. Ling described the experience:

> I struggled and Hill struggled also. We were entangled and I had to
> move Bucket. I remember I stretched up my arm to push him
> forward and away, and two of my fingers went through the hole in
> his skull, into the warm softness within. I wiped my hand on my
> blood-drenched clothes.

## TANK ON TANK

Having endured long-range enemy anti-tank and artillery gunfire, tanks
could close on tanks, seeking individual advantage from tactical

manoeuvre. Like naval actions, platoons of tanks working in teams of twos, threes and fours would change course and steer to achieve the advantage of appearing on the enemy's flank or rear. Tank-on-tank engagements would begin at ranges between 1,000 and 800 metres on level desert terrain, where the 50mm guns of the Panzer Mark IIIs would come into their own. They fired a greater weight shot at higher muzzle velocity than their 2-pounder equipped adversaries. British tanks could only begin to exact a certain toll from about 300 metres. 'Although we only had a 2-pounder,' remembered Sergeant Arthur Wollaston of the 3rd Royal Tank Regiment, 'we evolved tactics whereby we could dash in as fast as we could, and get round the back or side of the enemy tanks where they were more vulnerable.' Trooper Geordie Reay of the same unit likened it to a rugby match. 'We were like a lot of flyweights fighting hulking heavyweights. We had to run round them and tackle them broadside on. You learned that by trial and error.' But it could be a costly process. 'In the middle of the day,' a War Office training note advised, 'the heat haze is usually so great as to make accurate fire difficult.' Italian M11s and M13s were more vulnerable because of their weaker flank armour. Engagements below 500 metres would often be sporadic and dependent on ground conditions.

The enduring image retained by most participants was of chaos. Fighting could begin as much by accident as intent. 'We spotted some other tanks quite near, which we assumed were ours,' recalled Powell Jones, an M3 Stuart driver with the 4th County of London Yeomanry during the November 1941 battles. So did the Germans, and it was not until they were on top of each other that realisation dawned. 'Instant pandemonium!' declared Jones: 'Tanks milling about and firing away madly at other tanks and knocking out their own side's tanks . . . yelling and screaming both in English and German on the wireless, both being so near to each other.'

Jones also dryly observed, 'It was my commander's first tank battle as commander and I don't think he really knew what to do.'

'In a tank battle, you see, it is very difficult to identify who are your tanks,' said twenty-one-year-old Sam Bradshaw. 'It was the same for them as for us.' He was with the 6th Royal Tank Regiment at Sidi Rezegh. 'You are all milling around, firing, sometimes you find yourself abreast of a German tank, you see the tanks going up, the wounded, people burning – it's just chaos! Smoke is going up, ammunition exploding – it just went on and on.'

To the inexperienced eye the result was virtually incoherent. An RAF pilot flying across the tank battle at Sidi Rezegh in 1941 provides a vivid commentary:

> Guns were blazing on all sides as these land cruisers made for each other. It was impossible to pick out, from our position, which was which. Most of them were on the move, but there were several stationary and no longer firing. Several hundreds of them appeared engaged in a grim showdown. It was like looking down on some huge prehistoric arena with fire-breathing scaly-sided monsters pitted against each other in a terrific struggle, lumbering slowly forward, swinging this way and that, each intent on the destruction of the other. It must have been a concentrated hell of shell against shell and steel against steel.

German and Italian tanks were trained to pause, fire, and then move. Many British crews, until experience taught them otherwise, attempted to fire on the move. To some extent this was because the range inferiority and the inferior power of the British 2-pounder shell meant that they had to hit their opponents on a weak spot or from the rear. British gunnery was not that precise. In any case, judging distance in the swirling dust and shimmering conditions was extremely difficult and came only with experience. Rash charges were the order of the day, to close with the enemy as rapidly as possible. Tank driver Jako Wardrop admitted 'quite frankly, I was not so strong for this charging business . . . but off we went . . . storming right up to these tanks, firing as we went.' One gunner, Eric Pearson, observing these reckless assaults, claimed 'it was murder . . . to see these tanks having to go in time and time again, only to get shot up, the whole area ablaze with burning vehicles, knocked out tanks and men on fire.' Many of the tank losses resulted from mechanical breakdowns, but the average loss inside every tank destroyed in fighting was one dead and one to three wounded from each five-man crew. Survival was directly proportional to the efficacy of a tank's design, its construction and the thickness of its armour.

The ability of British officers to lead effectively against an enemy who appeared not only to have superior machines but was also more tactically effective raised inevitable questions. There was a social gulf between officers and men in any case. 'The seniors and lads from A Coy were not allowed to mix,' declared Bert Rendell of the 1st Royal Tank Regiment, an '*esprit de corps* in reverse, I thought'. Many of the rank and file in the desert army nursed unspoken suspicions about pre-war officers, who they believed were 'Colonel Blimp' caricatures, not quite in touch with the practical realities of their profession.

Public-school-educated officers were, however, beginning to be replaced by grammar-school commission candidates, often more practical men with engineering apprenticeship backgrounds. Expansion and the casualties of war brought with them a perceptible change in the sociological balance of the army. Officers from working-class backgrounds and others promoted through the ranks meant that in time the old-fashioned cavalry officer would be the exception rather than the norm, swamped by newcomers committed and read into the latest concepts of armoured and motorised warfare.

There was also a psychological difference between the regular army that had fought the first rounds in the desert and the conscripts now superseding them. At the start of the desert conflict Wavell had between 80,000 and 100,000 men to confront the Italian Tenth Army. By November 1941 Auchinleck had 750,000 between Libya and Iraq, with 140,000 in and around Cairo. Further reinforcements streamed into theatre. This new mass of men had to be quickly assimilated into what was previously a tight social, almost tribal regimental hierarchy. Conscripted amateur soldiers were gradually diluting core regulars and many regarded this war, after the 1914–18 experiences, as something that needed to be quickly fought to a successful conclusion, so they could go home. Whatever their background, they were all subjected to the same crucible of armoured combat faced by the regulars that preceded them.

Scenes within tank hulls and turrets during combat were claustrophobic, highly uncomfortable and surreal. 'Mingled with the detonations of high explosive and my own cannon,' one British tank commander said of Sidi Rezegh, 'I could hear that terrifying swish of armour-piercing shell, and sometimes get a split second glimpse of tracer going by, taking the breath out of my lungs with the vacuum of its passage.' The crew of five had to stoop and bend awkwardly to avoid moving machinery parts, which preyed upon unsuspecting hands and feet if they were not properly placed when the gun recoiled or the turret revolved this way or that.

The driver would sit in a small compartment with about the same amount of room as a pilot encased in a closed aircraft cockpit, with his gear and steering levers to hand. Forward of him was the bulkhead with dials, speedometer, revolution counter and pressure gauges. These he constantly monitored while he drove, peering through a letterbox-size slot so small it could be easily obscured by a splayed hand. It was difficult to extricate himself from this compartment under normal circumstances, never mind if wounded. Hermann Eckardt from Panzer Regiment 8 recalled one of his drivers being transferred to the infantry because he could no longer bear the conditions inside a tank.

The radio operator generally sat to the left of the gun mass, completely blind and reliant on his crewmates to tell him what was going on. He frequently doubled as the loader and had to locate the correct shells, fumbling around in the interior if spares were on the floor, and keep the gunner re-supplied from racks around the turret, remembering in the heat of battle to give advance warning when ammunition was running short.

Dominating the main part of the turret was the gun apparatus itself, which in the case of the M3 Stuart reached almost to the back of the turret ring. Attached to the rear of the gun was a metal deflector guard, protecting the crew from its recoil, another object to dodge on pain of severe bruising as it jerked back a foot following every gun report. A large canvas bag hung from the deflector to catch the ejected shell cases that would metallically ring as the loader, enveloped in escaping gas and fumes, would slide in another.

Inside the turret at head height was the gunner, his face pressed into the telescope eyepiece, adjusting a range drum to one side and turning the wheel or operating a lever for the mechanical turret traverse. His job was to identify the target indicated by the commander and engage it as quickly as possible. All this activity occurred amid a cacophony of sharp sounds and pungent smells that were almost physical in their intensity. The sharp crack of the main armament would be interspersed with the chatter of machine-guns and the clattering of tracks. After all the hatches were closed down, dust and fumes would fill the fighting compartment as each crew fought its individual team battle. Tank commander Robert Crisp described the frenetic activity within a Stuart M3 turret at the height of a tank battle.

I heard my gunner yell, 'I've got one, sir', and it sounded good to hear his elation and to see the slow smoke curling up from the Mark III and the men bail out. The gunner was all right. He was picking his targets with an occasional word from me as I watched the tracer searing towards its target: 'Keep on that big bastard that you've just hit until you stop him.' The loader was all right, too. He would be too busy to be scared . . . tugging the next shell out of its bracket, pulling down the ejection lever, whipping in a new shell with enough force to close the breech, bending under to tap the gunner in the 'gun ready' signal, and then starting all over again as he heard the shot and saw the recoil next to his face.

Anyway he couldn't see what I could see and the gunner could only see a small part of it. The driver was the chap I felt sorry for. He would be squeezed back and to one side, getting as far away from the driving aperture as possible, inactive and frightened to death, staring at that advancing line of tanks with an awful fascination, wondering when the shell would strike that would carve his body into little pieces . . .

Leutnant Joachim Schorm of the 6th Company Panzer Regiment 5 declared, 'The war in Africa is quite different from the war in Europe.' His unit had been part of the *Blitzkrieg* thrust to the Channel coast less than a year before. 'It is absolutely individual,' he said. 'Here there are not the masses of men and material. Nobody and nothing can be concealed.' A vehicle on the move raises a huge spume of dust, so it is difficult to identify what it is. Both sides were looking for each other's tanks. Schorm called it 'fighting, face to face, each side thrusting and counter-thrusting'. Panzer commander Erich Muller saw tank conflict in a detached sense. 'It wasn't a war of one man fighting another. There was no such war.' As far as he was concerned, it was a question of eliminating tanks. 'In a place like Africa, tanks and the range of their guns was the decisive factor.'

Cyril Joly described the 'dull metallic thud' of a hit that failed to penetrate his tank 'and the following crash of the explosion stirred up all the dust in the tank, making it difficult for a few moments for us to see each other'. Leutnant Schorm experienced 'a crash just behind us'. A strike from the rear would cause immediate concern because the engine and petrol tank, the most vulnerable parts of a tank, are positioned there. Being closed down in battle poses the dilemma of whether or not to bail out and risk being shot in the open. 'The tank must be on fire,' he thought. There are only limited chances of spotting the damage with restricted vision. 'I turn round and look through the slit. It is not burning. Our luck is holding.' Schorm survived this engagement and later extracted an amour-piercing shell from the Panzer Mark III's right-hand auxiliary petrol tank. The petrol had drained without igniting.

Quite frequently tanks were struck by high-explosive rounds, which did not penetrate, but broke off a 'scab' of metal that ricocheted around the fighting compartment, with devastating consequences. Captain David Ling recalled the typical 'blinding' associated with this phenom-enon, when the kinetic energy of such a strike blew out a fragment. It came 'from an instantaneous flash of great heat from within the turret, burning all exposed hair and searing the surface of the eyes, even though the projectile did not pierce the armour'.

If hit by an armour-piercing shell a tank could be immobilised by the hard-core slug piercing the outer casing of the hull or turret. The metal core of the round preceded a jet of molten metal; if the jet struck ammunition, a catastrophic explosion might result, often blasting the turret off with the pressure release and setting off a series of conflagra-tions and smaller eruptions. This would satisfy the assailant tank, who could confirm a kill and switch attention. 'I'd never seen so many tanks knocked out in so short a time in all my life,' declared Alf Davies with 1 RTR, describing the 'Cauldron' tank battles in the spring of 1942. 'Nowadays you'd think it was an atom bomb – a phoof – a plume of smoke, they were going all over the place.'

Common to all tank crews was fear of fire on being hit. 'It's a particular nasty form of ending one's days when one is trapped inside a tank and the tank brews up and is on fire,' said one tank crew veteran. 'You'll never lose the awfulness of screams of men trying to get out.' So traumatic was the event that British tank crews with typical gallows humour termed it 'a brew' – the same expression used to describe making a cup of tea. Radio operator Peter Roach of 1 RTR described 'our own particular dread, a very real dread of the tank brewing up when hit, so that if you were not wounded you had to move very fast to avoid incineration'. Fear of fire was all-pervasive. 'We had all seen and smelled the burned-out tank,' recalled Roach, 'and seen the charred remnants of the crew'.

Escaping a knocked-out and burning tank had to be worked out and practised during training. Newly arrived raw crews had no idea of the psychological pressure they would be subjected to when it happened. Each tank type had its own unique exit possibilities, and these could be complicated if the way out was under enemy fire. Bodies of dead crewmen were sometimes hauled in place as a shield against incoming fire. New crews, unversed in the ritual of carefully and systematically stowing personal belongings, only appreciated its importance when their exits were blocked. Time was brief. Indecision was an unaffordable luxury when flames were sucking the oxygen out of the fighting compartment. All escape routes were confined and required bending and stretching, particularly if wreckage impeded the exits.

In general panzers appeared to have better designed crew space; the Mark III and Mark IV had turret side escape hatches. This obviated the need to climb out of the top like the British and Italians. The British did not match these superior escape avenues until the introduction of American models, for example with the bigger opening side doors of Grant tanks.

Testimony to the superiority of panzer emergency exits can be found in surviving wartime photographs, where one sees open turrets and daylight showing through side hatches. British and Italian tank hulks stand forlornly by with open top hatches and, all too often, bodies of crew members nearby.

For crews squatting within the claustrophobic confines of their closed-down, noxious-smelling tanks, assailed by dust and cordite fumes, the shock of an armour-piercing shell strike was a brutal experience. Cyril Joly recalled the chaos on such an impact.

There was a clang of steel on the turret front and a blast of flame and smoke from the same place, which seemed to spread into the turret, where it was followed by another dull explosion. The shock wave which followed swept past me, still standing in the cupola, singed my hands and face and left me breathless and dazed.

Looking down inside the turret he saw 'a shambles'. Two thoughts might enter deranged minds: there would now be another hit, there might be a fire. Once an enemy tank had registered a hit, it had correctly estimated the range. If the victim had halted, the attacker would fire round after round until there was evidence of smoke or the crew bailing out, confirming a kill. Inside crippled vehicles, this knowledge, alongside shock and panic, urged surviving crew to get out. This was not easy. Slumped casualties and twisted metal from the impact might well have rearranged the physical geography of the confined space inside the tank. Smoke would hinder visibility, choking and smarting eyes. Joly continued:

> The shot had penetrated the front of the turret just in front of King, the loader. It had twisted the machine-gun out of its mounting. It, or a jagged piece of the torn turret, had then hit the round that King had been holding ready – had set it on fire. The explosion had wrecked the wireless, torn King's head and shoulders from the rest of his body and started a fire among the machine-gun boxes stowed on the floor. Smoke and the acrid fumes of cordite filled the turret.

Joly's gunner, totally shaken and losing self-control, urged him to get out, while the commander was still in a state of shock and was blocking the way. As they called to the driver to bail out, another round slammed into the front of the now stationary and vulnerable tank, tearing his chest wide open. Two of them got out, with the gunner attempting to claw his way past the commander, and restricted by the tangled wreckage around them.

'The flames shoot up 30 to 40 feet high, and if you're not out in a few seconds you are dead,' recalled Corporal Peter Watson of the 2nd Royal Tank Regiment. He and his crew climbed out of the top of their tank, eluded German infantry dispatched to capture them and dodged back the half mile that separated them from their own line.

I felt a queer feeling on my face, so I put my hand up and water was pouring down. I had blisters as big as saucers, and I'd lost my pride and joy – my moustache. That went for a Burton, my eyebrows went, my ears were burnt, the whole of my face.

A medical sergeant, attempting to comfort him, offered, 'I'll cut that off for you, Corporal,' to which the mystified Watson responded, 'Cut what off?'

He said, 'Good God, man. Look at your arms and wrists,' and I looked and hanging down about a foot was skin on both arms, like an umbrella.

The sergeant cut off the scorched gristle and threw it away. 'Then it hurt,' recalled Watson, before he was dosed in morphine and placed on a lorry to take him back.

## DISENGAGEMENT AND THE WOUNDED

War Office 'theatre notes' written at the time pointed out that various methods of evacuating wounded from tanks had been evolved and practised, but 'it is a fact of practical importance that not one instance can be found of any of these methods being used in actual battle.' Teaching had advocated the methodical construction of slings attached to equipment harnesses, but they were impractical and complicated. They were, not used because the War Office itself had already realised that 'the enemy always concentrates his fire on an immobilised tank.' Tank crews already knew this. Cyril Joly described what could happen with only a momentary delay in evacuating. His tank was immobilised as the crew sought to recover one of their members. 'Before the rest of the crew had recovered from the disaster, the tank was penetrated, killing the driver and mortally wounding the gunner just behind him,' Joly said. 'Only the operator, who climbed over the dead and dying, had escaped.'

'It is amazing,' continued the 'theatre notes' smoothly, 'that even badly wounded men managed to get out of their tanks unaided.' Fear of further strikes and fire motivated them. Speed of removal is the primary consideration, but by this time many tank crew were becoming oddly aware 'that most injuries when first inflicted cause remarkably little pain.' Veteran soldiers on both sides had begun to appreciate the extent to which shock can anaesthetise pain. Even extensively injured crewmen were crawling, clambering or allowing themselves to be roughly hauled out of crippled tanks, and 'consequently the necessity for great care in removal', the training note explained, 'appears to be of less importance than was supposed.'

Delivering casualties to medical care before nerve endings numbed by shock began to register pain was a trying experience. Sam Bradshaw was badly wounded and evacuated from Sidi Rezegh by ambulance. 'You've got to imagine,' he said, pointing to rough terrain during a post-war interview, 'driving over ground such as this over here.'

> You would suddenly be bounced up on the stretcher. If you were wounded in the back or the legs or anywhere in fact you had to endure this terrible pain, and this would go on without end.

Even worse was jolting about on the hot rear engine decks of tanks being utilised for evacuation, covered in noxious fumes and dust and likely under fire. Lieutenant Coglitore of the 12th Italian Bersaglieri Battalion, observing M13 tanks turning back from the combat zone, 'still managing to move slowly even under enemy fire,' saw that:

> They have dead and wounded aboard, some of them seriously hurt. They stop a short distance from us, where the other wounded and other fallen soldiers have been collected from the battlefield by vehicles from the tank regiment. They are unforgettable sights of how much the human body can be mutilated. The wounded are entrusted to the ambulances while the dead are to be buried on the spot.

At the end of the casualty evacuation chain was the Field and then General Hospital. 'When we were taken into hospital it was so different,' remarked Bradshaw, exuding the visible relief he felt. 'Beautiful clean sheets, nice clean-smelling English nurses, it was such a change from the desert.'

Back at the front, failing light generally obliged opposing tanks to gradually draw apart. The War Office 'theatre notes' assessed that it was unusual for actual fighting to occupy more than three daylight hours, 'the rest of the time being spent in patrolling and waiting, and preparing for an attack'. Harassing fire often prevented both sides from cooking, brewing or resting. As the tanks finally withdrew they would face a two- to three-hour night drive after breaking contact with the enemy, having been awakened at first light.

On the battlefield the process of recovering partially damaged tanks and mechanical breakdowns would then commence across a surreal landscape. The detritus of war scattered around included every conceivable object imaginable, from discarded equipment to burning vehicles. The stench of gasoline and burning oil and the pungent smell of ash rose up from burned-out tanks and vehicles, mixed with the sweet, cloying smell of dead bodies. Colonel Oderisio Piscicelle-Taeggi, commanding the Italian 132 Artillery Regiment, described the aftermath of a day's fighting in November 1941:

> Here two tanks clashed with bows locked, they remained half suspended like rampant lions. Together they burned. One, two, three at a time, machine-gun rounds exploded with short sharp reports, like bits of wood cracking in the fireplace. A few feet away another tank had its turret thrown off and lying to one side, like the top of an orange sliced off with a knife, and smoke slowly emerging from the damaged hole. And with the coming of dusk, more fires became visible. All around fires were burning and occasionally an explosion would occur with a flaming eruption.

British units tended to withdraw to some distance at night before establishing a leaguer, relying on darkness and deception to cloak their movements. Occasionally tracer was fired into the air to guide incoming stragglers. The Afrika Korps operated differently. They leaguered within the vicinity of the battlefield itself, lighting up the skies for miles around by constantly firing star shells and fairy lights to light up the security areas they sought to visibly observe and defend. Their intention was to aggressively dominate the site, recover their own tanks and administer the *coup de grâce* to British mechanical failures. Cracking tanks' hulls with explosives or fire rendered them irreparable.

Joachim Schorm's diary refers on numerous occasions to minor aggressively fought actions to save tanks. After an attack on Tobruk on 1 May 1941 he described how 'an anti-tank gun has to be kept in check by constant fire' while 'at last I move steadily off with tank 624 in tow, through the gap and on 800 yards.' He announces: '250,000 Reichmarks saved' and 'the crew is delighted to have its tank back.' On the following day he is recovering tanks again. 'We got out both of the Panzer Mark II tanks – 800,000 Reichmarks saved.'

It takes a particular brand of courage to continue fighting the tank when confronted with visibly accurate incoming anti-tank fire. All felt fear and everyone had his own personal way of dealing with it: bravado, quiet determination, denial or often quiet hesitant chats with comrades who knew because they had experienced the same rush of conflicting and terrifying emotion.

After any battle or long-term strenuous operation a form of physical or mental reaction would set in. 'It is generally agreed under such conditions the fighting efficiency of crews falls off very seriously after a week's continuous fighting,' was the official conclusion. Tank commanders were under particular pressure following the trauma of a crippling strike. If they survived, they were morally obliged to take over a subordinate commander's tank. This exacted a huge psychological toll. Even after the nightmare of losing half his crew in particularly grisly circumstances Captain Cyril Joly 'knew that I should not go back but that I should take over one of the other tanks of my troop.' He did so, moving on foot across the searing desert to his subordinate tank – 'the heat and the recent shock sapped my strength and determination,' he admitted. He need not be noticed and likely would not be blamed, but 'there was still an inner spirit which urged me to do what I must.' Joachim Schorm's Panzer Mark III was knocked out by a mine under fire outside Tobruk. He endured two more mine strikes before transferring to another panzer, still under fire, and continued the action. The new panzer drove 'back through artillery fire for 100 yards' before piercing the enemy line. British and German commanders were required to lead in all circumstances.

Combat fatigue, or post-combat stress disorder, occurred in the First

World War and it now appeared in the Second. Cowardice, a difficult concept in societies less stoic than those of the past and more discerning in their perception of pain and suffering, was rarely discussed by officers. Soldiers, ever more prescient, had few inhibitions about expressing their true feelings. Officers at the front tended to be more compassionate and understanding. NCOs and men enduring the same conditions were less generous. A coward or – worse – an inept soldier or leader could compromise their own survival chances. 'Windy' operatives within tank crews were a cancer that was better quickly removed before it spread. Such an individual diluted the effectiveness and thereby safety and survival chances of the team. Lance Sergeant Bert Rendell of the 1st Royal Tank Regiment, leading a troop of tanks against a German captured 25-pounder, recalled good support from his left-flank tank, 'but the one on my right during the important time ran behind a sand dune that gave him no hope of aiding me but was safe for himself.' His own tank was knocked out as a consequence and the left tank damaged with wounded. He furiously complained to his CO that a new corporal was responsible and 'I wanted him removed'. There was little debate. 'On explaining why, the CO did just that.' On another occasion he had a driver who froze after receiving a dangerous order. 'I am going to die,' he repeated and refused to move until, Rendell recalled, 'I gave him a couple of heavy blows to the head and he came to.' War was nasty and brutish, as was the communal response in the event of non-compliance.

Anything that disturbed the symmetry of the crew was to be avoided. Cowardice, or personal likes and dislikes, were only one aspect. Combat effectiveness was dependent on technical expertise. Poor training brought with it further potential threats to group cohesion, as well as increased vulnerability. Putting an inexperienced crew into battle before they were ready was not just dangerous; veterans, who were well aware of the implications, regarded it as criminal. Bert Rendell recalled:

I could go on talking about men who should have been in a canteen serving cups of tea, and they were given to me as a fighter, after ten minutes on this and ten minutes on that, two thousand miles out from England and straight into the attack. It was frightening, and this

187

is where I would like to do so much before I pass on. I'd like to get it to the BBC, to tell people so that they understand that a lot of boys who had parents that idolised them never had a chance from the moment they left England to go to war.

The vast majority of soldiers stoically endured the pressures, held together by an intense community of spirit: comradeship. This intangible manifested itself time and again in the fiercest of combat. Captain David Ling recounted an example, in the loss of one of his tank commanders at Sidi Omar:

> Donaldson died well. His tank hit and raging with flames, he told his crew to evacuate as the ammunition exploded and bit into their legs and bodies. Out went the radio operator, and Donaldson, demanding to go last, passed with all his strength his gunner over him and heaved him up badly wounded. They fell to safety to see their commander lift himself and fall back into the spluttering steel, his last strength spent.

Heroism in a commander was not always welcome. Ling, under pressure from General Freyburg VC during Operation Crusader at Sidi Rezegh, was obliged to follow orders that seemed futile to him and caused casualties. Looking at Freyburg's biography after the war, he saw that alongside a remarkable record of a VC and three DSOs was a note stating 'he was noted for his complete disregard for danger'. Ling commented: 'He was one of the lucky few who showed this "complete disregard". Ninety per cent are soon dead and bring death to their fellow soldiers.' As for himself, Ling felt he was always 'cautious and somewhat in fear', which he believed to be the right balance. 'The right amount of fear makes a prudent commander.'

Men were subsumed by machines in the need to feed the forward armoured battle. Going in again after the trauma of being knocked out was the equivalent of inviting a gladiator at the Roman games to engage in a rematch after surviving mortal combat. It was with a sinking feeling that NCOs like 'Buck' Kite of the 3rd Royal Tank Regiment received the invitation to go back. 'There's a fit tank there, Corporal Kite, will you take it over?' he was asked by the Motor Transport Officer after surviving bailing out at Gazala.

'It was fine; we didn't have a tank,' remembered Corporal Peter Watson with the 2nd Royal Tank Regiment. 'We didn't have to fight. Wonderful. We got a ride on the back of a lorry and had some tea. It was lovely. Then they sent for us. They said they were taking over Brigade tanks.' He had to go in with his crew again.

Bert Rendell, the tough twenty-nine-year-old regular tank troop commander with the 1st Royal Tank Regiment, remembered when they were 'running away from Knightsbridge [a track crossing], there were only six of us left out of fifty-odd tanks. It was all flames.' Racing down the macadam road to Bardia they came across ten tank crewmen sitting on their kit bags. Rendell, who was looking for a replacement for his dead gunner, realised that none qualified, so they were left behind. 'Off we go, driver,' the sergeant recalled saying, 'I couldn't use any of them.' They might be picked up by German tanks, but he knew that behind him were other British tanks also seeking replacements, who might want them.

> You can lose any one man on a tank but the tank is still running. If there was two killed on the tank and three left alive you laid them in a safe place and noted the position on your map . . . You carry on, because the tank must not fall into enemy hands and you might find more crew for it.

Rendell could show compassion, but he was also a survivor.

At the conclusion of a day's combat both sides took emotional stock and likely marvelled that they still lived, any elation clouded by a niggling concern that their luck might not last. Jake Wardrop was shot out of ten tanks in the space of thirty days in 1941, losing one crew member dead and one or two wounded each time. Captain Robert Crisp was knocked out six times in November 1941. Depression always accompanied the death of a special friend. As Joly described it:

> Each day's fighting took a mounting toll of killed and wounded. New tanks and new crews arrived and were lost almost before the

men were known by name. With growing dismay I wondered how much longer the old members of my squadron would last. As each night we saw them again in leaguer I began to hope that their skill and experience would keep them always out of trouble.

Combat stress manifested itself in irritability, jumpiness, slow reaction to orders and a tendency to hold back from combat. Constant exposure to gore and the wreckage visited on human bodies by war led to depression. Captain David Ling was particularly disturbed at the sight of Sergeant Bleadon, a troop sergeant with whom he had shared much. 'I was to see him grimy, with his left eye nearly gouged out and resting quivering on his cheek bone while he tried desperately to thumb it back.'

The impact was cumulative. 'In the main we were all silent and morose, withdrawn, tired, dejected,' explained Joly during the 'Cauldron' battles preceding the German advance to Alamein. 'I had reached the lowest ebb of my endurance and felt that anything would break my self-control.'

Bert Rendell recalled one of his drivers giving up, his nerves shot to pieces.

> I think he had reached the state a lot of people had – there was no need to go on any more. There was quite enough that killed themselves . . . they had reached the time when there was no more to do and it didn't matter if they were going to be shot; they would say *Let it be.*

The soldier was removed and sentenced to 110 days in the 'glasshouse'. Rendell saw him again after his sentence was carried out, recognisable but 'only a shadow' of his former self. 'Of course,' he remarked, 'they would never send him to the front again because he was useless.'

Once the tanks returned to their leaguers, vehicles had to be refuelled and re-armed, and minor repairs and general maintenance carried out. It was not just fuel and rations that needed to be replenished, the courage bank had to be restored, and this was achieved through friendly human interaction. German tank crews would gather around their mobile kitchens and check who had survived, talk to each other and psychologically regenerate. As

Leutnant Wilhelm Wessel with the Afrika Korps remarked, 'There, everyone spoke about the crises and the pleasure at meeting their comrades. One gladly gave what they had and took what was offered.' Photos were passed around, 'because for the men in the desert, wives and children lived in pictures.' Anyone who did not receive a letter got the news from the others, while 'anyone who received a photo would pass it from hand to hand.'

'The desert army,' explained British radio operator Peter Roach, 'was broken into thousands and thousands of little groups whose very core was a fire tin and a brew can.' Cyril Joly observed that 'during battle the night leaguer was always like home – there was food and hot drinks and companionship.' It was a period of psychological regeneration prior to the uncertainties of a day frequently only three to four hours' sleep away. 'There's more Christian feeling and comradeship in one leaguer in one night,' claimed Joly's regimental padre, 'than there is in many parishes during the whole week.'

As the tank crews indulged in a fitful sleep, similar emotional pressures plagued the wounded, who realised they would never be quite normal again.

The badly burned Peter Watson met a major – a skin specialist from Harley Street – when he got back to Cairo. 'You think you're going to look like an ape for the rest of your life, don't you, Corporal?' Watson had been thinking exactly that. 'I was in a terrible state; my lips were about an inch thick and all crusted, my beard had grown and sand had stuck on the burns.' So many burns cases were emerging from the front that the army had conscripted dermatologists and skin specialists from Britain. 'I'll tidy you up,' claimed the doctor – 'a smashing bloke' – who claimed that with treatment and creams his skin would grow and he would be 'as good as new'. 'And he was right,' exclaimed Watson, delivering his remarks during a lecture after the war – 'Look how handsome I am!'

Night-time regeneration was a trying period for the wounded of both sides. During a post-war interview Lieutenant Peter Vaux recalled the scene at dusk at a field dressing station. He had just been carried in when a young German soldier with infantry epaulettes was put down beside him. 'He was very badly hurt indeed,' he said. 'I was quite badly hurt, but he was worse.' Both of them received equal care and, after being injected with morphine shots, had labels attached listing how much they had been given.

As I lay there, I felt his hand touch mine and I grasped his hand and he held it and pressed it back, and as the morphine went over our heads we lay there holding hands like that. When they came to fetch me in the morning I saw that he had gone. 'What, has he gone?' I said. 'Have you taken him away?' And they said, 'He died – we had to take his hand out of yours.'

# 9

## THE RUSSIAN CRUCIBLE

### INVASION

As the German armies poised on the Russian frontier in June 1941 a new generation of panzer crews were joining the Panzerwaffe on completion of training. The sheer scale of forces required in the planning process for the invasion of Russia, code-name 'Barbarossa', required the formation of an extra eleven panzer divisions. German tank production could not keep pace with such an expansion and the dilemma was solved by cutting the number of panzer regiments in each panzer division from two to one. Each regiment now formed three battalions totalling 150–200 tanks. The Wehrmacht was to attack with a force of 3.6 million men. In support were 3,648 tanks and self-propelled guns, 7,146 artillery pieces and 2,510 aircraft. Across the frontier, arraigned in a semi-offensive stance in the Russian Western Military District, were 2.9 million Soviet soldiers with 14–15,000 tanks, 34,695 artillery pieces and 8–9,000 combat aircraft.

*Blitzkrieg* was to be tested in its refined form against its most determined and best-equipped opponent to date. Of the German panzers, 1,700 were completely inferior to Russian tank technology, although nobody was aware of this yet. Three massive German Army Groups were to strike simultaneously and a further twenty-four divisions waited in reserve. Success depended on the nineteen panzer divisions concentrated in four *Panzergruppen* (Groups), which also incorporated the fourteen motorised divisions. The newly formed *Ostheer* (Eastern Army) was the largest, finest and technically most proficient force Germany had ever committed to battle. With such a formidable cutting edge it was anticipated that the campaign would last eight weeks. As Hitler proclaimed, 'the World will hold its breath'.

Many of the newly recruited panzer crews had not tasted combat. Tank gunner Karl Fuchs was highly frustrated during training that he would miss the early *Blitzkrieg* successes. He wrote to his serving father: 'What are we doing here? We're sitting around at home like corralled horses and can only watch our comrades do our job.' After missing the French campaign he wrote again: 'I keep on hoping and I know that sooner or later it will be my turn and it may be somewhere in the east. What do you think?' Serving fathers were not always keen on their sons joining the Panzerwaffe, having seen gruesome remains of burned-out panzers in France. Otto Carius wanted to join the tanks, but his father, happy for him to join any other branch, even aviation, 'categorically forbade the panzer corps. In his mind's eye, he probably already saw me burning and suffering horribly,' he re-marked. Eighteen-year-old Ludwig Bauer was convinced by the *Wochenschau* weekly cinema newsreels and chose the *Fallschirmjäger,* or paratroopers. But his father, who had seen their casualties first hand while serving in France, 'was not convinced this was a good idea', so Bauer went for the panzers.

Ignorance was probably bliss. Amongst the Russians Aleksandr Fadin recalled shouting 'Hurrah!' at news of selection to the 2nd Gorki Armour Academy. 'Why are you so happy?' asked veterans who had fought at Khalkin-Gol against the Japanese and in the Winter War in Finland. 'You will burn in these tin cans.'

Western military observers had been staggered by the numbers and quality of the tanks they witnessed during the huge 1935 exercises held in the Kiev Military District, but Stalin's purges, which struck the army in 1937, beheaded the Red Army. Politically safe new military leaders were appointed. Former mechanised corps were broken up to create motorised divisions, designed to operate with horsed cavalry. Independent tank brigades were farmed out to the infantry.

Disastrous tank performances in Finland in 1939 and Germany's stunning victory in France convinced Stalin to reverse his tank strategy and mechanised corps with armoured divisions were re-formed from

June 1940. The outcome was chaotic, as tank Sergeant-Major Semen Matveev described:

> My corps was less than half its regulation strength. We had only bits and pieces. My tank battalion was in fact less than a company. We didn't have any trucks or tractors at all. An army is a huge organism, and the Germans had theirs up and running – and running well, I'd say – but ours had only just started to be built up. So we shouldn't be ashamed that they were stronger than us then. They were much stronger. That's why they often defeated us in the first year of the war.

'There's a distinct possibility, actually it seems like a 99 per cent certainty,' wrote Karl Fuchs in August 1940, having joined the 7th Panzer Division in France, 'that we're still going to cross the Channel.' The English were reckoned to be the next victim. 'If that happens I'll be ready to give my all.' Otto Carius of the 20th Panzer Division was meanwhile training 'with submergible tanks' at Putlos on the Baltic coast. He suspected 'England would be our next opponent'. Carius's tanks were in fact being prepared to wade the Bug River on the demarcation line marking the new frontier between German-occupied Poland and Russia. Rumours of designs against England assisted the deception.

Karl Fuchs met his wife Mädi when he was seventeen, wooed her while he was a trainee teacher before joining the army and married her at age twenty in 1940. When he saw her last in April 1941, she was seven months pregnant and it was clear he was going to war.

Seeking to compose his feelings before action, Fuchs wrote to his wife:

> We really have not yet had much of life and want the chance to experience a lot together. Once this war is over, once there's an end to all this madness, I want to work with you and our child. I want to create a happy and carefree life for us. I believe that fate has given me this task and I know that I will come back to you. My dearest, don't fear for me. I will return. I love both of you. Your Korri

Ten days before H-hour he received delightful news. 'The happiest day of my life is today!' he proclaimed. 'You have presented me with a boy! A strong baby boy! My darling Mädi, how shall I ever thank you?'

At 0315 hours on 22 June three German army groups moved into the Soviet Union. Karl Fuchs' Panzer Regiment 25 formed part of the spearhead.

A panzer division vanguard would be composed of a mixed battalion-size force of light panzers and motor-cycle and sidecar-borne infantry. These provided the eyes and ears preceding the next echelon, a battalion or regiment of medium and heavy panzers of over 100 tanks travelling with eighty or so lorries filled with light infantry, or mounted on armoured half-tracks. Bringing up the rear was a battalion or more up to regimental size of motorised towed-artillery.

Units moved in dust-shrouded columns several kilometres long. The fighting vehicles at the front were dispersed in *Keil* or wedge-like arrowhead formations anticipating a battle. The remainder drove in parallel file columns at best speed. Driving on choking dust-covered roads or within packed processions of vehicles made map-reading difficult. Crewmen slept fitfully wherever they could, bumping and lurching uncomfortably with the movement of vehicles. War correspondent Arthur Grimm, driving along with just such a *Vorausabteilung*, or vanguard, at the end of June, described the scene on the axis of advance ahead:

> The landscape stretches flat ahead with wave-like undulations. There are few trees and little woodland. Trees are covered in dust, their leaves a dull colour in the brilliant sunlight. The countryside is a brown-grey green with occasional yellow expanses of corn. Over everything hangs a brown-grey pall of smoke, rising from knocked-out tanks and burning villages.

Black dots moving like flies on the horizon often signified enemy tanks or fighting vehicles. Nobody was certain until the first flash, followed by a jet of flame and inky smoke bubbling skyward, signified that a tank battle had begun. The first sighting of an enemy tank might be a turret floating on a sea of waving corn. Inside the fighting compartment urgent shouts of range, direction and the type of shell to be fired ring out followed by a concussive bang that rocks the panzer on its chassis as a whirring noise indicates the round is cutting through the corn until a flash and distinctive 'plunk' denotes a hit. All this occurs within a fraction of a second as the turret fills with fumes. A metallic rasp indicates the sliding open of the breech block and a further shell is thrust within, snapped shut and a cry of 'ready' announces the next shot. Another round would follow and as many as it takes to convince the crew they have killed their opponent. Unless somebody bails out or they see flames, nobody can be certain. More reassuring are the colossal explosions that signify the penetration of the ammunition compartment. Compression from these bangs can launch turrets sky high, wobbling and gyrating in flight, with multiple flashes, bangs and reports as the rest of the ammunition crackles and flares, hissing and roaring like an upturned rocket motor until extinguished. Such an explosion can reduce the entire tank – turret and hull – to a few mangled metal slivers.

Arkadi Maryevski serving in a Soviet penal battalion claimed, 'With petrol engines these iron coffins burnt as easily as matches. Getting out of a tank in time was one of the most important skills to learn.' The thinly armoured BTs and T-26s which formed the main proportion of the Russian tank strength at the outset of the campaign were vulnerable to almost all German panzers and anti-tank guns at normal battle range. Vladimir Alexeev, who joined the tanks when he failed to follow his brother into submarines, was allocated a light T-70 tank, with a crew of only two. On being asked whether he felt vulnerable in such a light tank, his ironic response was 'Yes – it was really very difficult, but we weren't asked!'

Three days into the campaign tank gunner Karl Fuchs announced to his wife Mädi that 'yesterday I knocked off a Russian tank, as I did two days ago!' He was jubilant. 'If I get in another attack, I'll receive my first battle stripes.' These were the 'happy times' for the panzers. *Blitzkrieg* was working well. Close air support from the Luftwaffe preceded the panzer vanguards, shooting up the opposition and often catching Russian tanks on their rail cars. Combined-arms operational procedures, proven and tested in France, overwhelmed Russian defence lines before they could be established.

After piercing the line through the shock effect of aerial bombing and artillery, the panzers and mobile infantry broke into enemy rear areas and wreaked havoc. Villages were enveloped from both sides by panzer grenadier infantry who would break in supported by the tanks, artillery and their own forward anti-tank guns. The Russians were unable to cope with the focused precision of these co-ordinated strikes in tandem with waves of Stuka dive-bomber attacks. 'The Russians are fleeing everywhere and we follow them,' Fuchs proclaimed. 'All of us believe in early victory.' So swift were unexpected advances that trams still ran in some of the cities the panzers penetrated. Civilians lined the streets and cheered them, believing them to be their own.

By 17 July panzer spearheads closed in again at Smolensk, this time trapping three Soviet armies in the pocket. Nine days earlier the Supreme Army Command OKH calculated that it had destroyed eighty-nine of 164 identified Russian divisions. It was at this point that *Blitzkrieg* momentum petered out. There were no more German mobile units of appreciable size available to continue the eastward advance until the infantry divisions closed up. Despite staggering Soviet losses the *Blitzkrieg* impetus died just beyond the Smolensk 'land-bridge', a historical jumping-off point for the previous invasions heading for Moscow.

'Yesterday I participated in my twelfth attack,' wrote Karl Fuchs to his wife while pausing at Smolensk. 'Some of these attacks were more difficult than others. With twelve attacks under my belt, I have now caught up to the boys who had a head start in France! You can imagine that I'm very proud of this achievement.'

Karl Fuchs, like all soldiers, wrote what he thought his relatives would want to hear, rather than bleak truths. By 21 July his division had lost 166 of its 284 tanks, and his regiment had broken up one of its battalions to keep the other two up to an effective strength. One of the motorised infantry officers in the same division was more candid, writing the following week:

> The faces of the youngsters exude the same visage as First World War veterans. The long beards and filth of these days made many of them look older than they really are. Despite the satisfaction of sudden Russian withdrawals, this change in the faces of the soldiers is noticeable. Even after washing and shaving something different but difficult to describe has occurred!'

Panzer crews generally escaped their burning tanks, able to benefit from armoured protection even when hit. The infantry by contrast were naked and their divisions were bleeding to death.


## THE FAILURE OF BLITZKRIEG


A number of factors combined to dissipate the effectiveness of *Blitzkrieg*. Surprise did not just apply to the Russians; it was mutual. For the first time in this war the Germans reached the eight-week campaign target point and had not won. That was a surprise.

The first unpleasant shock was technological. On the second day of the campaign a solitary unidentified tank sat across the 6th Panzer Division's supply route and destroyed twelve German supply trucks. A battery of 50mm anti-tank guns was sent to deal with it and after closing to within 600 metres inflicted a succession of hits that all ricocheted into the air. The turret of the unknown tank type swivelled and remorselessly raked the battery with 76mm high-explosive shells until it was silenced. An 88mm gun employed in the 'fire brigade' capacity got to within 900 metres before it too was hit and its crew cut down by co-axial machine-gun fire. A re-supply crisis was emerging for the 6th Panzer Division, so a night raid was attempted with two satchel charges attached to the monster tank, and they were blown, but retaliatory fire indicated they had been unsuccessful. Dive-bomber support was not available in the morning, so it was decided to mount a joint attack, with light panzers feinting while a second 88mm gun was brought up to deliver the killing blow. The Russian tank was distracted by the duelling panzers until three 88mm rounds travelling at over 1,000 metres per second crashed into its rear. The barrel jerked skyward, seemingly signifying the end of the engagement. Excited and celebrating German infantry climbed aboard the monolith chattering animatedly. Suddenly the barrel rotated yet again and swept them off. Two assault engineers had the presence of mind to slip two stick grenades into a jagged hole pierced by shot at the base of the turret. Muffled explosions forced the turret lid open with an exhalation of smoke. It was over.

'New enemy tank!' wrote General Franz Halder, the German

General Staff Chief, in his diary that night. This was the Klim Voroshilov KV-1 tank, which mounted a 76.2mm gun. Only two of the 88mm rounds actually penetrated its armour, and the only evidence marking the unfortunate 50mm battery's efforts were eight blue carbonised strike marks.

The appearance of the new 34-ton T-34, not dissimilar in shape to today's modern tanks, caused consternation in the Panzerwaffe. Leutnant Rolf Hertenstein, now in the 13th Panzer Division, recalled how 'the next morning we saw the T-34s and, boy, we were impressed!' In his opinion 'the T-34 was the best tank in the world at that time, bar none! It weighed about 26 tons, and it had sloped armour, which was thicker than that of our panzers.' A 12-cylinder diesel engine gave it considerable speed over 'wide tracks that allowed them to go through soft terrain that our panzers couldn't go through. The T-34s went through as if it was nothing.' Otto Carius was a loader in a Czechoslovakian Panzer 38t, which constituted 25 per cent of the invading panzers. 'We felt practically invincible with our 37mm cannon and two Czech machine-guns,' he proudly recalled. 'We were enthusiastic about the armour protection and didn't realise until later that it would only serve as moral protection for us.' The appearance of T-34s as 'hit us like a ton of bricks'. Surprise was complete. 'How was it possible that those at the "top" hadn't known about the existence of this superior tank?' Carius asked. The one way to deal with it was to work in co-operation with the 'only salvation': the 88mm Flak gun. 'We thus started paying the utmost respect to the Flak troops,' he remarked, 'who previously had sometimes received a condescending smile from us.' Carius ruefully reflected that 'the feeling began to sneak up on us that it was no longer possible to count upon a quick end to the campaign.'

The second surprise contributing to the failure of *Blitzkrieg*, was a dawning realisation that this was a different type of opponent. Surrounded Russian pockets chose to fight to the death rather than surrender. General Günther Blumentritt, the Fourth Army Chief of Staff, detected this unusual behaviour on watching the initial encirclement at Minsk. 'The conduct of the Russian troops, even in this first battle, was in striking contrast to the behaviour of the Poles and of the western allies in defeat. Even when encircled the Russians stood their ground and fought.'

As a consequence panzer momentum slowed around Minsk at the end of June and stagnated outside Smolensk, the second major encirclement on the way to Moscow. Fifty per cent of the mobile offensive forces of Army Group Centre were taken up fighting defensive battles to hold the Russians inside the rings. Two weeks later 60 per cent of the offensive mobile forces and thirty-two infantry divisions were fighting to achieve the same outside Smolensk. Panzer and motorised divisions were neither structurally suited nor indeed practised in defence. They were manoeuvre units and bled vital machines and specially trained men until the mass of the marching infantry battalions could close up in forced marches. Panzers delivered the pockets; the infantry were configured to systematically demolish them, and this at considerable cost. Interestingly, veteran accounts of the fast-moving opening stage of 'Barbarossa' refer more to desperate holding actions than to a war of movement. Unceasing grind exacted a psychological toll.

'Believe me, dearest, when you see me again, you will face quite a different person,' confided Karl Fuchs to his wife, 'a person who has learned the harsh command: I will survive!' Panzer crews and infantry alike were astonished at the ferocity and staying power of Russian resistance even at this early stage in the new war. When the panzer spearheads closed in on Smolensk five weeks into the campaign, Russians were still holding out at Brest-Litovsk on the River Bug at the invasion start point. During the first twenty-four hours storming Brest, the German 45th Infantry Division lost two-thirds of the number of men it had lost in the entire six-week French campaign. 'You can't afford to be soft in war; otherwise you die,' emphasised Karl Fuchs. 'No, you must be tough – indeed, you have to be pitiless and relentless. Don't I sound like a different person to you? Deep down in my heart, I remain a good person and my love for you and our son will never diminish: Never!'

Fuchs's panzer regiment had fought its way down the Ostrov road in western Russia at the outset of the campaign. Fluttering by the roadside amid the debris of war was Russian tank crewman Alexander Golikow's last letter to his wife.

I can see the road, green trees and colourful flowers in the garden through the holes in the tank. Life after the war will be just as

colourful as these flowers and happy . . . I am not afraid to lay down
my life for this . . . do not cry. You will likely not be able to visit my
grave. Will there indeed be a grave?

Nobody would know; the only certainty is that the letter was retrieved
by German soldiers searching the shell-scarred tank hulk.

Geography and mass made up the third surprise that inhibited the
effectiveness of *Blitzkrieg*. In relative terms the four *Panzergruppen*
followed by their supporting marching infantry represented arrow
shots into empty space. The 1,200km-wide new front expanded to
1,600km as the Ostheer approached Moscow, the objective 1,000km
in depth. It is calculated that 280 divisions would be required to man a
continuous tenuous front across these distances, and the Germans
invaded with 127. The logistic effort was stymied by the inability of
the Wehrmacht supply system to support effectively beyond its 500km
sustainable rail and lorry reach.

Russian tank training establishments and armour schools were
evacuated to the interior, utilising the immense depth of the Soviet
Union. Vasili Bryukhov trained at the Stalingrad Armour Academy.
'Deep in the heartland of Russia,' he remembered, 'we didn't feel the
tragedy of the retreats and defeats of 1941. We were quite far from the
front.' With the advantage of geography and the limitations of German
strength, 'we started to realise,' he explained, 'that the war would last
for a long time.'

As the panzer advance was resumed beyond Smolensk, Leningrad in
the north was reached in August and encircled the following month. At
the same time an unprecedented drama unfolded in the south around
Kiev. Hitler confounded the Russians, who believed Moscow was the
next objective, by swinging Guderian's Army Group Centre *Panzergruppe* south, while directing the southern *Panzergruppe* under von
Kleist northwards. The battles around Kiev netted five Soviet armies,
fifty divisions, the size of Army Group Centre when the campaign
began. It represented the pinnacle of *Blitzkrieg* success, history's largest
battle of annihilation, replicating Hannibal's Cannae victory of 216 BC.
The Russians could not see it coming because of the unprecedented
distances involved. The pocket formed between Kiev, Kremenchug
and Trubchevsk in southern Russia was an area of 135,000 square

kilometres. Inside were between half and three-quarters of a million Russian soldiers.

Contemporary German soldier accounts refer to horizon after horizon of cornfields and sunflowers. Orientation in Russia was as difficult as the desert. 'The landscape here is bleak and desolate,' wrote Fuchs. 'If we weren't here to fight and were only here to live – I mean exist here – we would become imbeciles.' Otto Carius was likewise depressed: 'Our orders were: move on and on again, day and night, around the clock. The impossible was demanded of drivers. Soon even I was sitting in the driver's seat in order to relieve our exhausted comrade for a few hours'.

During the smooth period of the advance Carius recalled: 'We scarcely noticed how dog-tired the exertions of the march had made us.' There was a cumulative toll. 'Only when we halted, did we drop where we stood and sleep like dead men.'

Fuchs, like many German soldiers, was accustomed to short campaigns and returning to the comparative luxury of their barracks. He hated the filth. 'If I only had some water to wash myself!' he wrote. 'The dirt and the dust cause my skin to itch and my beard is growing longer and longer. Wouldn't you like to kiss me now!' he asked his wife. 'I'm sure you can see the dirt on the paper on which I write.' Over a month later he complained, 'We have bedded down at night without a roof over us, and for the time being we are holed up in tents.' They were homesick. 'We have forgotten what a house and a nicely furnished room looks like.' Russia, unlike the developed infrastructure of France, offered little respite from physical discomfort, whether at the front or not. Fuchs and his crew complained, 'No matter where you look, there is nothing but dirty, filthy blockhouses.' Peasant squalor added to the inherent belief in racial superiority already beginning to permeate this grim campaign. 'You can't find a trace of culture anywhere,' moaned Fuchs.

Carius, riding outside his panzer, irritably exclaimed, 'If only there hadn't been that unbearable dust!'

We wrapped cloth around our noses and mouths in order to breathe through the clouds of dust which hung over the roads. We had long since dropped the vision blocks in the armour so we could at least see something. Like flour, the fine dust penetrated everything. Our clothes, drenched in sweat, clung to our bodies, and a thick coating of dust covered us from head to toe.

And so it continued. Constantly rationalising that the damage they were inflicting dwarfed the casualties they were sustaining, the *Ostheer* swept eastward. They were convinced the next victory would be the one that finally collapsed the Soviet edifice.

The primary factor leading to the failure of *Blitzkrieg* was identified by the commander of the 18th Panzer Division as early as July. He warned that the heavy casualties of men and equipment should not be allowed to continue *wenn wir uns nicht totsiegen wollen* – 'unless we want to "victor" ourselves to death'. Only twelve tanks remained of his original complement of 212. They re-equipped in August only to lose all the replacements again by November. 'This is no longer the old division,' its chaplain lamented. 'All around are new faces. When one asks after somebody, the same reply is always given: dead or wounded.'

'It happened like greased lightning,' recalled Otto Carius, who had to bail out for the first time on 8 July. 'A hit against our tank, a metallic crack, the scream of a comrade, and that was all there was!' The initial daze and shock of the impact cleared with the noxious smell of scorched metal. A large piece of armoured plating had been holed next to radio operator's seat and had torn part of his left arm away. 'No one had to tell us to get out,' Carius recalled, and as he ran he checked over his own body. 'We cursed the brittle and inelastic Czech steel that gave the Russian 47mm anti-tank gun so little trouble.'

A diary entry from an officer in Fuchs's division early the following year complained that 'since 22 June thirty-four officers from the panzer regiment have been killed'. The arrival of snow on the Eastern Front accentuated the sense of foreboding now permeating the *Ostheer*. *Blitzkrieg* became subject to the vagaries of the weather, and momentum again squelched to a halt amid the mud of the autumn rains and the first snow. The last intact Russian field armies standing in the way of Army Group Centre were surrounded and annihilated at Bryansk and Vyazma in October and final victory was trumpeted by the German press, but German losses made it a pyrrhic victory.

Troops and equipments were worn out. The 18th Panzer Division had to form columns of horse-drawn *Panje-wagons* for logistic support as early as September. At the end of October the 6th Panzer Division reported average driving mileages of between 11,500 and 12,500km for its heavy and light tanks. Cannibalisation of spare parts was all that kept its Czech 35ts going. 'This means,' read the report, 'that after the retrieval of the panzers that are scattered around the terrain, a maximum of ten can actually be fixed out of the forty-one reported needing repair.' One month later there were no Czech tanks or Panzer Mark IVs left in the regiment.

Heavy casualties meant that fewer survivors stood more guards for longer, creating a vicious circle of sleep deprivation for soldiers already worn out by long road moves and combat. Living conditions worsened in the bitter weather. Food was insufficient, and the men, weakened by the rigours of the summer campaign, were easily susceptible to frost-bite. The 18th Panzer Division lost more men from frost-bite in November than from enemy action. Yet still the *Ostheer* struggled towards Moscow. Even the ever-optimistic Karl Fuchs admitted to his wife:

> We've received orders to move on in a few days and again the direction is further away from home. I guess this means that our dream of coming home at Christmas is over. Therefore you at home must pull together even more and be brave.'

'The cold was a problem with our panzers,' recalled Leutnant Rolf Hertenstein of Panzer Regiment 4; 'how do you keep them running?' There was anti-freeze but insufficient. Engine compartments were covered in canvas, straw 'or whatever we had'. The only way to keep the engines running was to operate them over four hours and power up the batteries. This went on day and night and was so wasteful in fuel that it was decided to place little catalytic stoves in the engine compartments. Hertenstein's crew positioned six for the night and still it took twenty-four hours to get started. Blasting tank scrapes into the rock-hard ground with explosives to get out of the wind also failed. One morning they found their tracks frozen rigid into the mud. Crews had to de-link the tracks, drive the tank off, and then use blow torches to melt the tracks from the ground's icy grip. 'If the Russians had attacked us that day, we would have been defenceless,' Hertenstein recalled. 'Fortunately they didn't.'

'We were issued some heavy greatcoats for the winter, but it was still not enough,' complained Hertenstein. 'We didn't even have any winter footwear.' His unit was with Army Group South and was often able to purloin houses for shelter. 'We went outside as little as possible, only when absolutely necessary.' Their tanks occupied hides behind the line, bulldozed inside houses and barns, providing 'fire brigade' support forward. 'I feel sorry just thinking about our infantry-men outside in their fox-holes. How they survived is beyond me,' he admitted. All the panzer crews felt the same. 'One look at the infantry,' declared a 20th Panzer Division crewman, 'was enough to change our minds if we ever felt compelled to complain.' Observing the shadowy figures shambling past their tanks in grey white-out blizzard conditions with temperatures of around -20°C by day and plummeting to -35°C at night filled them with helpless compassion.

Fighting tanks during the final desperate probes towards Moscow in early December were, because of the weather, exhaustion and worn-out equipment, small-scale efforts. Gone were the panzer vanguards of the previous summer, advancing in multiple columns of hundreds of vehicles. They were replaced by small combat teams of half a dozen tanks and accompanying infantry with anti-tank guns probing the forest belts around Moscow.

Tank actions were chaotic, deadly, fog-shrouded occurrences. Freezing conditions dulled reactions that needed to be at their sharpest for survival. 'There could be as much as two centimetres of frost inside the turret,' recalled Ludwig Bauer of Panzer Regiment 33. A particular problem was un-jamming shell cases stuck in the breech by ice. They had to be warmed up by mini blowtorches which operated like powerful cigarette lighters – 'a dangerous practice,' Bauer conceded. Cold and ice reduced the operational pace to a laborious slow-motion tempo. Any administrative task such as refuelling and maintenance, every routine action, took twice the normal effort to carry out in the stultifying cold.

'Today our boy is five months old,' wrote the homesick Karl Fuchs to his wife on 11 November. 'I suppose that is a birthday of sorts.'

He referred to his son's baptism, which needed to be organised, and local news. 'Our former residence advisors in Würzburg,' near where he taught before the war, 'Adam Hoos and Gerg Unkelhäuser, were killed in battle,' he reported. This must have upset him, because he added, 'I think a lot of them these days.' Karl was clinging to his emotional equilibrium: 'I love you for ever,' he wrote, 'you alone and Horsti', his little son. Sanguine as ever he wrote to his mother the following day, 'We know no fear. The cold is going to be a factor, but we shall endure that too. One of these days,' he concluded, 'we will meet again and no one is looking forward to this more than I.'

Karl wrote frequently and eloquently to his wife and parents, averaging a letter a week despite operations and more when combat conditions allowed. Then there was a gap of over two months before Mädi Fuchs received a letter from Leutnant Reinhardt, Karl's company commander. 'I have the sad duty to inform you,' he wrote, 'that your husband was killed on the field of battle on 21 November 1941.'

The day before, the 7th Panzer Division driving to encircle Moscow from the north cut the main Moscow–Kalinin road. Having outrun the rest of the division, the panzers came up against superior T-34 tanks for the first time and fought an unequal and bitter skirmish. Karl Fuchs's burned-out 38t tank, with its distinctively bent barrel showing evidence of flank damage, was photographed by the roadside near the village of Syrapkoje 26km west of Klin, surrounded by a forlorn group of figures, their hands thrust deep in greatcoat pockets as they dismally survey the wreckage. His crewmate Gefreiter Leon Schiller was buried alongside him. A snapshot of the graves with simple birch crosses and a frost-encrusted helmet placed between them was sent to his family. Karl never managed to hold his five-month-old son.

Fifteen days later the Russians launched a counter-offensive with eight tank brigades, fifteen rifle divisions and three cavalry divisions, transferred from the Far East. The Germans, unaware that these fresh forces had arrived *in situ*, were driven back 100km. The first phase of the Soviet counter-offensive cleared the Germans before Moscow, but the second did not succeed in destroying the *Ostheer*. Soviet operational inexperience resulted in some reverses before a tortuous yet continuous German front was shored up by April 1942. Army Group Centre had lost its offensive capability.

## CRUCIBLE OF EXPERIENCE - MACHINES AND MEN

Out of the maelstrom of experience from the Russian front came changes that would reshape the nature of tank forces and the men that manned them. Tank warfare was evolving into a technological slogging match between tank and gun and was also inevitably bound up in the dilemma of having to reconcile quality with mass production.

The tank changed shape as a result of these lessons. A bigger gun was needed, plus a greater turret to house it and thicker armour to protect it against more effective guns. All these improvements had to fit in larger hulls with more powerful engines to propel them and wider tracks to provide the mobility such heavy vehicles needed to cross soft and undulating ground. Both the German eastern and British desert experience convinced them of the need for sufficient space to fight a trio of commander, gunner and loader in the turret supported by a driver and radio operator in the hull below. A technical arms race began once the Germans appreciated that the Russian models, derisively assumed to be primitive, were in fact better than their own. Leutnant Helmut Ritgen of the 6th Panzer Division recalled the impact of meeting the previously unknown KV-1 and T-34 in combat:

That day changed the character of tank warfare, as the KV represented a wholly new level of armament, armour protection and weight. German tanks had hitherto been intended mainly to fight enemy infantry and their supporting arms. From now on the main threat was the enemy tank itself, and the need to 'kill' it at as great a range as possible led to the design of longer-barrelled guns of larger calibre.

The T-34 was the most influential tank design of the Second World War. Its revolutionary design gave it a gun, armour and mobility superior to any known medium tank at that time, it had sloping armour 32mm thick, a compact powerful diesel engine less capricious than its petrol predecessors and a turret cast in one piece rather than cold rolled steel.

In January 1940 a prototype T-34, mounting a 76.2mm gun, drove all the way from Kharkov in the eastern Ukraine to Moscow for a demonstration to the leadership at the Kremlin. It then motored on to Finland to demonstrate its firepower against captured Finnish bunkers. Another punishing return drive to Kharkov via Minsk and Kiev underlined its impressive mechanical reliability. It was accepted.

One interesting consequence of the 1939 Russo–German Non-Aggression Pact was the presentation of a Panzer Mark III to the Russians. The German Liaison Officer in Moscow assured his hosts it represented the pinnacle of the German armoured inventory. It was immediately dispatched to the GABTU Russian tank-proving grounds at Kubinka for evaluation and found to be inferior in firepower, armour and mobility. The investigation report derided it as 'a pretty toy, over-engineered and needlessly comfortable for the crew'.

Internal wrangling with the military resulted in production delays, and only 115 of 600 planned T-34 tanks were produced in 1940. During the following spring a torsion bar system was introduced to upgrade the Christie suspension, a longer and better 76.2mm gun was fitted and the frontal armour was strengthened to 60mm. Increased space in the turret and hull created better fighting conditions for the crew. By the time the Germans invaded, just under a thousand T-34s had been delivered.

The T-34's sloping armour meant that only 75mm rounds could get through. It was easier for drivers to get out from beneath the massive hatch at the front of the hull. Powerful engines increased mobility, and the diesel fuel appeared less susceptible to flame when hit.

The problem with the T-34 was that until just days before the invasion few crews had even seen it. Most of the early fighting was not tank against tank but infantry anti-tank versus these inexperienced Russian crews. Tank gunners were especially poor, armoured units performed badly, tanks were not effectively recovered, and there were production defects and a lack of spare parts. Reconnaissance was also poor, and all too often tanks were caught and bombed on flat rail cars before they even got to the front. The 32nd Tank Division, fighting near Lvov in the first month of war, lost thirty-seven out of forty-nine KV-1s and 146 out of 173 T-34s, with 103 dead and 259 wounded.

Still, Leutnant Rolf Hertenstein of the 13th Panzer Division was pessimistic about the Panzer III's inferiority. 'For us to have any chance at all against a T-34, we had to get as close as about 200 yards' while they could be knocked out from 1,000. 'For the first time during the campaign in the east,' declared Freiherr von Langermann in a 4th Panzer Division report, 'the absolute superiority of the Russian 26-ton and 52-ton tanks was felt over our Panzer III and IV.' Incoming rounds were delivered from 1,000 metres with 'high accuracy and enormous penetration energy'. Wide tracks conferred greater mobility and von Langermann praised the 'exceptional' diesel motor, recalling twenty panzers broken down on the road between Glnebow to Minsk during the advance but not a single Russian engine failure during retreat. Otto Carius, by now a panzer commander in Panzer Regiment 21, admitted that 'the feeling of being practically defenceless got to us'. There was a general realisation that something had to be done; otherwise 'the previous aggression and spirit of our panzer crews will be weakened and lost due to a feeling of inferiority,' warned von Langermann. 'Fortunately,' Carius observed, 'the first 75mm long-barrelled Mark IVs and the more heavily armoured 50mm long-barrelled Mark IIIs started to arrive in small quantities from the home front. That was the silver lining on the horizon, a lining which so often allowed our hopes to be revived in Russia.'

The German infantry felt totally naked:

Use your rifle? You might as well turn round and fart at [the tank]. Besides, it never comes into your head to shoot; you just have to stay still as a mouse, or you'll yell with terror. You won't stir your little finger, for fear of annoying it. Then you tell yourself you may be lucky, perhaps it hasn't spotted you, perhaps its attention has turned to something else. But on the other hand perhaps your luck's right out and the thing is coming straight for you, till you lose sight and hearing in your hole. That's when you need nerves like steel wire, I can tell you. I saw Hansmann of the Ninth get under the tracks of a T-34, and he hadn't dug his hole deep enough; he had been too bloody tired to shovel. The tank just turned a bit off its course, and that skidded just enough of the ground away. It had him. The next minute there he was, flattened out like a bit of dog-shit you accidently put your foot in.

There was one other hope – a new German technical response. In early 1941 the Army Office commissioned experts from Henschel, Daimler-Benz, Porsche AG and MAN to construct a 30-ton tank with a minimum 75mm gun. The *Heereswaffenamt*, the German Army Weapons Staff, was in effect raising a 'monster' specification, half as heavy again as the heaviest current German tank, the Mark IV. Two companies, Porsche and Henschel, were eventually commissioned to complete and produce competing prototypes in time for Hitler's fifty-third birthday in April 1942. It was a tall order – eleven months from drawing-board to prototype – that would have knock-on technological implications. British and Allied designers were averaging six years to achieve the same.

Hitler immediately issued add-on requirements. The new tank should have 100mm of frontal armour with 60mm on the side and be able to withstand a hit from any known Allied tank. Further, it was to mount an 88mm gun. Henschel had virtually to redesign its prototype, then undergoing trials. Porsche ordered a Krupp turret able to accommodate such a gun, the first to be fitted with a double-action muzzle break, reducing turret fumes. Henschel fitted the gun by widening the upper hull to extend over the tracks.

This was a match of competing design personalities. Professor Porsche, the colourful and genial inventor and Volkswagen designer, held an intrinsic advantage in that he knew Hitler, who enjoyed his company. The bald, bespectacled Dr Erwin Aders, by contrast, was a serious man with a bookish temperament and a pedantic exactness. Porsche worked with an energy bordering on excessive, constantly proposing novel and interesting solutions to the technical conundrum they had been set.

As the projects came to fruition, fitters, foremen and engineers went without sleep. Aders strove for systematic precision, Porsche for creative and ever more exacting ideas from pressed staffs.

The designers mortgaged the future to achieve the short-term fix. As Aders later admitted, 'To have geared up for mass production such as the Americans, as well as the Russians, appeared to be pursuing, would have meant recommending a revision of production plans which, instead of the actual nine months, would have required about twenty-four to thirty months.' The newly designated future Panzer

Mark VI was to be handmade rather than production-line produced. Every imaginable short-cut was taken. Dr Aders did not even personally check and sign every blueprint.

Both prototypes were loaded aboard specially constructed flat rail cars and transported to the Headquarters at Rastenburg in East Prussia for Hitler's birthday celebration. Snags arising from short-cuts taken during the blueprint race began to emerge. Porsche's prototype was unable to turn through 90 degrees and had to be assisted by the crane to do so, before recurring fires in the engine compartment cut short its debut. Henschel's version exhibited teething problems but was clearly the superior of the two. Reichsminister Albert Speer formed a panel that selected the Henschel version.

Unusually the Germans gave the new tank a name – *Tiger*, for its menacing appearance. It was huge, ten times the size of Germany's first tank and as high as but one third wider than the largest Allied tank, the US Grant. The revolutionary system of interlocking road wheels spread its 57-ton weight. The 88mm gun fired a shell with a case the size of a thin golf-bag (the Panzer I main armament fired a candle-size round).

The Tiger became, for the Allies, the most feared member of the German arsenal. Its feral counterpart the *Panther* was to follow, featuring sloped armour, a superior power pack to drive it and a devastating 75mm long-barrelled gun. The evolution of these machines now impacted upon the tank men required to fight them in a rapidly evolving technical environment. The Germans, having demonstrated in earlier campaigns that technical shortcomings can be compensated for by crew excellence, now sought technical solutions because their reserve of maturely trained crews was fast dwindling.

Trained officers and NCOs, not easily replaced, made up one third of the thirty-eight dead of Panzer Regiment 5 in Poland. Eighty per cent of that killed in 1941 were junior officers and NCOs. In Russia after four months of fighting the *Ostheer* had lost one third of its leadership.

*Auftragstaktik,* or 'mission command tactics', lay at the core of German *Blitzkrieg* success. It was a flexible system of command whereby the commander was given a mission. *How* the mission was achieved was dependent on the commander's initiative. He was not – unlike the British and Russians – prescriptively told in orders how to do it. But this initiative could only be exercised with training and experience, and this was bleeding away. By the end of 1941 there were few reserves. Commanders were reluctant to allow platoon commanders to take risks as they were less able to be saved if it went wrong. Less risk-taking denied tactical flexibility. Close co-ordination between panzers, infantry, air and artillery was dependent on specialists who made it work, and many were dead. German experience, which took three years on average to replace, was losing ground relative to Russian learning capacity. As the strategic situation worsened, Hitler's reaction was to start looking at technology rather than men for solutions. But Tigers and Panthers are manned by men.

Both sides appreciated that survival chances increased in proportion to the ability of the crew to work together. 'Tank commanders,' panzer gunner Ludwig Bauer recalled, 'could personally choose who they were prepared to work with.' This was an equitable practice that suited everyone.

Russians too realised that experience was the key to survival. Tank commander Vladimir Alexeev recalled, 'When we were retreating during the initial stages of the war, we had peacetime-trained soldiers, but they were all killed in the initial battles.' Not until later 'after Moscow, Stalingrad and Kursk did people become more skilful and professional on operations'. The Germans, he acknowledged, were more experienced. 'Even the commanders did not have sufficient experience to conduct combined operations,' he emphasised 'and this caused heavy losses. The Germans were very quick to call air support down.'

Bauer of Panzer Regiment 33 pointed out, 'We were always short of good veteran officers because so many had fallen.' Promotions could only occur when there was a vacancy, for example for a company commander. These were *frei-geschossen* or, literally as Bauer ironically observed, 'shot-free'. A regular officer was promoted every six months if he was suitable – and if he survived, as was the case with reserve officers. Panzer officers became younger and younger as casualties thinned their ranks. 'The best NCOs were ex-Reichswehr,' Bauer commented, 'they were always more correct and knew the form.' They assisted young officers but were becoming increasingly scarce.

Newly promoted Leutnant Otto Carius fluffed his first action. Half the crews of his four tanks were absent from their vehicles eating when a sudden Russian attack developed. Carius panicked, climbed into his driver's seat and reversed the tank out of the wood they were defending. His other tanks immediately followed, thinking his radio had failed and the infantry and a solitary anti-tank gun were abandoned to fight off the Russian assault. He was confronted by the anti-tank commander when he sheepishly returned. 'Man, what a bunch of heroes!' he declared. 'If that's all you can handle, then you'd be better off not even coming to the front!' Carius was crestfallen. 'I stood there with my tail between my legs.' He never forgot the experience. Veterans remark that a gradual baptism of fire is always preferable to a disaster in the formative days in order to develop later resilience. 'That experience still weighed heavily on my mind for many days afterwards,' he remembered. 'How easy it is to make such a hasty decision; how badly it could have ended!' This highlights the importance of nurturing future experience and gives some indication what the crucible of the Russian front exposure meant for the tank men.

The spring thaw of 1942 coincided with a fresh Russian tank-led offensive to recapture Kharkov and disrupt a potential German summer offensive. Fourteen of Russia's twenty tank brigades cracked open the German line between 12 to 17 May and penetrated 30km. Von Kleist's 1st Panzer Army sealed off the penetration, took 250,000 prisoners and destroyed virtually all the Soviet armour. Denuded of 75 per cent of his armoured potential, Stalin could do little to oppose 'Operation Blau', the German summer offensive that crashed into southern Russia. Stalin mistakenly placed reserves around Moscow to the north, the anticipated objective. The Russians were totally unprepared to resist General Hoth's 4th Panzer Army drive on Stalingrad, spearheading General von Paulus's 6th Army Group. Distance and the sheer scale of the advance created problems when the panzers outran over-stretched supply lines. German forces were unnecessarily sucked into street fighting at Stalingrad on the River Volga, while von Kleist, denuded of resources for the drive into the Caucasus, became stranded hundreds of miles apart in a huge salient, without reaching the oilfields.

Throughout the autumn of 1942 the Russians built up their resources, feeding in just enough reinforcements at Stalingrad and the Caucasus to prevent any decisive German breakthrough. On 19

November, yet another surprise winter counter-offensive destroyed forces holding the line north and south of Stalingrad. Within days von Paulus's entire 6th Army was encircled, along with elements of the 4th Panzer Army. It surrendered in February 1943, its siege barely providing time enough for von Kleist's stranded forces to get out of the Caucasus.

It appeared that the final lesson to be derived from the Russian 'crucible' was that the Germans dominated the summer operations but the winter belonged to the Soviets.

Leutnant Otto Carius rode in the passenger car behind the steam locomotive hauling lines of massive, tarpaulin-covered flat wagons behind. It was summer 1943. They were heading east. 'Occasionally, we looked at the monsters hidden under the tarpaulins with something approaching love,' he recalled. 'At least we could do something with these! The Tiger was the heavyweight of our fighting vehicles,' he declared.

Germany had previously relied on her tank men. Hitler now looked to his new machines.

# 10

## DESERT COMEBACK

### NEW MEN

'Gippos were not the British Army's best friends!' declared Eric Allsop, a young officer recently posted to the 8th Royal Tank Regiment. He was hinting at the ambivalent nature of their relationship with their Egyptian 'hosts'. Reinforcements were streaming into theatre, and Cairo and Alexandria were teeming with an expatriate population of British men and some women, aged on average under thirty. As Allsop explained: 'All men's sexual instincts are aroused when he is in danger, so he was going to have a woman before he was killed.'

'As a single young man I never gave post-war life a thought, living from one day to another or, at most, to the next leave,' declared Trooper 'Butch' Williams, the Matilda driver who had survived *Blitzkrieg* in France. There was a popular leave routine in Cairo. Rides in horse-drawn gharries; a visit to eat rich cakes at Groppi's or another emporium; trips to see some of the hundreds of Cairo's ancient monuments such as the Pyramids or the Citadel, followed by a visit to an open-air night-club to watch non-stop live performances by belly-dancers. Trooper Bright of 51 RTR climbed on top of one of the Pyramids. 'We were told to watch it as two Australian soldiers had fallen to their deaths just a week before.' British soldiers carved their initials at the top, just as Napoleon's Grenadiers had done a century before. Bright's crew got a week's leave in Alexandria. 'It was quite lively there. A few of us went in the Hole in the Wall dive. We all had a few and we felt like bashing a few wogs,' he reminisced.

The antics of soldiers on leave in Cairo are less understood in the socially cushioned conditions the young enjoy today, but at the time there was general recognition that war marked men. Tank troop commander Keith Douglas of the Nottingham Sherwood Foresters said of his squadron second-in-command: 'Someone who knew him before – which I did not – said that he went away a charming and entertaining young man, and returned a hardened and embittered soldier.'

Leave for Germans in Tripoli was not so exciting, but to men who had only seen towns and villages in Germany, it was still an adventure, Oberleutnant Harald Kuhn of Panzer Regiment 5 recalled a new rest camp set up near Marsa Luch. Its location had less to do with idyllic surroundings than with its strategic positioning for 'fire-brigade' operations at Sollum or Tobruk.

> True, it meant we always had to be at readiness, but despite that we had a few weeks to escape the interminable monotony of the endless grey desert and see the green of a few palms and the changing colours of the sea – and were able at any time to dive in!

German soldiers did not approach the fairer sex with the total gay abandon exhibited by their British counterparts. 'More than anything else,' explained Panzar driver Armin Böttger, 'the young recruits and soldiers had no experience, as a rule, in areas of sexual activity. Without a doubt the more mature men who had slept with women were way ahead.' They had departed school without their parents explaining anything. 'Now we wanted to hear something, and in fact daily, about the "top topic" and gather experience.' As a consequence 'We hung on their words, if they explained anything about relationships with women, and the practicalities of any sexual experience.' At the same time 'We had an awful fear of the shame and risk of infection, because that meant twenty-one days under arrest, which had an especially shocking impact.'

Sex-starved British troops coming in from the desert transformed Cairo's oldest profession into a major service industry, focused on the run-down quarter of Clot Bay, just north of Ezbekieh Gardens. Cairo 'was vivid, loud and garish, which was just what the troops wanted when returning from the desert,' remembered Peter Roach of 1 RTR.

' "Give Us The Tools And We Will Finish The Job!" ' was the cheeky sign one Cairo brothel owner erected, mimicking Churchill's famous 1942 appeal to the United States.' The Cairo area medical report gloomily noted in the first quarter of 1941 that 'the increase in VD in March coincides with the return of the 7th Armoured from Cyrenaica'. Life for the tank men was likely to be short. Every opportunity was taken to make it sweet.

The new desert army composed its own vocabulary, which was a mixture of many tongues including Arabic, to express its unique circumstances. It also had its own distinctive and scruffy mixture of civilian and military dress. 'The Scruff' was the Desert Air Force, so called for allegedly being even more dirty and unkempt than the army. 'Jerrycans' were the superior pressed-steel containers that 'Jerry' used for fuel and water. The British used 'flimsies', which were fragile and leaked 30 to 40 per cent of their contents, but which provided an efficient and safe method of cooking and 'brewing'. The 'Benghazi Stakes' or 'Handicap' referred to the annual advance to and – until the winter of 1942 – retreat from Benghazi. There was the 'Debollicker' anti-personnel mine, which described the damage it inflicted at waist height. 'Fart-arsing around' or 'swanning about the Blue' was the practice of moving around the desert landscape without knowing where one was. 'Bint' was Arabic for girl, an expression that still survives, while a 'Burka' was a brothel, taken from Sharia el Burka, a Cairo street. The 'Blue' was the name given to the desert and the 'Blue Train' was the transport that ran from 'Alex' (Alexandria) to the desert, eventually reaching as far as Tobruk. It was rumoured there were more hangovers on this train than anywhere else on earth.

Egyptians were 'Wogs' or 'Ahmeds', which for the uninitiated stood for 'Wily Oriental Gentlemen', but actually was a relic of Empire and Lord Cromer's day referring to the clerical 'effendi' class 'Working On Government Service'. 'Ahmed' was the name they were all called.

The peculiar physical conditions of the desert affected the fighting men in different ways. Heat afflicted them all. It was 'incredible, incredible', recalled Paul Rollins of 40 RTR:

I mean the sweat comes through your shirt, it dries. You have a drink of tea and that comes out again. You wear the same shirt and it gets dust on it with the sweat. It sticks on your face, the dust's on your face, you're covered in dust, and there's nothing to wash with.

The Italians hated the desert and appeared to try and civilise it, building stone houses in their camps and laying out paths and little gardens. The Romanesque Arco dei Fileni on the Libyan–Tripoli border, a grand triumphal arch passed through by both sides during the see-saw desert phase, seemed to encapsulate the futility of the attempt. The Germans, with their stores full of foot powders, eye lotions, insect repellents, mouthwashes and disinfectants, appeared to try and regulate the desert by science.

British soldiers coped, pragmatic as ever. 'I used to have a chameleon in my tent,' confided the resourceful Trooper Bright of 51 RTR. 'I used to have it on my head when I walked around, to keep the flies away.'

One loved or loathed the desert. Major A.E. Flatow of 45 RTR found he was 'always stirred by the vastness of it – the endless miles of stones and sand unrelieved by any life apart from the odd lizard'. There were exquisite sunsets, 'quite breathtaking' and brilliantly lit moonscapes by night.

It was as much a crucible of experience for British tank men as Russia was for the panzers. They were perceptibly changing from the army of 1940. 'Many senior officers were soft,' declared Lieutenant Eric Allsop of 8 RTR, 'until Monty sorted them out.' This comment marked the insidious transition under way. Surviving was a factor of experience matched with professional capability. New arrivals were less prepared to put up with hierarchical tribal regimental norms if it remotely affected their survival chances. The best of the old blended with a more uncompromising and realistic new. Public-school officer attitudes became diluted through casualties by the arrival of intelligent and focused ex-grammar school boys with a different approach. Men in their twenties arrived, capable personalities, who but for the accident of war would have followed successful civilian careers. They were keen and took to fighting and, as Allsop commented, 'were prepared to wipe out any Germans they confronted so they could get back to civilian life'. They were taken in hand by the 'old sweats', Senior NCOs and Warrant Officers, who were 'first class', Allsop judged.

Personal effectiveness became more important than the outward trappings of rank and tradition in a Darwinian winnowing whereby the incompetent were blown away by casualties, leaving the fittest standing.

New arrivals in theatre soon appreciated that their preparation in England had not qualified them for what was required in the desert. 'I was very green and I wasn't really trained,' admitted Eric Allsop, recalling his arrival in 8 RTR. 'I did not know the difference between a Panzer Mark III and a Mark IV.' 'The training I had was all free of the menace of battle because the men teaching us hadn't seen it either,' he said. Training was elementary and much more might have been done, 'as we had had an armoured division out in the desert even before the war'. Allsop keenly observed his squadron commander, whose Military Cross and bar was reassuring. A single glance around the Mess was incentive enough. 'There were a lot of chaps burned and put together by doctors,' he saw. Like many of the new tank men he 'felt naked before his first shot in anger and it would be dishonest to say otherwise'.

Sergeant-Major Bill Close was commissioned a lieutenant in his parent battalion 3 RTR. Experience worked to his advantage. 'I was received very well by all the other officers,' he recalled, 'who were mainly commissioned people and from public schools.' He had twice survived the destruction of his battalion and knew what he was talking about. The Panzerwaffe similarly focused on combat experience painfully evolved through three campaigns. Oberst Müller, the new commander of Panzer Regiment 5, arrived without much of his lower arm, lost in Poland. Dr Selmayr, the new medical officer, was immediately subjected to a no-nonsense preliminary interview by his commanding officer Oberstleutnant Stephan. It started with 'Take off your sunglasses, I want to look at your eyes – and now tell me about your life.'

Turret life was a social leveller. Traditional cavalry and the mechanised orientated Tank Regiment elements learned to co-exist. Despite class divides ex-public school merged with ex-grammar school, and selected sergeants appeared in commissioned guise in the Officer's Mess, a development that became more pronounced as the war progressed. 'It's quite democratic in any army, isn't it?' commented tank commander Paul Rollins of 40 RTR on the ease with which tank crews could be rotated. 'If you're not happy, or I wasn't happy, I could get rid of them and get a replacement, and the same applies to the crew. If the driver didn't like it he could ask for a transfer out, because you have to rely on each other. And that was a very sensible thing, that was.' The end product was priceless in combat and human bonding terms and prolonged life. It meant much to those who experienced this peculiar brand of comradeship. 'I know the names of my tank crew to this day,' declared eighty-six-year-old Eric Allsop, 'I forget a lot else!'

The final stage of evolution from cavalry public-school old to grammar-school new Tank Corps was the final blending of Territorial with Regular, which took longer and could be more painful. Training Major A. Flatow of the 45th Territorial Army (Leeds Rifles) Royal Tank Regiment recalled that 'the regiment in which I had served since 1937 was to be broken up and the officers and men sent as reinforcements to various field units'. Many of the officers had to even drop a rank. 'But I will not labour the point: there the fact was,' he resignedly wrote later, 'the three regiments of the brigade were split up and that was all there was to it.'

### NEW MACHINES

The new British tank men urgently needed a new fighting machine. Lieutenant Stuart Hamilton was derisive about the recent low-silhouette Valentine tank. It had three and a half inches of armour but was 'unfortunately armed with a piddling little 2-pounder pop-gun and Besa machine-gun'. British tank crews had already realised it was 'bloody useless' against the 50mm long-barrelled Panzer Mark III and the powerful 75mm Mark IV long barrel. So fearsome was the latter that German crews veiled the barrel silhouette by driving with it fully depressed on the front deck in order to coax the British out to engage.

British tank crews felt exposed in their vulnerable tanks. Hamilton summed it up as 'really like being a lightweight in the ring with a heavyweight'. German tanks were 10mph faster and had five-man crews against the British three or four.

Feedback from active-service crews rarely reached the tank design workshops. 'Most things were on an off-chance basis,' confessed Bert Foord at Wood Lee. He did recall Major Berkley-Miller, fresh from North Africa, 'full of beans' and totally uncompromising. Foord's mock-up for a new Matilda with thicker armour was roughly re-arranged by Berkeley-Miller, who broke up the wooden seat and tossed it out declaring, 'All I want to sit on is boxes of ammo!' Foord listened. 'He was pretty ruthless and knew what he wanted.' But they were not overwhelmed with new ideas. Mr Symonds, his supervisor, admitted that 'they were in a terrible state with tanks', so much so the original First World War design team was invited back to contribute. This was a desperation measure. There was no systematic blueprint to production process. War Office direction, Foord claimed, was a simplistic 'this is what we want', such as ten rounds in one minute, twenty-four rounds in four, or basic direction on protection.

The desperate need for a more heavily armoured tank was partially met with the 102mm armoured Churchill tank. The Prime Minister imposed an impossible deadline on Vauxhall motors to produce 500 by March 1941. Short-cuts in the nine-month gestation period from design to production led to the delivery of prototypes that resulted in technical nightmares for receiving units. They still mounted the ineffective puny 2-pounder, a stopgap, until the new 6-pounder came into production. The Churchill's spacious hull, hill-climbing ability and solid protection were to endear it to future crews. Six prototypes reached theatre in time for the battle, but one of them was promptly knocked out by uninformed British anti-tank crews in an inauspicious debut. None of the twenty-eight prematurely committed to the catastrophic Dieppe Raid of August 1942 managed to crawl off the pebble beach. Foord wryly remarked that the incensed Winston Churchill 'wanted his name removed after the Dieppe disaster'.

British tank design was in a sorry state compared to the quantum leaps in Germany. 'General Martel [the Director of Armour] used to come down with a party of officers to swarm all over our prototypes,' Foord remembered. Constantly plied with questions, he frequently could only answer, 'No, mister – you can't do that.' British tank design inexorably slipped behind, 'but the pressures did not trickle down as far as me,' Foord admitted. 'We were all pretty well in the dark until after the war.'

His statement could well have applied to the development of the new Allied tank. 'We heard of a very hush-hush tank called a Sherman,' recalled Major Flatow of 45 RTR, when he arrived in theatre in July 1942. 'It was so hush-hush, instead of calling it by its real name we had to refer to it as *Swallow*.' There was hope at last. 'We were warned it was a court-martial offence to call this tank by its real name.' It was also a mystery to Bert Foord's design personnel. 'We didn't know much about US tanks,' he admitted. Then they heard that Jack London, an important importer of caterpillar tractors from America, had taken delivery of a huge packing case, probably at the docks at Woolwich Arsenal. Inside was a Sherman tank named *Michael*.

The Sherman was a derivative of the M3 General Grant. US tank development required approval by Army Ground Forces (AGF) headed by Major-General Lesley McNair, an artilleryman with prodigious administrative skills but no combat experience. McNair subscribed to a 'tank-destroyer' doctrine, totally at variance with mass mobile firepower advocated by panzer theorists. McNair saw tanks as a breakthrough instrument supported by infantry. They were not designed to fight other tanks; that was the tank-destroyer function. These perverse philosophies were to dog American tank excellence from the start and eventually lead to a compromise between mass production and technical quality. A First US Army report would later complain that what was needed was not tank killers but killer tanks.

The US M3 Grant was the first effective tank the British were able to field against the Germans and it caused some consternation. *Feldwebel* Hermann Eckardt recalled that Panzer Regiment 8 lost eighty-six panzers the first time they came up against 'the Pilot', as they called it, because they needed to close to 300 metres to penetrate its armour. Eckardt was knocked out by a Grant, which he and his fellows found a considerable technical shock, running counter to the diet of invincibility they had been fed by propaganda newsreels. 'For the first time, after this experience, I started to believe that the war was not going well,' he admitted. The Grant, however, was an interim solution while its superior M4 successor was evolved. The new Sherman M4 was designed around a large cast turret capable of mounting an M3 75mm tank gun. The first one was completed in February 1942 and production began to roll five months later. President Roosevelt announced a suitably ambitious programme for 45,000 tanks in that year alone. By 11 September 318 Shermans had arrived in Egypt.

'Some Swallows are arriving,' recalled Major Flatow as two squadrons in 45 RTR were warned off to receive the new tanks. Rumours were rife of a large battle approaching, and it was hoped 'they would be an unpleasant surprise for the enemy on *Der Tag*' (The Day). Most of the tanks arrived from the States packed with 'goodies' for the crews: chocolate, boxes of biscuits and notes from American workers stating 'Give 'em Hell' or 'To Hell with Hitler'. 'But as the tanks were first reached in the holds by ordnance and stevedore personnel, all these things were taken by them,' Flatow recalled. 'The poor tank crews got nothing.'

Bill Close of 3 RTR recalled the response of his other tank commanders to the new Shermans. 'It's a bit too bloody big,' said Geordie Reay, 'the panzer gunners and 88s will have a field day.' They were all pleased, however, with the capacity of the new 75mm gun mounted on a fully traversing turret. It could fire both high-explosive and solid shot.

With new tanks and men came a new commander with a different mindset. There would be no more 'fart-arsing' around. 'People were told at Alamein,' recalled Eric Allsop:

> They were to get the idea at last, they were not going to 'swan about' the battlefield in columns. No more fluid this and that, go around the back of them and all that stuff. Monty said we are going to fight in divisions, how we are trained to fight. The tanks were well sited and told, 'You are not going back.' Rommel was very unpleasantly surprised.

Rommel launched his offensive against the newly established Alamein line with four German and six Italian divisions on the evening of 31 August 1942. When the 15th and 21st Panzer Divisions, supported by the Italian Trieste Division, breached the minefields and drove the 7th Armoured Division back, they reached the ridge but were repelled by an unexpected combined-arms mix of tanks and anti-tank guns, supported by artillery and infantry, and, significantly, air attacks. By the evening of 2 September little progress had been made and Rommel's armour was short of fuel. A retreat was ordered the next day. Montgomery chose, contrary to previous practice, not to pursue and hurl his armour on the German anti-tank defences. Instead, heavy air attacks were directed against the retreating Germans.

This was a new experience for the Germans. They were at the very limit of their logistic capability and Rommel characteristically gambled all on a quick attack to pierce the British line before Cairo, before it could coalesce. Dr Alfons Selmayr with the II *Abteilung* Panzer Regiment 5 recalled final assault orders. 'Last conference with the battalion commander – save petrol and ammunition. What good is that in an attack?' Selmayr described what happened after they were rebuffed:

> Now the British air force began to have an effect. We had never experienced anything like it before. Without pause they came over us like squadrons at a Party demonstration and wherever they could see even a few vehicles together they unloaded. My panzer shook at the seams. A Company commander's tank received a direct hit on the turret in front of me. The commander and loader were badly wounded and later died; the gunner and radio operator were seriously injured. And apart from a few bandages I had no more medical equipment.

'This fun,' Selmayr recalled, 'lasted from nine o'clock in the evening until five in the morning.' It marked a particular turning-point, after which panzer crews looked skyward as frequently as they watched out for ground threats – for the remainder of the war. The psychological fear of air attack, which had been unleashed by

*Blitzkrieg* on Germany's enemies, was in future to apply just as much to the Panzerwaffe.

Having failed to break through the Alamein line into Cairo, the onus now shifted on to the Germans to stop the English from breaking out. German logistics were under constant air attack. In September 1942 Rommel requested 9,000 tons of ammunition, 12,000 tons of fuel and 6,000 tons of rations. He received 1,000 tons of ammunition, less than half the petrol and one third of the food. That month alone 22,000 tons of Axis re-supply was sunk crossing the Mediterranean. Mussolini's *mare nostrum* was grimly renamed the 'German swimming pool' by the soldiers.

By contrast, more and more British reinforcements and equipments streamed into Egypt. By 23 October, the date chosen for the opening of the offensive against Rommel, Montgomery commanded 230,000 men and over 1,000 tanks against the Axis 100,000 men and 500 tanks. British air superiority was now about 5:3. A new drive and confidence had been injected into Montgomery's reorganised and re-equipped forces. Trooper T.A. Bright of 51 RTR remembered, 'We were given all the details of the coming battle, which was the first time that everybody had been put in the picture.'

Desert landscape is profoundly disorientating. Ridgelines on the battlefield were barely perceptible, but fought over because they offered a field of view worth fighting for. Distances were deceptive and the terrain appeared at distance to offer absolutely no cover. Martin Penck described this desert fighting as 'a war in landscape totally devoid of cover, in great heat, in a land where no wound healed and where the impact of weapons had a completely different impact from anywhere else'. Nevertheless, he reflected, 'This past year has shown me that one can endure anything if one only has the will.'

Nerves rising in anticipation of the coming battle manifested themselves in different ways. Major Flatow noticed those troops who had never been in battle before were in an excited state, which 'made them sing, laugh at any silly joke and work like stallions'. When it came to the second time, 'the same excitement is noticeable but with it there is grimness'. It lay over them like a spectre, but was not discernible to the uninitiated. Trooper Bright concentrated on his driving and staying within the prescribed lanes in order to get to the departure position, which took all his attention. 'It was one hell of a noise,' he remembered. 'Dust blotted out visibility to just a few yards.' After they halted, 'everything quietened down to an eerie silence,' Bright recalled. 'A quietness came over everything – no movement was seen in the wadi below us where all of the 8th Armoured Brigade were concentrated,' observed Major Flatow.

'I can remember standing up on the front seat of my tank when there was a gunshot and the next minute I was fairly lifted off the seat by a thousand guns which opened up together and started the battle of El Alamein,' said Trooper Bright. Montgomery launched a new type of battle for the British. Meticulous planning had gone into a detailed combined-arms division orchestrated battle. The different supporting elements – mine clearance by engineers, artillery, tanks and anti-tanks, fielded in concert with the infantry and with air support – were to be played in unison like so many musical instruments. A massive artillery barrage symphony preceded it, as described by Flatow:

At 2200 hours it started with a hell of a bang! The whole western sky was lit up with reds and blues and greens and white flashes. Even as far away as we were, the ground shook slightly and the bangs and crashes were continuous. From this distance it sounded as if hundreds of kettle-drums were being beaten. It lasted hours. An hour later the word was given to advance and we moved towards the noise!

Rommel was away on leave in Germany. Hermann Eckardt remembered 'a huge unbelievable barrage on the Ariete position; it set off the minefield and was demoralising'. Helmut Heimberg recalled the utter helplessness under such a deluge of fire. 'It was terrible for us to lie there for six hours and not be able to do anything.' Rolf Volker nearby accepted 'that the war was lost' as a consequence of this experience. 'We had nothing to fight back with against this mass of material.' The Afrika Korps was quite literally ground into the dust as Volker described: 'It stank of cordite. The ground was peppered with shrapnel. With every shot there was a cloud of dust which lasted for minutes. The earth was completely obliterated. There was nothing left'.

Four British infantry divisions moved into the assault. Heavy fighting broke out as the Germans committed the 15th Panzer Division to hold the break-in. Eckardt remembered that 'fourteen days of hard operations and counter-attacks followed'.

Major Flatow was able to observe the cumulative debilitating effect that prolonged fighting and fatigue began to have on 45 RTR. He recalled that on the third day, 'I occasionally walked about and found tank commanders fast asleep standing up in their turrets. God, how tired we were,' he confessed. Lieutenant-Colonel Parkes of their sister battalion 47 RTR 'who when I had been speaking to him had seemed restive and over-worried, had a breakdown that morning'. He was taken to an advanced field dressing-station, where he was killed by a bomb while sheltering in a slit trench. Courage, it appeared, can collapse if over-taxed. Fatigue and strain had a cumulative effect on tank commanders. 'The layman has no idea how tiring life can be in a tank,' declared Flatow, 'especially for the commander when he is standing up all the time or jumping in or out.' Repeatedly clambering up and down the high Shermans became an effort after a few days without rest. 'Towards the end of the battle you saw tank commanders swaying about trying to climb up their tanks and being helped into the turret; it certainly happened to me,' Flatow confessed.

Adding to fatigue was the physically draining effect of emotive sights and the fear they induced. Random death shook them all. Corporal Blackwell was the first to die in Flatow's squadron. As he stood up after brewing tea next to his tank a dud shell ricocheting at an unpredictable angle bounced along the ground and took his leg off. 'It shook us all a bit as we had got rather contemptuous of all the shelling and so far we had seen little casualty caused by it,' Flatow admitted. Cross-radio German intercepts caused further uncertainties. 'Get ready, here they come!' heard Flatow among innumerable other transmissions – he could speak German fluently. Radio offered a horribly revealing insight into other tank crews' desperate battles if the intercom was left on. Lieutenant Keith Douglas recalled hearing 'shouting, almost screaming' amid normal radio traffic:

'Bloody good shot! You've 'it 'im. You've 'it the bugger. Go on, Lofty, give 'im another. Go on. 'It 'im again . . .' rising to a crescendo. Then the inevitable angry voices of other stations: 'Get on I/C. Bloody well GET ON I/C and look to your BLOODY procedure.'

Even worse were ring-side transmissions of death. Effusions of fear and the screams of comrades shouting for mothers and loved ones might ring out across the net as men burned to death in anonymous turrets that were as audible as public places.

By the second night of the battle, when the crews 'were nearly dropping from fatigue', Flatow and the other 45 RTR squadrons were ordered to take the 'Pep' tablets carried by unit doctors for this contingency. During refuelling they each took one and a half tablets and 'felt fine, fighting fit, ready for anything'. What they did not appreciate is that twelve hours after taking Benzedrine and two more doses 'it was a different tale'.

Momentary hallucinations followed the second and third Benzedrine doses. 'I kept seeing things which didn't exist,' declared Flatow, and these merged into images he did not want to see. 'I will never forget,' he reflected 'a black-faced Highlander on his back with both his legs off at the knee.' Another distraction was a troop commander Norman Rounce's tank suddenly bursting into flame – 'and it was not a pleasant sight'. Two of them managed to get out, one died next to the tank and his friend Norman, appallingly burned, died in hospital. 'God, how horrible it was,' Flatow declared. 'I cannot go into details; it is bad enough thinking about them.' The psychological impact of grisly casualties and the terrors of three days of intense fighting tired them out. Benzedrine had them wandering in a drug-induced daze and was badly affecting their reactions. 'Allan Duggin, who was moving one of his tanks, spent ten minutes trying to wake a man up in his path before he realised he was dead.' Then the whole tenor of the battle changed.

Something happened that made our bowels cling and our mouths dry up – some Shermans, 'diesel' Shermans, appeared over the ridge in front of us, some reversing, some facing us, some in flames – they were odd tanks of the 41st and 47th battalions retreating, coming out of it. Some stayed with us, blocking our view, getting in our way; others passed through us and went away.

Over the air came the battalion commander's voice stating, 'The regiment will not retire one yard but will stand and fight where it is.' Dismay was expressed at the accuracy of the 88mm guns. 'I don't know what we are fighting for,' commented soldiers who remonstrated with each other on intercoms audible to all. 'Obscene words were thick in the dialogue, and believe me it was incredibly demoralising,' said Flatow. He switched off the radio for fear his crew might be influenced. 'As it was they were already rather windy'. With no idea why the other regiments were retreating, they expected German tanks to come into view at any moment. 'I really felt it was the end,' Flatow admitted. 'It was a most peculiar feeling and one I don't want to have again.'

Rommel, who had returned, continually counter-attacked with the 21st Panzer Division on 29 October and brought another division forward to help the one assailed on the coast. Despite resourceful generalship Kidney Hill was taken and Montgomery launched his decisive counter-stroke from there on 2 November. The 2nd New Zealand Division, supported by the 1st Armoured, launched an attack that developed into a violent tank battle with the 15th Panzer Division, supported by the 21st and some Italian armour. Rommel's panzer losses were so heavy that he felt obliged to withdraw that night, but Hitler forced him to hold on. Counter-orders added to growing German confusion. That night an attack by the 51st and 4th Indian Divisions levered open the deadlock. Rommel, down to thirty-five serviceable panzers, stared breakthrough in the face, and by 4 November the 7th and 10th Armoured Divisions were streaming into open country devoid of enemy.

'Shot up panzers lay all around,' declared Dr Alfons Selmayr with Panzer Regiment 5. 'Tommy stayed outside range but with his wide reaching and superior guns he bested us convincingly.' The Shermans were proving their worth. 'For the first time,' Selmayr admitted, 'we noted the enemy's material superiority.' The new M4 was the equal of the long-barrelled Mark IV and superior to the Mark III. In the south Selmayr could see huge smoke and dust clouds. 'Everywhere it was burning,' he recalled, while from the east he observed enemy tanks attacking *en masse*. Down to only thirty panzers 'against a good 300' they urgently requested support from Panzer Regiment 8. Instead they were ordered to counter-attack across a 'table-top' flat approach against 'Tommy, who was not only superior in numbers but also in armour and guns'. Selmayr overheard the radio exchange between *Hauptmann* von Senfft, commanding the regiment, to his own battalion commander Oberleutnant Mildebrath, who was being ordered to attack. 'An attack is nonsense!' he responded, but Senfft was having none of it. 'Correct,' the metallic radio voice agreed, 'but an order is an order!' Selmayr, who was providing medical support, hung back as the first of the panzers began to burst into inky conflagrations after barely 100 metres. The Italians fared no better. 'Despite their light armour they drove forward with magnificent daring and were of course heart-rendingly shot to pieces.' The Ariete Division was almost destroyed as Rommel began his withdrawal along the coast.

On the fourth night Flatow's crews fell to the ground and slept whenever they stopped 'and it took a long time for them to be awakened'. Flatow was completely exhausted, but the Benzedrine had set his nerves on edge and he was unable to sleep. They were easily disorientated, worsened by the misdirection caused when the turret is swung in a different direction from that of the moving tank hull. 'The moonlight, the desert, the ridges all whirled round,' Flatow recalled, 'and I absolutely had no idea where I was or which direction I had to go in – whether to the left or right.' So exhausted was the regiment that the Colonel went to division and objected to orders for yet another dawn attack – 'although it cost me a bowler hat', he confided as he went. 'Only half my brain seemed to be working,' Flatow declared.

Apart from the men the machines were about exhausted: the wireless sets had been on continuously from the very beginning and were now too hot to touch. The wretched operators and tank commanders had had their earphones on all the time and our ears were sore and our heads singing from the noise and crackle of the sets.

Men were a little depressed. 'So far the generalship had not been very bright – tank regiments had been flung into unrecce'd ground on to good dug-in enemy anti-tank positions and it looked like it was going to happen again.'

By the fifth day both their sister tank regiments had 'nearly ceased to exist', losses among officers were proportionally higher and there were isolated groups of unhorsed tank crews all across the tracks of their line of advance. Summing up their condition Flatow said, 'We could walk and talk and move our tanks but our minds were sluggish – they refused to work or think things out, and with all this fatigue all the horrors of the past five days were on top of us.' They were the victors, but had yet to realise they had won.

The inner core of the Afrika Korps was ripped out at El Alamein. 'Let me tell you I have cried a few times already for my comrades who were killed in the war and are here at El Alamein,' admitted Erich Müller, a panzer commander, during a commemorative post-war visit. 'My best personal friend, schoolmates – they are all here at Alamein.' He apologised as he wept. Dietrich Kohl, another veteran accompanying him, pointed to two lines written at the foot of an English gravestone, put there by family members. 'Lines meant to characterise this man,' he commented, 'which I find very moving.' He continued, 'Any who fought here and still alive today could have been buried in such a cemetery. We have every reason to thank the Lord every day.'

RSM Jack Watt of 3 RTR summed up his attitude at the end of a chaotic day.

> In the light of the day the extent of the night's disaster became apparent. The blackened mangled vehicles, a few sad soldiers aimlessly sifting through the debris, and I was still stuck in the minefield. 'The best laid plans' and all that . . . What a bloody mess.

The Eighth Army had suffered 13,500 casualties.

## NEW TERRAIN AND THE AMERICANS

'The bugle had blown and we couldn't stop!' exclaimed Sergeant Jake Wardrop of 5 RTR: 'There were thousands and thousands of prisoners.

If we happened to stop beside any, we nipped out, pinched their watches, binoculars or anything they had and carried on.'

Montgomery at first hoped to trap Rommel by encirclement on the coast at Fuka, and the 21st Panzer Division's remaining armour got away at Mersa Matruh on 6 November. 'And then it started to rain,' remembered Jake Wardrop, 'and didn't it pour down for about four days.' By 7 November Montgomery accepted that it would be a long chase but resolved to give the Germans no rest. 'We fought in the mud, got stuck in it, swore, drank rum and chased,' declared Wardrop. Rommel kept ahead of the pursuing British for over 1,600 miles until he reached the temporary safety of the Mareth Line in Tunisia. Most of the manpower of the German divisions was preserved although many infantry were lost. Surviving panzer crews were lorried away to fight another day, while virtually all the tanks were lost or abandoned as the columns retreated, harried by Allied aircraft the whole way. The Italian formations effectively ceased to exist.

The 'pendulum war' was over. 'It was nearly a thousand miles from Alexandria to Agheila,' pointed out Jake Wardrop, 'and in the two previous pushes the administration broke down. There was no stuff to carry on with and there had been a counter-attack.' This time was different. 'The fact that we were there with fifty almost new tanks was a change, and there were more,' he said. 'Like many people who had chased or been chased up and down the desert, the idea of riding triumphantly into Tunis had its attractions,' admitted Bill Close pursuing with 3 RTR. 'At the same time there was a feeling of relief that for once we would not be in the van.'

As they advanced west the terrain began to change perceptibly. Peter Roach, a tank radio operator with 1 RTR, noticed 'no longer the gentle vistas but a more rugged country, with hills and steep wadis, olive trees and more vegetation'.

The Afrika Korps got to Tunisia first and conditions changed: 'No longer a coverless desert empty of people, with no conspicuous features and without established roads, like in Libya; now a hilly, densely settled area with a thicker road network'. There were areas with trees and shrubs offering covered approaches for armoured troops, while large stretches were planted with vegetables, corn and fruit trees. Water was more plentiful as also were people. Rommel gained sufficient strength for a vigorous defence of Tunisia. But he was no longer alone.

On 8 November an Anglo-American Task Force code named 'Operation Torch' landed in French Morocco and Algeria. On board were two US armoured divisions, nearly four infantry divisions and a further British division. A build-up followed. While the Allies sent troops by air and sea from Algiers, the Germans dispatched elements of three German divisions from Italy to form the nucleus of a new 5th Panzer Army that was to operate in concert with Rommel's retreating Afrika Korps. Facing them was General Eisenhower's First Army in Algeria and Morocco, advancing on Tunis, and Montgomery's Eighth Army, hastening northward across the Western Desert and stalled at the Mareth Line south-west of Tunis. As Jake Wardrop observed, this was no longer good tank going. 'The country was becoming very rough, hilly with steep crevices which, in places, we could not cross.'

The combat debut of the Sherman tank with its dual purpose 75mm gun firing both high explosive and armour-piercing had been so encouraging that a cable signed by Montgomery to the War Office days after Alamein claimed 'the 75mm is all we require'. This was regarded by the General Staff as a virtual command. It reversed a former War Office policy of producing a first-class anti-tank gun, a 6-pounder or heavier, to outclass future enemy tanks they were likely to meet. 'In view of the evidence to date,' wrote the War Office, 'that the 75mm tank gun in use in American medium tanks is the best dual-purpose tank weapon yet produced', and to achieve standardisation, 'the 75mm should be adopted as soon as practicable as the main armament of the majority of British tanks.' The War Office was willing even to consider 'if necessary, the adoption in the UK of American medium tank design'. This decision had a drag effect on Allied tank design and production in 1943, even as worrying developments were identified in German workshops.

A British Intelligence report on 3 November 1942 noted that a new type of tank, the Kpfw VI, was in the offing. 'This confirms as expected, a new tank, heavier than III or IV, is being built.' The report's author Major Shallard urged 'both Middle East and the Mission in Moscow to take urgent steps to obtain precise information on the characteristics of the Pz Kpfw (*Panzer Kampwagen*) VI'.

The weight of this 'new German super heavy tank' was identified as 57 tons, the armour probably 100mm and the gun the fearsome 88mm. This represented a quantum leap from the 'agricultural tractor' Germany went to war with, and placed her in the forefront of design, ahead of the Russians. Characteristically the Russians volunteered no information until after April 1943, by which time the British had captured a Panzer VI in any case. The Russians had engaged Tigers outside Leningrad in August 1942, three months before the information request from their allies.

Hitler meanwhile dispatched thirty-four Tigers to assist Rommel and 5th Panzer Army in North Africa only six months after the batallion had formed up. Piecemeal reinforcement continued with Battalion 504 in February 1943. By mid-January two of the 501 companies were ready for action. Hitler said to General Walther Nehring commanding 5th Panzer Army 'that the six Tigers that would be arriving would be decisive to the war'.

When the first 501 Battalion Tigers trundled through Bizerte in Tunis they were scooped by the press, and a report complete with picture appeared in the German *National Zeitung* newspaper on 11 December 1942. Now the secret was out of the bag. British Intelligence employed a technical illustrator to draw an image scaled to the buildings identified in the background of the press photograph, to estimate the tank's likely dimensions and it was realised that the 1943 policy decisions on Allied tank production and design were likely invalid. Britain was now third or fourth in the armour-design race, having led for the previous decade. The *Daily Mail* headline from its Reuter correspondent in Tunis rubbed it in – *62-Ton German Tanks Arrive* – depressing reading for those only too aware of the significance of the new 'land battleships'. The troops remained oblivious until they came up against the Tiger on the battlefield.

Lieutenant Peter Gudgin arrived in Tunisia with the heavily armoured Churchills of 48 RTR early in 1943. They were not well informed.

When we were coming over in the ship to land in Tunisia we were given a book about the Middle East – a briefing book, and we were given an intelligence briefing. And I think the Tiger was mentioned in that briefing but not as to what it consisted of, you know, its larger calibre gun and so on. We went into this campaign having no idea.

As their train steamed past the sidings and the logistic paraphernalia of war, they spotted burned-out hulks of tanks. The whole railhead was littered with the wreckage of their parent brigade's Churchills, knocked out by Tigers or 88mm Flak guns. 'We were horrified, absolutely appalled,' Gudgin declared. 'I mean, nobody had told us anything about this – it wasn't fair!' The new leviathans could be knocked out, but the odds were frightening. Gudgin appreciated later with experience that their tanks needed to be within 600 metres range and on the flank or rear to penetrate. Unfortunately the 88mm could comfortably dispatch them from out to 2,000 metres. It was not uncommon for one Tiger to account for as many as ten Allied tanks in a single encounter.

'We were told about about the German MarkVI, the Tiger, a 60-ton tank with a stepped up 88mm on it,' recalled Sergeant Jake Wardrop, 'they were very bad medicine.' As all veterans do, they proceeded to discuss how best to deal with it. 'It was thought that if we ever fought them, by having a superior number and doing some manoeuvring, we could make something of it.' Desperate measures were required to bridge this technology gap. They began to practise shooting to hit the barrel and to innovate with delayed high-explosive rounds. One technique was developed whereby they would 'bounce' the shell in front of the tank so that it would explode, they hoped, at cupola height, which might 'part the commander's hair with a bit of luck'. However, luck and skill did not always operate in tandem. The best outcome was not to meet one.

If the British were misinformed, the new American tank men were *un*informed. Little in the United States could prepare them for their first experience of combat in Europe. Americans were committed to their nation's war goals and convinced after Pearl Harbor that they were fighting for the forces of good. Their last sight of America was the first their immigrant fathers had seen, the Statue of Liberty, on departing New York harbour. Lieutenant Belton Cooper, leaving for Europe with the 3rd Armoured Division, watched her head slip beneath the horizon. 'This final vision of New York had a profound effect on me and probably all the other troops,' he admitted. 'I'm sure that many were wondering if or when we would see our country again.'

Like other tank men they were attracted by the size and power of the machines they served. 'For a neophyte like me, entering a tank park for the first time was a thrill,' admitted Captain Norris Perkins of the 2nd Armoured Division. He recalled engine start-ups at dawn. 'As the air-cooled radial engines cranked up, blue smoke filled the park, the ground shook, and this was life!'

In 1939 the US tank force was smaller than in European armies like those of Italy and Poland. Yet within two years, spurred on by the collapse of its role model, the French Army, the US Army created sixteen armoured divisions and more than sixty separate tank battalions. Two years separated its formation as an armoured force in 1940 from its first large-scale deployment to North Africa in November 1942. During this period it trained on huge manoeuvre areas, mostly in Louisiana, Tennessee and southern California. Training was hard and thorough, with space allowing more practical manoeuvring and live field firing than their constrained European counterparts. Four men died and twenty-one were injured in the first major exercise near Fort Benning in May 1941. When 'Barbarossa' started in June 1941, the 2nd Armoured Division was conducting a two-week exercise in Tennessee involving a rail deployment and 78,000 men, over 140 miles, much of it at night, again resulting in four fatalities. There was a 420-mile march by 2,500 vehicles by train and road in North Carolina the following November and a 223-mile road march during another Louisiana manoeuvre. Mishaps occurred during this early training phase, one being the spectacular demolition of a two-storey City Hall in Tennessee. Only minor bruising to the tank commander's head was the outcome, recalled Captain Norris Perkins, but the entire building and its furniture collapsed around the tank. 'We uncovered the tank and it drove away,' he remembered. 'The locals were impressed.'

American tank men probably possessed more mechanical and technical expertise than their European counterparts. The initial cadre for the 3rd Armoured Division forming in the spring of 1941 came from the agrarian south-eastern states and had experience with farm machinery, tractors and cultivators. They were reinforced by a further cadre of men from the Midwest, with industrial backgrounds, who had knowledge of manufacturing and industrial machinery.

Although the training was technically proficient it was, according to one official account, 'an ocean away – psychologically and physically – from what was to come'. A 741st Tank Battalion history described a tank company attack demonstration laid on for the battalion and invited civilians. 'Immediately following this,' the report noted, 'tanks were available for members of this battalion to give tank rides to members of their families.' Homer Wilkes, a lieutenant in the 747th Independent Tank Battalion, recalled, 'There was no training with the infantry, no training with artillery, no training with air support, and no amphibious training.' Training was also unrealistic when it did occur. An exercise report from the 743rd Battalion claimed that during one manoeuvre they knocked out thirty-six enemy tanks, five half-tracks and six wheeled vehicles in a mock armoured assault, while friendly forces only lost one tank and a half-track. Further examination of the battalion's training records show that most units were not exercised in accordance with known German technical or tactical capabilities.

British tank crews and were respected and liked by their American counterparts and had interested regard for each other on arrival in North Africa. Language differences were seen as 'quaint'. 'You're just about used to his speech when you realise that he doesn't speak much,' commented Sergeant Burgess Scott, writing about the British in *Yank*, a wartime American magazine. 'When he says, "I'll lay on a lorry", he doesn't mean he's going for a nap. That's his way of saying "I'll go rustle up a truck".' Mercifully, watching Hollywood films was something both sides could identify with. 'He wants to know if all our girls are like movie stars,' reported Scott. 'Nothing ruffles his military calm,' he observed, 'but try and put anything over him on him, and you have a righteous uproar on your hands.' Respect came with an appreciation that these men had already fought several campaigns. Scott made his point by describing the contents of a wounded British soldier's letter home. 'It read: "Dear Dad: I'm knocked about a bit, but I'll be all right. Don't worry".' 'That guy had an arm off and an eye out,' Scott remarked. 'Tommy's like that.'

In contrast to British doctrine, the Americans did not see the defeat of German panzer divisions to be the primary role of their armour. The head of the army ground forces, General Lesley McNair, was convinced that anti-tank artillery was the antidote to the panzers, not tank-on-tank fighting. His interpretation was not shared by much of his own army, because they saw that anti-tank cordons had failed to stop the panzers in Poland, France and Russia. Manoeuvres in the United States in 1941 reinforced McNair's conviction that the towed gun or self-propelled 'tank destroyers' should be used to defeat panzers. The role of the US armoured divisions was not unlike the Soviet 'Deep Battle' concept of exploiting infantry breakthroughs, racing deep into the enemy rear, decapitating command posts and logistic links and demoralising the enemy by cutting off his line of retreat. Three types of armoured unit evolved as a consequence: armoured divisions to exploit breakthroughs, separate tank battalions to work closely with the infantry to achieve them and Tank Destroyer battalions to defeat enemy armour.

US Armoured formations arrived in North Africa after two long years' thorough technical training and uninterrupted formation development with competent technical and logistic personnel. Convinced at the senior level that they had the answer to the panzer menace, they brought with them the most up-to-date Allied tank, demonstrated at Alamein to be the equal of any panzers they might encounter.

A highly personalised, indeed extrovert command style reinforced American confidence. US generals could be larger-than-life figures, promoting a brand of loyalty verging on cult status from obsequious personal staffs. This contrasted starkly to the equally political but more publicly subdued English and German style of command. General George S. Patton, an armoured general who had served in tanks during the closing stages of the First World War, quickly earned the soubriquet 'Blood and Guts'. His colourful ability to express combat principles in earthy language endeared him to soldiers who enjoyed a character. 'Grab 'em by the nose and kick 'em in the ass' was his assessment of fire and manoeuvre. He was endearingly direct. 'Don't have compassion for the enemy. If you are confused and scared in the attack, all you've got to remember is that the enemy is more scared than you are if you are attacking,' he said. Patton could be totally ruthless. 'You will have more casualties per hour,' he predicted, 'but fewer casualties per day' if you are aggressive. His nickname came from his characteristic 'pep-talk' containing the advice: 'You young officers have got to get used to the idea that there are going to be blood and guts all over the battlefield.'

These larger-than-life personalities were emulated in style by their subordinates. It was both a strength and a weakness. Philosophical uniformity was rigidly imposed and seen as a factor of loyalty. Strength was provided by uniformity of purpose; the weakness was a tendency to gloss over details if the accepted standard was questionable. Indeed, battalion and higher executive officers tended to filter out opinions inimical to their commander's views. Patton sincerely believed 'the enemy's rear is the happy hunting ground for armour', and nobody was going to disagree with him. Bonding among the tank crews was therefore slightly different from the British and German practice. There was a more formal style; officers seldom used first names when speaking to each other or to their men. Crews were equally gregarious but the atmosphere was slightly different. Extrovert leadership can inspire subordinates to super-human efforts, but at a certain command level it can promote divisions if personal loyalties are allowed to get in the way of the taut teamwork essential for success in war.

During January 1943 fighting in eastern Tunisia was sporadic while Allied naval and air pressure interdicted the Axis supply route from Italy. Montgomery remained blocked at the Mareth Line for months as uncoordinated attacks and counter-attacks occurred through the Atlas Mountain passes further north. Both sides were coming to terms with the tactical differences of operating in this mountainous terrain, which with its stony ground exacerbated the shrapnel effect of artillery. Lieutenant Michael Pope, with the Churchills of the North Irish Horse, found it 'rough, extremely steep, flaming hot and very dusty'.

'If wars have to be fought,' wrote twenty-two-year-old 'Jimbo' D'Arcy Clark, with the Queen's Own Yorkshire Dragoons, 'they should be reserved for . . . desert and [other places] like it, where there is no living thing to be ruined by destruction. In fact desert seems a fitting place for wars.' His almost poetically composed letter to his mother juxtaposed the odd asymmetry of their changed surroundings, 'lovely countryside' with cultivated areas, and a stark background of burned-out tanks. As a flock of 'pheasants or partridges' suddenly flew up from the road around him he was moved to write:

All seems such a mix-up – war seems so far removed from country such as this. It makes one realise what England would look like in the circumstances, the grim-looking wreckage and destruction left behind by a retreating army. Somehow you feel and say to yourself, 'People can't have been burned to death in that tank in this lovely country road where trees and flowers are growing and birds singing, or that aeroplane can't have been shot down in flames in the middle of that field of hyacinths.'

On 14 February the 5th Panzer Army launched the 10th and 21st Panzer Divisions against the American II Corps between Faid Pass and Gafsa, attempting to push through the Atlas Mountain passes. Sergeant Debs Myers captured the essence of this brutal experience for the Americans, writing later in the war: 'He learned the ache of loneliness, the ache of exhaustion, the kinship of misery. From the beginning he wanted to go home.'

The advancing German tanks, including Tigers, had moved slowly without raising dust and manoeuvred into advantageous positions before their presence was revealed. The American 1st Armoured Division was poorly deployed, split into four separate combat commands scattered over an excessive 60-mile front. The command relationship between the II US Corps and the British First Army was disjointed. Personalities played a role. The division commander was quiet and well liked by his men but detested by an irascible corps commander, with all that entailed for subordinate executive commanders, in a personality rather than functionally driven chain of command. After penetrating Faid Pass the 21st Panzer attacked Sidi bou Zid with 150 tanks. Preoccupied with air attacks, the Americans missed the flanking and rearward approaches.

*Hauptmann* Heinz Rohr, leading the I *Abteilung* of Panzer Regiment 5, was moving around an American-occupied hill when he spotted a large dust cloud converging from the west. 'It was an American tank division that appeared a little too late on the battlefield.' His fifty panzers were drawn up in line next to him, behind was the sun and the American-occupied heights. 'I gave the most satisfying radio order in my life,' he recalled. 'No shooting, no more movement – only I give the order to open fire'.

American tank veterans frequently refer to the German panzers crews' ability to catch them with the sun in their eyes. They were shocked at the accuracy and engagement speeds and the brutal power of the German anti-tank guns. At Faid Pass Bill Haemmel a Sherman loader with the 1st Armoured Regiment recalled 'in short order ten of the seventeen attacking tanks were hit and disabled', and eight immediately began to burn. 'The attacking tank soldiers were greatly handicapped as they had the early morning sun shining directly into their eyes.'

Tank Sergeant Gordon O'Steen also found his vision obscured by sun and heavy dust. Unable to discern what was going on and receiving no orders by radio, he glanced at the rest of the company to the south, only to 'dimly see what looked like the rest of the tanks in the company all burning!'

Sidi bou Zid was another disaster for the 1st Armoured Division. 'The Americans could not pick out our panzers against the sun,' remembered *Hauptmann* Heinz Rohr. 'It was a catastrophe for the enemy as I gave the order to open fire at 500 metres'. His I *Abteilung* lined up against the hill claimed seventy-eight enemy tanks. Sergeant Clarence Coley, the radio operator in the 3rd Battalion 1st Armoured command tank, admitted, 'I didn't see too much and didn't know much about what was going on.' Momentary glimpses through the vision slits revealed many of their tanks hit and set on fire. 'Sometimes two or three men got out. Sometimes no one.' They changed position and were engaged again. 'We were getting it hot and heavy. I did not keep the count on them, but we received many hits on our tank.' Nerves became taut as 'I could feel the shock and hear the loud noise as those projectiles bounced off.' Eventually 'our luck ran out'. A round jammed in the barrel, rendering them helpless unless they could clear it. For a moment Coley was bent behind his seat trying to pull out the last of their ammunition, whereupon a shell slammed into the left side of the tank, through the petrol tank and ricocheted around, landing precisely where he had been straining to reach ammunition from the racks. 'I remember it well – sitting there watching that bit of hell standing on end, spinning like a top, with fire flying out of the upper part of it like it was a tracer.' Coley became momentarily snagged as he attempted to bail out, then tore himself free. As they ran, their tank

*Texas* spectacularly exploded. They had managed to knock out four panzers.

Desperate American crews learned what all the intensive training in the United States had not been able to impart, which was the horror of exiting the cloying and claustrophobic confines of burning tanks. Wreckage blocked exits and snagged their clothes as the flames sucked away the oxygen around them. Air was consumed in seconds, emptying lungs shrieking for help. Captain Norris Perkins of the 2nd Armoured Division confessed, 'One great fear of tankers was of being burned up before they could get out of a tank.' Training had only introduced the problem. In the event of propellant fires 'the temperature inside the tank could go to 5,000 degrees within five seconds'. His crew preferred to keep the turret lids open. 'We never locked ourselves in the tank.'

The isolated American combat command near Sidi bou Zid was crushed. Another Combat Command sent to relieve them was shot to pieces by elements from both veteran panzer divisions. They coolly stood their ground when the Americans charged text-book cavalry fashion into the teeth of precisely co-ordinated combined-arms fire. The panzers pushed on in *Keil* formation, advancing through the open expanse of the Kasserine Pass.

The American II Corps was driven back 50 miles, and the offensive petered out on 23 February, ironically this time because of German command personality differences as well as devastating US artillery fire. Some 183 tanks, 194 half-tracks, 208 guns, 560 trucks and 2,459 prisoners were lost to the panzers, alongside nearly 200 killed and over 2,600 wounded.

After the battle the Americans completely reorganised the structure of their armoured divisions. Instead of light and medium tank battalions, all were based around a structure of three medium tank companies and one light. 'They fought with great doggedness,' commented Hans von Luck. 'I will never forget the sight of a few Tiger panzers with their superior 88mm gun knocking out one Sherman after the other, as they tried to advance through a pass to the east, and couldn't understand that they were hopelessly inferior to the Tigers.'

'They didn't have a very good reputation,' observed a more cynical Paul Rollins serving with 40 RTR. 'They were all right, the Yanks, as long as they'd got a lot.' Rollins typified the hard-bitten approach of many bloodied British veterans:

> They're not tenacious, shall we say? Well, that's my opinion, I may be wrong. They didn't do very well at Kasserine Pass in North Africa. They got out of their tanks and left them and the Keil Division took them . . . They didn't destroy them, they didn't put a hand grenade in or anything, just got out and fled and left them. They were shot at, they lost some tanks and they panicked.

In fairness Rollins added: 'Mind you, as far as I know, I don't think they did that again. That was their baptism, as we say.' Hans von Luck stated that 'we admired the courage and the élan' with which the attacks were conducted and 'sometimes felt sorry for them at having to pay for their first combat experience with such heavy losses'. 'They had the wrong type of people probably,' surmised Rollins, 'the wrong leaders and all that. I'm not decrying that they were all like that by any means. But that was just one occasion – but it's true that they don't mess about. They are very heavy-handed, with everything. Sledgehammer to crack a walnut.'

Within two and a half months of the Kasserine battle the front was re-established, concentric attacks were mounted on Tunis after the Mareth Line was breached and Bizerta and Tunis were captured on 7 May. Some 125,000 Germans and 115,000 Italians became prisoners, and the general surrender took place six days later. Rommel had been invalided through illness and flown out the previous March. The Axis presence in North Africa was at an end.

Panzer crews were surreptitiously flown out of the shrinking pocket by forward-thinking regimental staffs at the end of March as it became increasingly apparent that surrender was the only option. Sickness, leave, career courses and other administrative ruses were quoted to get them out.

'There was no gloating on our part,' reflected Captain Bill Close of 3 RTR, 'only a sense of achievement in having beaten men who, in my opinion, had fought with distinction and skill, even decency, if such a word can be applied to the battlefield.' 'We were never licked,' wrote Sergeant Jake Wardrop, who summed up the essence of the fighting in the desert. 'Sometimes we had fought and lost, but the spirit had always been there, and when the time was ripe we showed them and we shall show them again.' What the desert campaign repeatedly demonstrated was the ability of the Wehrmacht, and in particular the panzer arm, to recuperate and resurrect itself after set-backs. The 'pendulum war' finished at Alamein, but still the Fifth Panzer Army had mounted a dangerous counter-offensive in the Atlas Mountains only two and a half months before capitulation. This ability to regenerate was time and time again to be under-estimated.

The demise of Germany's African army was eclipsed by the publicity of the greater surrender at Stalingrad three months before. Tunis was icing on the Allied cake. Even after this catastrophe in Russia a surprise German counter-stroke spearheaded by panzers was mounted by von Manstein at Kharkov in March 1943, and this restored the Russian front to a certain equilibrium, roughly corresponding to the pre-Stalingrad situation. It left a vulnerable Russian salient, about the size of Wales, sticking out into the German line in the Kursk and Belgorad area.

The impact of the Russian crucible on the Wehrmacht and Pan-zerwaffe was significant in operational and technical terms. Only a fraction of the German potential was set against the Anglo-American forces, who suffered significantly in the process. Operations in Europe on the Eastern Front in 1943 would be conducted on a far different scale against substantially larger German contingents.

# 11

## TANK ACTION EASTERN FRONT

### ASSEMBLY AREA - WAITING

The assembly area was the place where units massed and organised themselves before going into battle. It was a place where tank crews came to terms with their fears. They did this in different ways. 'One guy was extremely silent, didn't say a word, the second was very hungry,' recalled Georgi Krivov, who was in charge of his company commander's tank, awaiting action. 'I was just over-excited and couldn't sit still. The company commander himself was breathing heavily and sniffing.' There was always time in the assembly area to reflect on what might be. 'Of course, there were fears other than the fear of death,' remembered Krivov. 'Men were scared of getting crippled or wounded. They were afraid to go missing in action or to be taken prisoner.'

Tanks and the hundreds of wheeled vehicles that supported them were generally dispersed over hundreds of acres, preferably in forest or woodland, where they were invisible from the air or could be made so by the use of branches and foliage as camouflage. After the failure of *Blitzkrieg* both sides could only rely on temporary local air supremacy. The scale of the forces committed on the eastern front was massive. At the Kursk salient in July 1934 the Germans and Russians committed between them four million soldiers, 69,000 artillery pieces and mortars, 13,000 tanks and self-propelled guns and 12,000 aircraft.

The Soviet reserve at Kursk, the 5th Guards Tank Army, numbering 650 tanks, occupied a zone 200 miles from the front line. All these forces came together within their assembly areas and trained, were briefed, and logistically and administratively prepared for battle. In the words of tank driver Aleksandr Sacharow: 'Preparations in the field took place in total secrecy. Right down to NCO level, efforts were made to ensure all were combat ready.' Most of all, he added, 'they needed to be morally and psychologically prepared for a particularly heavy battle'.

Material and emotional reserves had to be replenished. Panzer gunner Ludwig Bauer recalled 'being in principle day and night in the panzers'. There were always pauses and quiet times, but he always slept either inside or under the tank. The crew dug a ditch about two metres wide and half a metre deep, inside which the five-man crew lay alongside each other. The panzer was driven over the top for protection, and a canvas bivouac erected alongside and fastened to the vehicle.

There was very little sleep at any time of year, but Bauer thought the summers more wearisome: 'It was always light very early, so sleep was automatically too short. By 0200 hours the Russians had often already started shooting.' In between was one or two hours' sentry duty and panzers had to be serviced and maintained and weapons and working parts stripped down, cleaned and oiled. Expended shells had also to be replenished, lifted and passed up in a crew chain on to the tank deck and then laboriously taken inside and stowed around the turret and hull. 'Apart from huge physical exertions from combat this was one of the heaviest and hardest times for us – we were often at the end of our resources,' recalled Bauer. Crews were tired out even before battle commenced.

Distractions from this hard routine were welcome. 'Shortly before the battle [around Kursk] began,' battalion commander Gerd Schmükle of the 7th Panzer Division recalled, 'I organised a party for my battalion; we had gypsy music and dancers.' It became one of those indelible images lighting up the approaching darkness:

It took place during a marvellous summer night. About 500 soldiers were sitting around the stage where the dance acts were performed. We all felt this was a party between life and death, between hope and despair, because it was clear that at least one third of us would be killed in action or wounded in the next few days.

'When on earth did we have spare time?' asked Russian Lieutenant Aleksandr Fadin. Battle pauses in assembly areas were likely the only occasion. Entertainers might visit the front with concert parties, and sometimes even films might be shown. Many tank men were too fatigued to participate in much; they would gather around radio sets to listen to the latest war news or read front newspapers. Men wrote letters home.

Certain letters were unwelcome, to write and to read. After Ludwig Bauer was promoted company commander in Regiment 33, writing condolence letters was the most distasteful of his tasks. He insisted that his crews write home, otherwise 'the only letter the families might receive would be the casualty notification'. Formulating death notices was taxing 'because one had to avoid describing exactly what happened'. Horrific injuries witnessed inside burned-out tanks defied description. Worse still, Bauer confided, was explaining why their son or husband had not made it, whereas he had. There were other complications exacerbating already sensitive issues. Scorched or partially melted watches, rings and valuables recovered from burns cases could hardly be returned, 'and then they always asked, why not?' Bauer resolved never to get involved in such exchanges, devolving responsibility to the unit chaplain or as a last resort the local Nazi Party functionary.

Accurate responses were further dogged by the sheer numbers of the dead, wounded and missing to be accounted for and whose families had to be notified. Karl Fuchs's wife Mädi heard about her husband's unfortunate death from his over-taxed 7th Panzer Division company commander. He thoughtfully and compassionately added the sentiment: 'We commiserate and are saddened that fate did not allow Karl to see his little daughter of whom he was so proud.' This was doubtless heartfelt, but constituted one of scores of letters this weary officer had to write amid the snow and ice of a failing front before Moscow. Karl Fuchs's only child, never seen because he had to leave a heavily pregnant wife, was in fact a son. Bauer recalled stories of panzers burned out and left behind during the advance. The letter would be written when the hull had cooled down and the remains recovered, but by this time the unit might have marched a hundred kilometres beyond. 'Then the inevitable question would arise,' he explained, 'why – when he died so far away – didn't you trouble to write far sooner?' The unstated accusation was that he had not bothered about their son or husband's welfare. Tank commanders' emotional resources were therefore already tapped before even mounting their tanks for action.

A unique feature of Russian tank units was that they included women within their ranks. Living together in a tight crew community within the assembly area, or indeed in battle, raised sensitive issues. About 800,000 women served, mostly in the Red Army, during the Second World War, and some were tank crew, mainly drivers. 'It was easy for the men because there were so many of them,' declared tank driver Ekatarin Petluk of the 3rd Tank Army. 'Whenever we stopped for five minutes they would surround and distract me, while one by one they went off to do their business. But what could I do surrounded by men?' she asked. Women and girls came mainly from the *Komsomol* Communist Youth Organisation. They were young and innocent and on the whole unworldly, and they had to adapt. Some problems, however, could only be endured:

> I must say conditions were really very hard. For me, a woman, the worst time was my monthly period. There was seldom enough cotton wool or bandages. I had to improvise and use whatever I could find. And you must understand I was young and very shy. I had to keep my dignity and femininity, surrounded by so many men.

Females could be divisive. One tank man, Arkadi Maryevski, bluntly declared, 'We had a shortage of women and the top brass got them all.' Tank platoon commander Aleksandr Fadin agreed:

> Top brass, I mean commanders, got all the girls. Company commanders that had girlfriends were an exception. A platoon leader or tank commander was a different case. We weren't so much fun for the girls. We were always getting killed and burned.

Most contemporary accounts agreed that 'men and women were shy with each other then'. But the expectation of death provided a spur to intensify whatever remained of life. 'I lost my virginity before a big battle,' admitted one woman:

My boyfriend asked me if I had ever known a man. I said, 'Of course not.' He told me he had never known a woman. I know this sounds silly, but we didn't want to die without experiencing it!

'Obviously it was difficult to have sex,' recalled one woman, 'to do so you need the time and the place' and 'during the war we seldom had either – there was absolutely no privacy.' If there was, another commentator remarked, 'the conditions were hardly conducive to sex anyway. We were filthy, exhausted and hungry. We were just trying to survive.' Inevitably there were cases of married men falling in love with girls at the front. The prospect of losing one's life encouraged men to review their relationships with wives and sweethearts at home, and if there were doubts they did not return to their families afterwards. 'So we weren't entirely popular with everyone when the war ended,' one female observer dryly commented.

'At night-time everyone agreed as they said goodbye, "Whoever survives must write to the relatives",' remembered tank driver Aleksandr Sacharov. Russian tank crews like their German counterparts, were emotionally sustained by their comrades when facing the prospect of random death. 'We treated everyone as our brother,' said Vladimir Alexeev, 'we shared everything, never argued.' Russian tank men quickly appreciated that their survival depended on this mutual interdependence. Nobody else could watch out for them. As Sacharow explained:

> Others from outside cannot really help us in a serious situation. You can only assist from within the confines of one's own crew to get people out if the tank has caught fire. Crew members are closer to each other than brothers. Tank soldiers are like a family sticking very close together. One always watched out for the others and would never leave them in the lurch in a crisis.

Despite genuine compassion for each other, Russian tank men did not bond in quite the same way as panzer and western Allied tank crews. Suspicions exacerbated by ideological currents could haunt relationships in a Russian crew. All were aware and afraid of the influence exerted by political commissars.

Russian losses of crews and tanks at the beginning of the war caused such fast crew rotations that unit commanders cared less about keeping crews together as a group. As a consequence many fell apart before even getting into action. Suspicion lurked beneath turret relationships, and it had a divisive effect until crew stability increased along with front successes. Polyanovski evaded German encirclement, and on his return after an epic escape and odyssey lasting several weeks he was locked up in a cellar by the counter-intelligence officer of the 5th Guards Tank Army. They never seemed to believe his protestations that he had not been captured. 'Fine, you haven't been in German hands – sign here,' he was told. 'But still, what mission did the Germans give you?' They kept at him for three weeks.

Anatoly Kozlov, also serving with the 5th Guards, acknowledged 'you were considered a traitor if captured'. He tried to explain the emotions that did bond tank men beyond the 'brotherhood' holding them together in extremis. 'It is difficult to describe how people keep going,' he said; 'it's a combination of patriotism, propaganda and the personal – namely, families at home.' In his opinion 'fear was the driving factor above all'. This was less the fear of personal death or suffering than of what the party might inflict on their families in the event of disgrace or failure. They might be denied rations and other vital assistance, which was tantamount to a death sentence in winter. Russian crewmen never wanted to stand out or 'rock the boat', preferring to keep their thoughts to themselves rather than share them with other crew members. Care was taken. 'You were shot if you picked up enemy propaganda leaflets, you could not even use them for cigarettes or toilet paper.' Soviet tank men read the Communist Party's propaganda and were in broad terms patriotically convinced by it. Above all else their fear was for their families – 'that they should have a better future'. Kozlov summed up by saying that Russian tank men were very patriotic and followed a pragmatic 'live and let live' philosophy. Authority was not regarded as menacing unless things went wrong.

This corrosive influence was less apparent to panzer crewmen, although they served an unequally uncompromising regime. At the top of the German military hierarchy there might be dedicated Nazis, ideologically motivated or simply seeking professional advancement through party sponsors. Alexander Stahlberg remembered the commander of the 29th Panzer Regiment delivering a party homily on the eve of 'Barbarossa', as if he 'was at a party rally at the Berlin Sports Palace: ranting of Germany's future in the dawn of the East'. He did not approve; in fact 'it had been insufferable, and also incomprehensible, that our panzer regiment should have been entrusted to such a fanatic,' he complained. With the exception of those hard-core Nazis, panzer crews were in general politically apathetic. There was little time for ideological reflection at the front. Otto Carius was shocked to see that Jewish businesses had been plundered and demolished 'just about everywhere' shortly before their arrival in Lithuania. 'We thought that such things could only be possible during a *Kristallnacht* in Germany.' They condemned the mob's antics, 'but we didn't have a lot of time for pursuing these thoughts' because 'the advance continued without a break'.

When asked about combat motivation Leutnant Ludwig Bauer of Panzer Regiment 33 insisted, 'National Socialism had nothing to do with it.' They watched the *Wochenschau* newsreels 'but had nothing to do with the party, even in the final stages of the war'. After the attempted assassination of Hitler in July 1944 every battalion, he remembered, had to appoint a political party officer. 'This was widely treated as a bit of a joke in the regiment,' Bauer commented, 'because the unit chose their own. All the unfortunate picked for the task inherited was a load of political paperwork.' Unlike the spectre-like influence wielded by the Soviet commissar, the Nazi party did not gain entrance to the German fighting compartment. Bauer recalled the arrival of a young officer appointed to the regiment who was also a high-level party functionary. 'Virtually nobody would have anything to do with him', mainly because of his lack of professional experience. For guidance he was obliged to serve under another lieutenant, a platoon commander who did have combat experience, and this 'rather punctured his pride'. His company and battalion commander conspired to get him posted out 'and he soon disappeared from the scene'.

Otto Carius, serving in a heavy Tiger platoon, found Nazi political officers 'becoming an increasing nuisance to us at the front'. Not too serious, however, because 'they usually hung around division headquarters'. 'It would have appeared idiotic to me,' Carius acknowledged, 'if I had said "Heil Hitler" to my men at morning formation.' He accepted that the crews were made up of different types. There were 'Nazis', 'opponents of the regime' and 'completely disinterested parties'. Comradeship was what united them, and so far as he was concerned 'it was completely unimportant whether one did his job for the Führer or for his country or out of a sense of duty'. They were there to fight.

Religion was another issue for troops preparing themselves in assembly areas on the eve of battle. Atheism and faith in one's own strength, knowledge and professional capabilities was the typical response to questions about God on the Russian side. Vasili Bryukhov, a nineteen-year-old T-34 tank commander, was shot out of his tank nine times and destroyed twenty-eight German tanks by the time he finished his war in Austria. Having seen his share of horror and mayhem, he was fairly non-committal about his religion:

Some men had crosses, but at that time it wasn't fashionable, so even those who had them tried to hide them. We were atheists. There were some believers, but I never noticed anyone praying among the multitude of people I saw during the war.

Panzer crews were offered church services before going into battle. Ludwig Bauer remembered it was at just such a gathering and blessing that 'for the first time in my beliefs, for want of a better word, I began to have doubts in God. I could not understand how God could allow such a war with all the many dead on both sides. We then prayed He might protect us.' Unable to accept the contradictions of 'asking for victory and protection so that we could better kill Russians and they us', he resolved, after much discussion with his friend Sepp, never to attend such a service again. 'I don't believe in anything now,' he confessed, 'and about half the people thought as I did.' Not all, though. He remarked that 'in the middle of a battle we had a loader who did not load because he was praying, which was totally unhelpful'.

As with the Russians, the Nazi regime was ambivalent in its attitude. Italian war journalist Curizio Malaparte commented:

In the Wehrmacht religious feeling exists and is in a sense very strong; but its basic elements, its underlying motives, are different from the normal. In the Wehrmacht religion is regarded as a private matter, wholly individual and personal. And German Army chaplains, whose numbers are restricted to a minimum, fulfil a function that bears little relation to the usual one of religious ministration.

The Nazi regime by its very conduct and example was irreligious but perceptively accepted that many of its soldiers – over 90 per cent and many of the population at home had beliefs. As Malaparte concluded, chaplains 'affirm a presence, they constitute a living witness, but that is all'. Even the most pragmatic and self-sufficient tank man, though, would not voluntarily reject any possibility of increasing his survival chances, from wherever it might come. Many prayed on the eve of battle that their cocoon of armour be supplemented by the sloping armour of God's protection.

'We're all sitting in this ravine,' wrote twenty-eight-year-old Soviet officer Nikolai Belov in his diary. 'It will be a month soon and there's just silence at the front.' Only activity could break the tension that was always a feature of waiting for battle in the assembly areas. Both sides refined their zeroing and optics by shooting any available practice ammunition into the burned-out hulks that always seemed to litter the ground nearby. Fear was handled in various ways. 'Probably none of us was free from fear,' admitted Leutnant Otto Carius. 'Before some operations, I did not feel my best.' Some form of physical activity always provided a little release. Crews almost willed the start of an operation, so they could get moving and get it over and done with. 'At the front you tended to make use of the good time and not think about "later" and "for how long".' Veterans recall the small details of waiting. Nikolai Belov remembered the desertions he recorded while they awaited the Orel offensive in the summer of 1943. 'Today another two have gone over to the enemy side. That's eleven already. Most of them are pricks.' Another tank veteran prior to the battle of Kursk watched his friend spreading fat over a chunk of bread with some relish. He did it slowly, taking his time, oblivious to his comrade's concern at the prospect of imminent action. 'Don't rush me,' he remarked with an uncanny awareness of his eventual fate. 'I'm going to enjoy this. It's the last meal I'll eat in this world.'

Then came the order to move.

## OPERATIONAL MOVE

Vast space in the Russian theatre of operations meant that the move to the front was often an epic enterprise. Much of the Wehrmacht after the losses of 1941 had reverted to horse-drawn logistic support, so rail became the preferred option for a move if it was practical. Vulnerability to surprise enemy action on the move had to be balanced against the mechanical benefits of saving track mileage, mechanical breakdowns and wear and tear. To execute such a move tanks had to be assembled, driven to rail yards and manoeuvred on to flat rail or goods wagons, an especially demanding task for the drivers. Rail moves exposed tanks to air attack or, worse, unanticipated ground actions while the vehicles were still on board. This was not unusual when the front might unexpectedly shift scores of miles in a single day. Arriving at a contested unloading point aboard a flat rail car in the middle of an action was the tank man's worst nightmare.

Panzer Regiment 33 entrained for Shisdra in southern Russia to deal with a Russian breakthrough in August 1942. Ludwig Bauer recalled that as their steam locomotive puffed into the station, Russian tanks, which had unexpectedly broken through, began pumping shells into the rail carriages. 'Complete chaos broke out in a free-for-all during which we opened fire still positioned on the goods wagons,' he observed. Moreover, because 'with good reason' owing to the fluid situation the tanks were not tightly roped down, the concussive recoil reports of German return fire was sufficient to topple some from the cars. The shock impact of each round fired at the enemy from this lofty perch began to break up the carriage. 'Naturally,' Bauer commented, 'all this did not occur without light and occasionally heavy damage sustained by the panzers.' Within minutes the station was engulfed by the fiery conflagrations of knocked-out tanks from both sides. Then the Russians, having caused absolute pandemonium, disappeared.

The Russian theatre of operations was fluid and constantly shifting.

Quite often scattered mobile tank forces had to assemble and march to deal with changing trouble spots and then reconstitute elsewhere. These redeployments involved long and uncertain road moves. Physically driving a tank under such conditions could be a demanding, wearisome task. Leutnant Otto Carius often sat to the left of the 88mm Tiger gun, with the gunner on the other side. 'By doing that,' he recalled 'we could see better in the darkness and help the driver.' But he often dozed off and on one occasion he 'suddenly tumbled past the driver's hatch on to the road'. Fortunately his driver Baresch 'reacted as quickly as lightning and braked before the track could grab me'. He was luckier than the dispatch rider who cut in front of the tank to turn right. Losing control in a pothole he was run over and mangled before anyone realised what had happened.

Night marches were especially tricky. 'Night operations were three to four times more demanding in nerves, more intellectual pressure, organisation – everything', recalled one officer.

Light and smoking discipline was essential. Leutnant Ludwig Bauer believed that cigarettes 'were the most dangerous threat to security', so he would attempt to recruit non-smokers for his crew. Trundling along during one stealthy night march he detected the distinctive odour of Russian cigarette tobacco. He fired a Verey pistol and illuminated a group of twenty to thirty Russian infantry bunching ahead in the snow. They were swept aside by machine-gun fire.

Lieutenant Anatoly Kozlov with the 5th Guards Tank Army was in the Steppe Front assembly area at Ostrogozhsk-Novy, west of the River Don in July 1943, awaiting the outcome of the battles around Kursk. T-34 Tank Commander Vladimir Alexeev with 101 Tank Brigade in the same location recalled the normal practice was to form the tanks in a circle for security or simply disperse in order to rest. He like Kozlov had occupied forward positions ready to advance. 'The commander and driver would gain some sleep,' he said, 'while the other crew members stood watch.' They suddenly received the order to move forward to prevent a threatened decisive junction of two German Army Groups at Kursk. Political commissars ominously warned of 'a very severe battle about to come', he recalled. Kozlov remembered the surge of adrenalin when the prospect of battle became a certainty. 'During the period of getting ready there had been time to think' but the inevitability of approaching combat meant they 'had now to do their best'.

As the 5th Guards Tank Army tanks and vehicles poured out of the subsidiary forest tracks and roadways on to hard gravel roads leading to the front they were wreathed in dust and the blue-grey mist of exhaust fumes. Ahead lay a very long march. Anatoly Kozlov remembered the generous equipping of Allied lend-lease wheeled vehicles meant that for once they could move forward on tracks and wheels instead of the more familiar and vulnerable rail transports. They formed three huge armoured columns that thundered day and night through villages and forested areas for three days on an epic 380-kilometre journey. With 850 tanks and self-propelled guns and probably six times that number of wheeled vehicles, dust clouds obscured the sun and made individual navigation virtually impossible. Each vehicle followed the one in front. The urgency of their task forced them to accept the risk of driving in broad daylight.

'The move to Prokhorovka was a nightmare,' Lieutenant Alexeev recalled. 'It was really hot beneath huge clouds of dust from the three columns of tanks.' Motoring through forested areas was especially uncomfortable. Low branches trapped the compacted hot air, making it 'worse to breathe' in the intensely humid atmosphere. A tank track move over long distances with no regard for the air threat communicated the urgency of the situation to the crews. It meant there would be a battle at the end of it, and tensions rose. Thoughts inevitably turned to the enemy they were likely to meet.

'We were well aware of the atrocities the fascists had committed,' recalled female tank driver Ekatarina Petluk of the 3rd Tank Army, 'not only against our soldiers but also against civilians and prisoners of war. We knew the things they had done.' Many veterans, like platoon commander Nikolai Zheleznov, rhetorically asked, 'How should we treat the Germans? We treated them in a natural way: we gave them a proper beating. We hated them bitterly.' In hindsight some veterans acknowledged they were barbaric to each other. 'Being over eighty years old,' confessed Aleksandr Bodnar, 'I now feel sorry that we treated each other in such a barbaric manner in the war. They dragged our dead from the roads into swamps with prime movers, and we did the same.' Most veterans detected a change from the young, healthy and insolent German captives taken at the beginning of the war. 'They didn't care about world domination any longer,' commented Kirichenko, 'they all looked a bit confused – though they fought hard until the end.' Tank men like Aleksandr Fadin maintained a certain detachment. Suppressing emotion would be more likely to keep them alive. 'At the front I looked upon them simply as targets,' he said, 'so I just fired at those targets.' Revenge certainly played a role in the excesses committed by both sides. Hatred turned to pity when the Red Army eventually raped and rampaged its way across the Reich, reaping the whirlwind suffered by Russia on the hapless German civilian population. Men like Bodnar, who saw depredations committed by both sides, later temporised. 'We weren't so civilised either,' he admitted. 'We would come to their field cemeteries, destroy the grave crosses and move on.'

Panzer crews dwelt on similar themes as they approached the front. They were supremely confident in their professional capabilities, but as Wilhelm Roes, a Panzer IV radio operator with the SS *Leibstandarte* Adolf Hitler (LAH), admitted, 'We weren't easily frightened in my unit but we were terrified of being captured. We expected to be shot or we expected to be tortured.' This fear was universal among panzer crewmen. 'We'd find some comrades of ours tied up with barbed wire, dead, so that our worst fear, which remained in the background, was of being captured.' Panzer commander Ludwig Bauer argued, 'We were totally free of hate.' His was not an ambivalent attitude, because he had seen the best and worst in Russia. He recalled the friendliness of some Russian people; and that the women were as beautiful as the scenery. Russia also had its dark side, as he revealed in an incident following the capture of a Russian bunker after a local counter-attack:

A German officer came out and motioned me inside. There were eight to ten Russians in there, and the officer kept telling me to look in the corner, where apparently a German lieutenant was lying on the ground. I could not discern anything, but when I got closer it was clear an empty cartridge case had been hammered into his forehead and one other in each knee. He was not yet dead. The Russians were asked to point out who had been responsible. They fearfully indicated a commissar. Luckily for me my gunner entered the bunker at that point and called me out to answer the radio in the turret. This lieutenant belonged to the unit that rescued him. I have no idea what followed – and neither do I wish to!

Both sides feared each other and both sides exacted revenge.

An interesting characteristic of these journeys to the front is the assurance with which men drove to battle. Lieutenant Anatoly Kozlov remembered that his commander 'was confident' prior to the long march to Kursk and Prokhorovka. Vladimir Alexeev thought his commander 'well prepared mentally'. His tank crew had been together for about three months, had frequently experienced battle and were veterans. During their time at the Ostrogorhsk-Novy assembly area they had test-fired their guns and conducted crew training, including confidence tests allowing themselves to be run over by their own tanks in trenches. They were ready. Alexeev was philosophical about his chances and did not permit himself to dwell on the negative. 'A person only lives once,' he liked to say.

Despite the fact the Germans were aware that their massive concentration of tank forces around the Kursk salient was an open secret, they too were confident of victory. At the end of the approach marches Wilhelm Roes gazed about him as the II SS Panzer Corps began to shake out into assault formation for the coming attack on 4 July 1943:

> I saw the silhouettes of our panzers in the distance against the setting sun with apparently no end in sight and said to myself, nobody will be able to resist this might. We were so confident of winning, as we had always done before. It was a dead certainty for all of us.

While 988 panzers and self-propelled assault guns were to attack north of the salient, a force of 1,377, of which Roes was part, were to push up from the south. At dawn they crossed the start line to begin the first phase of the battle, the advance to contact: to seek, find and destroy the enemy.

## ADVANCE TO CONTACT

As the panzers lurched into motion across undulating steppe land they immediately fanned out into *Keil* or 'spearhead' formation. This arrowhead shape widened on sighting the enemy but tended to operate with one platoon of four to five tanks leading, followed by two further platoons of about ten tanks in depth, and then other arms such as anti-tank or panzer grenadiers in armoured half-tracks. The latter would come to the front to lead the way across close or wooded terrain. These formations were replicated at battalion and regiment level, whereby companies would open up into a huge *Keil* formation up to two or three kilometres wide. Armour was concentrated until it found the enemy, whereupon fighting occurred as the requisite number of panzers skirmished with their opposite numbers until, with the arrival of greater and often mixed combined forces, battle was joined. Tank battles on the eastern front were not, as often in the west, constrained by urban conurbations and close-wooded or cultivated hedge-lined fields; they were open-space duels conducted on a massive scale.

Trundling and bumping along, all the time scanning the approaching horizon for signs of the enemy, was tense and both physically and emotionally draining. Orientation was always difficult. There are few landmarks on the open steppe, with dry water-courses or *bulkas*, ravines, to ensnare the unwary. Tank columns ploughing the ground ahead can totally transform the landscape, making recognition difficult. Tank commanders constantly scanned undulating ground ahead for hidden enemy anti-tank or hull-down tank firing positions across their axis of advance. Panzers were kept in formation by hand signals, and by radio when out of sight. 'One always felt fear,' declared Leutnant Ludwig Bauer, 'it would be false to declare otherwise.' Even the sound of engines starting up was enough to stimulate the adrenalin rush, a sense of impending nervousness before battle actually started. 'When it came to the attack, believe me, nearly everyone had to quickly go and 'spend a penny', confessed Kurt Sametreiter with the SS LAH Panzer Regiment. 'You just got the urge, it came from fear; it came from fear,' he repeated. Foreboding revolved around the basic conundrum 'Will I live – or be injured?' Vladimir Alexeev remarked, 'but when battle started, you forgot fear because you were completely caught up with moving and fighting the Germans.' At least advancing was a physical release from the waiting, and crews could immerse themselves in a myriad of technical tasks that demanded immediate attention.

Panzer driver Helmut Steiner remembered the precise direction given by his Panzer IV commander Leutnant Thiemann, a Knight's Cross holder. Rapt attention was paid to the veterans because it improved the odds of surviving. 'To avoid confusion when in action,' he instructed, 'each crew member will be called by his functional name, that is: driver; wireless operator or front gunner, according to which job Hans is carrying out at the time; loader; and main gunner'. Having established the essentials, he continued, 'There will be no needless chatter over the intercom. I will give all necessary directions.' Crew members were confined to speaking only on matters of operational importance, such as 'warning of enemy approaching'. Other valid reasons for crew to speak, Thiemann stated, were 'spotting anti-tank positions, or reporting malfunctions of equipment within the tank, either of the driving function or any of our armaments'. Nobody was to get out in an emergency until they heard the order 'bail out!' If Theimann became a casualty, the gunner, who was the nearest, 'will deputise for me and give all necessary instructions'. Should there be anything else, or in the case of Steiner, who had just joined the crew, 'do only what I tell you,' the commander emphasised.

It was not the same for the Russians, for whom a shortage of radios made control during an advance to contact immensely difficult. 'Follow me – Do as I do' was the practice remembered by Vladimir Alexeev, who was commanding a T-34 platoon. Signal flags could be employed, but they were 'impractical', Alekseev recalled, and 'hardly ever used'. The practical way around the problem was to give the crew or other commanders a preliminary indication of direction, such as a lone tree coming up ahead. When a deserving target was identified, the initial direction might have been 'watch my tracer'. Tank commanders developed their own simple communication methods. Ivan Sagun of the 2nd Tank Army had decided:

I directed the driver by tapping him on the shoulder with my foot. On the right shoulder meant go right, on the left shoulder go left. A prod in the back meant stop. That was the simplest steering system we had.

Such a procedure was workable because commander and driver could still focus their attention on what they could see through their restricted vision slits. The other rudimentary signals were a distraction that disadvantaged crews in the fast-moving pell-mell conditions of tank-on-tank combat.

As for the gunner, I'd signal to him through the noise. A thumb meant an armour-penetrating shell, two fingers for a shrapnel shell. The index finger also meant I needed a shrapnel shell, but if we were facing another tank he often knew which shell to use.

All this of course required considerable presence of mind during battle. Crews developed their own fighting methods, but common to all these intercom improvisations was mutual trust in each other's capabilities. As the Germans' spearheads advanced, regimental, battalion and company commanders regularly communicated with each other by radio, as did the accompanying infantry, artillery and Luftwaffe. The Russians opposing them also used radios but less capable ones. Crews did not worry themselves with the niceties of command. Their concerns were basic. 'The company commander gave platoon commanders orders to move from one reference point to another in the direction in which the company was supposed to advance,' recalled Soviet tank driver Nikolai Zheleznov. 'My task was to drive that distance and stay alive.'

Tiger platoon commander Otto Carius followed a simple guideline in the advance, which was 'shoot *first*, but if you can't do that, at least hit first'. The difficulty was to spot the enemy before he spotted you. Soviet T-34 commander Alexeev had long realised 'you could not see in a tank that was closed down, particularly if attacked from the air'. Carius, an equally experienced commander, felt the Russian tendency to close down in battle placed them at a disadvantage. 'Tank commanders who slam their hatches shut at the beginning of an attack and don't open them again until the objective has been reached are useless,' he criticised, 'or at least second rate.' Vision blocks impeded the breadth of view needed to pick out the enemy and respond. Many panzer officers followed this maxim and sustained head injuries as a result. Carius accepted this as a calculated risk. 'If they had moved with closed hatches, then many more men would have found their death or been severely wounded inside the tanks.' The Russians saw it differently. 'Fortunately, for us, they almost always drove cross-country buttoned up.'

Mines were the first obstacle that tanks encountered. At Kursk the German panzer spearheads had to penetrate minefields up to 60km deep. They tended to disable rather than destroy a tank, but were invariably covered by artillery and anti-tank guns. Being marooned after a mine strike could be just as lethal. Millions of mines were employed in the Soviet anti-tank belts protecting the Kursk salient in 1943. Sapper Aleksandr Vishnevsky of the 5th Guards Tank Army recalled the sensitivity of the Russian types, 'because they were made in such a hurry'. He preferred German mines, which were so valuable that they were prepared to crawl into no-man's-land to recover them. 'They were well made and very safe,' he recalled. 'We could move them several times. You couldn't move our mines about. If you tried, you'd blow yourself up.'

A mine explosion was often the first indication the enemy was nearby. The next event was the ear-splitting shriek and crump of artillery fire. Near misses could lift a panzer and shake up the occupants, while a direct hit on the thin armour on top could be catastrophic. Ludwig Bauer's Mark III was hit by just such an artillery strike as his tank was crossing the start line for an attack in the summer of 1942. The impact split open the cranium of his Viennese tank commander Leutnant Sirse:

As I turned to him after the strike, he sat higher than me, he tumbled forward on to my upper body, pressed down on to my shoulder and his entire brain spilled out on to my field jacket. I was completely covered in blood and Sepp [the radio operator] thought at first that I had been rubbed out too. I opened my jacket and at the same time the brains fell on to the floor of the panzer. The attack carried on without us. We pulled the dead out of the tank and laid them on the rear engine deck.

After a three-day pause, he and his friend Sepp were put together in another panzer crew and carried on.

The real enemy in the advance to contact was not so much other tanks, which could be more easily detected, as hidden anti-tank guns. An anti-tank projectile would hit before the gun could be heard, which meant without warning if the flash was missed. Leutnant Carius insisted 'a tank commander's eyes are more important than his ears'. One never heard the dry bark of an opposing anti-tank gun amid the deafening reports of artillery explosions in the vicinity. Carius, being a canny commander, would occasionally lift his turret lid for a quick look around. 'If he happens to look half-way to the left while an enemy anti-tank gun opens up half-way to the right, his eye will subconsciously catch the glimmer of the yellow muzzle flash.' This was a matter of seconds and rarely was there a second chance. 'His attention will immediately be directed toward the new direction and the target will usually be identified in time.' Gun positions were always difficult to locate because of their low height above ground and good camouflage. 'Usually we didn't make out the anti-tank guns until they had fired their first shot,' Carius admitted. They had to rely on the Tiger's formidable armour and 'keep as cool as possible' and engage before another shot was fired. Keeping one's nerve was paramount but not easy because the guns would operate as a minimum in a pair and often many more. Official score keepers only counted other destroyed tanks as successes, but panzer crews always included the anti-tank gun tally, because they 'counted twice as much to the experienced tankers', Carius remarked.

Anti-tank guns were protected by infantry. At Kursk, and often in large-scale tank battles, the infantry tended to get left behind by tanks pursuing other tanks. Russian infantry were particularly tenacious. 'The worst was the anti-tank hunting detachments which came in between T-34 attacks,' claimed Wilhelm Roes, who as radio operator manned the hull machine-gun of the Panzer Mark IV. 'You had to pay them particular attention – if they got through you were finished. An explosive charge and up you went.' Gerd Schmükle, the 7th Panzer Division battalion commander, recalled the safeguards employed to counter this problem. 'It was the cruellest thing,' he admitted:

The Russians normally took cover in the trenches we had passed with the tanks or with artillery or other parts of our division. They would fire from behind, and then we or the tank was lost. Consequently we turned [the panzer] around on the trenches, and by doing this they were injured or killed.

The interviewer, not certain he had heard correctly, asked what he meant – 'ground down in the trenches?' – implying horror at the awful nature of the death. 'True – a terrible thing,' Schmükle admitted, 'war is always a terrible thing.'

## MEETING ENGAGEMENT

Once the *Panzerkeil,* or spearhead, working with air and artillery support and with infantry, breached the anti-tank belts, armoured meeting engagements would occur as Soviet tank formations attempted to plug the German breakthroughs. These sudden tank-on-tank confrontations were unpredictable in nature and fully tested the professional resourcefulness of the crews.

Lieutenant Vladimir Alexeev's T-34 battalion started such an engagement at dawn on 12 July 1943 at the huge tank battle of Prokhorovka, south-east of Kursk. About fifty Mark VI Tigers participated in this battle from around 128 involved in the Army Group South thrust on Kursk. Another 200 Mark V Panthers were also engaged in the fighting for the Kursk salient. The mainstay of the panzer regiments was in fact the 75mm long-barrelled Panzer IV. Panthers had an improved version of the 75mm, and the Tigers the 88mm. 'The German tanks could fight it out at very long range,' Alexeev admitted, 'they could open fire at 1,200 metres and easily hit our T-34s, we could only hit at a distance of 800 metres.' German tanks backed up with superior optics and practised fire-control measures were lethal. 'Just try to approach them and they'd burn your tank from 1,200 to 1,500 metres!' declared Lieutenant Nikolai Zheleznov. 'They were so cocky! In essence until we got the 85mm gun we had to run from Tigers like rabbits.' These superior guns dominated the eastern front tank battlefields in 1943. Material inequality had a pronounced emotional and by necessity tactical impact on the fighting. As Alexeev recalled, 'the tactics between the two sides varied a lot'.

Poor Russian radio communications meant the Russian tanks operated not unlike traditional horsed cavalry. They attacked in echelon or in battalion or even regiment-size groups, numbering scores of tanks, and in the absence of control could degenerate to charging tank masses that might number hundreds. Battle became mass versus tactical guile. Once launched, like cavalry they could not be recalled and only simple manoeuvres like change of direction were achievable. The panzers, by contrast, operated in tactical platoons or bands of four to five tanks. Good communications enabled the platoon groups to be quickly assembled into company and battalion-size formations to achieve specified objectives.

The gentle crest lines of the terrain favoured anti-tank defence but the guns were vulnerable. Tanks could take advantage of good shoots at maximum ranges 'hull down', which means only the turret showing. Kursk, according to panzer radio operator Wilhelm Roes after breaching minefield after minefield 'was actually a battle in the first few days always against high ground, Hill 230.5 and whatever'. It was a question of holding these crest lines with only a long-barrelled tank gun firing across the top. As Roes explained, 'Then on the right thirty T–34s would break through, then from the left fifteen, then would come eight, completely festooned with infantry.' German tank crews were often taken aback at the quantity of Russian tanks that would suddenly charge them. Cool precise fire control was required to exact punishment at maximum range, beyond effective Soviet fire, before they could close in. 'We said we can't hold out against a thousand tanks,' Roes claimed at Kursk; 'they were going to roll over us – but they didn't.'

Ivan Sagun described what an unequal contest it was for a T–34, with these restrictions, up against a Tiger:

I had an encounter with just such a tank. He fired at us from literally one kilometre away. His first shot blew a hole in the side of my tank, his second hit my axle. At a range of half a kilometre I fired at him with a special calibre shell, but it bounced off him like a candle, I mean it didn't penetrate his armour. At literally 300 metres I fired my second shell – same result. Then he started looking for me, turning his turret to see where I was. I told my driver to reverse fast and we hid behind some trees.

'The turret of our tank was electronically motorised, which meant we could rotate it faster than the T-34s,' claimed Wilhelm Roes, 'which was a huge advantage.' The aim was to maintain distance if possible between the Soviet tanks and systematically pick them off through judicious and well-directed fire control. Such nerve was not easy to sustain. Tiger gunner Gerhard Niemann, who was with Heavy Battalion 503 at Kursk, recalled sitting at the commander's feet, headset and microphone in place, awaiting direction. 'Nervously I once again check the triggers for the main gun and machine-gun and the hand wheels for the elevating and traversing mechanisms. My hands tremble a little as I quickly set the various ranges on the range scale.' Panzer gunner Ludwig Bauer remembered that 'after the first few rounds, the fear went'. Thereafter he worked hand in glove with the commander, pressing left and right to align the gun according to fire control direction. The other occasion he felt fear was when the infantry ahead fired flares, 'meaning other tanks about, and then the adrenalin pumped again'.

Once battle was joined, actions in the turret became as automated and impersonal as the machines they served. Gerhard Niemann described the sequence of mechanical actions that caused such fearful Russian attrition:

Achtung, (watch out), two o'clock, bunker! – High explosive!
My foot presses forward on the pedal of the turret traversing mechanism. The turret swings to the right. With my left hand I set the range on the telescopic sight; my right hand cranks the elevation hand wheel. The target appears in sight. Ready, release safety – Fire! The target is shrouded in a cloud of smoke.

'I never experienced German tanks moving at high speed like us,' recalled T-34 commander Vladimir Alexeev. 'They would move, pause and fire – a very lethal combination.' It was this precise jockeying just below crest lines that exacted such a high toll on the Russian tanks.

'How could we overcome this problem of 400 metres?' rhetorically asked Alexeev, referring to the range disparity of the T–34. The only option was to 'cover the difference at high speed until we were all around and in amongst the German tanks – this was our tactic'. The Russians sought a tank mêlée. It was the tactics of desperation, and Soviet commanders were prepared to trade off quantity to match quality and accept the human cost. They would swamp the panzers by numbers alone.

'The T–34s came straight for us at full speed with hardly time even to fire, as though they had gone mad,' recalled Wilhelm Roes, at Prokhorovka near Kursk with the SS LAH. 'I had the feeling of being suffocated, suffocated by the sheer number of tanks.' *Obersturmführer* (SS lieutenant) Rudolf von Ribbentrop, a company commander in Roes's regiment, claimed, 'What I saw left me speechless.'

From beyond the shallow rise about 150 to 200 metres in front of me appeared fifteen, then thirty, then forty tanks. Finally there were too many to count. The T–34s were rolling toward us at high speed, carrying mounted infantry . . . Soon the first shell was on the way, and with the impact a T–34 began to burn. It was only 50 to 70 metres from us . . . The avalanche of enemy tanks rolled straight towards us: tank after tank!

T–34 commander Lieutenant Vasili Bryukhov recalled the crowded battlefield at Prokhorovka. On 12 July 186 German panzers and self-propelled assault guns engaged 850 Soviet tanks in an area confined to 50 square kilometres. 'The distance between the tanks there was below 100 metres – it was impossible to manoeuvre a tank, one could just jerk it back and forth a bit'. Evgeny Shkurdalov of the 5th Guards Tank Army described how 'our tanks got in amongst the German ones and the Germans got between our lines. They were firing virtually at point-blank range – like boxers fighting close in, inflicting terrible damage on each other.' 'It was a slaughterhouse of tanks,' concurred Bryukhov. 'Everything was enveloped in smoke, dust and fire, so it looked as if it was twilight.' Telephone cables wrapped around their tracks and 'our radio was jammed'.

Blindly charging in an attempt to inflict damage resulted in terrible attrition for the Soviet tanks; the Germans stood their ground and shot them to pieces as they closed. Tanks could not fire accurately on the move. The Germans retained their edge even during the close-range mêlée. 'We had only one slim chance,' Rudolf von Ribbentrop assessed, 'we must remain constantly in motion.' As panzers lost sight of each other in the dust and obscuration of battle, they could at least check identification of friend and foe by radio. Any Russian tank displaying radio antennae received concentrated German fire. 'A stationary tank would immediately be recognised as enemy,' explained von Ribbentrop, 'and fired upon, because all the Russian tanks were rolling at high speed across the terrain.' Lieutenant Bryukhov exclaimed, 'That was Prokhorovka! If a tank stopped in that battle, you had to bail out immediately. If you weren't killed by the first round, another tank would drive up and finish you off.'

The sights, smells and sounds of a close-in tank battle were awful and afflicted veterans with nightmares for years to come. The seeming inability to counter the random nature of death was disturbing. Wilhelm Roes described how vulnerable he felt sitting in the radio operator's seat with only his hull machine-gun to face a T-34 'that had broken through and was heading straight at us'.

My commander kept shouting, 'Shoot! Shoot! *Shoot!*' But the gunner at the back couldn't shoot because the gun was not loaded. So I had to crawl back to load the gun. After I had done that four times the commander shouted, 'Thank God – we've done it!' We all heard him through the intercom, otherwise we couldn't have heard anything in all the noise.

After the battle they saw the tank had come to rest eight metres away. 'I still don't know why it had not fired at us,' said Roes.

Panzer Mark IV driver Helmut Steiner of the 9th Panzer Division recalled that in his very first battle a panzer next to them blew up in an orange sheet of flame. Shaking uncontrollably, he nevertheless kept his foot on the accelerator and drove 'until the bones in his foot ached under the pressure'. Activity and clear orders helped him to suppress his fear during this baptism of fire. Nightmare images remained indelibly in his memory. A momentarily blinded Russian tank crew survivor blundered into his path while he frantically tried to manoeuvre the tank out of the way at the height of the action. He glimpsed the poor man's face through the vision slit, 'a frozen picture compounded of shock, terror and astonishment – before he disappeared beneath the tracks'.

Most veterans comment at some stage on the intensity of battle noises, mixed with fumes, and how intimidating and disorientating it can be. 'The engine would be roaring so one couldn't hear the explosions outside,' remembered Vasili Bryukhov, 'and when I opened fire myself I didn't hear anything that was happening outside the tank.' He only realised he was being fired at when the crack or thump of an armour-piercing round or fragmentation round sounded against the armour. There was the constant rattling sound of metal peppering the hull with near misses or the sharper and more violent thwacking of machine-gun fire splattering against the armour. Each time a round was fired, choking blue-grey cordite fumes would penetrate the turret fighting compartment and sting sweat-rimmed eyes. So intense were the fumes inside a T-34, according to veteran accounts, that loaders would pass out. Bryukhov, realising his loader was not forwarding 'fragmentation' on request, would glance down below, where 'he'd be lying unconscious on the ammo storage, poisoned by the exhaust gases'. 'Few loaders could last out a heavy fight to the end,' he commented.

Tank fighting transformed pleasing and peaceful scenery to desolate landscapes of ploughed tracks polluted by the stench of burning oil, lubricants and human flotsam. Wilhelm Roes has always remembered the distinctive odours of the Kursk battlefield:

> There was the smell of the heavy Ukrainian soil which had been churned up and then soaked by rain. Then there was the strong stench of smoke, of gunpowder, and the burning tanks. You could smell burned leather and dead bodies that were still smouldering. It was a mixture that I cannot really describe.

Smells triggered memories of disturbing sights. Viewed from far away the tank battlefield was a dramatic and at times colourful spectacle. Lines of tracer criss-crossed dark silhouettes within the engagement area, some of the fiery threads moved more slowly, denoting heavy-calibre machine-guns. Gun reports cracked out, expelling slivers of gleaming metal that languidly arced across flashing lines of tracer until splashing in a cascade of sparks atop a target or spinning off violently at acute angles, to drop glowing to the ground again. Smoke reduced these spectral flashing images to the semblance of rolling thunder squalls. Close in, the images were brutally ugly.

It was the images that blighted future minds more than anything else. Lieutenant Aleksandr Fadin remembered the death of fellow T-34 platoon commander Konstantin Grozdev, whose turret was blown completely off the hull of his tank in a catastrophic Tiger strike. 'Konstantin bailed out – more accurately, the upper part of his body bailed out: the lower part remained in the tank.' It was a picture he would never erase from his mind. 'He was still alive. He looked at me and his hands scratched the ground. Can you imagine such a sight?' Ludwig Bauer is haunted by the images of two close friends he lost, tank drivers, both decapitated by in-coming anti-tank shells. 'I had always wondered about the guillotine in the French Revolution during history classes – and that is what I witnessed!' One lost his head completely, the other was sliced in half.

'Have you burned yet?' was a common question that Soviet tank men asked each other on greeting the first time. 'Everyone's fear was to be burned alive,' confessed tank commander Vladimir Alexeev. Lieutenant Nikolai Zheleznov recalled burying burned tank crews, grown men reduced to mummies the size of children. 'The skin on their faces was reddish-bluish-brown. It was scary to see then and it's very disturbing to recall now.' There was a dark Russian joke in which a 'politruk'(commissar figure) tells a young tank soldier that almost every tank man in his group died that day. 'I'm sorry,' the young man replies, 'I'll make sure that I burn tomorrow.'

'The tank was on fire, I couldn't breathe,' remembered Nikolai Zheleznov, who lay on the turret floor, after being struck by a Tiger. From here he saw the driver's shattered head, while the loader's arm had been torn off and the gunner was also dead, having soaked up the shrapnel that otherwise would have hit Zheleznov. Fire was consuming the oxygen in the tank and licked at him while he hung in the commander's hatch trying to get out. His left leg was broken at the knee, preventing him from climbing. 'My legs and butt inside the tank were already burning,' he recalled. A mass of blood covered his eyes and to his horror 'my eyes got burned on top of everything else'. He appealed to two men who were passing by to get him out. 'Zheleznov?' they disbelievingly asked. 'That's me!' He was unrecognisably burned. They tugged him out by the arms and his boots, snagging on the turret edge, dropped back inside. They slapped out the flames on his clothes as the tank exploded.

'Thirty-five per cent of my skin was burned!' he declared. He was denied water but did receive alcohol to deaden the pain. Skin hung down from his face. 'The biggest problem was that I could not see anything, my entire face got swollen. My eyelids grew together and they had to cut them open. I'm not going to talk about it or I might start crying.' It was the end of his war. He had one satisfaction: 'I'm even with the Germans. I lost three tanks and burned three of theirs, plus an armoured personnel carrier.'

Rolf Hertenstein's panzer with the 13th Division was hit by two Molotov cocktails as it was about to run over infantry in a trench. There were two explosive fireballs and fire and burning liquid seeped into the interior. Despite being under fire they were forced out 'because we couldn't breathe any more'. As the weather was hot the crew wore only their grey uniform shirts and not field jackets. 'Sticky stuff from the Molotov cocktails was running all over our necks, shoulders and arms,' he recalled. The panzer was completely incapacitated.

Concussive blows from incoming shells paralysed the senses. Dazed men could not hear shouted commands. Once the tank burst into flames the overwhelming urge was to get out, but Vasili Bryukhov explained the need to stay calm. 'The temperature increases right away, and if flames envelop you, you completely lose control.' It was especially hard for the driver. 'He had to take off the hooks, and open his hatch, and if he panicked or became enveloped by flames – that was it, he'd never be able to bail out.' Claustrophobia was pervasive enough without the threat of a fiery end. 'Radio operators burned the most,' declared Bryukhov; it was easier for the commander and loader, 'but for the others it all depended on their luck'.

Guilt figured prominently because will power could not always match the physical capabilities of rescuers. This accounted also for the puzzling phenomenon of crew who sometimes fell back inside burning turrets at the very point when it appeared to horrified onlookers that they were going to make it. Animal-like cries indicating failure haunted men for the rest of their lives. When tank driver Aleksandr Sacharow's T-34 was hit, he recalled, 'the tank commander was on fire' and 'the commissar's head was ripped off'. Visibly forcing himself to tell his story, he continued: 'The mechanic, the radio operator and I were the only ones who survived. We jumped down from the tank and our uniforms were still burning.' Even though it was years since the event Sacharow began involuntarily slapping and brushing at his clothes as he said, 'At the same time we smothered the flames – we helped each other.'

'You wouldn't have thought that the metal could burn so fiercely,' recalled Dr Olga Borisenko, a female doctor with the Medical Corps attached to the 5th Guards Tank Army. 'We had a dreadful time helping the wounded crews at the battlefield. Many of the men would come in covered in dirt. They'd tried to put out the flames by rolling on the ground. As a result their wounds got dirty and became infected.'

Crews not only burned, in their desperation to escape they would launch themselves from upper decks and hulls high above ground level. On hitting the ground burning, many of them shattered limbs, which further impeded their ability to move in order to douse the flames.

Fighting often petered out at the end of the day, or paused prior to the next. Emotional reaction set in as a consequence of the physical energy and mental reserves expended during the day. Despite the German qualitative superiority at Kursk, resulting in the successful tactical holding action at Prokhorovka, there were always more Russians to fight the next day. Gerd Schmükle, commanding a battalion in Panzer Regiment 25, described the intimidating effect of Soviet numerical superiority:

One morning in the early twilight we were alerted by our night watches and I saw a spectacle I have never seen before. We saw hundreds of Russian tanks in front of us; they must have been camouflaged before. Now they were lined up as if on parade, side by side in a very deep formation. It was a terrible, terrible view for us

273

because our tank regiment was now very small; we had lost a lot of tanks. And now suddenly we saw this armada in front of us.

German retreats now began. 'It was a very wise decision,' Schmükle declared, 'because the Russian armada started to move forward slowly, extremely slowly – I don't know why – but we were saved by this, I believe.'

## AFTERMATH

Sixty-three years after the event Lieutenant Vladimir Alexeev found the spot near the nondescript village of Andreerka, 8km west of Prokhorovka, where his T-34 was destroyed on the second day of the battle. It was an emotional point on a journey he had not attempted since the war. 'The terrain has changed a lot over the past sixty years,' he declared. 'The battle was in the field to the left,' he indicated, 'I can say for sure, and the remains of the houses destroyed on the right.' Vladimir and the gunner helped the driver, 'Papa Sergai' – so called because of his thirty-six years – out of his hatch. Both legs were smashed, 'parts of the leg were joined only by the sinew of the trousers,' Vladimir remembered. He was visibly upset recalling this. 'He got out as far as his waist and then lost consciousness' he said. The loader Nickolev, aged twenty-three, had to be left inside the blazing tank. 'I could not imagine how I survived,' Vladimir concluded, 'it had been a very severe tank encounter.' They spent the entire day sheltering in a shell hole waiting for medical assistance. Vladimir never saw his driver again. His crew had lived cheek by jowl for three months. 'This is how the day ended for me and my crew,' he wistfully remarked.

At the end of a typical day's tank fighting on the Eastern Front scores of groups of surviving crew from both sides sought to return to their lines. This might take days because of the distances involved and the fluidity of front changes. 'It took some time to relocate them,' Alexeev said of the crews. 'All the officers and platoon commanders, there were about forty,' he recalled, 'were all loaded on to two trucks and driven to the 3rd Guards Tank Army near Orel.' He was to spend the rest of his war with this unit.

'Dejectedly we plodded back two or three miles, smoking cigarettes to steady our nerves,' recalled Hans Becker of the 12th Panzer Division. The previous day his crew had knocked out six tanks before being hit and bailing out themselves. This day they had gone to battle again with a new reserve tank, the same model Mark IV but 'unfamiliar in small ways, and all of us were suffering from the after-effects of the previous evening'. There was no time to paint their score rings on the gun barrel, a talisman of 'superstitious significance for us'. After four and a half hours' fighting they destroyed two more Soviet tanks, but this time they were shot into flames and two of Becker's five crew were dead. 'We were all spattered in blood from the effects of the enemy shell.' Even today there is a scar on his chest the size of a coin where his identity disc was driven into his chest bone. 'In avoiding death by a disc's breadth here surely was a sign to confirm my belief that I would survive the war.'

Day's end brought with it emotional stock-taking. How did one measure success after such carnage? 'How many tanks did we destroy?' asked tank driver Aleksandr Sacharow. 'How do you remember how many you have knocked out throughout the war?' as if to ask, what was the point? 'There was firing and there were hits – or at least thought to be. Perhaps you didn't hit, the tanks don't always burst into flames.' Vasili Bryukhov, a battalion tank commander, remembered 'we didn't always accurately record how many [of our own] tanks were destroyed', but they believed the daily reports gave an indication of how many the enemy had lost. His brigade Chief of Staff, however, indignantly responded, 'If I believed all the reports of battalion commanders . . . we should have finished the war six months earlier, as we'd destroyed the entire German Army.' After submission numerical claims were halved as they proceeded up each headquarter chain.

The real issue was, as Sacharow intimated: 'it is always painful to remember people who have died next to you, died for nothing and again nothing, and that goes exactly for our own people as also the Germans.' Panzer radio operator Wilhelm Roes remembered the headquarters panzer that took a direct hit alongside his own, because 'inside were people that I had served with during training'.

Two people were killed instantly. One Untersturmführer (SS lieutenant) Beckman climbed out. He only had one leg and jumped
down from the turret to the ground and made it. The Russian
infantry were soon on him and he took out his pistol and fired,
hitting two of them. The other Russians charged up and sorted him
out with the bayonet. That was hard – *very hard*!

Stress and combat fatigue had become ever more prevalent as a consequence of longer campaigns after the failure of *Blitzkrieg*. '1942 was
absolutely the worst year of my life,' declared Lieutnant Ludwig Bauer.
He had been knocked out for the first time at Tula, outside Moscow, the
year before; the driver and radio operator had been killed, and he was
severely injured, nearly losing an eye. In June 1942 his driver was
decapitated by an anti-tank round at Tim. Nine days after that his Panzer
III was rammed three times by a heavy KV-1 and shot to pieces in a tank
battle around Vorenesch. Six weeks later at Shisdra an artillery strike
destroyed his tank, with more grisly deaths and wounded. A four-month
relative pause followed, after which his Panzer III was hit again near
Rschev, with the driver and gunner killed and the rest of the crew
wounded. He recalled writing in his diary that autumn how deeply
depressed he was at losing so many close comrades, and he unburdened
himself in a compassionate interview with his company commander.
Bauer was a survivor with that essential zest for life. There was no other
option he appreciated except 'to keep going, but he knew not how'. It
blighted his faith in God and he resigned himself to accepting that his life
would be short. 'I always thought with certainty I would not survive,' he
confessed. The next strike on his panzer would probably be the last.

   Nightmares afflicted survivors, not only at the time but in perpetuity.
Panther driver Helmut Steiner was recovered hanging half out of his
escape hatch with the rest of his crew dead. Weeks of mental anguish
followed as he languished severely injured in a military hospital in
Dresden. Like many survivors he was assailed by irrational feelings of
guilt. 'Why did I survive when all my comrades had died?' he asked
himself. He longed to return to action to ease the torment. 'After the
war I dreamed not once but a hundred times that I was again on the
battlefield at Prokhorovka,' confessed Wilhelm Roes. Crews had
always been intimidated by the vastness of Russia:

But I was alone and I had to get home from Prokhorovka through 1,500 kilometres of enemy territory. I was constantly thinking 'how can I do it?' In my dream there were always burning tanks. It was always the same picture, this landscape rising up to a tank trap, a few tanks on fire, but I was alone, wondering how I could get back home, through the forests, how I could hide.

Dreams like this continued for years, always interrupted by his wife. 'She would wake me up and say, 'You're dreaming of Russia again.''

Recovering wounded tank crew, often unable to get themselves out of the obstructive twisted metal confines of damaged turrets, required super-human effort. Russian female nurses found this especially demanding. Nina Vishnevskaya of the 32nd Tank Brigade at Prokhorovka remembered girls weighing 48 kilos struggling with incapacitated dead-weight crewmen weighing 70 kilos. 'It was difficult to drag out a man, especially a turret gunner . . .' and if the tank was moving 'you had to keep your feet clear of the caterpillars so you wouldn't get dragged in.' Vishnevskaya still kept a tank crewman's helmet hanging in her living-room in the 1980s.

Transporting wounded to hospital from a tank engagement could be a dangerous and often ad-hoc affair. Infantrymen were also given lifts. Tiger commander Otto Carius recalled carrying some on the rear engine deck. 'They were dead tired and scarcely capable of walking anywhere.' They sat above the cooling vents where the warm air was expelled from the engine compartment. 'They soon fell asleep and suffered monoxide poisoning,' recalled Carius. 'Despite immediate resuscitation efforts three of them couldn't be saved – at that time we hadn't known any better.' As it was often too dangerous to lay the injured in the open on the engine decks, infantry wounded were stowed inside. Ludwig Bauer recalled how violently they reacted to their involuntary claustrophobic confinement. 'Get us out of here – I'm not staying inside!' they would shout, tugging at his legs as he stood maintaining balance in the turret cupola and trying to pick out enemy threats through binoculars.

Conditions in the field hospitals were physically and emotionally disturbing. Wounded and nurses alike were confronted with the most appalling sights, sounds and smells imaginable. 'Sometimes they amputated as much as a whole leg,' confided Nurse Maria Bozhek, 'and I could barely take it to the basin. I remember the limbs being very heavy. I would take it as noiselessly as possible, so that the wounded did not notice, and carry it like a baby . . . I used to have dreams that I was carrying a leg.'

When tank commander Evageny Shkurdalov was knocked out at Prokhorovka, his driver managed to get the tank out of the line of fire despite a smashed hand, but the rest of the crew were dead. 'My left side was torn open and I had wounds all over my arms and legs,' he recalled. He was transported to hospital but was bleeding to death on arrival and blood supplies had run out. In one of those rare uplifting battlefield moments, Olga Borisenko, the female doctor, volunteered a direct blood transfusion in order, without realising it at the time, to save her future husband's life:

I lay beside him on the operating table and my blood was pumped directly into my tank commander. I must have given him about 300 grams of my blood, because when I looked over he started moving and said, 'Where am I? Why aren't I in my tank?' 'Well,' I thought, 'everything's fine, I've brought him back to life.'

Out on the bleak, tank-scarred field of battle recovery crews laboured in darkness to retrieve salvageable tank hulks. Both sides were prepared to fight its other's teams to achieve this. Urgency permeated the German side because their material reserve was so much smaller than that of the Soviets. Getting one tank out often meant the rescuer could become bogged down. Tigers, because of their mass and weight, were especially difficult. 'The recovery of a tank after an operation usually cost more in nerves than the operation itself,' admitted Tiger commander Otto Carius. Often they gave up in order to spare infantry casualties. To keep it out of enemy hands, the hulk would be shot into flames.

Back in the assembly areas the cycle prior to the next action would start again. Company commander Ralf Tiemann of the SS LAH recalled that 'for four days and four nights we didn't leave the confines of our panzers. We had to be awake the whole time.' His company destroyed seventy-nine enemy tanks in twelve days of battle around

Kursk. He was twice knocked out, suffering crew deaths each time, and climbed into three new tanks in the course of a single day. He had now to carry out 'the sad and painful duty to write to the families of his fallen comrades'. It was an unenviable task. 'I want to write personally and full of heart in each and every case.' How could he do this when he was so emotionally and physically spent himself? 'Although I wrote every letter with great effort, it was somehow unavoidable that in twenty cases a cliché came up.' Three platoon commanders had died, so that 'there were moments in action when I had to lead every single platoon'. One of them was *Untersturmführer* (SS lieutenant) Weiser, whose death he admitted 'struck me especially deeply'.

Rolf Ehrhardt had been part of Weiser's Panzer Mark IV crew. He remembered that Weiser 'came from leave in the homeland and was wearing his dress uniform as he still hadn't any opportunity to change into his field uniform'. All the emotion Tiemann recalled was because 'he had come back two days before the beginning of the offensive from vacation, from his honeymoon'. Wieser had proudly passed the wedding photographs around the crew. 'We checked out his wedding pictures,' said Ehrhardt, a poignant sharing of memories because 'everyone tried to find some contact with home', especially prior to a big battle.

Receiving tragic casualty notifications at home in Germany was disturbing and the frequency was becoming emotionally draining. Housewife Hildegard Gratz remembered that 'being a postman suddenly became an unpleasant occupation, he became the bringer of bad news. There were these terrible letters, and the postmen told stories of pitiful scenes of grief. The postman came to dread his round if ever there was one of those black-edged letters to be delivered.'

Even the SS Secret Service took an interest, particularly focusing on the opinions of women in the Reich. 'Total War', as expounded by Goebbels after Stalingrad, required their acquiescence and support if their menfolk were to fight. Their opinions were canvassed and accorded immense respect in daily reports submitted to Reichsführer Himmler, the head of the service. It was clear from numerous reports that female opinion was uncompromising and voiced fearlessly once they perceived the extent their menfolk were suffering at the front, particularly in Russia. 'Two particularly crass cases' of casualty notifications 'were reported from Düsseldorf', noted an SS Home Front Survey investigating condolence letters. A death notice inserted with the normal mail through a letterbox after the postman received no answer at the door resulted in the housewife discovering her husband was dead as she sorted the routine mail with the children present. Another unfortunate woman was given the tragic news at a tram-stop with her children, as the unsuspecting postman continued his round. She allegedly screamed and collapsed in the street. Numerous changes to procedure were officially recommended, but could never mitigate the emotional impact of such news.

The battles around Kursk marked a turning-point on the Eastern Front. The deadly cycle, beginning in the assembly areas and proceeding through movement to the front line, then crossing the start line and going into combat, was to continue for a further two years, constantly retiring westward. The Panzerwaffe became increasingly reliant upon the technical superiority of its machines, served by a hard core of veteran survivors who, man for man, became increasingly lethal and proficient as the war progressed. Soviet tank men, too, became ever more capable. As Panzer General Hoth confided to von Manstein, the Commander of Army Group South, after Kursk: 'The Russians have learned the art of war from us.'

Heavy casualties were to be inflicted on every Russian advance. In 1943 and 1944 the panzers destroyed an average of eight Red Army fighting vehicles for every tank lost. Gathering together in the emotional mill ponds of assembly areas prior to these battles, the Red Army sang its haunting choral melodies around evening camp fires. Lieutenant Vladimir Alexseev quoted from a favourite soldiers' song that expressed the guilt all survivors felt at still being alive:

> If I am not killed in action or burned in a tank,
> It is not my fault I have remained – maybe next time.

# 12

## MASS VERSUS TECHNOLOGY

### PREPARING MASS

The Allied invasion of Sicily in July 1943 obliged Hitler to block the deployment of von Manstein's panzer reserve at Kursk. Local success that could conceivably have brought operational advantage was frittered away by inaction, allowing the Soviets to grip the strategic initiative, which they proceeded to do, despite appalling tank losses. In the East the Germans were on the defensive.

Italy followed Sicily in September, as the Allies grasped a toehold on the boot of Mediterranean Europe. This was a different war for the Allied tank men. 'In the desert, then, I do not recall being, what I would say, really frightened,' confessed twenty-three-year-old Lieutenant Stuart Hamilton of 8 RTR. 'Scared, yes – but in Italy, well I was bloody terrified.' 'We crossed the Volturno and fought our way slowly on,' recalled Peter Roach of 4 RTR. 'There seemed endless rivers, streams and dykes which frustrated our advances.' Tactical ingenuity aided by a completely different terrain from the desert enabled the Germans to conduct skilful withdrawals. 'Jerry was as thorough as ever,' emphasised Peter Roach, 'and made us earn our advance with here a tank and there a man.' Mines and hand-held bazooka weapons now came into their own. Infantry could stop tanks by themselves. The endless round of heavier casualties in shorter periods of time promoted war-weariness. 'Things were deadly grim by now,' reflected Hamilton.

Eric Allsop, a subaltern also in 8 RTR, recalled numerous differences from their recent desert experience. Civilians were now in the way; there had been none in the desert. They lived in the easily fortified small farmhouses and in small and large towns, 'and learned by experience to get out of the way'. Others stayed to eke out a living and survived by selling produce to troops. Built-up urban areas required different techniques to overcome. More reliance was placed on high-explosive than armour-piercing shells. 'The Sherman was a very good gun platform,' explained Allsop, 'you could put a round through a window or door and unlike artillery you could make it go through precisely the same place.' Of 100 rounds carried in a tank, seventy were now high-explosive (HE); they did not expect to encounter armour often.

The new terrain was a nightmare compared to the flat expanse of the desert, and brought peculiar pressures with it. 'After the desert, which is open country, you have to keep your head down – it's no good looking out of the turret when you're going through villages,' explained Paul Rollins of 40 RTR. 'Snipers up telegraph poles, in trees, in church spires – you'd get a nice little hole there,' he said, indicating his forehead. Snipers were ubiquitous, deadly to tank commanders and maintenance crews, and generally disliked. Rollins explained how one sniper perched atop a water-tower had been 'popping them off' until apprehended by a patrol. 'He wanted to give himself up, but they stuck a bayonet in his guts and left him to die.' Rollins was unperturbed. 'He'd knocked off so many blokes. Snipers are a nasty swine, aren't they?' He described a prevalent attitude. 'Nobody gives them any quarter, snipers; they're fair game, you know.'

Allsop explained that gradients were now assessed in terms of 'what will your tank take? How do you get over a crest without getting mown down by a bunch of 88mms?' He pointed to an unfortunate example: the Queen's Bays, who lost twenty tanks in a few minutes – 'Awful,' he declared. It was now especially difficult to pick out enemy under cover. 'I found it very demanding indeed,' confessed Allsop; 'attacking well-sited and long-prepared mountain positions, dangerous slopes under fire with water obstacles at the bottom and bridges destroyed. Crossing under fire and then uphill, always against the grain of the country.' He admitted, 'I was very near the end of my endurance; I think I might have cracked up.'

Allsop had tremendous admiration for the ambulance drivers – conscientious objectors – who were 'driving past blazing houses in the battle zone in soft-skinned vehicles. Quakers not prepared to take up weapons, admirable people, in a class of their own!'

Finally, as Allsop pointed out, the climate was very different – 'hot dusty summers with the fruits of the earth in abundance but in winter worse than England'.

His squadron commander was very much aware that 'as one of the few "old desert hands" left I was expected automatically to show coolness, confidence and complete disregard to anything "unpleasant".' He found this to be 'a very heavy responsibility under these conditions'. A combat law of averages was operating inexorably against them. 'I had seen so many good friends and good men "get the chop" by then that I felt my number must be coming up soon.' Western Europe had to be the next major theatre of operations, and a number of desert-wise, combat-experienced Mediterranean divisions were thinned out for return to the UK and replaced slowly with fresh ones. Those that were left continued the grind up the steeply undulating boot of Italy. Hamilton now began to think and say when warned off for further operations: 'Christ! Not us again! Not my squadron! Not me! Isn't some other bastard fighting this bloody war!'

In March 1943 the Allies decided their Second Front would come ashore in Normandy. Part of the training and build-up required the homecoming of the 7th Armoured Division, the 'Desert Rats', and other veteran armoured units to stiffen the spearhead for the coming assault. These men only spent a brief time in the United Kingdom before participating in the Invasion. Many had been away from home for up to five years. Briefly reuniting with wives and sweethearts was perhaps not the best preparation for emotionally revisiting the spectres that were uppermost in their minds. 'We had mainly come to terms with our life and with the many faces of death,' declared Peter Roach, returning with 4 RTR. This set them apart from the norm and especially the 'green' armoured units that stayed behind and were condemned to train in England for three years. 'We had lived with the thought of the dignity and warmth of Britain' which had sustained them during the hard times in the desert and Italy, 'and we desperately wanted to be part of it again,' recalled Roach. But their experience of combat had marked them immeasurably, because 'here we are strangers in a strange land'. Captain Bill Close returned after three years to find that his wife Josie had joined the ATS, which meant that his son Richard, 'now a sturdy lad', had to be looked after by his parents. 'I was not particularly happy about this arrangement,' he admitted, but realised his wife wanted to 'do her bit' for the war effort. He only managed a few days' leave in these circumstances and 'was not unhappy' when he had to rejoin the battalion.

'Jacked me in for a civvy,' remarked one soldier returning from years overseas. 'I got home; no one there, no furniture, nothing.' Apart from the emotional upsets of finding unfaithful or now indifferent wives and girlfriends, there were other niggling occurrences that served to set them apart. Trooper Robert Whitehead of 44 RTR recalled that wearing the African Star campaign medal ribbon 'was both an honour and a disgrace'. This was because 'one of our respected lady MPs had warned the girls of England to be very careful having relations with soldiers who wore the Africa Star, because of the possibility of contracting VD from them'. There was also the inevitable difficulty of readapting to changed circumstances. Trooper Whitehead remembered that at first it was difficult to make conversation with his parents, 'and long pauses became an embarrassment'. Normality came but, with it, unanticipated pitfalls. 'My tongue made a nasty slip and the word "f–k" came out' while he was animatedly recalling his experiences. His father simply invited him to 'help him with the drinks' in another room. Jake Wardrop, back from Italy, queued for ten minutes in the local fish and chip shop, only to be informed 'We only serve regular customers'. After giving them 'a short talk' reminding them there would have been no regulars or otherwise 'if certain members of the great British nation had not been spending the past three years scrapping the Germans', he came out with five shillings' worth, grumbling, 'They certainly do not overdo the hospitality in East Anglia.' Wardrop and his mates were heavy drinkers. 'We certainly shook Suffolk out of its customary tranquillity,' he declared. The practice was to assemble as many as ten or twelve men in a pub and drink as hard as they could with one eye on the clock. 'The reason given for this was invariably that they were just making sure that they still liked it.'

The feeling among returning units was that they had done their bit in war and now it was someone else's turn to risk their lives. This stance was further exacerbated by the relatively safe existence many other armoured units based in the United Kingdom had enjoyed.

Lieutenant Eric Allsop believed the desert veterans destined for Normandy 'did not want to go, they had lost their dash'. Major-General George 'Bobby' Erskine commanding the 7th Division agreed: 'There was undoubtedly a feeling amongst a few that it was time somebody else had a go.' He was reluctant to admit this attitude, to which he 'had to pay considerable attention', but he was a realist. 'With 7th Armoured Division it was no use trying to pull the wool over their eyes. They knew war too well to take it light-heartedly or carelessly.' Peter Roach recalled that 'truly the Regiment was tired, yet like an old war-horse at the smell of powder it raised its head and would not be left behind.' They would get on with it. 'Being human,' he remarked, 'we wanted it both ways.'

These innermost thoughts were rarely discussed. Combat fatigue, despite what had been learned in the First World War, was still not freely discussed or comprehensively addressed in the Second. Even the 'green' units like the armoured battalion of the Coldstream Guards drank heavily; its Medical Officer commented: 'I thought a great deal too much drinking was done'. Subalterns, many under twenty, were spending £20 per month on whisky and port. The imperative was to 'eat, drink and be merry for tomorrow we die', and 'sadly that was to be all too often the case'.

Men returning from the desert and Italy were visited by nightmares of fluttering hands seeking hatch covers that cannot be opened or desperately banging hatches snagged by gun barrels trapping them within. They saw ghostly charred effigies half poking from red-oxidised turret openings – and drank to forget. Modern volunteer armies often see an exodus of personnel after periods of prolonged combat, but this was not an option for conscripted armies in the Second World War. Ken Rice of 48 RTR was knocked out in a Churchill during a night advance near Pieve in Italy:

> Almost immediately an explosion rocks the tank and a huge wave of heat is carried into the turret from the driving compartment. I can see molten metal which looks like 'golden rain' spraying into the tank from the right-hand side of the driving compartment. Then black-ness as the interior lights are fused and I am struggling to breathe since all the oxygen has been taken out of the turret.

The tank ran downhill and began to tilt over when its right track ran up a bank. Rice struggled with the hatch clips and was suddenly out and fell into the road because the tank was heeling at a steep angle. 'I am within yards of the tank, which is burning fiercely, and the sounds and smells are like a scene from Dante's *Inferno*.' Certain domestic cooking smells were quick to trigger acute discomfort and initiate bad dreams for certain returning veterans. 'The reek of a brewed-up tank is never forgotten by those who have experienced it,' declared Rice. 'A mixture of hot metal, burnt electrical circuits, rubber, paint, webbing, leather, oil and petrol, high explosive, ether and death. These combine to make a cloying cocktail which lingers in a burned-out tank long after the inferno has cooled off.'

The evocative detail of Rice's description, expressed fifty years after the event, is some indication of the pervasive horrors it held for him. He describes 'muffled explosions' as the ammunition is consumed, and the 'roaring, whooping, crackling cacophony of sound' as ammunition propellant burns, 'accompanied by the flames changing hue' as Verey lights and magnesium from flares ignite. 'Kettle-drums boom twice' as two 75-gallon fuel tanks erupt one after the other in the engine compartment.

Two men failed to scramble out. 'I can now hear other sounds that freeze me with horror,' Rice recalled:

These are the sounds which emanate from an overheated domestic oven when a large joint is being cooked. A combination of sizzling, splashing hot fat sounds, and wheezing eruptions. When the full implication of these noises registers with me I vomit on the ground.

His face 'feels drawn' and he realises it is burned, together with his hands. These memories never left Ken Rice, who nevertheless says that, despite the awfulness, they are 'insignificant compared to the fact that I am still alive'.

Such experiences were not shared with anyone other than fellow veterans. More people had been killed on the home front by German bombing than lost in action in the desert in any case. It would have been inappropriate to raise such issues. Indeed newly arrived United States units toured bomb sites as part of their instruction during training in dealing with the reality of war. Discussing personal horrors in drawing-rooms would needlessly disturb loved ones and bring no respite. Even sharing misgivings with mates could be misinterpreted as 'windiness'. Most kept their thoughts to themselves and endured their personal fears in silence.

Fears built up remorselessly at the prospect of impending action. Occasionally something had to give. Bill Close was promoted to Major and likely because of his experience in the ranks he was approached by a friend, Geordie Reay. Reay was a seasoned tank soldier, who had been awarded the Distinguished Conduct Medal (DCM), yet realised his courage bank was exhausted. 'I want to get out of the Army, sir!' was his unexpected request, which took Close completely by surprise. When asked, 'For what reason?' Reay honestly confided, 'I don't think I am fit to command men in battle, sir. I've lost my nerve.' Close referred the matter to his commanding officer, whose predictable response was: 'I'm afraid you'll have to carry on like the rest of us, Reay.' And so he did.

Domestic exposure to wives, sweethearts and parents who had no idea of the grim realities behind strange behaviour did not alleviate tensions. Without it being apparent, the soldiers' baptisms of fire placed them in a world populated only by other soldiers. Modern experience has since demonstrated that it is emotionally more stabilising to keep soldiers with their own kind as they unwind, because only they understand the issues. Sympathetic pity from those they love in a domestic setting has little impact. Lieutenant Eric Allsop of 8 RTR suspected that 'the Second Front was cruel to those who were at home for several months and got to see their wives and children before battle again. It made the prospect of assaulting well-defended beaches even more emotional.'

Most veterans dug deeper into dwindling courage reserves. Lieutenant Keith Douglas of the Nottinghamshire Sherwood Rangers Yeomanry was such a man. Much of his anguish was expressed in some of the finest poetry and prose to emerge from the war. He enjoyed a sort of respite at the end of the desert war with the German surrender at Tunis:

The strain, the uncertainty of tomorrow, the fear of death: it was all over. We had made it. We stood here on the safe side of it, like swimmers. And Guy lying under the flowers in Enfidaville cemetery, Piccadilly Jim [his CO] buried miles behind us, Tom, and all the others back to the first casualties, during Rommel's attempt to break through to Alexandria; they didn't make it, but it's over for them too.

Douglas was distressed by the loss of men like his friend Tom, 'another institution gone, and someone on whom I now saw that I had come to rely'. His friend, who had been a great success in the regiment, always sharing plans for horse dealing and equestrian honours for his two little daughters, was 'wiped away by one shell burst: as if by one devastating, cynical comment of God'. Lieutenant Stuart Hills, who had joined the regiment after the desert, was 'a little nervous' at the prospect of action and recognised that Keith Douglas, who had been seriously wounded and lost many friends, 'also had to confront ghastly recollections of burned and maimed men on the battlefield'. He himself had the advantage of 'simply not knowing how awful war could be'. But he saw that Douglas would carry on; indeed he was pleasant and assisted him as a newly joined officer. Hills suspected 'that he was weary of war and felt that he had used up most of his luck in North Africa'. Douglas seemed visibly to pull himself together. 'This produced a mounting fatalism as he thought about the hard and dangerous campaign ahead', which for Douglas would be unmercifully brief.

There was a sense of tedium and frustration for the tank men who had been left at home. Lieutenant Peter Balfour, with the Churchill-equipped Scots Guards, remembered, 'We had been training now for nearly three years and we thought we were quite good.' But 'we wondered whether anything was going to happen'. Trooper Stephen Dyson joined 153 Regiment RAC with his twin brother Tom because 'we became bored stiff with soldiering in England'. Trooper Patrick Henessey recalled his friend complaining in the 13/18 Hussars that 'in this regiment, if it moves you salute it – if it doesn't, you polish it!' Too much time was arguably spent on troop lectures and maintenance in and around the vehicle park and not enough time on manoeuvres. Training land was scarce in England and even less so in the build up to D-Day.

Ken Tout, a young trooper with the Northants Yeomanry, claimed, 'Because of the requirements of British farmers every battle seemed to be an eyes-to-the-front, straight back and forward situation.' Later experiences in Normandy were to confirm his view that 'war is geographically messy' and that training limitations in England led to shortfalls. 'German Mark IV tanks cheated and did not approach from up range,' he wryly recalled. They later lost an entire tank troop to an attack by a single German panzer from the rear at Caen.

One advantage to be derived from so much time spent together was, as Trooper Ernest Hamilton with the 15/19 Hussars commented: 'One got to know what made your pals tick.' Bonding cemented the camaraderie that sustained them in the difficult days ahead. Hamilton explained that you got to know 'their likes and dislikes, problems, how many girls were left at home and most had two parents in those days. Any letters from home were sometimes read out loud.' One veteran pointed to certain unwritten rules regarding conduct. Abuse was kept within carefully understood limits. A man's honour, courage, honesty, truthfulness and morals might be torn to shreds with impunity: he could be humorously accused of being cowardly, lying, cheating or stealing. 'But nothing could be said that reflected upon his social status, his ability to pay his share, his personal cleanliness or his family.'

The tank crew was a special relationship and in many respects a social leveller between officers and troopers. The replacement of ex-public schoolboys with ex-grammar schoolboys in the commissioned ranks, a processs accelerated by casualties and the expansion of the armoured corps, was felt on the tank park.

Michael Trasenster, a subaltern with the 4/7 Royal Dragoon Guards (RDG), dryly recalled how the oddest of acquaintances managed to get on together during basic training. 'The borstal boys were let out with the public schoolboys together; because both were away from home they could cope quite well.'

Eccentric officers remained but were steadily sidelined by a more capable and pragmatic new breed intent on getting the job finished and returning to normal life as soon as possible. Trooper Fred Sprigg of the 6th Guards Tank Brigade recalled being accosted by his commanding officer, a retired cavalryman in charge of training at Pirbright. He was testing out his Churchill turret, revolving it round and round. 'You must not turn that round half a dozen times,' declared the old colonel, 'without turning it the other way to screw it back on again!' Lieutenant

Ian Hammerton remarked the senior officers at 61 Training Regiment RAC seemed 'to me mostly fairly elderly men who had served in the Great War, and all, I think, were cavalrymen'. Lieutenant Andrew Wilson described the sudden departure of their previously uninspiring CO and the arrival of a new peacetime stockbroker and Territorial to command 141 RAC. The 'Old Guard' were ousted and a 'bitter unspoken conflict' ensued, 'yet the outcome was never in doubt'. The new CO was pragmatic and tightened up training. Ernie Cox, a soldier in the same unit, recalled that Colonel Waddell 'hit the place like a small hurricane'. Everyone had now to pass two trade tests, and failures were sent back to the infantry, while the additional pay would 'buy five pints of beer or fifty cigarettes'. All were satisfied.

'Regiments would get rid of officers who were no good,' explained Lieutenant Michael Trasenster of the 4/7 RDG. This was achieved without friction as attitudes were changing with the realisation that nobody could be carried once in action. Trasenster pointed out that regiments had a proportion of old, who might appear prematurely dated, but actually extolled order, tidiness and discipline. They mixed well with enthusiastic younger officers. 'The former sometimes knew nothing about mechanical things and this knowledge was supplied by the younger,' Trasenster explained. Qualities were complementary because 'tidiness and order was pretty essential to effectively fight a tank'. Territorial Army (TA) battalions had a similar mix. Officers who had administrative ability and were good at staff but had few professional or leadership attributes 'did the regiment well', Trasenster commented. 'Others were just plain useless and the colonel would get rid of them at any price – but they often turned up in odd places and were a menace,' he declared.

NCOs sustained the whole fabric, cementing the fighting power required of the tank crews. As Paul Holbrook, a yeomanry subaltern, explained, 'the sergeants fathered the subalterns'. Increasingly classless and occasionally faceless young officers came and went, they were promoted, killed or replaced, 'but the stability, order, and enterprise of the Army was with the sergeants, kind, hardened, versatile and careful older men, working-class fathers mostly'. These were the men, Holbrook noted, who sustained patrols and found their way about chaotic battlefields supporting and standing by their subalterns. They provided the essence of family to the regimental 'tribes'. 'The bravery of the young officers was made possible by the devotion and reliability of the sergeants and corporals' and as Holbrook concluded 'the best sergeants were fathers to their young leaders'. They underpinned the fighting power of the British tank men. Trooper Ernest Hamilton of the 15/19 Hussars believed on the eve of D-Day, 'We were a good team under our troop leader Lieutenant Mike Roderick.' They were confident after long years of training. 'As time passed we wondered when it would be the day to try our skill at the Germans,' reflected Hamilton, 'we did think that we were superior to them.'

This belief was shared by their opponents across the Channel massing to block the anticipated invasion of Western Europe. German strategy in 1944 rested on the assumption that decisive offensives in the East were no longer possible and that the growing strength of the western Allies made an invasion attempt virtually certain before the end of the year. With the war going badly a failed invasion could prove a political turning-point and at least enable a substantial transfer of divisions to the East. Hitler felt that his panzer divisions, the instrument of crushing victories in 1940 and 1941, would provide the means for a decisive counter-stroke. Mobility provided time to identify where the attack would come in order to throw it back into the sea. The Allies would soon face a new opponent not encountered *en masse* before, the SS panzer divisions. They were formed for this eventuality in late 1942 and 1943, despite General Staff reservations. Hitler was impelled by politics. The SS manifested the political reliability he sought over, in his opinion, lesser performing Wehrmacht formations. The Allies would not only face superior tanks; they would be manned by different tank men.

The formation of the 12th SS *Hitlerjugend* (Hitler Youth) Panzer Division was a controversial decision, even in the Reich. It was recruited from teenagers aged sixteen and a half to eighteen years and immediately nicknamed the 'Baby' Division, whose insignia was purported to be a baby bottle. Such junior soldiers it was assumed would not be able to withstand the physical and mental demands of modern warfare. 'The Reichsführer [Himmler] gave the *Hitlerjugend* Division to Hitler for his birthday. It was a warped birthday present,' commented SS volunteer Günther Adrien. 'It didn't occur to me then that it's monstrous to give children as a present, just so they can be sent to die.'

These divisions formed in the context of Germany exploiting its final manpower reserves. They called upon a youth already physically and mentally prepared in certain respects. 'Nobody wants to be a mummy's boy,' declared Hitler Youth member Günther Damaske, 'myself included, so we cut the apron strings.' The Hitler Youth movement was established on Hitler's accession to power in 1933. He exploited their rebelliousness and taught vocational skills such as motor engineering alongside a competitive element always present in their activities. After 1942 they began to enact small-scale military manoeuvres: marching, assault boat training, grenade throwing, shooting and basic field-craft. Many had dug a fox-hole and knew the rudiments of camouflage and concealment on joining. They grew up in an era of rapid technological change as well as war, and experienced losses and dislocation at an early age. 'In those days it was dangerous to be eighteen years old,' remembered Franz Müller, 'one of us had an eye shot out, and another lost an arm.' 'I can still see the board with the roll of war dead at my High School,' recalled seventeen-year-old Karl Kunz:

> The art teacher wrote six names on an old drawing-board – that was after the Polish campaign. Then about six more names after the French campaign, and quite soon the board was full. So a second board was hung below it, then the next one to the left, and another board on the right – it got faster and faster.

'Coffee-table' literature and cable TV documentaries tend to cloak the SS in an aura of myth. They were highly motivated and effective divisions, but even during historical high points, such as Kursk in 1943, they were deployed in combination with regular army units. SS exploits were considerable, but the twenty other panzer divisions in army units fought in similar hot spots and scored like achievements with the same or better equipments.

The character of both the Wehrmacht and SS panzer divisions evolved with expansion. Recruiting had less to do with National Socialist spirit, more the need to compete over a declining manpower pool. The 9th SS Hohenstaufen and 10th SS Frundsberg Panzer Divisions were specifically established to defend the West against the Allied assault projected for 1943 and were compulsorily recruited from the Reich Labour Service (*Reichsarbeitdienst RAD*). Kurt Sametreiter from the SS LAH Panzer Regiment was influenced by future civil employment considerations when he announced to his father he intended to join the Waffen SS. 'Listen,' he said, 'how about if I went into the SS? All I would need to do is four years, like an apprenticeship, and then I could be a civil servant.'

The Wehrmacht criticised the early SS as all show and lacking discipline, while the latter considered the Wehrmacht as cautious and old-fashioned. Self-sacrifice was also a Wehrmacht axiom, but the SS were more convincingly portrayed in propaganda, and subsequently in the media, with their smart black uniforms. Both could be ruthless in action, the SS more so on the Russian front. In reality the SS became more like the army and the army more like them. Ludwig Bauer in Panzer Regiment 33 declared, 'The SS were soldiers like us and sent their people to our panzer schools.' Courses were combined and he was so taken by their comradeship that he considered joining. If he did he would have to relinquish his Leutnant rank and serve as a *Junker* officer cadet. 'I was not prepared to be chased around all over again as an officer cadet when I was already serving as a Leutnant in an active panzer regiment', so he declined.

'We had to parade in the yard,' recalled Burkhard Köttlitz, barely a teenager. An SS officer came along and said: 'Right, now I expect you're all going to volunteer for the Waffen SS. Or is there anyone here who doesn't want to volunteer?' SS *Standartenführer* (Colonel) Kurt Meyer, initially a regimental commander with the *Hitlerjugend* until called upon to command, recalled that the first 10,000 youths who arrived at Beverloo Camp in Belgium included some 'more or less persuaded' to join. Bernard Heisig, who joined the division, mentioned that 20,000 teenagers were directly recruited from the Hitler Youth, but 'many of them were forced'. Many of his comrades 'had enlisted for the Air Corps or whatever and ended up fighting in Normandy'.

Paucity of resources meant that initial training began with youths dressed in mixed civilian or Hitler Youth uniforms. The only tanks available were four damaged Panzer IVs, two knocked-out Panzer IIIs and two still mobile captured Russian T-34s clandestinely 'acquired'. Training could not start until July 1943 – which meant the majority had just nine months' training from basic to unit level standard before being committed to battle. 'When it was founded, we didn't like the name at all,' declared Bernard Heisig. 'We wanted to be real soldiers you see. The youngest among us didn't get any cigarettes – well they didn't smoke anyway – they actually got sweets.' Not all the volunteers made it. Albert Bastion, beaming with pleasure, told his mother he had joined, but her tearful and angry response was: 'But they're all criminals!' She saw to it her boy did not go into the SS. 'They're only children,' she raged. 'Have those men no respect for anything?'

Ideological bonding was still important for some. Jürgen Girgensöhn joined the SS Viking Division 'convinced we were conducting a just fight' and 'convinced we were a master race. We were the best of this master race and that really does form a bond.' As the SS divisions promoted camaraderie, survival as a group and fear of retribution provided the bonding element. Josef Schoenecker joined the 5th SS Panzer Regiment Viking impressed by 'smart uniformed soldiers recruiting for the Waffen SS' who picked up on his Morse signal experience because he was training to be a railway station-master. This expertise was urgently required. He only completed five to six weeks' additional signals training before being dispatched to his division in Russia. There was no tank training apart from on an obsolescent Mark III in Russia on arrival. Even this was interrupted when he was abruptly rushed forward in a jeep to the front and told, 'That's your tank, get in it – no introduction or anything.' They immediately drove forward to repel a Soviet attack and Schoeneker did not know how to operate the hull machine-gun. 'I did not meet the crew until the attack was repelled and we were filling up with diesel.' Manpower had clearly overtaken ideology as the overriding imperative.

Six Waffen SS panzer or panzer grenadier divisions provided the core of the German defence in Normandy. Much of this force would face the British. Training in the *Hitlerjugend* Division was considered especially comprehensive bearing in mind the short time between establishment and committal. There was a shortage of junior officers and NCOs, and the core of these came from the other SS divisions already struggling with manpower deficiencies. This leadership was the key to its effectiveness. Training in the SS was hard. 'You see in training we were really drilled in some very brutal methods,' explained tank loader Jürgen Girgensöhn of the Viking Division. 'Not everyone was able to endure it. There were some who wanted out and the only way of doing that was through suicide.' Many young officers and NCOs had been brutalised by service in Russia. 'After a few years they became so desensitised,' explained Gerhard Stiller, a twenty-two-year-old panzer officer with the SS LAH,' that they didn't even notice any more, given that they were capable of just bumping someone off without batting an eyelid.' These were the men the unbloodied British tank men would meet in battle. 'Let's just say that they would need to develop a lot of their humanity again,' Stiller wryly observed, 'and that takes time.'

An indication of the difference between the new panzer crews and British tank men forming up is revealed by the differing experience of the Fife and Forfar Yeomanry, who had trained in the UK for three years, and Gerhard Stiller's *Leibstandarte* Regiment formed in 1942. The two were to clash on the Normandy battlefield. Bill Close viewing the Yeomanry described them as 'well trained and raring to go' but 'untried'. The latter after forming up were in action in Russia by January 1943 following six months' training. After winter campaigning they fought at Kursk in July and were transferred to Italy in September, where they engaged in low-level skirmishing and disarming the Italian army. By early 1944 the regiment was back in Russia and fought defensive battles at Vinniza, Tscherkassy and Tarnopol. In April it was transferred, decimated by casualties, for rest and refit in the West. Half its company and platoon commanders had been killed during a span of uninterrupted action. War-weariness was less a problem than in British tank units, because the German philosophy was to fight units to virtual extinction and then re-form. Hard-core survivors formed replacement cadres which effectively bound new arrivals. Personnel management was less troublesome. Few mentally disturbed crew lived long enough to experience war-weariness before being replaced with fresh blood. The chain was crudely effective in physical and spiritual terms. Units formed up to fight benefiting from veteran cadre guidance at all levels. Many British tank units such as the Fife and Forfar Yeomanry had yet to be bloodied and they waited and trained on limited and constrained training areas. On the Continent their opponents had space to roam and an average of three campaigns under their belts.

The 12th SS *Hitlerjugend* was able to face down veteran British armoured units after only nine months' training, a statement of the technological lead established by panzer design and an effective training regime. German training was inherently flexible, benefiting from constant infusions of veteran knowledge. It was accepted that the normal superior/subordinate relationship might not be appropriate for training teenagers. Officers and NCOs, explained Kurt Meyer, a regimental commander, instilled a relationship 'between those who were older and a little more experienced and those who were new'. This paternal approach, treating officers as role models and mentors to young soldiers 'to emulate the close relationship of a family in as much as that was possible in the circumstances of the war', worked well. Combat training in a combined arms context 'under the most realistic battle conditions possible' was the focus. The result was that 'the young soldiers went to war superbly trained', as was acknowledged by numerous and initially sceptical superior officers.

Robert Boscowen, destined for the Coldstream Guards, remarked on the unrealistic tank training preparation at Sandhurst in the summer of 1942. 'At times we bicycled along the lanes in close groups of four, pretending to be tank crews sitting in the real thing!' he declared. 'We saw little of the tanks themselves and, for the most part, drove in trucks.' Trucks with broomsticks sticking out were an early expedient, but the quality of training never appeared to reflect a veteran input. 'A good way of training tank crews,' remembered Lieutenant Richard Carr-Gomm, 'was to drive across [Salisbury] plains chasing rabbits':

> Doing this would train the gunner, who kept his unarmed gun on it, the commander in giving directions and the driver in speed and handling. Often the rabbits just gave themselves up and sat waiting in dejection; then we would let them go.

These were 'handy hints' rather than structured training and are reflected in British training films of this period. *Ten Tips for Tackling Tanks* by the Directorate of Army Kinematography [1941] was amateurish, teaching infantry to decoy blind tanks over precipices like prehistoric mammoths. Other tips included tossing bombs from trees and trucks used as pseudo tanks with an earnest infantryman pointing a flag to represent a gun. *Wrong Lessons,* released in 1942, offered a stark contrast to the gritty reality of German training films that offered practical lessons in tank killing and staying alive, such as *Men Against Tanks* produced by the Wehrmacht Film Studio after 'Barbarossa'. The latter demonstrated how to disable a Soviet T–34 tank in close combat using a variety of weapons including grenades, satchel charges and Molotov cocktails. Many British films demonstrated a fictitious capability of accurately engaging enemy tanks on the move which desert veterans quickly realised was unrealistic. Corny humour and clipped BBC 'old boy' commentaries did not convince audiences, while German films hinted that ignoring advice or not paying attention might prove fatal.

Most British veterans are neutral at best and uncomplimentary at worst about the training regimes they followed. Trooper Ken Tout claimed his 1943 crew never trained using live ammunition or with any simulated conditions of battle noises, lights, wireless confusion or injuries. 'Everything was neat and orderly according to the training manual', and the squadron commander 'was more than once in trouble' for departing from the literal letter of the manual. 'Wounding,' he wryly observed, 'meant a joke badge to wear, a chance of a fag and a day sunbathing on Salisbury Plain.' Desert veterans were unimpressed. Jake Wardrop of 5 RTR was sent to Bovington to learn about the Cromwell tank 'from some gallant warriors who had been driving them around the moors and roads of Dorset for the past three years'. Wardrop dismissed them as 'base barnacles' with 'every second person a sergeant-major or staff sergeant', with 'an unlimited number of officers and you can take it from me that they are on a very good thing'. Newly returned desert warriors delighted in giving the instructors the 'ab–dabs' or 'hobbing it out', slang for any number of introduced 'red herrings' or seemingly innocent distractions. Nevertheless, the veterans introduced a sobering note to training proceedings. No amount of training was going to close the tank technology gap that had opened and appeared as wide as the Channel they were going to cross.

## MASS VERSUS TECHNOLOGY

Peter Roach, serving with 1 RTR, recalled disturbing classroom periods of instruction: 'I will always remember a vehicle recognition class taken by our OC in which we questioned him about the thickness of armour, weight of projectile and muzzle velocity of the respective tanks, ours and the Germans'. They were not happy with the response. 'He was an honest man and when he had finished there was silence. Each man sat quietly brooding. Again we were to be hopelessly outgunned, and after our period of equality, this was a bitter blow.'

Sergeant Jake Wardrop, receiving instruction on the new Cromwell tank, acknowledged it was fast, 'but apart from that it was a disgrace'. Those who had seen action asked more disturbing questions than those who had not. Some veteran tank commanders were cross-posted to green units to share their experience, but in the main men were blissfully unaware of the technology gap. Veterans saw little point in unsettling them as they would find out soon enough. It was thought that an experienced driver could safely drive the tank around a Panther, which had a slow traverse. Its cyclic gearbox enabled it to turn on a circle. Carson had to 'jump' the tank during driving demonstrations to show off its Christie suspension. 'No one went into details about the shortfalls,' he explained, 'we simply knew the Germans were bigger.' Jake Wardrop was less compromising. 'I hold the designers of that tank and the men who ordered its production personally responsible for the deaths of hundreds of men who fought in those tanks and had a lot more guts and common sense.'

During the spring of 1943 both the Allies and Germans were given the opportunity to exchange notes on technological progress. On 14 February, while fighting near Kasserine Pass with Panzer Regiment 5, panzer gunner Werner Fenck hit a Sherman tank with a high-explosive round. It caused little damage but the crew bailed out. It was dispatched to a proving ground near Berlin where it was rigorously tested alongside the Panther tank for combat efficiency and durability.

Three months later 48 RTR managed to capture the intact 'Tiger 131' at Djebel Djaffa. A fluke 6-pounder Churchill shot had ricocheted beneath the gun and stuck in the turret ring, jamming the traversing mechanism. Lieutenant Gudgin, who was knocked out by one of the tanks in its group, was subsequently appointed to the team responsible for its evaluation. 'It was a quantum jump ahead of our stuff' was the immediate impression. There were many improvements he could see from a crew perspective, including more 'room to move and lie down if you needed to on a long observation stint'. Power-assisted steering made it a comfortable tank to drive. 'We had these extraordinary Churchill tanks,' which were by contrast, he explained, 'very narrow between the tracks, and you couldn't get a big enough turret to mount a decent gun on it anyway.'

The Tiger was shipped to the UK after rough trials in Tunisia and passed to the School of Tank Technology at Chertsey for thorough examination in October. By February 1944 the researchers had assessed it as 'basically an excellent tank'. The only criticisms were weight and width limitations and its small range of action. The verdict was: 'It presents a very formidable fighting machine which should not be underrated.' These scientific observations did little to alleviate the sheer feeling of physical menace the colossus aroused among veteran and other tanks crews allowed to view it. Captain Bill Close saw it in Tunisia: 'a captured specimen, which looked grim even on a sunny day undisturbed by any war-like noises'. Bill Close never wanted to meet one. 'I looked at the long 88 sticking out from the massive turret and swallowed hard.' Technical reports suggested it was prone to breakdowns, and Close reflected, 'I sincerely hoped so.'

Tiger 131 was ominously displayed on Horse Guards Parade near Whitehall in November. Many tank soldiers viewed it. 'It looked pretty formidable,' recalled Michael Trasenster with the 4/7 RDG visiting with a group of troop commanders. The optics were superior to anything they had. Lieutenant Boscowen of the Sherman-equipped Coldstream Guards 'found its size and weight of armour and the deadly 88mm in the turret quite startling'. The engine, he appreciated, was 'almost twice as powerful as anything we had' and even if not as reliable it was 'nearly as fast as our Shermans'. Green officers who knew little better did not really accept the harsh technical realities that the monolith represented. 'We still had faith in the Sherman,' recalled Michael Trasenster, 'which we thought a good tank.' But it was obvious the Germans now had some that were better. 'Tigers, captured in Tunis, had been sent home, but apart from being gawped at and swarmed over by a bunch of base barnacles,' commented the irritated Sergeant Wardrop, 'little had been done about it.'

There was a kernel of truth in Wardrop's dismissive statement. Lieutenant Peter Beale, who served with Churchills in 9 RTR, felt 'tank crews were murdered because they were sent into battle so ill prepared'. Decisions had been taken that interpreted quantity as being a quality in its own right. Montgomery had decided 'the 75mm is all we require', and that meant accepting 1943 production priorities stemming from this decision. Correspondence with the Vice-Chief of the General Staff in August that year disclosed that a technological gun gap had opened. 'We are badly behind the Germans in this respect,' he admitted. 'The enemy can engage our tanks at ranges at which it is hopeless to reply with any hope of success.' His suggestion was to break with past practice; previously, he wrote, 'we have tried to fit the gun into the tank. Instead we should select the gun and build the tank around it.' There was little time to do anything about it before the invasion of Europe. A stopgap solution of up-gunning a small percentage of Sherman tanks with the newly developed 17-pounder was proposed. These 'Fireflys' could only be produced on a scale of one per tank troop in Sherman armoured regiments. The remainder would have to fight with what they had.

Bert Foord in the British tank design department at Wood Lee described the haphazard gestation of fitting a bigger gun on the existing Sherman turret. There had been gradual improvements in the design chain in 1943, when a tank hull design department was established at Chobham and another for suspension and tracks. Armour plate was being tested and electronics experts were tasked to design electrical and traversing gear.

'While at Wood Lee we got a Sherman and we were told to put a 17-pounder in it,' Foord recalled. A gun mount was designed but he needed to procure the steel tubes he identified for the recoil system. Tank design still operated on the lines of a cottage industry or 'a small-shop way of doing business', Foord explained. A small croft tin mine in Cornwall 'dabbled in hydraulics' and held the required steel tubing. 'I got in my car and collected some,' recalled Foord, 'sent it to Colonel

Stacey in the workshop who pre-fabricated a cradle' to fit the gun. Now they needed a specialised machine to cut the ports. A 'spare machine' was located on the other side of Kingston, near Chessington, and 'three of us went to Chessington and bought it straight away'. After they had cut the ports and assembled the new gun cradle 'they took it to the sand-pit and fired the first shot and shook every one's windows'.

The 17-pounder was likely the most highly effective high-velocity tank gun in the western theatre in the Second World War, and its tank mount was produced 'on the back of a fag packet'. Its haphazard production exposed the dichotomies of British tank design in that pragmatic ingenuity overcame bureaucratic inertia. Foord described the bizarre methodologies sometimes employed in turret design, such as when 'the tallest and smallest chaps were brought down from the armoured school to test the fighting compartments'. Nevertheless, it worked. Sufficient 'Fireflys' were produced to hold the technological ring in Normandy as Allied tank crews came to terms with the technological shock of meeting new panzers. The Americans, stymied by their own development decisions, had nothing that could effectively duel with the heavy German tanks.

The remaining British tanks were inadequate. Just under 50 per cent of those produced in 1943 had no operational value in terms of gun calibre effectiveness against German tanks. Production promises agreed in 1942 were furthermore unrealised in 1943, which meant that 26 per cent of tank production was shortly going to be obsolete. Broadly only about 25 per cent of 1943 tank production could be termed acceptable to those required to use them in the field. Peter Beale, a wartime tank man who researched these figures after the war, concluded: 'The thing that should make us angry and indignant is that with a little thought and planning these murders could have been avoided.'

The Soviet Union decided likewise to continue with the mass production of existing tanks but strove to up-gun the T-34 to 85mm. Meanwhile it was mass versus technology on the eastern front. An American tank trial was also conducted at Tidworth in the UK in January 1944. A completely new main battle tank was proposed, the M-26 Pershing, heavily armoured and mounting a 90mm gun. It was enthusiastically received by the many field officers present who had fought against the Germans in North Africa. Brigadier-General

Maurice Rose, who had led a Combat Command in the 2nd Armoured Division and faced the Tiger, felt strongly they should have the Pershing as soon as possible. Lieutenant-General George Patton, who commanded US troops in North Africa and Sicily and was the highest ranking armoured commander in the European theatre, declined. Imbued with the tank-destroyer philosophy of avoiding tank-on-tank fighting, he felt the Sherman M4 was lighter and, in requiring less fuel, was agile and better equipped to perform what he felt to be the primary mission of armoured divisions, penetration in depth. Being determined and highly opinionated he got his way. SHAEF notified Washington to 'de-emphasise' production of the M-26 heavy tank in favour of mass production of the M4 Sherman. American tank men were thereby condemned like the British to tackle a new generation of heavy German tanks with lightly armoured and under-gunned tanks. Mass was favoured relative to technology for a variety of reasons. The Americans chose not to switch mass production lines and the British were unprepared to compromise the delicate balance of their tank 'cottage industry'. The human consequences of pitting mass inferior tanks against superior German technology appeared to have been readily accepted.

Germany went to war with the Panzer Mark I 'agricultural tractor' or training tank. In 1940 hardly any German tanks could hold their own in a duel against heavy French or British tanks. Now, in only three years, the Panzerwaffe had not just caught up in the tank design race, she had overtaken, with tanks five to six times heavier than her first variants and projecting four times the amount of firepower. The Tiger was a 57-ton 120mm thick monolith mounting an 88mm gun so intimidating it was reported some Russian crews bailed out before engaging at Kursk in 1943. The Panther was barely mature at Kursk but its post-production problems were quickly resolved. Its sloped frontal armour was as thick as the Tiger's and its 75mm gun marginally superior. Significantly, the forty-three out of 200 Panthers that did function at Kursk between 9 and 15 July accounted for 269 Soviet tanks. Despite weighing 43 tons, it was the fastest German tank. Panthers were less well known to the western Allies, who had yet to meet them in appreciable numbers. German performance at Kursk demonstrated that the Soviets had fallen into a technological 'hole'. Russian T-34 tanks, superior to most Allied models, could be knocked out frontally at 2,000 metres, Panthers could knock one out from the flank at 4,000 metres. Not only was the German tank fleet modernised with superior tanks, training had inextricably harnessed the fighting component 'man' with the 'machine'.

Whereas the turret provided a gun platform for Soviet guns, in the Panzerwaffe it was the 'brain' commanding itself and many other tanks and assets. Five men crewed German panzers against four in Soviet tanks. Turret functionality and 'fightability', aided by radio, raised panzer duelling capabilities further. Extensive combined-arms training resulted in effective fighting mixes with other arms. The Russians and the western Allies massed artillery while the German practice was more integrated. Luftwaffe ground-air support was particularly effective at Kursk. Henschel HS 129 ground attack aircraft flying alongside 'tank-busting' Stukas especially adapted to this role were so effective as to obscure the true effectiveness of the new tanks and other ground weapon systems. Much of the Wehrmacht, however, had yet to experience the full impact of western Allied air potential.

The Panzerwaffe paid as much attention to the human component in the turret as the optics and hardware itself, demonstrating emerging maturity over its Allied counterparts. This was in stark contrast to more ponderous training methods in the Allied armies. Trooper Patrick Hennessey, for example, recalled trainees chanting the fundamentals of their engines, singing out: 'Induction-Compression-Power and Exhaust!' General Heinz Guderian, the new Inspector General of Panzer Troops, introduced two comic-strip training manuals or 'bibles' of handy hints illustrated with comic pictures and written in catchy rhyming couplets to drum home tactical, maintenance, logistic and personal advice. They included AFV recognition pictures complete with simple charts identifying the weak spots panzer gunners should aim for. It provided every panzer crewman with the basic information he needed to fight his tank more effectively than his opponent. They were issued alongside the new tanks in 1944.

Peter Roach and his desert comrades working their way through Cromwell introductory courses 'knew that many of us would die because the tanks lacked a proper gun'. Lieutenant James Carson, with the Welsh Guards armoured battalion, had not seen action but knew about the Tiger's 88mm. His verdict was: 'It's only 13mm greater than the 75mm Sherman – so what?' There was no shortage of cynical veteran comment, but as Roach pointed out, 'The experts who brought the Cromwells were no help, for they insisted that all was well and that we knew nothing.' Inconvenient facts were swept under the carpet as the decision to dilute quality with mass employments was already taken. There was awareness that the human dimension would have to be handled carefully. Sergeant Jake Wardrop of 5 RTR commented on the replacement of General Erskine, his division commander, and Brigadier Hines. 'The story did get around, for what it is worth,' he recalled in his diary, 'that both of these officers had been quietly eased out of their commands by the War Office, because they had complained of the Cromwell and objected to men being sent into battle against Tigers and Panthers with such big odds against them.'

'How does a Churchill get a Tiger?' one newly arrived officer asked his superior, recalled Lieutenant Andrew Wilson. 'It's supposed to get within 200 yards and put a shot through the periscope' was the response. 'Has anyone ever done it?' the eager young officer enquired further. 'No,' was the bleak retort.


## BELIEFS AND CONCERNS

In the autumn of 1943 the 1st and 2nd US Armoured Divisions arrived in the UK, followed by the 4th Armoured in December and a number of independent tank battalions. By the following month it was said that every tenth male in the UK was an Allied soldier. Two million US soldiers settled in to 1,100 locations, occupying 100,000 requisitioned buildings, constructing another 160,000 Nissen huts and erecting thousands of tents. American tank soldiers were confident in the Sherman, convinced it was the equal of anything the Germans could field. Charles Evans of the 3rd Armoured Division recalled its introduction: 'After what we had gone through it was like a blessing, some of us would stay in it all night just to get acquainted with it.' One of the lessons of Kasserine Pass in North Africa was to reduce light tanks in an armoured division to a reconnaissance role. The Sherman 'heavy', Evans felt, 'was brand new and it had everything we had been missing'.

J. Ted Hartman joined the army in May 1943 and earned the princely sum of $65 a month. Nine out of ten US servicemen earned above the $50 average they received in civilian life, which gave them the equivalent of £750 per year, much more than the £100 the British were given. American soldiers were urged to spend some of this on war bonds which would pay a handsome interest within ten years; a co-owner had to be listed, and many chose their parents. 'Suddenly, I realised,' Hartman recalled, 'that they were telling me that I might not survive the war. What a blow to a teenager who expected to live for ever!'

Life in the United States prior to embarkation was easier and more pleasant than Europe. Civilians were generous to soldiers in uniform, and Hartman recalled that many of his minor bills were frequently waived. The Home Front was tangibly seen to be supporting the war. Every family with a serving relative advertised the fact, displaying the stars and stripes prominently in a window or flying it from the house. Training was thorough. Hartman benefited from the Army Specialist Training Program, a form of university further education. During their training period people had to cover long distances throughout all parts of the United States, and travelled by train. This ended for Hartman and others with their sudden departure on an overcrowded troop-ship bound for England. The Atlantic crossing and news of close friends killed in the Pacific theatre concentrated his mind on the perils ahead. If he got 'bopped off', he wrote to his parents on departure, 'you are entitled to six months of my pay plus all that they owe me at the time, but you have to apply,' he reminded them. 'Please remember this.'

New Shermans were issued on arrival, followed normally by up to six weeks' training on Salisbury Plain. Hartman was impressed by his new tank. 'The hulls of these tanks were made of two and a half inch thick steel plates welded together,' he observed. 'This seemed like great protection.' American gunnery was good. Each tank battalion in the 4th Armoured Division was allocated twenty training rounds per tank, a lavish amount given wartime restrictions and far more than the British.

Hartman's military indoctrination would have been very different if he had been a black man training in the 761st Independent Tank Battalion. Despite being at war with a clearly racist Nazi Germany,

President Roosevelt refused to end segregation in America's armed forces. Johnny Stephens was a black tanker from Georgia who joined at nineteen. 'Living in the South in those days,' he described, 'was not really an experience you would want to go through twice', and little changed on his arrival at the 761st training barracks:

> If you were a soldier and in uniform and went to town you had to ride on the back of a bus, you had to eat in a black restaurant. If you wanted to use the facilities in a bus or train station you had to go in the part that was marked coloured. You wore the same uniform, you were there for the same reason but we couldn't do the same things.

They signed up for the same reasons as white tank men. Leonard Smith joined in 1942 'because I was doing things wrong at school. I had a choice, either mess up or go into the services.' He opted for tanks because they were not taking any more recruits for the air force. His companion E.G. McConnell, also black, was motivated by 'patriotic duty, I wanted a piece of the action'. McConnell looked so young that he stencilled a pencil-thin moustache with eye make-up on his upper lip. His mother, who accompanied him, remarked to the recruiting sergeant on passing him over, 'You take care of my boy.' 'Good God, was I embarrassed!' McConnell admitted.

There were interminable troop-train journeys, as for Hartman, but Stephens had to ride forward where black people normally sat 'where you got all the smoke and the smut and the fumes'. They were cautioned to lower the blinds because 'red-neck Hillbillies' had taken to shooting at black carriages as they passed. There was official reluctance to end segregation but awareness that they needed black people for the war effort. Reluctance to employ black soldiers in combat kept the 761st Tank Battalion training in the US until crippling American tank crew casualties resulted in their passage to England in October 1944 becoming unavoidable. On arrival they learned that the army had spread rumours about black troops. Johnny Holmes remembered:

> When we landed in England they told the English people or whatever European people we came into contact with, we were monkeys. We had tails and we couldn't fight and we were just

bringing up the tanks for the white boys to fight with . . . You wouldn't think your own countrymen would do this to you but they did.

It was a beautiful spring in England. Stretching ahead for the tank crews was a period of limbo, living on borrowed time, insecurity underscored by the wonderful weather. There was uncertainty for the uninitiated and scepticism for veterans weighing up the chances of death and injury. This mixture of questioning and stoicism permeated the waiting camps. What would combat be like? Trooper Patrick Hennessey was consumed by curiosity and wondered how he would cope when under fire from an equally determined enemy. He felt impelled to ask his Squadron Sergeant-Major, a veteran who had seen action in France in 1940: 'What's it like in battle, sir?' He received a typically phlegmatic response: 'Bloody noisy, mate!'

Air raids were a concern to everyone. Sociological surveys testify that motivation had little to do with abstract notions of freedom and patriotism but much with protecting personal values: sweethearts, wives and families. In addition to conventional bombing raids the arrival of V1 Flying Bombs over London in late June 'was a great worry to those of us with families in the capital', declared tank crewman Stephen Dyson from north London. 'Although it was a worry for lads from the Smoke [London], a certain court martial awaited anyone caught AWOL [absent without leave] attempting to go and see their families.'

Similar home concerns disturbed the teenagers of the 12th SS *Hitler-jugend* Division that moved into France, ready for action, in April 1944. *Oberscharführer* (Sergeant) Karl Friedrich Hahn watched apprehensively as the vapour trails of high-altitude American bombers traced their webs across brilliant spring-blue French skies *en route* to Germany. 'It is a terrible feeling to have to passively watch,' he recalled, 'as they fly undisturbed on their way to reap havoc in our homeland.' As the panzer divisions waited inland for the coming invasion, tragic news from home frequently trickled through. Leave was constantly granted to men who lost family members or indeed entire families to Allied bombers. Mothers of the regiment's teenagers often withheld permission for them to join without the concurrence of absent fathers fighting at the front. Four years of war meant that many of the fathers were dead, while mothers worked outside the home and teachers and Hitler Youth leaders had long since departed for the front. Bombing dislocated the youngsters' normal environment, destroyed their homes or caused them to be evacuated. Some had already seen war as flak auxiliaries. The *Hitlerjugend* Division offered an oasis of emotional stability among other teenagers bound by the same experiences. This bred not so much fanaticism as a grim determination to confront the perpetrators of their ruined lives. Those without a family future resolved to sell their lives dearly. Repelling the coming invasion might open up political and diplomatic options to deal with the West while holding in the East. Generaloberst Fritz Bayerlein, the commander of the Panzer Lehr Division, was told by Rommel, 'Your objective is not the coast, your objective is the sea!' A new front could not be allowed to form.

Many panzer divisions formed up or were refitted in France after the occupation because there were fewer air attacks and food was more plentiful than in Germany, an important consideration for developing young recruits. The SS *Leibstandarte* Adolf Hitler Division began its training at Wildflecken and Paderborn before being moved to Evreux in France. 'Better an ass full of tacks than another day in Wildflecken,' wrote Heinz Freiberg in his diary, commenting on complaints about primitive accommodation and worse food. Evreux had space for live firing and manoeuvre – and a better quality of life. Young soldiers took full advantage of the opportunities. Acquiescence was gained from the local French railwaymen, after initial reservations, to raid the wine transports that halted at the local station. New recruits quickly learned that the Sergeant-Major's 'cinema trips' normally constituted the core of the next fatigue-work detail. Otto Carius, forming up with one of the new Tiger battalions in Brittany, recalled the extent to which 'red wine was a part of our stay in France as well'. Austrians in his company were especially partial to it, and 'there was hardly an evening where I didn't have to get up again and put my Austrians to bed'.

A posting to France was the best a German soldier could hope for, and Paris, including leave, was the jewel in the crown. Panzer crews were on leave prior to the next operational tour, likely Russia, while

Allied tank men waited three years for action. Whatever the interval, leave was exploited as if it might be the last. In Paris there was a garrison of 25,000 German soldiers, few of them panzer. When Carius visited, he saw 'our troops in Paris acted as if the war had already ended and been won'. With the typical contempt front-line soldiers reserved for their garrison counterparts he commented: 'This behaviour was unbelievable to me. I wasn't able to forget that in a few weeks we would be slugging it out with the Russians again.'

Attitudes in Paris were changing with the increasing likelihood of a Second Front, but this made little difference to soldiers on leave. Officers dined in style at hotels such as the Georges V, which like all fine hotels was requisitioned as an officer's club. *Soldatenheime,* or soldier's hostels, were set up to accommodate holidaying troops. These incongruously tramped the cobbled streets around Montmartre in uniformed jackboots led by earnest civilian-attired French guides. Shopping was better than Germany: lingerie, sweets and perfumes and all items that were scarce in the Reich were picked up at a preferential exchange rate in flea-markets. One function of the *Soldatenheime* according to an observer was to ply soldiers 'with heavy German victuals that are deemed to be Nordic and virile, as distinguished from the degenerate, tasty French diet'. German quartermasters monopolised the Paris potato supply, foraged to rarity in the city's markets, and German troops were nicknamed *doryphores,* or 'potato-bugs', by the Parisians.

The real attraction for the uniformed tourists was the opposite sex. It is estimated that 85,000 illegitimate children were fathered by Germans with French women. *Soldatenheime* were strategically located, like one near the Moulin Rouge, to facilitate easy access to night-life. The best brothels were reserved for officers, but the soldiers had little difficulty soliciting street-walkers in the Montparnasse. The coming invasion influenced reserve but not business. The erotic floor show continued at the Shéhérézade night-club, with scantily clad ladies circled by men in grey Wehrmacht uniforms sitting at tables and seemingly taking cover behind a multiplicity of champagne buckets and bottles. In the Moulin de la Cralette the audience was totally close-cut uniformed grey, with the occasional panzer black enjoying the floor show. The highlight was the strong-man who could lift two jackbooted German soldiers into the air with one arm.

In England, 'war aphrodisia' lightened the load for those waiting in limbo for the coming battle. Local girls 'seemed to become more liberal with their favours the nearer the Second Front appeared to be', remembered Trooper Stephen Dyson with 107 Regiment RAC. 'Make the most of it while you can!' Three-ton trucks taking soldiers into town on 'R and R' [Rest and Recuperation] were nicknamed 'passion wagons'. Barbara Cartland, the romantic novelist, working as a voluntary welfare officer, remarked on the spate of war-time weddings. These rushed affairs with snatched forty-eight-hour honeymoons were explicable because girls feared becoming widows even before marriage. 'By this stage in the war love was about the only thing left unrationed,' she remarked.

The Americans conducted their own 'Sweet Invasion' prior to D-Day. British soldiers jibed that the Yanks were 'overpaid, over-fed, over-sexed and over here'. The Americans did not disagree, retorting that Tommy was 'under-paid, under-fed, under-sexed and under Eisenhower'. The American soldiers 'were not welcomed by the British men,' declared one woman, 'but to the English girls they were wonderful.' Her view was that the Yanks brought 'a wave of glamour, romance and excitement that has never been experienced before or since'. Allegedly over 20,000 fatherless babies provided silent testimony to this 'Sweet Invasion'. Even so, the US Army Postal Service was to record that one quarter of the letters from Normandy in the first four weeks after 6 June were posted to addresses in the British Isles, and by the final year of the war some 20,000 English girls had applied to become wives of American soldiers.

Tank crews were in the thick of the hostilities that broke out for female favours during the waiting for approaching battle. 'One fly in the ointment,' according to Trooper Robert Whitehead of 44 RTR were French Canadians billeted nearby, who 'did not like to have to share the local women with us'. Three Canadian soldiers beat him up to make the point, until 'they finally picked on the wrong soldiers'. He recalled a Royal Marine Commando from a unit recently returned from Italy was knifed and killed. 'The Commandos retaliated by raiding the Canadians' camp, and seriously injuring large numbers of them'. After the Canadians were removed to another part of the country 'it became a paradise for us, with plenty of dances to go to, myriads of wonderful young girls in attendance, and very little opposition to our charms'.

'London's West End was bursting at the seams with British and foreign troops,' recalled Trooper Stephen Dyson. 'The Piccadilly "floozies" had never had it so good – business was booming.' 'Hello Yank, looking for a good time?' became a much parodied wartime joke. The most brazen 'Piccadilly Warriors' swarmed around the entrance to the Rainbow Club, opened for the American troops in 1942 in the old Del Monico's on the corner of Shaftesbury Avenue. High-level official letters sent to the Metropolitan Police Commissioners expressed concern at the 'vicious debauchery' conducted in the blacked-out Leicester Square, 'the resort of the worst type of women and girls consorting with men of the British and American Forces, in which the latter seem to predominate'. 'Piccadilly Commando' antics were discussed at Home Office level. A leaflet entitled *How to Stay Out of Trouble* was issued by the US Provost Marshall with stern warnings about 'females of questionable character', which of course became an indispensable guide for those GIs attempting track them down. American slang subconsciously permeated the English language even further. 'SNAFU' became the army slang expression for bungling, translated as 'situation normal all fucked up'. 'Wall jobs' became part of every GI's wartime vocabulary, as a result of the curious predilection of 'Piccadilly Commandos' to engage in illicit sex standing up, fully clothed, in doorways, based on the erroneous belief that they could not get pregnant. 'It was Second Front fever,' explained Trooper Stephen Dyson, 'and everybody was caught up in it'; yet at the back of everyone's mind was impending bloodshed.

Farewells were heartfelt. The Dyson twin brothers with 107 Regiment RAC finished their last night in the local pubs singing the Great War homily 'Goodbyee, goodbyee, wipe the tears from your eyes, don't cryee'. As Stephen recalled 'it was the obvious and spontaneous choice: if this was to be our last communal booze-up before embarking, it would be one to remember'. 'Britain had been at war for five years bar a few months,' recalled Lieutenant Robert Boscowen of the Coldstream Guards. 'So the war-weary British were utterly browned-off and longing to get on with it, to reach final victory and bring the boys home.' Stephen Dyson had finally to say goodbye to his twin brother as they separated,

Tom to go with the spare crews in echelon. 'Please God,' he reflected, 'only *au revoir* to Tom.' They sailed on separate ships.

Lieutenant Andrew Wilson with 141 Regiment RAC visited his parents two days after D-Day. He would soon be in battle. His mother was crying a little because she thought he was 'already over the Channel'. His father had lost an arm and the sight of one eye in the First World War and his mother nursed him through the years of pain and distress that followed. 'War had twisted and ruined their lives,' Wilson reflected, 'but they didn't mention it.' They accepted this war like the last with 'unquestioning patriotism'. It was Wilson's twenty-first birthday. 'Many happy returns,' his father said, wrestling open the cap of a bottle of whisky with his one strong hand while he secured it with his knees. 'God bless you,' he added. They had their drinks 'and tried to find things to say, but in reality there was nothing,' Wilson recalled, 'for the future – even the immediate future – was unknown, and the ordinary topics of conversation had no meaning any more.'

## TECHNOLOGICAL SURPRISE – THE 'FUNNIES'

One of the ironies of the invasion battle, given the tank design gap, is the extent to which the Allies achieved technological surprise on the beaches with Major-General Percy Hobart's 79th Armoured Division. Swimming DD or duplex-drive tanks preceded a variety of specialised armoured vehicles nicknamed 'Funnies' that crawled over the supposedly impenetrable Atlantic Wall in Normandy. The need for such vehicles had been dramatically illustrated by the disastrous performance of the Canadian Calgary Tank Regiment equipped with new Churchill tanks at Dieppe in August 1942. Marooned on the pebble beach, the tanks were unable to break through the German obstacles, leaving the assault infantry exposed to withering fire. Successfully landed Allied tanks in Normandy two years later were to be equally surprised by the excellence of the German heavy tanks and anti-tank guns they were to encounter inland. 'We just could not understand,' declared SS Leutnant Fritz Langanke, a Panther commander with the 2nd SS Panzer Division, 'how countries with the highest degree of industrialisation, sitting apart from those European powers killing each other for so many years, would not come to Normandy with the very best tank in the world – we just couldn't understand it.' The Americans had rejected the M-26 Pershing with a 90mm gun in favour of more numerous Shermans. Yet when Allied tank crews saw the technical vision exhibited by the 'Funnies' there was no reason to doubt that the Shermans, as they had been assured, were the equal of the Germans' tanks. Moreover as the floating harbours and other technical innovations supporting the land-ings began to unfold around them, it appeared that victory in Europe could soon be in the bag.

DD tanks wore canvas flotation collars raised on steel arms and were equipped with rear-mounted propellers powered in the water by the tank itself. The tank commander needed a periscope to see over the floating screen side. Entering the water was perilous, and then there was the danger of water swamping the screen once under way. Crews were unenthusiastic. 'Being a bloody sailor in a bloody tank was taking patriotism too far' was the majority view expressed by Lieutenant Stuart Hills of the Nottinghamshire Sherwood Rangers Yeomanry. Lance Corporal Patrick Hennessey recalled the doleful view of the Chief Petty Officer who taught them underwater escape drills: 'Rather you than me, mate!' The task of the DD tanks was to land just ahead of the infantry and engage beach pillboxes and to provide supporting fire as they attacked.

Next in line were the 'Crab' Sherman flail-tanks, with massive chains revolving at high speed detonating mines, creating gaps in minefields for the assaulting infantry. This concept likewise elicited scant en-thusiasm from crews warned to anticipate a two-thirds casualty rate. 'At least sixteen of the troop might be wiped out,' recalled Lieutenant Ian Hammerton. 'Nor were we to stop to care for any wounded. Not very cheering.' They were even less happy to discover that the tank gun had to be reversed during the vulnerable operation and they would be completely reliant on other tanks for protection.

When the assault waves reached the sea walls, Churchill AVREs [Armoured Vehicle Royal Engineers] armed with a 290mm mortar ejecting a 40-pound projectile called a 'flying dustbin' would engage pillboxes and blast obstacles at close range. Other AVREs were to follow with fascines to fill anti-tank ditches, lay 'Bobbin' non-slip carpets of coarse material to negotiate slippery slopes and other mobile

313

trackways and ramps to climb up sea walls and bridge gaps. The plan was to land the assets in sequential order on the beaches; an ambitious undertaking.

Lieutenant Andrew Wilson, serving in the HQ Squadron with 141 Regiment RAC, was frustrated by the secrecy surrounding mysterious courses and exercises the sabre squadrons were conducting of which he had no knowledge. Field Security Police even operated in civilian clothes in local pubs around the unit lines. Once he discovered the unit had a 'Crocodile' role, he was invited to sign the Secrets Act and at last gained access to a practical demonstration of what the unit would be doing across a mock-up battle-run. He saw a lone tank:

> It went towards the first target, a concrete pillbox. Suddenly there was a rushing in the air, a vicious hiss. From the front of the tank a burning yellow rod shot out. Out and out it went, up and up, with a noise like the slapping of a thick metal strap. The rod curved and started to drop, throwing off burning particles. It struck the concrete with a violent smack. A dozen yellow fingers leapt out from the point of impact, searching for cracks and apertures. All at once the pillbox was engulfed in fire – belching, twisting, red-roaring fire. And clouds of queer smelling, grey-black smoke.

It was the stuff of awesome science fiction, a Churchill flame-thrower tank towing four hundred gallons of viscous flame fuel in a trailer behind. Liquid was projected through the 75mm gun nozzle under a nitrogen pressure of 350lbs per square inch. The rod of fuel was ignited by a jet of burning petrol that passed over two electrodes giving the flame a range of 90 yards and could 'flame' for two minutes. Twenty-year-old Ernie Cox in the same unit recalled that the first practical demonstrations 'came as quite a shock for we had never seen the likes of it'. The flame could be bounced around the corners of zigzag trenches. The demonstration included houses and various structures and was profoundly sobering. When it finished Wilson noticed a spot of the liquid had splashed on to his boot, where it 'clung and burned', however hard he tried to shake it off. In the end he wiped it off, still burning, on to the grass. What it might do to a human being was unimaginable.

On 4 April six tanks of the 4/7 RDG 'drowned' with the loss of six men in a very heavy swell off Poole. 'We remained anxious, about what the state of the weather and the sea would be like on the great day,' recalled Lieutenant Stuart Hills. Lieutenant Michael Trasenster remembered 'the hurt and the shame' that resulted from the 'obscene judicial acts' cloaking the obsessive secrecy of the DD project. The squadron commander could only write to the widow of one of the drowned men 'in the vaguest of terms that her husband had died bravely at dawn'. He promised he would write again in more detail when he could. Unfortunately the squadron commander was killed early on in Normandy. 'Nothing more was heard from the poor widow for over fifty years,' Trasenster recalled, 'until she was found by one of the old comrades. It transpired she had felt too ashamed to make further enquiries or ask for any benefits, because she thought that he had been "shot at dawn" rather than drowned.' Such were the inequities of war.

Above the noise of the 'tremendous roar of gunfire' off the British Sword beach, Lance Corporal Patrick Hennessey heard the order over the ship's tannoy: 'Down Door Number 1'. 'We knew this was our cue' and on D-Day 6 June at 0730 hours the first DD tank trundled off the ramp of the landing craft and nosed into the choppy, grey, threatening waves. Hennessy followed, and as they wallowed upright he could make out the shore line some 5,000 yards away. 'It seemed a very long distance and in a DD tank, in that sea, it certainly was.'

All the crew sat on the deck of the tank while the driver, several feet below the water line, was nervously intent on keeping the engine running. If it stopped they were finished. There was only the thin flimsy canvas screen keeping the waves at bay, and water ominously lapped over, to be ejected by the co-driver energetically operating the bilge pump. To their right they saw Captain Noel Denny's tank wallow into the water. With their hearts in their mouths they watched as the landing craft, pushed on by the swell, crept up on it and involuntarily forced it under the water. Only one head bobbed on the surface, Captain Denny; the rest of the crew perished.

Off the American Omaha beach, B and C companies of the 741st Independent Tank Battalion had launched 32 DD tanks more than fifty minutes earlier, five to six kilometres from land. The seas were rougher than any they had encountered in training. Captain James Thornton, the B Company commander, saw the tank behind immediately swamp, as did the fourth to launch. After only a few yards struts snapped and canvas tore and water flooded his engine compartment and his tank went down. He and the crew got out. Within two to three minutes of launching, twenty-seven tanks had foundered. Few of the 135 men struggling in the water off the coast were saved. Only two tanks swam to the beach and three remained on their landing craft as they had collided when they tried to exit. It was a disaster.

Hennessey recalled being 'buffeted about unmercifully, plunging into the troughs of the waves and somehow wallowing up again at the crests'. The wind was behind them, which helped. As they struggled to keep on course the shore line became more distinct 'and before long we could see the line of houses which were our targets'. It took more than an hour of hard work before they wallowed on to the beach 'and it was a miracle that most of us did'. They leaped into the tank and within a minute 'had fired our first shot in anger'. A puff of smoke and brick dust denoted the strike on the first fortified house. They remained at the water's edge while 'the beach, which had been practically deserted when we arrived, was beginning to fill up fast'. Infantry were wading ashore all around.

German defenders were flabbergasted. Complete technological surprise was achieved. One tank driver recalled, 'I still remember very vividly some of the machine-gunners standing up in their posts looking at us with their mouths wide open.' The 'Funnies' had made a considerable impact. At the end of the first day the British had driven six miles inland at the cost of 3,500 British and 1,000 Canadian casualties. The Americans, using few DD tanks and no specialised vehicles, suffered 6,600 casualties and penetrated only two to three miles. There was a cost. Ian Hammerton managed to get his flail tank ashore but it was flooded by the incoming tide. He recalled a lot of dead and dying Canadians around them as they landed. On the sea wall he observed 'a man with the lower part of his face blown away and the padre was comforting him. The man wanted to smoke but there was nowhere to put the cigarette – that shook me up a bit.'

The majority of the tank men were still back in England when the invasion started. They gazed open-mouthed at endless fleets of white-striped planes and gliders flying overhead toward Normandy. 'We could start the countdown for our own D-Day,' Stephen Dyson realised. Lieutenant Robert Boscowen was on a route march with the Coldstream Guards armoured battalion 'to keep us fit and out of mischief', he recalled, when 'all of a sudden people came out of their houses and down their gardens to greet us on our march'. They were jubilantly shouting, 'Our forces have landed, the Invasion has begun!' 'This was the first we had heard,' he remembered. 'The day we had all been waiting for had arrived.'

Between 1,500 and 2,000 panzers were warming their engines with crews attending last-minute maintenance at various locations in the French interior. Like the majority of tank men in southern England waiting for the call forward, the panzers paused. They still anticipated the main Allied attack to come across the Pas de Calais. Within days the 1st SS *Leibstandarte*, the 12th SS *Hitlerjugend* and Panzer *Lehr* Divisions began to move towards Normandy to establish contact with the 21st Panzer Division already in the thick of the fighting. The battle of Normandy had begun.

# 13

## NORMANDY TANK FIGHTING

### UNREALITY TO INVINCIBILITY

Lieutenant Peter Balfour of the 3rd Scots Guards Churchill battalion was constantly vexed by the dilemma of 'how one is going to behave'. He explained: 'Whether I am going – you know – to disgrace myself or whatever. I remember being terribly surprised, looking back on it, we were terribly green. I mean we had no experience of people shooting at us, who meant to kill us.'

Tank veterans who fought in Normandy discerned, in retrospect, a number of identifiable stages that led to battle fatigue. Memories of Normandy are of pulverising battles of attrition, not mobile armoured operations. Close fighting developed as a consequence of the *bocage,* or hedgerow, countryside of Normandy confounding the planners on both sides. Peter Balfour reflected, 'We knew a lot and we were quite good at what we did, but we had no battle experience and we didn't really know what it was going to be like.'

Lieutenant Michael Trasenster, who landed on D-Day with the 4/7 RDG, described the corrosive impact cumulative operations had over ensuing weeks and months:

> The first day is unreality, the second stage you probably feel invincible. At the third stage you see a few tanks brewed up and they're your friends and that's probably when you are at your best. Then the next stage you go through very carefully, I mean everyone does. It's a funny thing, people think the first tank is likely to be brewed up, but very often it gets through, and it's the second one that is brewed. One was told as troop leader you should always lead – it didn't apply further up. Then you became slightly bomb happy –

pretty wary. Then you got to the final stage where you didn't care and hoped you would get wounded. By that time you should have been taken out of it if you had a decent squadron leader.

This description was mirrored to some extent by scientific neurological surveys taken shortly after the war. R.L. Swank and W.E. Marchand developed a combat efficiency chart measuring the impact of exhaustion on the combat efficiency of the average US soldier. Combining veteran views alongside scientific analysis close to events offers an insight into the emotional impact that the technological arms race had on tank men in Normandy.

The first transition stage was from a form of 'dream-like unreality' to what Trasenster described as a 'feeling of invincibility as if in a tournament'. Lieutenant Stuart Hamilton, fighting in Italy with 8 RTR, called it 'battle initiation' to 'battle hardened', the first of 'various stages, with each stage getting progressively worse the longer one was up the sharp end'. He claimed, 'Once one went through the first shock of battle and survived it, then this was OK.' The Swank and Marchand study assessed that it took about ten days for a soldier to become 'battle wise'.

During the initial ten days after D–Day the Allies established a secure foothold but not more then 10 to 12 miles deep. This period of village fighting along 55 to 60 miles of front line along the coast indicated that the Allied landing was successful, but the German defence would not be easily overcome. Stalemate ensued, signalling the extent to which both Allied and German plans went awry. German operational orders no longer included the stock phrase of 'throwing the enemy back into the sea'. The compromise intent became to restore the situation sufficiently to muster forces for a counter-stroke. At the end of June seven and a half panzer divisions faced the 2nd British Army, with only half a tank division in front of 1st US Army. The operational aim to draw German armour off the American front was developing. Germany had to accept the ground war it feared, on two fronts, in the west and east. The battle of Normandy began in earnest.

It literally began with a bang for Captain Alastair Morrison of the 4/7 RDG. 'The leading tank stopped and a great plume of flame came out of its turret'. He recalled being amazed. 'One person jumped out, landed on the ground, and then a great black column of smoke climbed up about 200 feet in the air.' This was unexpected. 'While I was watching it, another tank stopped and exactly the same thing happened. We had no idea until then that a Sherman could blow up in this way.' Michael Trasenster in the same unit likened this period to an 'unpleasant dream'. 'You feel you are a spectator the whole time,' he said, 'the whole thing is such a shock to the system.' It was the feeling of an observer, not a participant. 'This was enhanced by an unwarranted trust in the armour against battlefield hazards outside and an isolation caused by being deaf to most external noise from wearing radio headsets and the general noise of tanks.'

Unreality was a distraction that needed to be quickly overcome, in order to be supremely alert on a tank battlefield. Slowness and dullness were harbingers of death and crews were acutely vulnerable at this early stage. The American 743rd Independent Tank Battalion lost sixteen tanks, or 17 per cent of its total wartime losses, on D-Day alone. Another battalion, the 737th, entered Normandy on 14 July and lost twenty-three Shermans in three days, 35 per cent of its total losses for the war. Inexperience was the primary killer.

Lieutenant Belton Cooper of the 3rd US Armoured Division described this 'dullness' as being incapacitating, in that 'Your mind tends to boggle after a constant series of shocks and trauma, and apparently it reaches a different psychological level. This tends to become inert to further shocks.' The future, because it was less likely to be achieved, diminished, and with that went the past. One was fixated on the present. 'I decided,' he reflected, 'that this was nature's way of reducing anxiety and worry and providing a safety valve for maintaining psychological balance.' Life reverted to the simple axiom of getting through each day.

Lieutenant Peter Balfour, sitting on his Churchill tank in reserve smoking a cigarette, whimsically observed 'S' Squadron the Scots Guards deployed on a ridge 400 to 500 yards away. He was experiencing the 'empty battlefield' phenomenon. Little of interest could generally be seen. People were hidden and, when action did occur, it was generally in the form of a series of interrelated skirmishes rather than the epic spectacles seen on cinema screens. Balfour had yet to experience his first action and learn how to 'read' a battle. 'We suddenly noticed that tanks were going up, were blowing up, and this was the first time I had actually seen this happening.' At first he was mystified. 'We thought, God the mortars are accurate, they must be dropping them through the hatches.' It wasn't until he saw the Panthers emerge from the flank festooned with infantry that he appreciated this was a tank engagement. Infantry on board to him signified surrender. Even death was unreal. He watched his friend Nigel Bease climb out of his tank and try to get his crew out. 'His tank was on fire and, as he got out, suddenly something swept him away, just like that.' Seven or eight tanks were knocked out before he appreciated that this was an actual tank-on-tank engagement.

There was curiosity about the enemy, and attitudes toward him were ambivalent. 'The extraordinary part,' Peter Balfour wrote to his father, 'was that from beginning to end you probably saw no more than two to three live Germans at the most' in any engagement. There were attacks 'where I saw none at all'. On one occasion 400 bodies were picked up after an advance in which 'I saw nothing!' He did not like Germans, especially the SS:

> They were the real hard nuts to crack and partly because they had always behaved in a disgusting way. When you went into a place where the SS had been, they had shat on the floor and you know, crapped the whole place up entirely. We didn't distinguish between Nazis and Germans. They were all Germans and bad news. We didn't feel about them politically at all – we just felt they were the enemy.

Condemnation of the SS was almost universal. Lieutenant Belton Cooper of the 3rd Armoured Division reported men shot in cold blood. 'This enraged our men and undoubtedly resulted in severe retaliation later against other SS troopers.' The 12th SS Division were alleged to have murdered at least 130 Canadians in Normandy and received little quarter thereafter. Bodies were dragged on to roads to be crushed by tanks to hide atrocities. Lieutenant James Carson of the Welsh Guards, on reaching one of his tank crews cut off by the *Leibstandarte*, 'saw my five boys laid out in a row, Sergeant James [the tank commander] at the head, each with a bullet in the head and with their boots removed'. Absolutely incensed, he admitted, 'I did not take a prisoner and I am ashamed of that.' Nowadays, he commented, he would 'have been pounced upon and condemned by the media before being court-martialled'. He had nightmares about these five men for some time after.

Cruel events formed part of the unreality in which tank crews found themselves. Lieutenant Andrew Wilson lost his friend Harvey to the SS. 'Harvey with his big, bear-like body and a trick he'd had at parties of being able to waggle his ears.' It was incomprehensible. 'The idea of him facing an SS firing squad was utterly incongruous. He wanted to shout aloud, to do something to deny that it was possible.'

Lieutenant Michael Trasenster was phlegmatic, 'I had no enmity against the Germans,' he claimed, 'you were just put in to fight.' He saw there was a 'certain degree of chivalry with front-line troops' whereby 'both side's tanks would often not machine-gun troops who had bailed out – but the infantry would, though.' This was illogical, he surmised 'because Shermans were expendable and only good crews were in short supply'. Treatment for prisoners he remarked 'got worse the further they moved to the rear'. It was only when tank gunner Ken Tout saw them close up that he realised they were like themselves. 'A few minutes before we had been trying to kill the lot of them,' he remarked, recalling how they had captured a group; 'now they were human beings like us.' Prisoners had an ability to immediately establish a rapport, something that politicians could not. 'The first thing they would do was to take out their wallet,' he observed, 'and say I have got some kids at home and here is a picture of my family.'

The technical shock of German armour and the power of German anti-tank guns compounded the strangeness of the situation. Trooper Ernie Cox of 141 RAC the Buffs recalled the surprise when a recovery team towed in a disabled Tiger. 'We were over it like a rash,' he declared. 'Look at the width of those tracks and the thickness of armour and that bloody great gun – no wonder the puny 75mm would not dent it,' they agreed. Somebody took out a tape measure to measure the length of the gun 'and 18 feet 2 inches came to mind'. 'Eighty-eight, a figure we came to dread – I'd even duck when I saw an 88 bus coming in later life,' he recalled.

Leutnant Richard von Rosen of Tiger Battalion 503 was dismissive of the Sherman. 'We had fifteen Shermans against us and they started to fire,' he recalled. 'I received some hits on my turret and I could feel this inside, but' – and he shook his head disdainfully – 'I'm feeling, this is not dangerous.' Only the British 17-pounder Firefly could penetrate the Tiger and Panther frontally, and there was only one per tank troop. The Americans had none; limited British production capacity meant none were available.

The Americans were equally shocked at the technical excellence of German tanks, having been assured the Sherman was their equal. 'I had been told it was the best tank going and I believed it,' claimed Lieutenant Belton Cooper of the US 3rd Armoured Division. 'I believed it was better than the German tanks'; and he felt it was a 'tragic misunderstanding' when on arrival they found 'it was the other way around'. The result was 'fantastic losses', he complained. 'We lost eighty-seven tanks in the first seven miles of those hedgerows. It was just horrendous!' Sardonic German humour soon labelled the Shermans 'Tommy Cookers', owing to their propensity to burn. One Panther with Panzer Regiment 33 knocked out twenty-three Shermans in a single day.

Tank crews desperate to survive plunged into 'Heath Robinson' modification schemes to ward off the unavoidable. Belton Cooper observed American tankers taking sacks of cement from an abandoned factory and mixing crude concrete patches to reinforce the front glacis plate. Other crews stacked sandbags or anything that could be purloined. Lieutenant Peter Balfour was introduced to this feverish activity as soon as their tanks arrived on the first day in a field near Bayeux. 'Everybody was welding on pieces of track to their tanks, which was a device for setting *panzerfausts* (bazookas) off before it actually hit the main armour.' This prematurely detonated them before they could penetrate the armoured plate. This went on for two or three days until 'the whole thing looked like a hedgehog in the end'. It made no difference.

Beyond this, all crews could do was improvise to narrow the technology gap. 'The Panzer *Lehr* records criticised our shooting as being too low,' declared Lieutenant Michael Trasenster. 'But we were going for the sprockets and tracks with the 75mm, otherwise their tanks were immune.' It was the only way to immobilise them. Sydney Radley-Walters of the Canadian Sherbrook Fusiliers found you could kill a Panther if the shell hit a four to five-foot strip of armour directly beneath the gun mantlet. This produced a favourable entry point by bouncing a round from above into the thin armour covering the driver and co-driver, 'in most cases killing or badly wounding' and knocking out the tank. He destroyed nineteen.

The Normandy *bocage,* or hedgerows, was a landscape beyond the training experience that was conferred by the flat and open Salisbury Plain. Hitler constrained panzer flexibility, insisting they fight as near the coast as possible. They became entangled in the ensuing stalemate fought among a belt of dense apple orchards and small fields the size of football pitches, dissected by a network of hedgerows on earth banks concealing sunken lanes. Trooper Fred Sprigg with the 6th Guards Tank Brigade recalled:

Banks were about five to six feet high, on top of which grew dense hedges and trees. Narrow twisted lanes were sunk deep in the banks. You couldn't find your way around – sheer impossibility – and at this time of the year the trees and hedges were at their thickest with green foliage. There were a few hamlets and farms whose hundred-year-old walls were quite capable of standing up to shell fire, let alone trying to get through them. It was no wonder that the Germans thought it was impregnable.

Peter Balfour, a subaltern with the Scots Guards, thought 'it was terrible country for tanks – very close – all orchards' and 'you can never see more than the other side of the field which is about 100 yards away'. Keeping in touch with other tank troops or infantry was tricky because visibility was often down to 40 or 50 yards.

The network of banks provided ready-made trenches for the German defenders. Parallel hedgerows covered each other and provided communication arteries. Lurking behind leafy screens were anti-tank guns, self-propelled guns and dug-in tanks, covered by a network of machine-gun posts with well-surveyed artillery and mortar defensive fire zones. German defenders did not sit still; they employed aggressive mobile counter-attacks with tanks supported by infantry carrying *panzerfaust.* The average was 14 hedgerows per kilometre in Normandy, and they had to be captured one at a time.

The moment tanks and infantry broke cover to advance there were tremendous losses. Roads generally provided the centre line for attacks so that supporting vehicles could travel behind to provide fire support, supply ammunition and pick up casualties. Tanks were constrained to using roads because they could barely cope with the extremely ponderous cross-country ride.

The first Sherman of the 737th US Independent Tank Battalion that tried to ram through a hedgerow 'was flipped on to its back and lay like an up-ended turtle' according to one observer. 'Trial and error' tactics were employed to deal with the new tactical conditions because, as the battalion's CO was forced to admit, 'We've spent years studying the book and practising, and then in our first action we had to throw away the book, and everything we learned in practice was no good to us at all.' This was the experience of all tank men in Normandy. Schemes were employed to breach hedgerows, starting with bulldozers and explosives, until the Americans deployed the 'Culin' hedgerow device named after the cavalry sergeant who designed it. This was a set of 'dozer' teeth mounted on the nose of a Sherman which enabled it to scoop its own path though the hedge-lined earth banks, thereby achieving some mobility. One unforeseen advantage of the close *bocage* was that it neutralised the long-range advantage of German tank guns. They were, however, hidden in ambush waiting for Allied tanks that had to break cover to advance.

The 'battle hardened' state, following the initial 'unreality' of combat, which Lieutenant Michael Trasenster felt conferred feelings of 'invincibility' or confidence, was the position that veterans had already reached. This was why they were wanted, because their impact was immediately beneficial. Stuart Hamilton, a subaltern with 8 RTR in Italy, described it as 'a good stage as one had become experienced and knew what it was like and what to expect. One could trust one's crew, squadron, equipment etc and, above all else, one's self.' Veterans could 'read' developing combat situations, but the down side was that they knew what was dangerous and might therefore be cautious. Measuring combat readiness against fatigue was an imprecise art. Battle-hardened crew might be a stage or two ahead in terms of weariness, depending how much rest and mental 'softening' occurred during leave.

German mental preparation, developed through hard and thoroughly realistic battle inoculation, put them ahead of some Allied units. *Hitlerjugend* teenagers could hold their own even against battle-hardened units. They were bonded by a hardbitten and largely desensitised veteran cadre. Nineteen-year-old *Hitlerjugend* trooper Bernhard Heisig declared, 'When the war broke out we were all mentally prepared.' They were impatient. 'We were young and thought the war would soon be over, but we really hoped we would get a go.' 'I had a friend,' he recalled, 'who said in all seriousness, "I want to die in battle." ' Not only did the teenagers intimidate their opponents, local civilians were also wary at their presence. 'They machine-gunned every window, every flutter of a curtain,' remembered Jacques Vico, who was living in Caen. 'They were bare-headed, singing in their armoured vehicle. You could sense their determination and absolute fanaticism.'

The *Hitlerjugend* gained the grudging acceptance of other German units, initially cynical about the reasons for its formation and suspicious of what the 'baby division' could actually achieve. 'At first we thought – my God, now they are taking the children,' recalled Wolfgang Filor of the SS Division Das Reich, but then he observed them in action:

I saw them myself on the stretch from St Lô. I had my sights on an American tank and was going to fire, when to my horror I saw a German soldier waving his bazooka to stop us firing. He then blew himself up with the tank, firing from underneath – he gave his life.

The period of 'maximum efficiency 'identified by the Swank and Marchand chart lasts twenty days or so beyond the ten-day initial orientation to the unreality of battle. This period encapsulated the repulse of the British 7th Armoured Division at Villers-Bocage between 10 to 12 June and 'Operation Epsom' at the end of the month, when attempts to cross the River Odon east of Caen were blocked. Allied troops ashore outnumbered the defending Wehrmacht after 18 June and Cherbourg was captured on the 27th. Many units were by now at a relatively efficient stage, where anxieties could be controlled reasonably well. Exhaustion gradually corroded efficiency but not confidence at this point. Those spearheading the advance were under greater stress. 'People don't realise what it's like to be in tanks and know the horrors of tank warfare, when your friends are being burned alive,' declared Trooper Fred Sprigg of the 6th Guards Tank Brigade. 'They're being killed and you always think, thank God it's not me.' Michael Trasenster appreciated that survival was a lottery. 'It sounds very callous,' he admitted, 'you really are rather glad it's not you – but he is your friend.' Guilt at surviving pervades many veteran accounts. 'I lost my first real friend to a sniper – he was going to be a doctor – while he was taking prisoners,' he remembered.

Perceptions of 'invincibility' became associated with 'fanaticism'. Human beings are generally reluctant to kill. It conflicts with normal behavioural patterns in civilised societies. On the battlefield though, soldiers are taught to kill if convinced there are reasons that make it necessary. Patriotism and a 'just war' motivated tank men, but so, arguably, did fanaticism. This can be a powerful tool in increasing combat effectiveness. Soldiers with a 'death count', veterans, are respected by peers, admired by subordinates and generally trusted by superiors. The majority of soldiers become desensitised and conditioned by combat. Some were alleged to be so desensitised, like the Waffen SS and notably the *Hitlerjugend*, that they were labelled fanatics. Hans Kauthold, a Panther tank commander in the 12th SS, was indignant that his unit was labelled fanatical:

> We learned we were called fanatics only after the war, it was so unapparent to us. There were so many of us who had lost their homes, their parents and all. The cities and even the smaller towns were being bombed. Almost everyone was determined to do his best and fight. None of us thought we were fanatics, we were good and hard fighting soldiers. We were fighting if necessary to the last – *Ja* – everyone was very willing to sacrifice himself. But whether this was a fanatic? It was always a strange word for me, and 'heroes' – that was also a word that wasn't used.

There is a fine dividing line between fanaticism and bitter determination. 'You had to admit they were well trained,' Canadian officer Doug Barrie reflected. 'What's more they were determined to do all they could to inflict the highest possible casualties on us.' Corporal Patrick

Hennessey of the 13/18 Royal Hussars remembered the door of a house opening in a village as their tanks drove through 'and a little boy came out – well, fourteen or fifteen [years] perhaps – carrying a *panzerfaust*'. He opened fire on a Sherman at point-blank range, no more than 12 feet. 'The sergeant from this tank looked out and was just going to shout at the boy when he hit the tank with such force that the tank was destroyed and the sergeant and all the crew killed.' Hennessey was dumbfounded. Barrie was convinced 'many of them were fanatics, especially the officers and NCOs they had behind them', because they had been indoctrinated in the Hitler Youth. 'The ordinary soldiers knew they couldn't retreat or surrender – they'd have been shot. German prisoners told us that if they'd run away their families at home would have been in trouble.' 'Vendettas sometimes sprung up between certain units,' claimed Lieutenant Michael Trasenster, 'such as the Canadians and the 12th SS.'

The impact of such intense resistance was unsettling. German units were in no doubt they were superior. Perhaps for them 'invincibility' was the precursor to death or glory, as distinct from the Allied appreciation of it simply preceding varying degrees of caution. 'At this time we felt superior,' remarked Heinz Kauthold, the Panther commander with the 12th SS, 'not only regarding tanks, but also in the quality of our training and so on.' German units were fought literally to extinction, unlike Allied formations, who would be withdrawn to rest and refit after excessive casualties. 'Sometimes we saw the casualties as proof of how tough we were, how hard we could be pushed,' remarked Bernhard Heisig, with some cynicism, about his time as a trooper in the *Hitlerjugend*. 'That was a crazy ideology.' Heinrich Himmler, the head of the SS, was obliged to write officially to Reich Labour Leader Konstantin Hierl to recoup his losses. He admitted:

The *Hitlerjugend* Division now has casualties of 6,000 including 2,000 dead. The painful truth is that, at the lowest estimate, one third of the wounded are amputees, since most of the injuries have been caused by artillery and dive-bombing. We must see to it that these divisions do not bleed to death totally, since they are – and this is a phrase I seldom use – in the truest sense decisive for the war.

Combat stress becomes less of an issue if death or injury predates the condition. Heisig explained that fighting like this was 'lemming-like behaviour' in that 'they run straight towards disaster, because the others are running'. Nazi ideology constantly extolled the value of the *Volk*, the 'folk' or group; this was group behaviour. Thinking was not required, 'at least not at that stage', Heisig reiterated.

Ken Tout, advancing cautiously with the Northamptonshire Yeomanry, saw a member of the *Hitlerjugend* lying in a ditch alongside the road. He appeared to be mortally wounded:

> We had to halt, so my driver and I got out and went over to see this lad, about sixteen to seventeen years of age, absolutely pale. He hadn't very many moments left to live. My driver got his water bottle and came over to give this lad a drink and I saw the boy making feeble movements. He was pulling out a pistol and he was going to shoot my driver. We grabbed the revolver and threw it into the field and went away and left him. He wouldn't take water from us.

Veteran status conferred a certain ability to cope. If one survived the initial 'dream-like' shock of tank combat, proficiency followed. Crews who learned quickly had improved chances in the combat lottery. Douglas Ambridge, a Sherman tank commander, quickly came to appreciate the power and lethality of the 88mm German tank gun. 'With 88mm solid shot whizzing about all over the place, I went behind a house to get out of its fields of fire,' he recalled. Within minutes he had to bail out with his tank in flames. 'The 88mm tank gun had fired through five walls of the house and still penetrated my tank and got into the petrol. So that showed you something of the power of that gun!'

'We were drilled to wait for the tank commander's order before abandoning the tank,' remembered Churchill tank crewman Stephen Dyson, 'but in action that's a joke.' Crew learned to clear the tank on the first strike. 'The survival instinct ignores the rules and asserts itself,' he declared. Lieutenant Andrew Wilson of the Buffs claimed Churchills caught fire three out of five times and could take up to ten seconds to burn through the turret from the engine-room. Shermans were nicknamed 'Ronsons', after the famous Ronson cigarette lighter advert that claimed 'they always light first time'. They took three seconds to burn. Turret crew had to ensure that nobody was trapped by the gun before they got out. Corporal Patrick Hennessey made the point, 'If your gunner is killed and you can't traverse then the poor old driver or co-driver has a genuine case of poor old luck.' He viewed the awful consequences when a tank from his own troop was hit and burned with the gun left at the 11 o'clock position over the driver's hatch. 'We could see the tank burning and exploding and you could see that hatch being opened by the driver. There was no way he could get out.'

Lieutenant Peter Balfour of the Scots Guards recalled the rash armoured tactics of the early days. Preceded by a massive air or artillery bombardment, infantry would capture key ground and armour would be ordered to pass through. 'Well we would get to the place and the armour would 'sweep through' about 200 yards down the road where it would meet a couple of Panthers who would quietly brew up the first six Shermans and there the matter would remain.' Tank co-operation with the infantry needed to be more closely developed. 'Tank crews,' Balfour explained, 'can very easily get into an attitude of mind where they think that not only does the whole battle depend on them, but if they suffer losses they are so important they need not go on.'

Eventually the tanks began to advance with infantry all around providing anti-bazooka and sniper protection, 'from hedge to hedge, making each hedge a bound', Balfour explained. Infantry would peer into a field to check for enemy tanks; if not, break through the hedge and occupy the one behind. All would 'then settle down to a quarter of an hour's speculative shooting up of the next hedge, HE into any likely looking places and Besa everything including the tree-tops'. This generally occurred under Spandau machine-gun and mortar fire 'but from nowhere could you pin-point it'. Houses were shot into flames and if there was no return fire the advance continued at walking pace. Using this deliberate method 'we advanced about five miles in about six hours'. If they encountered a tank or anti-tank gun 'you were almost bound to lose at least one tank as it was point-blank range and you could not possibly see them until they fired and frequently not even then.' This was exhausting and stressful work and they 'hardly ever saw a German'.

The concept of the 'tank ace' attracted little Allied media interest at the time but was certainly utilised by German propaganda. Medals and achievement badges play a role in the respect accorded to veteran prowess by their peers because they differentiate 'doers' from 'passengers' in combat units. There was colourful German media interest in achievements. It is interesting to view differing Allied and German attitudes to heroism. German crews were results conscious, as exemplified by the plethora of medals and badges awarded. Allied crews looked at destroying opposing tanks as a means of shortening the war and getting home. Allied wartime pictorial magazines such as the English *Picture Post* or American *Yank* magazines displayed scant interest in tanks, whereas German equivalents like *Signal* and *Die Wehrmacht* often displayed panzers on their front covers. German wartime magazines promoted heroism and sacrifice as typical Germanic ideals fighting for *Volk und Führer*. They aimed at inspiring the factory workers who produced the key weapon systems such as tanks, and the fighting men and others on the home front. German magazines counted tank kills as they did those of air aces. Allied publications showed aircraft tallies and naval successes and devoted a lot of space to the Russian Front, particularly human interest stories such as female snipers, but less to tanks. Some 'tank aces' encapsulated what cumulative skill could achieve; one example was the German tank killer Michael Wittmann.

Wittmann was a thirty-year-old SS *Obersturmführer* (Lieutenant) in the 1st SS Division at the time of the battle of Normandy. He had entered the Waffen SS in 1936 and by Normandy had served successive campaigns in Poland, France, the Balkans and Russia. He was a committed National Socialist, which produced an intimidating resolve in a highly experienced soldier. This background, combined with an equally veteran and competent panzer crew, produced a lethal capability that personified the Panzerwaffe philosophy of harnessing two fighting systems: 'man' together with 'machine'. Wittmann and his crew were at the 'invincible', combat-hardened level of the identified war-weariness spectrum when he faced a column of Allied armour single-handed at Villers-Bocage on 13 June, spearheading the 7th Armoured Division.

Lieutenant Cloudsley-Thompson, in a Cromwell tank with the 4th City of London Yeomanry, saw the tank ahead explode just before an armour-piercing shell whizzed between his head and that of his radio operator. He was convinced the projectile missed him by no more than half an inch. 'It was so vicious, a supersonic shell passing so close, and this was the first time, I think,' he recalled, 'I'd ever been frightened, really, really frightened, in my life.' He was completely intimidated. 'After that, I tended to feel nothing could ever miss me again.' Out of the smoke loomed the gigantic silhouette of a Tiger. Even though they fired at point-blank range, 35 yards away, their 75mm shots bounced off the armour. 'The Tiger traversed its big 88mm gun very slightly. Wham! We were hit.' The shot passed between his legs 'because I could sort of feel a tingling from it', sped into the engine compartment and engulfed the tank in flames. As they bailed out, the lone Tiger trundled by, its command hatch slightly ajar, leaving a choking trail of black smoke and destruction in its wake as it proceeded further on, systematically shooting up the column.

Wittmann knocked out twelve half-tracks, three light and six medium tanks. Inside two hours he was back, re-armed and with reinforcements, this time destroying twelve medium tanks, four heavy tanks and sixteen Bren-gun carriers. He became the darling of the German press. *The Classic Example: Man versus Mass!* was the heading for an article in *Signal* magazine. He was awarded the sword to the Knight's Cross, the equivalent of a bar to the British Victoria Cross.

How could one tank crew be so brutally effective? Wittmann certainly utilised his self-propelled assault gun expertise. His gunner *Rottenführer* (Corporal) Balthasar Woll was also a Knight's Cross holder, having knocked out eighty tanks and 107 anti-tank guns, and had an instictive aim. Gunner and commander stayed together in the Panzerwaffe whenever possible, longer than other crew members. Wittmann was renowned to possess a sixth sense in identifying potential anti-tank ambush positions, and he had a 'hunter' instinct.

Studies of air aces show that 1 per cent of US Army Air Corps fighter pilots in the war were responsible for 40 per cent of all kills. This pattern also applied to tank 'aces'. Luftwaffe ace Erich Hartman claimed that 80 per cent of his 351 victims never even knew he was in the sky with them. This provides a clue explaining tank crew success because the majority of successful engagements were simple ambushes, shot in the back or flank killings. Tanks 'stalked' their prey, without provocation, anger or emotion to empower the killings: Wittmann was a soldier for ten years and had been at war for six prior to Normandy. He was likely desensitised to killing. There is only anecdotal knowledge about his personality. He was described as 'modest' and 'gifted' by a previous SP gunner and well liked by comrades, doubtless impressed by his formidable score rate. He married, but there is no record of children, and he could only have spent weeks with his wife owing to postings. Totally committed to his Führer and country, he might be described as a serious, 'intense' man. Clicking his heels in the Nazi fashion as a tank instructor amused his students when it caused him to stumble but Wittmann, not so amused, handed out extra duties. He was a serious officer with a high sense of duty and very successful in decoupling emotion from his professional capabilities. Refusing the softer option of an instructor's post after his success at Villers-Bocage, despite being knocked out, he was decorated and promoted and returned to his tank company.

Wittmann was a tank killer. Like many competent operators, his ability and confidence were factors in his survival. However, his confidence eventually exceeded his ability. Within two months of Villers-Bocage he was dead, caught in the cross-fire of five Shermans, or hit by rocket-firing Typhoon aircraft. Whatever the cause, his Tiger was found with the turret separated from the hull and the entire crew wiped out. Myth has obscured his career, but he embodied the capability that could develop if a crew lived long enough.

Lethal tank crews were not sociopaths; their performance is explainable through a combination of aggression, responsive crew skills and a lack of empathy for others in the same predicament in battle. Such men inspired their own and engendered respect from the enemy. Peter Roach of 1 RTR admitted, 'We believed the tale of the leading regiment of our brigade who were ambushed in a cutting beyond Villers-Bocage.' The story had become myth. After trapping the column by shooting up the first and last vehicles, Roach claimed, 'The commander had then appeared from his turret, taken off his hat and bowed to the remainder. Such was the feeling of immunity given by this great gun and weighty armour.'

British crews were irreverent regarding medals and modest about achievement, often to a deprecating degree. 'VC Wallahs' were those who sought medals and were mistrusted because they were dangerous to their own crews. David Holbrook, serving as a subaltern in a Yeomanry regiment, described one crew's reaction to a series of close shaves to which their glory-seeking troop commander had subjected them. One of them pointed out tell-tale 88mm scoop marks gouged out on their tank armour and remarked: 'D'you know what 'e wants, Sir? 'E wants to get 'is fookin' VC. It's fookin' ooncomfortable . . . 'E's too bright, 'e is.'

Holbrook saw how 'the man's terror was expressing itself in this ironic clowning'. Such humour, however, was what kept men going at this time of acute stress. Trooper Bob Knight of the 1st East Riding Yeomanry described a tight spot they had been in while fighting around Caen. Several tanks had been hit and set on fire, and all were wondering 'who was going to be next' when the tank gunner called the crew commander over the internal radio and said: 'I would like to have my cards now, sir.' The remainder of the squadron heard the message because his radio was still on transmit. 'I heard that, Ellis,' called the squadron commander, immediately recognising the voice. 'Get off the bloody air, there's a battle going on.'

Motivation, bravery and a certain emotional blocking were what kept tank crews going from the initial unreal shock of battle until the combat hardened stage, when survival made them feel strangely invincible. Even the most ideologically motivated Germans realised that medals were an irrelevance. Weak and strong died, however brave they had been; the next stage to ultimate combat weariness demanded caution. The pointlessness of gallantry awards was poignantly appreciated by a medical officer in the *Hitlerjugend,* who recalled his best friend Otto Toll, one of the company commanders left behind as a casualty to fend for himself. 'I can still see Otto lying before me, unfortunately already dead,' he remembered. 'He had tried to make a tourniquet using the ribbon of his Knight's Cross and a flashlight to stop the bleeding from an artery.' It did not work.

## CAUTION TO FEAR

'By now a little of the "gung-ho" attitude had given way to a more cautious one,' explained Lieutenant Stuart Hamilton, recalling how he

Stuart Hamilton displaying the desert sores that afflicted many, serving with 8 RTR. He described the progressive stages of deterioration that lead to combat fatigue.

The cameraderie of shared hardship provided the main cohesion for tank crews, such as this British trio sitting astride their Matilda medium tank.

An American Grant tank crew, freshly arrived in Tunisia. The US forces were convinced they had the answer to panzer dominance, with their own 'tank destoyer' philosophy.

A view taken through the vision slit of a T-34 under artillery fire.

A hit on a T-34 turret usually blew up the shells stored within. The spectacular explosion
could lift the turret from the hull, seen here flying forward to the left.

The advent of the 'Swallow', as the Sherman tank was secretly called, at last restored technical tank parity briefly to the Allies in the desert. Staff officers curiously inspect the first arrivals.

Large-scale tank exercises conducted in the US in the early 1940s. Despite all its preparation the American army was in for an unpleasant surprise.

Otto Carius was a highly experienced Tiger commander who believed in fighting and commanding from an open turret.

Ludwig Bauer used up his proverbial 'nine lives' when he was knocked out nine times in action. The final strike was a 'blue on blue' from his own side during the final days of the war in Germany. He escaped with his life but with severe burns.

Karl Fuchs of the 7th Panzer Division alongside his wife Madi. He was killed outside Moscow in November 1941 before the birth of his son.

Heinz Guderian the 'father' of the Panzer arm and successful tank General (second from right) is completely dwarfed by the bulk of the Tiger tank he is inspecting in France prior to the Allied landings in Normandy.

Guderian intoduced comic-strip manuals to simplify training and education in the panzer corps. This example shows the basic maintenance required for a Panther tank.

A Tiger tank loader at work. Once the commander identified an enemy tank he ordered the loader to load with an armour piercing 88mm shell. Note the size of the shell and difficulty the loader has manhandling it in a restricted turret space.

A British tank driver observing mortar fire through the vision slit of his tank.

A German Panther tank, hit and destroyed by a US Pershing directly in front of Cologne Cathedral. top left: 1) the Pershing fires down a side-street at the Panther. 2) Crew start to scramble out in the few seconds before the Panther explodes. The commander emerges, burned by the flames already spewing from the turret hatch to his left. The rest of the crew below and inside are being scorched in the developing fireball. 3) Only three crew escape. The commander has jumped landing in the crouched position discernible forward of the tank. The driver is scrambling out of his hatch forward of the turret. 4) The third crew member is slower and obviously injured. He is seen sat on the turret and as he starts to roll off. The driver is fleeing the feared explosion top right. They are out in three to five seconds. 5) With three of five men out the propellent from stored shells begins to incinerate the turret. 6) Flames shoot 30 to 40 feet skyward as ammunition explosions spew fire from the turret and driver's hatches. Two men are incinerated within.

Desperate measures were employed to stem the flood of Allied tanks in Germany. Hermann Eckardt recalled units of boys armed with panzerfausts on bicycles 'in the slippery frost and snow of January 1945 – with only ten metres of effective range!'

By the time the Comet tank appeared, able to take on a Tiger on even terms, the Reich was collapsing, as evidenced by this white flag of surrender in a German town in April 1945.

and others of 8 RTR reached the next stage of combat weariness. 'Thinking a bit more of the possible consequences of being hurt' meant 'the excitement had been considerably dulled by then'. The Swank and Marchand combat efficiency chart estimates that combat exhaustion sets in after a thirty- to forty-day interval preceded by a period of over-confidence. In Normandy this included 'Operation Goodwood' between 18 and 21 July, when over three and a half days a British corps of three armoured divisions attacked over ten miles with 877 tanks, losing 437. This pinned down the defending German armoured reserves and created the conditions for an eventual break-out by the 1st US army five days later.

Lieutenant Michael Trasenster of the 4/7 RDG described this as 'the time when you start noticing your friends are becoming casualties and you think you might become one also'. Lieutenant Stuart Hills recorded that the Northamptonshire Sherwood Rangers Yeomanry lost forty tank commanders killed or wounded by 13 July. About twenty-four of these were officers and included many of his friends.

Losing friends was hard. Trooper Ernie Cox with the Buffs remembered having to restrain a man who thought he had lost his entire crew. 'We had been together for two or three years and knew them like brothers,' he reflected. 'To see them reduced to this was hard to take.' Stuart Hills remembered that the war poet Keith Douglas was caught by a mortar bomb within a few days of D-Day, 'killed while he was running along a ditch towards the safety of his tank'. He was twenty-four years old. Casual disturbing images viewed through letterbox-size observation slits became daily events. One trooper in the East Riding Yeomanry can still 'vividly remember an army padre weeping in a slit trench as he touched infantrymen crawling past in preparation for another futile attack'. Michael Trasenster listed thirteen of his contemporaries from Winchester College killed, thirty-nine survived, possibly wounded. There was a one in three chance of remaining untouched. 'Men I had known so many years gone before our eyes,' announced Sergeant Jack Parramore of the 1st Lothian and Border Yeomanry. 'No counselling in those days,' he ironically observed. It was becoming increasingly apparent to many that they might not survive.

Losing a brother was especially traumatic. Michael Trasenster's driver Reg Cox saw his twin brother's tank explode and burn barely 20 yards away. 'Reg and Ron were an inseparable pair,' he explained, 'both fine athletes and popular.' 'Reg was sitting in the driver's seat and sobbing,' Trasenster recalled. 'I gave him half a bottle of brandy.' It happened during a disastrous day that left only about nine tanks in the squadron. The remainder of the crew sat awkwardly by, sipping cocoa and milk. The radio operator Roy 'Wilco' Willets reminisced over the sad day, 'thanking the Lord we had come through it and not knowing what we were about to go through'. Willets was troubled by his friend Reg, who 'sat there sobbing, sobbing'. Eventually, he recalled, 'I put my hand through the turret cage and just gripped his shoulder', offering human contact. 'I didn't like to say anything else – I should leave him to his thoughts.'

The Wehrmacht was conscious of the bond between brothers and the emotional consequences if it should be broken. Ludwig Bauer, with Panzer Regiment 33 in Normandy, recalled the case of two brothers serving in a sister battalion. 'It was not allowed to have two brothers crewing the same tank; nor were they encouraged to serve in the same battalion.' This was sound practice because he had seen the potential implications in Russia. One of the brothers was in a tank that was hit and burned and the other, a panzer commander, learned of the incident on the radio and sped to the spot. His brother was trapped inside and the panzer was in flames. Moreover, all this was clear to the entire regiment because his stricken brother's throat microphone was on transmit. Desperately he appealed across the net to his brother, beaten back by the flames, 'Shoot me!' There was a pause, and he did. 'Can you imagine what he had to say to his mother?' Bauer exclaimed. Shortly afterwards the soldier suffered a nervous breakdown.

Bad news invariably came over the radio. 'You could hear all the talk on the radio from other squadrons doing different places,' explained Lieutenant Peter Balfour of the 3rd Battalion the Scot's Guards. 'I remember a particular friend of mine in another squadron. It was quite clear that he had been killed and that shook me up a bit.' 'People's voices changed as the tension worsened,' recalled Michael Trasenster of the 4/7 RDG. 'Some got more and more casual but, knowing them, you could feel the tension building up.' Paul Holbrook, a Yeomanry subaltern, described a turret-eye view of 'confused voices' that came over the air when radio transmissions were accidentally left on.

'Hallo able one Hallo able one. Enemy hornet is attacking my able three.'

'Fire at the bastard' – an angry scream.

'Hallo able two . . . Fire! Fire!'

Meanwhile a dull dogged voice here and there would be checking a net.

'The traumatic experience of hearing the click of a radio going dead in another tank on the net added to the horror,' recalled Trooper J.W. Howes with the Buffs. A dull metallic click on the air sometimes signified death. 'One wore the headphones at all times when in action,' remembered Ernst Hamilton of the 15/19 Hussars. 'If, for instance, someone reported "Able three" had been hit by an 88mm gun, everyone knew who this was and the faces of the casualties would flash through the mind.'

Wireless transmissions gave tank combat an unreal and distant perspective, while noise accentuated the feeling of exclusion from what was going on around. 'Little could be heard above the noise of the huge engine, the noise when a gun was fired inside, and the constant hiss in the earphones worn all the time,' recalled Howes. Despite their armoured protection tank crews were vulnerable to unexpected mortar fire. Only the infantry could hear the distant banging, signifying the barrel reports, and the whispering approach. A wary eye needed therefore to be kept on how the accompanying infantry were reacting to what was going on. Hatches closed as soon as they began leaping into cover.

Other senses, particularly smell, applied intangible mental pressures. The putrid stench wafting up from bloated farm animals and human remains was dispiriting. 'There were times when we would have to drive over them or in the dark may not have seen them,' recalled Trooper Ernie Cox with the Buffs. 'The vile-smelling mess would revolve around the tracks while inside we'd be trying not to vomit.' It was an enduring memory, 'the stench I can smell to this day', he claimed. The only recourse was to find the nearest field 'and begin to try and plough it up to try and get the mess off. It took a long time to go.'

Viewing the detritus of combat did more than anything else to raise the level of caution. Padre Leslie Skinner, serving with the Nottinghamshire Sherwood Rangers Yeomanry, was given the fearful job of recovering the remains of men he knew. In a diary entry for 17 August he wrote, 'Buried the three dead and tried to reach the remaining dead in tanks still too hot and burning.' It was, he explained, a 'fearful job picking up bits and pieces and reassembling for identification'. Debris was placed on blankets for burial. His squadron leader offered to lend manpower to help, but Skinner wisely declined. 'Less men who live and fight in tanks have to do with this side of things the better. They know it happens but to force it on their attention is not good.' Lieutenant Sidney Radley-Walters of the Canadian Sherbrook Fusiliers Armoured Regiment had already reached the same conclusion:

> We needed tanks badly and I was down to six or seven. This one had the motor still running in it and we could see where it had been hit and so on. When night came on I decided to get the body out. I had to go in and cut the guy in half because rigor mortis had set in. I took a machete and cut him in half and took him out in two pieces, we couldn't get him out in one piece. Well, that doesn't do you very good and I thought after doing these little tricks – but in doing your duty really – that came over me, none of the crews, including myself, should get involved in it again.

Tanks that did not burn out were salvageable. When a projectile penetrated a tank it resulted in a series of incandescent particles or scabs of metal showering the inside of the fighting compartment. At close range the slug might hit and go all the way through. This was the best result for the crew, who would avoid the terrible ricocheting effect inside. Gerhard Stiller, an SS Leibstandarte lieutenant, called the Panzer Mark IV the 'mess tin', complaining 'our armoured protection was not always the best'. German *Landser* (equivalent to 'Tommy') jargon chimed: 'Better a hit with a Panzer IV in and out than Panzer V (Panther) which gets stuck, and goes round about.' The latter meant the crew was eviscerated by the round spinning around inside. The tank could be made to run again, but at an emotional cost to the next crew.

Lieutenant Belton Cooper worked with the Maintenance Battalion with the 3rd Armoured Division and his job was to recover such repairable tanks.

As the tanks and other armoured vehicles were brought into the Vehicle Collection Point with broken and twisted bodies still inside, the horror of war began to settle into my being. When a tanker inside received the full effect of penetration, sometimes the body, particularly the head, exploded and scattered blood, gore and brains throughout the entire compartment. It was a horrible sight.

Helmut Pock, with the Maintenance Company of the first Panzer Battalion of the *Hitlerjugend* Panzer Regiment, was called out in the middle of a night's brief exhausted rest to repair a panzer's damaged steering gear. To get at the interior he had to climb into the turret and 'as I climbed up and was feeling for a hold, my hands gripped a wet slippery substance'. He asked the teenaged gunner what it was. 'Our commander was killed in action,' he replied. 'His head was ripped off.' He then added, apologetically, 'I know that the whole interior is a mess.' Pock realised this was his first time in action. 'It's all right, there's nothing you can do,' he said, and tried to console him. 'I slowly wiped my hands and was suddenly out of words to say.'

Belton Cooper recalled how the maintenance men then had to get inside and clean up the remains. Body parts were kept together in canvas shelter halves and turned over to the graves registration people. 'With strong detergent, disinfectant and water, they cleaned the interior of the tank as best they could, so men could get inside and repair it.' Even maintenance crews occasionally refused to work inside, but eventually someone would be persuaded to finish the work. Once repairs were completed the tank's entire interior was painted with a heavy coat of thick white lead. As Cooper explained:

> This covered up all the blemishes and pockmarks inside the tank, and at the same time the persistent odour of the drying paint tended to off-set the pungent stench left by the mutilated bodies. Some said the odour never completely left the tanks; however, by this time the new crew would have gotten used to the tank.

New tank crews were always reluctant to accept a tank in which men had been killed. For this reason numbers would be painted over and company and battalion designations altered, and then the vehicle was handed over. 'The new crew never knew its history,' explained Cooper, 'and we never told them.'

Burned-out tanks were a total loss but had nevertheless to be cleared of remains. Lieutenant Peter Balfour's letter to his mother understated the difficulty this led to when dealing with requests for news by loved ones of casualties. 'Anne writes to me that she supposes there is some hope for Sidney as he is only reported missing,' he wrote. 'I am afraid there is no hope. The tank he was in was in such a mess that nobody could be identified. That's the worst of these tank battles. If the tank gets brewed up and you don't get out, the results are very unpleasant.'

Padre Skinner, with the Nottinghamshire Sherwood Rangers Yeomanry, wrote in his diary nine days later: 'In Campbell's tank three bodies were still inside, partially burnt out and firmly welded together.' He was unable to get them out. Trooper Austin Baker of the 4/7 RDG looked for his best friend Wally Walters in a burned-out Cromwell tank:

> A brewed-up tank is always a grim sight – the outside is usually a dull, dirty, rust colour and inside it is a blackened shambles. There is a queer indescribable smell. The bottom of Jonah's tank had been blown right out, and we could peer inside from underneath. There was no trace of anybody in the turret, but some stuff in the driving seat that must have been Walker. There was a body on the ground by the left-hand track. Somebody had thrown a ground sheet over it, but we lifted it off. It was probably Brigham Young, but it was impossible to recognise him – he was burned quite black all over, and only part of his anklets remained of his clothes. Nobody ever found any sign of Wally.

By the time of 'Operation Goodwood' crews were becoming 'slightly bomb-happy', as Michael Trasenster described, and in need of a rest. 'Goodwood', which commenced on 18 July, was the largest deliberate armoured attack mounted in Normandy. Three divisions assaulted, two up and one back, following a massive air and artillery bombardment. The British had assumed they were tackling a three-mile-deep fortified locality across a corridor of flat arable land bordered by the Bois de Bovent to the east and the factory area of Caen to the west. The

Germans had in fact built four defence belts stretching back ten miles up to the Bourguébus ridge that dominated the approach, consisting of infantry positions, fortified villages, a belt of 88mm Flak and a mobile armoured reserve.

British tanks were steadily picked off as they traversed the flat ground and struggled across the three railway lines that radiated out from Caen. Fortified villages and the few hedges and tree lines spat out armoured shot as soon as the tanks crested any undulation. Major Bill Close of 3 RTR lost seventeen of his nineteen tanks in two days. Montgomery's 8th Corps received a bloody nose, losing 36 per cent of the British tank strength in France. It did pin down German panzer reserves, but failed in its ostensible mission to break out. Pressure was drawn off the 1st US Army to its right, seeking to pour into the French interior. Six panzer divisions were pinned down on the British front, leaving two on the American front when the breach occurred on 27 August.

Lieutenant James Carson of the Welsh Guard's Cromwells declared that when they saw the sheer extent of tanks in flames around them, 'We were bloody scared!' 'Pass sir a cigarette' was the advice from his driver Kennedy; it was the first time Carson had ever smoked. A shell case was passed through the turret, normally used for urinating when the tank was closed down, because the driver admitted 'he had already pissed his pants'. They had passed the stage when, Carson explained, 'you became more wary and crafty, taking great care where you placed the tank'. But now they were experiencing real fear. 'You grew up quickly in war,' he reflected, 'you miss something, you come back a man.' But the concern was to come back whole, mentally as well as physically.

Tank men by this stage of the war had identified certain fears. For the Allied tank crews it was German technical superiority: particularly their heavy panzers, the power of anti-tank guns and the infantry-carried *panzerfaust*. Fear for the Germans was the Allied material ascendancy in all types of firepower: heavy battleships and more especially air power and massed artillery, which unlike the Russians' was excellently directed and flexible.

The first panzer unit assessments on the Invasion front identified that the Allies were clearly ascendant in terms of air and material superiority, and aggressive, but not to the point of heavy casualties. The British were employing the same attrition tactics as in North Africa, which 'guaranteed' according to one situation report 'there would be no decisive battle'. It was quickly appreciated that the Allies were not going to be tipped back into the sea so long as the guns of sixty to seventy warships and overwhelming air superiority were not countered. 'The courage of the panzer troops cannot compensate for the absence of two parts [Navy and Luftwaffe] of the Wehrmacht's armed forces,' General Guderian, the Inspector-General of Armoured Forces, advised Hitler.

The real fear for panzer crews was air attack. Its emotional impact far outweighed the material damage, which was primarily upon the soft-skinned support vehicles. Although tanks often survived they were soon inoperable owing to logistic shortfalls. The first indication of how progressively bad it was going to get was during the nightmare trek to the coast when the panzer reserve was released to counter the invasion. Between 6 and 8 June the Panzer *Lehr* Division lost 10 per cent of its vehicles – five tanks, eighty-four armoured half-tracks and ninety wheeled vehicles – during its 120- to 200-kilometre march to Normandy from the French interior. The *Hitlerjugend* lost twenty-two killed and sixty wounded and over a score of vehicles while travelling 90 to 190 kilometres to the coast.

'We'll soon give it to Tommy!' was the initial banter among the troopers with Panzer Regiment 12 of the *Hitlerjugend*, recalled SS Sturmann Helmut Pock. A panzer division on the march is an intimidating spectacle, and troops were filled with confidence. Before long they began to drive past the debris left in the road by earlier air attacks, passing one shot-up half-track next to a bomb crater. 'The hatch to the rear of the vehicle was open, and from it protruded the leg and lower torso of a soldier, and what looked like a knee. Driving slowly past it became apparent that the top half of the corpse had been completely roasted.'

'Perhaps he had already been mercifully dispatched by a bullet,' Pock hopefully reflected. Confidence waned and real concern grew over a threat that they were powerless to contain. 'The fighters are about again, cleaning up the roads,' Pock described later. 'We are among the houses, partially protected and camouflaged.' Movement descended into a series of stop-start races from one area of overhead cover to another before the fighter-bombers reappeared. 'Outside the village a few vehicles must have been surprised by the aircraft,' Pock ruefully observed, 'because the machines dive down without pause, and badly aimed bursts are smacking into the walls and streets as far as us here.'

'Unless a man has been through these fighter-bomber attacks, he cannot know what the invasion meant,' declared *Hauptmann* (Captain) Alexander Hartdegen with the Panzer *Lehr* Division.

> You lie there helpless, in a road-side ditch, in a furrow on a field, or under a hedge, pressed into the ground, your face in the dirt – and there it comes towards you, roaring. There it is. Diving at you. Now you hear the whine of the bullets. Now you are for it.

Terror from strafing developed progressively. 'Suddenly they were there,' declared a Panzer IV crewman of Panzer Regiment 130; 'nobody knew where they came from.' Haphazard and totally unexpected, the unprecedented intensity of the air attacks produced acute stress. 'The first detonation thundered forward in the column,' recalled the panzer crewman. 'The thought registered on everyone's face. Is it one of ours?' Hartdegen described the apprehension:

> You feel like crawling under the ground. Then the bird has gone. But it comes back. Twice. Three times. Not till they've wiped out everything do they leave. Even if you survive it's no more than a temporary reprieve. Ten such attacks in succession are a real foretaste of hell.

By the time of 'Operation Goodwood' Allied air superiority was having a corrosive effect on German morale. Movement was completely stymied. Rail transports previously measured in days were taking weeks. Train journeys occurred on a stop-go basis. Twenty-year-old Karl Drescher of Reconnaissance Battalion 116 recalled, 'We heard on the BBC that Germany had been spared a day's bombing so that all the planes could bomb the Panzer *Lehr* – and now we had to fill the hole.'

'Goodwood' was preceded by a 1,500-bomber raid during which

68-ton Tiger tanks were turned upside down. Two tanks were neutralised and two others unusable because shock waves from the bomb explosions had bent the turrets out of alignment. Two suicides occurred during the bombing and a crew member had gone mad. Fear of the Allied air force and the pulverising potential of artillery, especially battleship guns, was beginning to suggest to panzer crews that their days were numbered in this match of man versus material.

Fear was entering a higher reactive stage for many tank men between the thirty- and fifty-day points after the invasion. A typical day would begin at 0430 hours. Fatigue affected Lieutenant David Holbrook, a yeomanry subaltern, who was waking each morning with feelings akin to a hangover:

> Above his head the scratched steel plates were sweated with moisture. Crusted and sandy with exhaustion, his eyes stared painfully at the colour returning to the wet grass and weeds in the hedgerow. He flexed his limbs in the sleeping bag, but they were like wooden things, twisted in his rucked clothes, and dull with the stiffness and sleep on the hard earth. His body did not want to emerge from the warm blankets and expose itself to violence and hurt.
>
> Buffeted on the shoulder by a sentry, he bruised his head on the metal roof casting about for his boots, and got moving.

Hugh Sackville-West, a squadron commander with 7 RTR, recalled, 'Until the break-out at the end of July we were either in action or ready for it all daylight hours.'

At dawn they would drive from the harbour area to a defensive position. If it was quiet, a snatched breakfast was prepared by one of the crew. Orders groups would follow, normally at the end of a short drive in a jeep or armoured car. Maps were marked, sketching rising tension. During the rest of the day operations would be conducted, often there was an attempted advance, and then it was time to dig in. Crews were frequently constrained to sitting at their tank positions all day while the commander stood at watch in the turret. 'Most of the time I was intensely bored, with short periods of fear,' Sackville-West recalled.

As it was mid-summer, darkness came late, when at the end of a long day tanks would pull back to a nearby harbour. Here they were met by logistic transport and the tanks were maintained and replenished: all physically demanding work. Refuelling a panzer in the combat zone at night, Leutnant Klaus Voss remembered, meant that the gunner, loader and radio operator each had to carry two canisters of petrol for about 100 metres, often under fire. Five hundred litres was required to refuel, which meant twenty-five jerrycans to be carried to the panzer, lifted on to the upper deck and manually poured into the fuel inlet: back-breaking work. Sleep was not possible until about midnight, and then it was broken up by guard duties. Commanders might be given additional orders or have to prepare their own for others. An average of two to four hours' sleep per night following a stressful and often demanding day led to cumulative fatigue, which further corroded the strength of character needed to master accumulating fears. Previously simple administrative tasks now became burdensome. 'The agony of dividing compo boxes each for fourteen men between tank crews of four and scout crews of two, when dead tired, cannot be imagined,' declared Peter Roach of 1 RTR.

Fear has certain characteristics. 'In 1944 we should have been told about fear,' declared tank gunner Ken Tout of the Northamptonshire Yeomanry, 'but we were not.' Pain is God's gift, he believed, alerting the body to danger, and fear plays a similar role on the mind. Its unknown properties caused even more dread and he felt if he had known more about its nature he would have benefited. 'In 1944 we needed a talk by a sensible psychologist more than we needed the Padre's routine lecture on VD.' Tout took forty years to learn that everyone had fear. He was surprised to discover that Captain Bill Fox in his squadron, who always sat unperturbed in his turret, and his squadron commander Major David Bean, languidly walking through artillery fire, were as afraid as he was. Meanwhile 'I sat or stood in my turret and branded myself a coward.' Recognisable symptoms were dry mouth, a rapid heart-beat, cold sweat, trembling, and a temporary inability to think clearly with diminished powers of concentration. Other physical characteristics could include vomiting, vertigo, stomach and headaches, muscle pain, difficulty breathing, incontinence, tired-ness and sleeplessness accompanied by depression and nightmares.

There was little information about fear and marginal official sym-pathy for it. 'Malingering' could attract a five-year sentence in the

Canadian Army. Much of the compassion came from immediate superiors or the tank crew itself. During the first ten days of the Normandy landings 10 per cent of British battle casualties proved to be psychiatric, and this rose to 20 per cent in July and September. After the break-out it fell again to 8 per cent. In 1942, psychiatric as opposed to battle casualties were less: at about 7–10 per cent, of which it was suspected that most, amounting to 5–7 per cent, were simply due to exhaustion. Infantry battalions were seen to suffer more.

Michael Trasenster of the 4/7 RDG was sympathetic toward the PBI – the 'Poor Bloody Infantry' – who had an unglamorous role and, lacking armoured shelter, suffered heavy casualties. 'They had to slog it out for months, and a wound was probably their best chance of getting through the war alive.' He claimed, 'One of the most moving sights I have ever seen was an infantry regiment decimated by terror.' Soldiers were retreating, with most of the officers alive and still with them; a few, 'Canute-like', tried to halt the unstoppable tide:

> Weapons were abandoned, people were clinging to the backs of Bren gun carriers, anything to get away from the German dawn attack. The regiment concerned had a horrific night, with a flame-throwing Panther tank driving around their slit trenches burying many alive and using the roaring flames to light their way around.

Montgomery withdrew the 6th Battalion the Duke of Wellington's Regiment from 49th Division at the end of June because its twenty-three officer and 350 other ranks casualties had broken its cohesion. Seventy-five per cent of its men were reacting adversely to enemy shelling and were jumpy, while officers and NCOs refused to display badges of rank for fear of snipers. Five cases of self-inflicted wounds were officially reported in three days, with more suspected. A post-war survey concluded:

> In the Middle East the great separation from home, the flat barren wilderness in which men lived, the poor food and water supply, the rarity of action, the occasional big battles dominated by the spandau, the 88mm, and the mortar, lasting only a few days, contrast with the battle of the Normandy bridgehead, which went on without remis-

sion for over two months in familiar green fields and crops, with scarcity of sleep, the multi-barrelled mortar and the continued carnage as the great stresses.

Tension immediately prior to battle was another characteristic of fear; Ken Tout called it 'the peril of the empty hours'. 'The tension before a set-piece battle was appalling,' claimed Lieutenant Andrew Wilson. As a Churchill Crocodile flame-thrower commander his vehicles would lead the way. 'The timing and direction of the whole assault depended on them,' he recalled. This represented a further dread of the unknown. Had the reconnaissance been conducted properly? Would the essential landmarks become apparent to show the way? Would you be able to pick out the target in the smoke and murky half-light of battle? 'All the while,' Wilson reflected, 'you saw in your imagination the muzzle of an 88 behind each leaf.'

Leutnant Ludwig Bauer of Panzer Regiment 33 admitted, 'One always had a certain nervousness before battle, but after the first few rounds fear went.' The crew were so intent on their functional business, commanders spotting targets, relaying fire control orders, communicating with other tanks, driving and shooting that all other thoughts were banished. Tout claimed that if the vacuum of the empty hours was not filled 'then legions of fear will come rampaging in'. Bauer remarked that a second fear surge happened when infantry ahead started firing flares skyward, 'indicating other enemy tanks – then the adrenalin rolled again!'

The horrific sight of gore magnified fear. Ken Tout witnessed the impact on a young trooper ordered to evacuate a badly wounded soldier from a house by stretcher. 'When he saw the mess of blood and intestines of the dying human animal in the house, he refused the order.' Tout was ordered to arrest him, but what impressed him most was that despite a spectacular battle raging around the trooper 'he stood transfixed, totally oblivious of the steel and flaming death about him, transfixed by an image of blood'. Such fears had to be overcome but they left an indelible mark. Tank commander Michael Trasenster, commenting on the fictional battlefield scenes he viewed in films and on TV, felt they 'may brutalise people and appeal to the macho image of young men and women; but it is a poor vaccine for the real thing':

It does not cover the stink of rotting flesh, one's clothing being covered in the blood of friends and throwing lumps of half-cooked flesh and guts of what was a man into a slit trench or shell hole and covering it with a few inches of soil. We were not supposed to do this, as it affected even the least imaginative as to what they could become in a few days' time. I only did it for one of my crews, but it was greatly appreciated by the father of an only son who was glad he was laid to rest by his own friends and that he heard through me rather than the War Office.

Claustrophobia and the terror of enclosure is particularly pronounced in a tank and contributed to the cumulative impact of stress. A Sherman tank turret occupied by three men was cramped. The commander, gunner and radio operator all had their heads within about two feet of the gun breech, occupying a domed enclosure not more than five feet in diameter and less than six feet from the turret floor. Physical secretions released under stress can usually only be broken down in the body by rigorous physical activity, but such activity cannot occur inside the body of a tank except by the loader. The imperative to move is overwhelming. Crew have to remain immobile, closed down under fire for long periods of time. All this is fenced in the acceleration of the metabolic process which caused exhaustion early, persistent thirst and gave the crew ample time to ponder: how long can I bear this? Meanwhile they viewed the carnage of battle around them, the gore magnifing the fear of death.

Yeomanry tank commander Paul Holbrook had unexpectedly to stand in for a loader caught up in the heat and confusion of battle. In an unfamiliar role, he found his mouth was dry, 'he twisted and turned in his seat, and hung on to his periscope, through which he could see nothing but the blue line of the wood, occasional bursts of flame, and the sky'. As tank commander he was used to seeing more. They were under intense fire from deadly 88mm guns well beyond their range, but fired back. Holbrook was then subjected to the inexplicable terror of confined combat, having to sense rather than see what was happening.

He slid each round into the gun, with a hysterical sense that away across in the wood a German gunner was sliding in the shot that was to tear him limb from limb. His hair stood on end and his limbs quivered in fearful anticipation, like those of a man condemned. His bowels were water with fear.

The gunner breathed tensely next to his ear saying, 'God, sir, we're next! God! God!'

They fought on, concussed by the gun, and choked by acrid fumes propelled into the turret every time the breech block was opened and a shell fell to the floor with a metallic clatter. Sweat poured down his body, 'his brain teemed, and he could not loosen its harrowing anxiety'. Then it was all over, 'the moment gone, and the memory of it as quickly suppressed and forgotten'. Physical reaction then set in as the metabolic cycles of the crew compensated for the adrenalin they had pumped through their bodies. The consequence was exhaustion bordering on apathy.

Nearly all crewmen's personal fears were handled by the compassion of the group, so exclusion in any shape or form could impact on survival. Domestic crises within the crew might impact upon its professional capability, it might provide a distraction, freezing the finger on the gun, obstructing the driver's mind at a vital moment or the commander's observation at the precise moment they were engaged by a German gun. Upsets, gunner Ken Tout explained, might turn upon:

A crew man's sanitary, or rather unsanitary habits, within the noisome den of the tank closed up for six hours without respite. It turned upon the gunner's asinine humour at appropriate moments. It turned upon the driver's habit of incessantly singing doleful hymns, or simply upon the fact that the cockney commander spoke with an assumed Oxbridge accent.

If you did not fit you were removed. The three most boastful and culturally crude men in Tout's regiment 'all turned and ran in one way or another', he explained. 'One, a loud-mouthed corporal driver and self-publicised sex exponent reported his tank out of petrol in our first action. He had simply switched off and, incidentally, left four men in a supporting tank to die.' Another 'braggart Corporal', he remarked, 'at least had the decency to drop a tank flap on his own fingers as the quickest way home'. Brave men tended to be quiet and introvert.

Crew cohesion did much to counteract the deterioration associated with combat fatigue and fear. Losing a tank was like losing a home; it was the focal point of the crew's existence. 'This 32-ton hunk of metal became our only home and, tortoise-like, we took it wherever we went,' declared Corporal Patrick Hennessey. There was a certain domesticity to crew routine, and this cosy arrangement tended to reinforce the tank man's false sense of security. Lieutenant Paul Holbrook called tanks 'American mastodon mothers in whose bellies they lived'. Private letters might be tucked behind the radio set as if it were the clock on the mantelpiece at home. 'Goodies' such as bars of chocolate and cigarettes were kept in handy and familiar places. 'It seemed hideously wrong that the mastodon mother herself could be destroyed,' declared Holbrook, 'and so the first sight of a burning tank dislodged a fundamental security in the trooper's soul.'

It was these little communities that held men together. Major Bill Close said, 'I got to know every man in practically every tank in my squadron personally and that helped considerably.' There were many diverse characters and they were difficult to judge. 'Very often you found that the strong footballer, hockey player or whatever wasn't as good as the little cockney chap who was a driver – ever cheerful and always able to cope with whatever situation.' This was rewarding and provided emotional reserves that could be drawn upon. Canadian tank commander Sidney Radley-Walters found:

> I think what I learned was an awful lot about ourselves. What I found out was that you did not necessarily fight for king or country. There was a whole bunch of chums out there, friends that you had joined up with, trained with and people you loved really. And when the chips are down, nobody but nobody was going to let the other guy down.

Bill Close, despite all the suffering, admitted, 'I still look back on it as one of the best times of my life. It's difficult to put it into words, but the friends that I made during the war are still my friends.' It was this emotional cohesion that kept Tout's 'dark angel' of fear at bay. 'I don't think you can ever alter the bond between tank crews,' Close claimed; 'whether you commanded, or whether you were a driver, the bond is always there – quite extraordinary.'

## FEAR TO SHELL-SHOCK

The 'higher reactive stage' of battle fatigue according to the Swank and Marchand study occurs at between thirty and fifty days, which was the period up to the savage fighting that preceded the Normandy break-out. This was achieved at the end of July and developed in early August 1944. Beyond this period was 'resignation' at the forty- to sixty-day point, presaging emotional exhaustion when complete lethargy sets in. Lieutenant Stuart Hamilton of 8 RTR called this 'battle weary' phase 'very definitely the worst stage of the lot and I was beginning to wonder just how much more I could take'. 'You saw a pair of boots sticking out from a blanket, and they looked exactly like your own,' reflected Lieutenant Andrew Wilson of the Buffs, gazing at the dead awaiting burial. 'There was no ground for thinking that the thing that had come to the owner of these boots was not going to come just as casually to you.'

Mathematical certainty juxtaposed against a perverted law of averages was leading many to question their chances of survival. Wilson concluded, 'It was quite against logic to suppose that you were destined to survive the law.' Such spectral calculations were beginning to trouble crews. Veteran desert units such as 5 RTR began assessing their chances long before un-blooded units. It only took until the end of June before Sergeant Jake Wardrop was confiding in his diary when 'Lofty' Whitby was killed and a few men were captured, 'I'm afraid there was a bit of flapping all round and sad to say one or two had bailed out without either being fired on or firing a shot themselves.' Jake, a pre-war soldier and desert veteran, had always succeeded in containing his fear and used his diary as an outlet. 'Waiting like that is very hard on the nerves, especially at four in the morning,' he wrote about a delayed operation. 'I found I had quite a shake on.' His innermost thoughts were confided to his 'egotistical diary' which was kept in a map case in the turret. Viewing these notes offers an unintended view of a steady decline that can be discerned from unconnected remarks on what was going on as the campaign progressed. Captain Daniels, he observed, came forward to bring replacements to the squadron, but 'I thought it was odd Danny being at B Echelon [the logistic tail] and the squadron still operating.' He should have been situated forward, but he chose to say nothing and neither did the officer, but it was clear to Wardrop that he was 'taking the well-known run out with the old nerves complaint'.

> It was a common complaint in those days and I had seen a lot of it. Anybody is liable to crack but it is not good that a man should be a captain, respected and looked up to because he was a captain one day, and the next he is sliding out of it with some spurious nerves complaints while troopers carry on and in lots of cases have been fighting for much longer than the others.

The deterioration continued. At the end of July Wardrop wrote, 'there had been a lot of changes in the unit, the major had slid out on the nerves excuse', Captain Daniels had gone, as also 'the funny little man called Clark' who had commanded a troop for only two days, had 'been reduced to a nervous wreck, and he was gone'. In August it got worse. 'Wilkie was in the guardroom for refusing to go into a tank', during which time 'A and B [squadrons] had lost between them 18 tanks and a lot of good men'.

Being selected as the point or leading tank on an advance reduced survival chances even further. Trooper Ernest Hamilton of the 15/19 Hussars recalled, 'If one's troop had been chosen to lead the squadron, we waited for what we considered to be one's last day on this earth.' Lead tank itself was even worse. If it survived the day or half day agreed, it would rotate to the rear of the column and the next tank would take its chance. Hamilton remembered, 'If you were given lead tank, sleep was hard to find that night; one hoped one could die in the short sleep to come.' At first light the nerve-racking day began with often an advance down a narrow road. 'The co-driver, the front gunner, concentrated on the left side, the driver right, the gunner dead ahead, the operator and commander all around.' *Panzerfausts*, anti-tank guns or the dreaded 88mm might be concealed on the verges. Teller mines were expertly laid. Even crossing an open field with track marks was not necessarily safe, because German engineers would dig out a track spur, lay two or three teller mines and replace the track pattern.

Crews worked out on the basis of losses and engagements per day that they had a one in four chance of being knocked out. There was an equal chance of dying because each tank lost resulted on average one killed and another wounded. They sustained hope from observing exceptions to the rule, veterans who seemed to go on for ever, so the common assumption was that it would always be someone else who 'bought it', never them. 'Dick Dexter was carted off in an ambulance,' observed Lieutenant Stuart Hills, who was with a yeomanry regiment. 'Nobody quite knew what had happened, but for some reason he would not come out of the tank.' He slept in it, ate there and would not even be coaxed out to play a game of football, 'which he loved'. Some crew men developed a form of 'armour-consciousness', needing to feel the security of being in a tank all the time. Hills surmised that he had perhaps 'drawn too deeply on his own particular well of endurance, had seen too many terrible sights, suffered too many vivid nightmares'.

The breaking-point could be sudden, unexpected and shocking to onlookers. In early August Stephen Dyson's Churchill tank squadron was due to conduct its third raid against Esquay. It was preceded by a trooper dropping a turret hatch on his hand on the start-line. He was sent back and 'we gave him the benefit of the doubt'. They could not do the same for a corporal tank commander 'who suddenly rushed away from his tank and crouched in a ditch, trembling as though shell-shocked'. His nerve had snapped completely. 'I could only feel pity as the members of his crew went over and did what they could to comfort him.'

Rest provided some antidote to combat fatigue. Fatigue always formed part of the deterioration, which was recognised by both sides, but could not necessarily be acted upon. 'A full night's rest in an undamaged field, getting some mail, having an opportunity for a proper wash, possibly a dip in a stream, was a wonderful sensation,' recalled Hugh Sackville-West of 7 RTR. Psychological surveys were in general agreement that rest could reverse some of the combat fatigue stages, and after it crews might re-enter action a stage or two down. Everyday things taken for granted assumed considerable importance. One armoured Guardsman recalled:

The enormous satisfaction of having a good wash from just a mug of hot water on the tank turret, having one's sponge bag handy with toothbrush and toothpaste, soap and flannel and razor. The important thing was to do things in the right order – teeth cleaning first while the water wasn't soapy, then washing all get-at-able areas with the flannel, and finally shaving when it no longer mattered if the shower bristles got into washing water. Then to be handed a mug of hot sweet tea and a biscuit or bread and jam.

Domestic routine composed raw nerves.

Mail provided an important part in this process but had the opposite effect if it brought bad news. Virtually all veterans in command appointments remember the strain of composing casualty notifications to next of kin.

Dear Mr and Mrs Welch,
    This is a sad letter to write and the fact that I have to write only too many makes it no easier.
    This is a specially sad one for many reasons. Your boy was killed at Noyers on 18 July. I am not allowed to write until it is clear that you have received official notification from the War Office. He was a grand lad. Happy, full of courage, a fine leader and a joy to meet at any time.

This extract from a letter sent by Lieutenant-Colonel Herbert Waddell commanding 141 RAC is typical of its type. It described the manner of death, how much 'everyone in his troop both liked and respected him' and never dwelt on pain or negative aspects. Every such letter written by commanders who had lived and trained with their men for some-times as long as three years took away a part of their emotional fibre. Composing the letters forcefully reminded them what had been lost. As Major Bill Close expressed it, every time a tank was lost in action under command he knew that some of his crew would have been killed. Some of them would have been old friends, 'who had been with me years ago when I was a trooper'.

At the time in action, you could not really think about the losses at that stage. It was only at later times, particularly at night when you were lying behind your tank under the stars, that you really felt that you had lost some friends as well as tank crews. Then, when you had a few days' rest and opportunity, you, as squadron commander, would find the need to write to wives and girlfriends. Some that you had already met and known. I found it a most difficult thing to do to put it in the right perspective.

'We were very close, knew each other very well,' recalled Lieutenant Peter Balfour of the Scots Guards, 'knew all about each other's families.' He developed a system where 'my mother and my sister would write to various people and keep them going that way'. Writing to the families of those who died 'was quite a difficult thing to do, but you had to do it and get on with it and do it quickly before it got too late'.

Officers found censoring the soldiers' mail particularly hateful. Lines were blacked out or cut out with a razor blade. Lieutenant Eric Allsop of 8 RTR said 'it was distasteful to read expressions of strong feeling by a husband for his wife and children'. They tended to quickly scan through and sign 'OK'. It was intrusive and resented. Lieutenant Richard Carr-Gomm of the 6th Guards Tank Brigade remembered reading a letter penned shortly before action that one of his guardsmen had written to his parents. 'He told them he was going to die and thanked them cheerfully and strongly for the loving upbringing they had given him.' He was then killed.

Yea though I walk through the valley of the shadow of death, I will fear no evil, for Thou art with me.

Lieutenant Belton Cooper of the 3rd US Armoured Division constantly repeated these biblical verses and derived comfort from them. Crying and under enormous stress after the initial shock of combat he repeated, 'Thy rod and Thy staff they comfort me'. 'I knew there would be terrible times ahead and would still be frightened,' he deduced, but 'I knew I would be able to cope with it.' The experience moulded his subsequent life; prayer got him through the stress. Michael Trasenster of the 4/7 RDG admitted, 'It sounds pompous and holy, which I am not, but I go along with: God is for mortals helping one another.' He applied it to life and on the battlefield. 'Though unnoticed,' he wryly observed, 'I don't think God takes sides.'

One study conducted in 1945 suggested that it was the fearful and less confident men who felt they were assisted by prayer. It found that 79 per cent of combat experienced men believed their army exposure increased their faith in God, while 19 per cent claimed the opposite. Of those actually involved in combat 29 per cent stated they became more religious as a consequence while 30 per cent said less so, an ambivalent figure. Anecdotal veteran accounts suggest overwhelmingly that prayer was rarely overlooked. Eric Allsop of 8 RTR confirmed that 'when the chips are down, quite a lot of people will pray'.

'I feel lucky and I prayed a lot,' recalled Harold Levy of the 2nd US Armoured Division. 'Matter of fact I carried rosary beads that my mother gave me, and to this day they are in my jacket. I think that helped me get through it.' Churchill tank crewman Stephen Dyson, now with the King's Own, was convinced religion carried him through also. He recovered a dust-shrouded nine-inch miniature statue of the Blessed Virgin Mary from a shattered home in the village of Cheux. Being Roman Catholic he cleaned the statuette up and retained it as a talisman, jammed between the smoke bomb ejector and metal wall inside the Churchill turret. It was positioned 'where I could see it and offer prayers for safety in battle'. It was soon tested when the turret was struck a glancing blow from an 88mm projectile, momentarily glowing red at the point of impact inside. On examination a clean and shiny bare metal patch showed against the grey colour of the rest of the turret interior, indicating near penetration just inches from the statuette. Joe Whelan, his crew mate and also a Catholic, grasped the significance of the scar: their prayer to the Virgin Mary had been answered. 'We were astonished!' admitted Dyson.

German resolve during this period of great strain for the Allied tank men seemed unshakeable in contrast, and still a break-out was not achieved. They were, however, subject to the same uncompromising laws of averages as the attackers, perhaps more so, because of material inferiority. Tank gunner Ken Tout recalled a counter-attack by combined infantry and panzers that shook them to the core.

We saw the German infantry follow the tanks and we began to fire at them at 300 or 400 yards range. You have to remember that the cornfields were in full golden ripeness and very dry and as soon as our tracer rounds went into the corn it caught fire. So the Germans were asphyxiated, they were being shot and burned but they kept coming, they kept coming and coming. So one wondered what one had to do in order to stop them reaching our positions. What actually happened was so many of them suffered either from the direct shooting or from the burning of the cornfield and smoke and so on that in the end it was more than flesh or blood could stand. As they were at that point when it seemed they were not to be denied it was like King Canute and the sea coming in. You kept saying stop, stop, but the sea kept coming in. At that point there was a feeling of tremendous terror and you hoped that the colonel would say 'Retreat', but he didn't – you had to stay!

German morale and resolve was likewise eroding. There were indeed limits to what flesh and blood could stand. *Sturmann* Hans-Ulrich Dietrich, a Panther gunner in the *Hitlerjugend* recalled that his commander's chest was 'completely ripped apart' by two shells that bore through the turret. They managed to reverse and Dietrich climbed down from the turret because the damage obscured visibility, in order to guide the driver. All the hatches had now been opened by the fearful crew, anticipating another hit, and the co-driver Hase climbed out and stood next to the turret on the enemy side. Dietrich tried to get him back below, 'but there was no way he would sit in the seat again'. 'So what had to happen, happened,' declared Dietrich. Another shell struck at turret level. 'It ripped off one of Hase's legs close to the hip and threw him high into the air,' recalled the gunner. 'I can still see it today, how he tumbled and then slammed into the ground.' Dietrich jumped down to attend to him and applied a tourniquet to the stump, using a belt. Hase only remained conscious for a few moments and during one of them he had a pistol in his hand. He said very clearly he wanted to shoot himself.

Wachtmeister Müller, a tank driver with Panzer Division 116, recalled that their Panther was surrounded and crippled by eight Shermans. His commander Leutnant Stetzka continued grimly to try and fight them off but they were hit again. Müller drove his burning Panther for 300 metres seeking cover, but the heat forced them out. Seeking shelter in the lee of the smouldering tank he saw the radio operator bail out and, after hearing his commander's voice, crawled over to investigate. He had lost both legs beneath the knee. Shock had deadened the pain, because he was not crying out. As Müller tried to bind the stumps Stetzka said, 'Leave them alone, it's pointless.' He could not pull him away from the tank because machine-gun rounds were bursting all around, so he appealed to the commander to give up so he could fetch medical assistance. Stetzka told him, 'Müller, take my identity disc and pay-book [key to his personal administration] and I order you to give them to the company.' He then asked him to give his love to his parents and told him to break out and get back to the company. Stetzka was outfought by eight tanks. Black German humour claimed that a Panther could knock out ten Shermans. 'Ja,' was the ironic response, 'but they always have eleven!'

Hill 112, overlooking the village of Esquay in the Odon valley region, was labelled *Kalvarienberg,* or the 'Hill of Calvary', by the Germans, an appropriate name in view of the battles of attrition fought around it. Trooper Ernie Cox in the Buffs recalled his Crocodile Churchill flame-thrower had a 'run away' gun during one assault. Once the valve stuck on the gun it was obliged to 'flame' for the full two minutes until the fuel tank towed behind was empty. During a night attack on the Le Bon Repos farmhouse it jammed. The outcome was termed 'the night of Dante's party'.

> It cascaded down the trees in a waterfall of flame. We felt we were about to be consumed by our own weapon. The leaves floated down like masses of fiery butterflies, the flames danced along the tracks and still the gun was throwing out the fuel. In the dark and in the gloom, the smoke that we were now adding to the flames was of a dull red. It was frightening, terrifying and awesome and yet in a way exhilarating, too engrossed in the moment to have any feelings. Then it stopped, 500 gallons of fuel was spent.

The gunner's voice came over the intercom – 'A bigger cock-up than Dunkirk.' The farmhouse was ablaze from end to end, but they had seen no one. 'Then we saw some people standing there and as we got closer they were Germans.' They were virtually comatose. An infantry Major came across and asked them if they wished to see their handiwork. They declined. 'At a guess he said there were three hundred in there.' The tanks started to grope back to their own lines in the dark. The Germans 'just stood there, no weapons, no helmets, in a complete state of shock; we just left them there'.

The German Army in Normandy was at the end of its emotional tether.

Dennis Young of 153 Regiment RAC was reduced to shell-shock after two actions three weeks apart. On 16 July his grim day began when his troop commander Lieutenant Hearle 'came to us very worried and shaken and told us we had a sticky job in half an hour's time and then hoped to be taken out of the line early in the morning as we were badly beaten up'. In the ensuing assault they were struck by an 88mm shell, Hearle 'was a ghastly sight, half his head was blown off and the turret a mass of blood'. The tank burned.

Dennis Young was dazed by the blast from the impact when the tank was hit. Veterans often speak of complete silence after the explosion. Often their hearing was gone, and some momentarily blacked out. Young recalled, 'after seconds which seemed like hours I heard distant voices of the turret crew which told me to get out'. He fell out of the side pannier door tangled up in head-sets. With two other survivors he crawled for a quarter of a mile under fire from mortars and German infantry, and then managed to scramble aboard another damaged tank withdrawing back to their lines. He was completely exhausted and languished unconscious or semi-conscious in a field hospital for three days. It was a traumatic experience, 'something I shall never forget'. Twenty days later he was being prescribed tablets to help him sleep at night, but they did not work. 'There was too much battle noise and a terrible smell of dead German bodies that lay around our harbour.'

On 12 August he was back in action, and this time his tank was obliged to withdraw to an empty field to clear a shell that was jammed in the barrel. They were hit four times by *panzerfausts,* and again he had to crawl away from his burning tank. Bailing out presented certain dilemmas. One either had to shelter in a hole and wait for the front to roll forward, or make an honest attempt to get back. No one could be blamed for hiding. Giving up offered similar relief, but mercy was not guaranteed, particularly after a bitter fight, and being reported missing subjected families to uncertainty and stress. Invariably the chosen option was to infiltrate back.

As Dennis Young and the survivors attempted to do this they were pinned down by machine-gun fire. 'The fellow in front of me got a bullet in a leg, the one behind got a burst in the back'. This was accompanied by loud cracks and grotesque whines as bullets sped overhead breaking the sound barrier, with multiple thumps of gun reports indicating that more was on the way. 'It was hell!' They had to abandon the seriously wounded crewman, who was dispatched by a sniper after they left. Young was incensed by what had happened and was restrained from assaulting a young German prisoner by medics. 'But when he looked at me so pitifully and I had seen what a mess he was in I went useless.' He offered him a cigarette instead, but saw that 'his head was in a terrible mess and his hands were bleeding and he was beginning to go a bit simple'.

Young was haunted by the experience of being hunted by persistent machine-gun fire, which the others had not avoided. 'I lost my head after the dirty trick Jerry played on us,' he reflected, 'because normally when a tank bails out they are helpless, and more often than not the crew are left to make things out for themselves.' Infantry by comparison were always helpless in front of tanks and would never pass up the opportunity of retribution if it arose. There was no chivalry in war.

Compassion, a front-line value, eased further to the rear. The final stage of combat exhaustion is resignation bordering on apathy. In this state it was difficult to differentiate or evaluate battle noises. Every exploding shell sent patients running for cover. Young's diary account described many of the accepted symptoms: minor upsets leading to outbreaks of fury, exaggerated elation over good news. 'Although feeling pretty rough,' Young recalled, 'I did not want to go to hospital but needed treatment.' Sleeping tablets were all that he could be given.

Lieutenant Peter Balfour recalled a crewman whose 'nerve had gone a bit' after he had lost his tank. His squadron sergeant-major, noticing the state he was in and that he was not badly wounded, instituted a regime of compassionate activity. He 'made him get up and do his kit properly, polish his shoes and then generally gave him a sort of barrack square discipline for twenty-four hours'. The sergeant-major sought to combat the bizarre by an excessive dose of the military norm, and it worked. 'He was quite all right to come back to his unit.' Comradeship was the antidote to most nervous problems.

When troops cracked they were sent to Battle Exhaustion Centres where treatment consisted of five to seven days' rest and recuperation with drug-induced sleep, hot food, clean clothes, quiet, games and discussions. Psychiatrists attached to 2nd British Army assessed that for every recorded case of combat stress, three or four ineffective men remained with their unit. Fatigue was the greatest impediment to mental resilience, and rest and relaxation was sufficient to get 30 to 40 per cent of cases back into the line. Denis Young wrote in his diary:

I suppose when I recover a little they will try and send me back, but I don't think I could ever get inside another tank, it's finished me this time. When you first get hit your mind goes blank for a split second. At least it did when I first got knocked out, but this time in that split second I lived that last experience all over again.

He did not want to do it again.

During the first week of August the Normandy stalemate was unlocked by the break-out by 1st US Army during 'Operation Cobra'. The newly created 12th US Army Group instituted a form of *Blitzkrieg* in reverse. Mass, it appeared, was about to triumph over technology.

# 14

## TANK MEN

### THE MARRIAGE OF MEN AND MACHINES

On 17 July 1944, 58,000 German prisoners of war shuffled silently through Moscow in a huge meandering column thirty soldiers wide *en route* to prison camps. Apart from the occasional jibe the shabby soldiers elicited little comment from crowds of silent onlookers. These men were the flotsam of a staggering defeat inflicted on the Germans that had begun shortly after D-Day, theatrically staged to coincide with the third anniversary of the invasion of Russia.

The scope of 'Operation Bagration' had been unprecedented and the outcome breath-taking. Its objective was a 400-mile penetration beyond the Pripet Marshes to seize the land-bridge between the Dvina and Nieman rivers. A long-range encircling manoeuvre by 166 divisions supported by 2,700 tanks and 1,300 assault guns resulted in the virtual annihilation of the German Army Group Centre in the Minsk sector. Three German armies ceased to exist. It was a classic *Kesselschlacht*, [a 'cauldron' battle of encirclement] composed and conducted perfectly. Seventeen German divisions were destroyed and fifty mauled to half strength. Minsk fell on 3 July when the 4th German Army encircled to its east lost 40,000 of 105,000 troops hopelessly trying to break out to the west. Seventeen days later there was an assassination attempt against Adolf Hitler.

As the western Allies broke out of Normandy during the first week in August, the First Ukrainian and first White Russian Fronts reached the line of the River Vistula south of Warsaw. The Poles rose in revolt against the German garrison. Russian units crossed the Nieman and Bug rivers to the north of Warsaw and briefly touched the German frontier in East Prussia in October. The war had been irretrievably lost for Germany in the east.

'I think it was the most exciting and sensational time I shall ever have in my life,' recalled Major John Stirling with the 4/7th Royal Dragoon Guards (RDG) describing the pell-mell break-out from Normandy in the west. They were swinging towards Argentan and the Seine and moving 'gingerly'. 'At every corner and every wood one waited to hear the familiar boom and snarl of a piece of 'hard' [armour-piercing shot]. But the noise never came.' Driving with the 3rd US Armoured Division Lieutenant Belton Cooper described it as 'classic armoured warfare. The situation was highly fluid, and it was extremely difficult to know where the friendly and enemy units were at any one time.' The VII US Corps breakthrough five miles to the west of St Lô had exceeded all expectations. Four thousand two hundred tons of bombs ploughed a 6,000-yard breach and the American armour was through. *Bocage* country was left behind as one corps swung into Brittany and the remainder of 3rd US Army drove east towards Le Mans and Chartres.

Four panzer divisions drove into the perceived fault line of the Allied advance and made some progress before the skies cleared. Massed columns of vehicles were then exposed to the full weight of the Allied air forces. German persistence in the advance merely further exacerbated the likelihood of envelopment by rapidly moving Allied armoured formations. First Canadian Army launched 'Tractable' but was unable to close the gap doggedly held apart at Falaise. It nevertheless became the calvary for the mechanised formations of three retreating German armies, though many troops did manage to extricate themselves before the vice closed on 19 August. Withdrawal across the Seine proved an equal disaster. Army Group B suffered half a million casualties and had 210,000 captured alongside the bulk of its 2,300 tanks and assault guns. Fighting on two fronts in Normandy and Brittany, Patton's Corps advanced 400 miles in twenty-six days.

'It seemed incredible after all these weeks,' said an exuberant John Stirling, that:

We could motor ten miles down a main road without being fired on. But the ten miles mounted to twenty and still there was silence and

363

still the speedometers ticked on. We could not understand that the rout of the German Seventh Army was now almost complete, that the Falaise pocket, round whose outskirts we were driving, was the scene of the biggest disaster the victorious Wehrmacht had ever experienced. This was the real thing. This was the Breakthrough.

Paris was liberated on 23 August and the pursuit to the German frontier was on. The British 2nd Army advanced 386 miles in eight days. 'To travel at top speed across hard, open country on a lovely morning, knowing that the Germans were on the run, was exhilarating to say the least,' declared Lieutenant Stuart Hills of the Nottinghamshire Sherwood Rangers Yeomanry. They were swept up in their success:

It was almost like taking part in a cross-country steeplechase or going on a pre-war motoring tour. In every village we passed we received terrific welcomes. Occasionally we would stop to receive the fruits of our success in the form of something to eat or drink, but usually we passed through in a cloud of dust, hardly able to see or hear the cheering groups of liberated French. No doubt we left them a little bewildered, wondering what on earth was happening after four long years of occupation and hardship.

The British captured Brussels on 3 September and Antwerp the following day. By 14 September the whole of Belgium and Luxembourg was in Allied hands. A continuous battle front now stretched from the Schelde River in Belgium through Alsace to the headwaters of the Rhine at Basel on the Swiss frontier. Hitler had comprehensively lost the war in the west.

Mobile armoured warfare had been restored to the two primary fronts in the east and west, while the southern Italian front route to the Reich was still characterised by positional warfare. The sixth and final year of the war provides a useful point at which to look at tank 'fightability'. A tank design revolution had occurred, inspired by World War, just as inspired as the 'lozenge' shaped boxes of 1916–18 had been. Tank men had come of age since the 1930s, and now bore little resemblance to the recruits who had first marched into brand-new Wehrmacht barracks or the motley bands of disorientated British newcomers who sought transport from nondescript Wool railway station to Bovington training camp. But the marriage of man to machine was not satisfactorily resolved by 1945.

The human dimension of mechanised warfare was not one that attracted close attention from Second World War tank designers. Warfare is recognisable to veterans as 90 per cent boredom and 10 per cent fear, and only a fraction of the latter in combat. It should come as no surprise that designers were prepared to trade off physical discomfort and human wear against optimal technical performance during those crucial battle moments.

Until 1943 tank design reflected a poor understanding of the man/machine interface. The exception was the Panzerwaffe who from early on adopted a philosophy whereby *Mensch* – or man – was part of the essential equation that produced the weapon. Incorporating three men in a turret in order to fight the machine effectively meant an overall crew of five. This conferred tactical battle-winning superiority during the 1940–1 *Blitzkrieg* period, even though German tanks were technically a generation behind.

According to Richard Simpkin, tank 'fightability' is based upon elements that recognise certain human needs within mechanised warfare that ease the interface between man and machine, enabling a full exploitation of technological advantage. Lack of this in the case of superior Russian KV-1 tanks and T-34s in the early 1940s, meant that technical advantages were squandered. The needs are good vision when the tank is closed down, ease of mechanical operation, clean functional interior design, habitability and fighting conditions, physical contact between the crew themselves and the ability to bail out safely when hit. Crews that live best fight best: it was a repeat of the lesson that had emerged from the first tanks in 1918.

Tank crew lethality was about the coincidence of crew skills to achieve a first-round kill. The commander especially, but also crew members in concert need to out-think the opponent and 'anticipate the moment'. The driver therefore exposes minimum frontage to the enemy, while the gunner has his sights pre-set to anticipated battle ranges so all he has to do is quickly assess and fire above or below that. The loader has already worked out the type of shell required, and the radio operator offers information on developing events. The commander instinctively 'feels' if any of this is not happening fast enough and mentally fights the tank through all the options quicker and more ruthlessly than his opponent. Holding all this together is mutual trust, loyalty to each other, in short, crew bonding. One modern tank veteran summed up all this by describing true commitment to several principles:

> We are all of one company who do as we ought, not what we want. Think through the situation to the finish, dare to be different in terms of initiative and dare to be totally honest with the crew.

This was not far removed from panzer crew standards, who it could be argued consistently fielded superior tank commanders throughout the war. Leutnant Klaus Voss of Panzer Regiment 11 believed that a good commander brought the ability to identify the enemy first and then get into a superior position to provide good observation and protection against fire. Towards the end of the war the Allies began to catch up, following brutal, costly instruction from their opponents. Doctrinal disunity hamstrung British armour from 1916 onwards; it crippled French armour in 1940. The Americans and Soviets developed some unity of thought, but this was primarily the unity of mass, accepting and doing what one was told. Unity of outlook from the tactical to operational level brought considerable success to the Panzerwaffe. Disunity at the strategic level and superficial logistic principles brought defeat, as their opponents learned.

Apart from dominating the man/machine interface in training preparation terms, the Germans created a tank technology gap which overtook the Allies in 1943. As superior German guns began to crucify opposing tank crews, the mass versus technology riposte adopted by the Allies was unconvincing. The closing years of the war saw considerable technical improvements to close the gap. Firepower was the shortfall, and the British Firefly 17-pounder on the Sherman and the Pershing with its 90mm gun provided the response. The latter was not as good as the German 88mm but far more effective than the Sherman 75mm. 'The 90mm muzzle blast rebound in the Pershing tank would suck the helmet right off your head if you didn't have the chin strap fastened when your head was out of the turret,' recalled Captain Norris Perkins of the US 2nd Armoured Division. 'Also, when the breech block opened for the 90mm during recoil, a tongue of flame and smoke would blow back into the turret.' Only a few of these tanks reached the front by the end of the war. By 1945 the British Comet, an up-armoured and up-gunned derivation of the Cromwell, was being issued to British tank units. The Comet was the precursor to the very successful post-war Centurion tank, but its appearance in December 1944 was too little and too late.

The Soviet T-34/85, mounting a far superior 85mm gun, was produced in some numbers in 1943 and was the first attempt by the Soviets to match German gunnery. By late 1943 the 'Joseph Stalin', more heavily armoured and also mounting an 85mm and later 122mm gun, appeared with the superior SU-100 assault gun, which T-34 commander Lieutenant Vladimir Alexeev labelled 'the best tank killer'. However, 68 per cent of Soviet tank production was still devoted to the T-34, fitted with heavier guns. Mass was to dominate Soviet tank tactics until the end of the war.

German appreciation of gun dominance on the battlefield became something of an infatuation as a multiplicity of bigger and more lethal tanks was produced. Heavy armour requiring even larger tank hulls to mount bigger guns resulted in the 'King Tiger' or Tiger II, which was in action on the Eastern Front by May 1944. It had an 88mm lengthened gun and sloping armour, more like the Panther than its square-built 'boxer-like' Tiger predecessor, with 260mm of armoured protection. Like many German tanks it was under-powered. More industrial effort could have been invested in the proven series of *Jagdpanzer,* or self-propelled guns whose name means 'hunting tanks'. These were cheaper and lethal because of their low silhouette, but without turrets the gun could move only a few degrees. The *Sturm-geschütz* series mounting 75mm guns were excellent tank ambushers, highly effective and more appropriate to Germany's increasing defence stance. Self-propelled derivatives came from the Tiger, a Jagdtiger mounting a 128mm gun at 72 tons, and the Jagdpanther with the proven 88mm on a Panther chassis. These tanks were becoming so heavy that bridges had to be tested and positions surveyed by jeep before occupation.

Surveys of Allied tank casualty rates based on an examination of 1,600 wrecks confirm the gun's mastery of the battlefield. Only 30 per cent of hits failed to penetrate the Sherman, but 50 per cent in the case of the Churchill, a safer tank. Fires resulted from 45 per cent of turret and 60 per cent of hull penetrations, and because 60 per cent of tanks were generally repairable, German crews often took the trouble to keep on hitting Allied tanks until they caught fire. If Allied tanks had been at least up-armoured at the front, sufficient (like the Churchill) to reduce penetration, 40 per cent fewer casualties might conceivably have been achieved. The human cost of superimposing mass over technology is auditable.

Balance was restored to the technical mismatch on the ground by the Allied air forces. Unlike the brutal German levelling of odds through armour-piercing fire, this outcome was achieved indirectly. Leutnant Ludwig Bauer with Panzer Regiment 33 offered a practical illustration of how panzer mobility was impeded:

One day I saw a low-level fighter coming straight at me across the ground. He could only have been 20 to 30 metres high. I could see what was coming and yelled 'Halt! Halt! Halt!' to the driver. As we stopped there was an explosion just under the front of the tank. It shook us around a bit but we were OK. A little further forward and the rocket would have come through the hull.

It was not easy for a rocket-firing Typhoon fighter aircraft to hit a defended target. All eight rockets were fired in a single salvo from a steep angle or ripple fired at a shallower dive at varying heights between 1,000 and 1,700 yards from the target. A direct hit on a tank with the 91-pound rocket usually caused irreparable damage, but it was a scatter-gun affair. Accuracy was difficult to achieve, and near misses as close as fifteen yards merely showered the target with mud and dirt.

German columns at Mortain trying to counter-attack the Allied break-out were rocketed for eight and a half hours. Werner Josupeit, an NCO with the 2nd SS Panzer-Grenadier Regiment, described a cab-rank of twenty aircraft which pulled out one at a time to deliver their attack before rejoining the circle. 'And so they continued until they had all fired. Then they left the terrible scene' and 'a new swarm appeared in their place.' A battalion commander with the 2nd SS Panzer Division pressed his thumb hard against the top of the table as he explained, 'Your fighter bombers simply nailed us to the ground.' Camouflaged aircraft were British. Silver were American. Those not there were German. 'Black clouds of smoke from burning oil climbed into the sky everywhere we looked,' recalled Josupeit. 'They marked the dead panzers.' Allied observers watching attacks claim that many panzer crews simply climbed out of their tanks and took cover away from them.

The impact of air attacks was as significant for their nervous effect as for numbers of vehicles destroyed. RAF tactical interrogation reports hint at how frightened German tank crews were of strafing. 'Crews are very aware that if a rocket projectile does hit a tank, their chance of survival is small.' Although the chances were reasonably remote 'this would hardly be appreciated by a crew whose first thought would be of the disastrous results if a hit was obtained'; particularly after evading eight and a half hours of merciless and unprotected strafing. Operational research sections from 21st Army Group investigated damage done to 667 German panzers, assault guns and other armoured vehicles abandoned around Falaise. They found that only 4.6 per cent were destroyed by rockets and bombs, whereas nearly 40 per cent were destroyed by their crews to prevent capture and 31 per cent abandoned undamaged. Most vehicles had run out of petrol. Nearly 28 per cent of 6,656 light-skinned lorries and cars investigated were destroyed by aerial bombing, and over 37% were left behind undamaged. It was the *indirect* impact of air attacks that was so decisive in complementing Allied tank inferiority, because it severed the logistic umbilical chord needed to sustain the panzers and drove the crews to nervous distraction, precisely what the Luftwaffe achieved in 1940 and 1941. Air attack denied the panzers the aggressive tactical superiority that training had granted and removed their offensive potential. Armoured protection was thinnest on top of the tank.

The Germans were able to hold sufficient terrain forward in north-west Europe to enable battered panzer units to rest and refit in the Reich. The western Allied dilemma of whether to advance on a broad or a narrow front was resolved when three airborne divisions laid an 'airborne carpet' across the last remaining river obstacles before the lower Rhine at Arnhem in September. The supporting ground advance to link up failed in the newly bared teeth of German resistance. 'Narrow front' was limited by terrain to a single tank corps advancing on an unintended lone tank front. Failure to capture the Antwerp approaches resulted in logistic famine until the end of November when the port could be cleared. American advances around Aachen, Lorraine and particularly the Hürtgen Forest were laborious and costly. The Siegfried Line was breached and the line of the Roer and Rhine reached in December, just as winter weather denuded the Allies of their main air advantage. The Allies were poised on both sides of the Reich.

Although new tanks dribbled into the line, the final battles would be fought with what crews had now. There were no technological short-cuts. Tank men fighting these battles bore little resemblance to the crews that formed up in 1939 and 1941.

Panzer crews had emerged from secret and obscure beginnings as a technical arm at Kazan in Russia, via the Spanish Civil War and pre-war international crises to become the darlings of the nation, and especially of the Führer, grateful for *Blitzkrieg* successes. Their development was characterised by cohesion, from operational leadership to tactical training, off-setting technical shortcomings. Germany went to war with a 6-ton 'Krupp's sports car' and within five years was fighting with 70-ton King Tigers and Jagdtigers, boasting an increase of ten times the firepower and protection. Early German recruits had been both mechanically minded and technically proficient. Subsequent expansion of Wehrmacht and SS panzer divisions resulted in panzer armies. Tempered by the crucible of the Russian front, the veteran survivors consistently provided a steel core to new panzer formations equipped with ever improving tanks and deadly assault guns. Successive strategic defeats had decimated their ranks, but *Kameradenschaft,* or comradeship, held them together. It was obvious the war was lost. They fought on for their families and themselves and in the increasingly vain hope that political compromise might be wrung from uncondi-tional surrender by inflicting costly casualties.

Early Russian tank crew leadership had been decimated by Stalin even before the invasion of Russia began. Exuberant tank men, whose imaginations were fired by modernism and the desire to be the 'warriors of the future', were long dead. Good crews perished early. Hope was denied until Stalingrad and not restored until the strategic offensive initiative was captured after Kursk in 1943. Plummeting morale had been addressed by shifting allegiance from the Communist Party to Mother Russia, which remained a patriotic ideal for many and was pragmatically fused within a new common resolve. Tsarist trappings were reintroduced into the army alongside an appreciation of the spirit of 'Borodino', the battle that had checked Napoleon's fortunes in Russia. Tank officers wore Tsarist badges of rank, and units designated 'Guards' armies were formed, apeing the imperial tradition of the armies that had resisted Napoleon. Tank schools and academies continued to turn out a stream of variably trained crews. Mass sacrifice had denied the Soviet tank arm veteran stability until the turn of the tide in 1943. More veterans survived despite breathtaking losses. New crews were cynically deployed with open acceptance that mass versus quality –fielding large numbers of inferior tanks against small numbers of superior German – implied sacrifice.

Soviet tank men came from a society where technology appeared to move selectively. They had complete trust in the T-34, their main battle tank. 'The T-34s that went into combat during the first days of the war and the T-34s that burst into the streets of Berlin in April 1945 differed significantly,' claimed Alexay Isaev, 'not only externally but also internally.' At the beginning its powerful gun, protective sloping armour and seemingly fire-retardant diesel engine promoted immediate confidence. By 1945 its high speed, mechanical reliability, stable communications and effective gun enabled them to fight the Germans on more equal terms than the western Allies did. In fact, foreigners and their tanks were mistrusted. 'To tell the truth, we were afraid of being posted to fight in foreign-made tanks,' admitted T-34 commander Aleksandr Burtsev: 'the Matildas, Valentines and Shermans were coffins.' Veterans like Burtsev had already noticed 'the driver could never bail out'. Another commander, Semen Aria, remarked, 'I saw the insides of American and British tanks, where the crew was in far more comfortable conditions.' He was unimpressed. 'Western tanks had petrol engines and burnt like torches'; moreover, 'they had a narrower wheelbase and would easily capsize on the slopes of hills.' Nobody wanted them.

Russian tank men were patriotic, seemingly stoic at their losses and, like many Allied tank men, they drank to forget. They fought for their families back home and bonded differently in some respects from their western counterparts. Affection was always tempered by the unspoken fear and influence of commissars and the apparent ease with which one might suddenly be transferred to a penal company. Nobody wished to stand out. Fear of failure and the likely implications for families at home, dependent on party goodwill to overcome wartime scarcity, intangibly stifled initiative. Decision paralysis often resulted when things went wrong. Hatred was directed at the enemy because of Nazi atrocities and eventually transitioned to pity during the excesses about to occur.

The Russian tank man in 1945 was different from his predecessors who had sought to contain 'Barbarossa' in 1941. 'Deep Battle', the Soviet equivalent of *Blitzkrieg*, likewise aimed to create mayhem in rear areas to paralyse the opposing leadership's will to resist. Eighteen months of high-intensity mobile operations after Kursk transformed Soviet professional capabilities. Tank corps were first formed in 1942, and tank armies the following year. Like the Germans, from whom they learned, tank armies consisted of a mix of light, medium and heavy tanks. The Allies' Lend-Lease Agreement with the USA provided new-found operational and strategic mobility with its generous allocation of wheeled support vehicles. Soviet industrial production was free to concentrate on tanks. Lieutenant Anatoly Kozlov with the 5th Guards Tank Army remarked that by this stage of the war his corps 'was 100 per cent equipped with Lend-Lease, from tanks to motorbikes'. He claimed that his 1st Guards Mechanised Corps had '210 tanks and other vehicles, Chevrolets, Studebakers, all types of equipment, including Harley-Davidson motorcycles with machine-gun mounts'. He saw it as a turning-point for the tank armies. 'Headquarters now paid great attention to combined operations, which was the secret for victory.' This alongside enormous technical strides in artillery, tank guns and rocket artillery as well as anti-tank and anti-aircraft improvements 'produced a capability totally unimaginable two years before in 1941'. The Germans had taught their enemies well, and 'the middle ranking staff became more experienced in handling military operations,' Kozlov emphasised. Expertise aligned with mass was to make the Soviet armoured juggernaut unstoppable.

British tank men had also changed beyond recognition from the ill-prepared crews that had been brushed aside by the German *Blitzkrieg* in

1940. Poor preparation was further exacerbated by the redundant tank-fighting philosophies conferred on British training methods by her pre-war tank thinkers. It was not entirely expunged by the desert experience, when costly punishment meted out by superior German anti-tank guns working in close synergy with panzers forced British tank men to pay greater attention to working together with other arms. Normandy demonstrated greater awareness, but the various arms still tended to fight alongside rather than *with* each other. A doctrine for fighting tanks in combination had now to evolve from open desert to close, heavily populated farming communities and urban landscapes, linked by a modern European road network, while applying air superiority.

American tank crews had entered the war late and confident in their particular home-grown tank-fighting philosophy. Successive Allied armoured set-backs prior to their arrival in theatre had not convinced them otherwise. They were better educated and technically more aware on joining the war effort. Normandy was a rude shock. Attrition in the *bocage* was as unexpected as it was grim. In late July the 741st Independent Tank Battalion lost sixteen men killed and sixty-four wounded – 10 per cent of its crews in little over two weeks. The 743rd lost nearly 20 per cent of its strength with twenty-five killed in action and 116 wounded in June and July. German tanks by contrast appeared impenetrable. 'We could outrun them, we could outshoot them on a straight run, but we could never, or very, very seldom knock them out,' declared Pete Abatto of the 2nd US Armoured Division. 'They would just bounce right off the tanks.' The 3rd Division's Combat Command B lost forty-eight of sixty-four tanks in one twenty-six-minute attack engagement on 16 November. Two similar combat commands in the 2nd Division lost about 100 tanks in similar circumstances as they approached the River Roer. 'If you hit 'em in the front, forget it,' claimed Abatto, 'it would just smash the shell in pieces and wouldn't even penetrate.'

Tankers who survived the odds in these first engagements fell back on wits and cunning to live. 'I had a short-barrelled '75,' declared Charles Evans of the 3rd Armoured Division, 'the main advantage being that you could go between trees, whereas long barrels got caught up.' This became particularly pronounced during the fighting in and around the Hürtgen Forest. 'We caught Germans because their guns were so long they couldn't swing between the trees. So whenever we saw they *were* in between trees, then we would go in from the side and try and get them through the turret – we liked that.'

Casualties between the Normandy break-out and the approach to the German border were low. The 743rd Independent Tank Battalion lost one man killed and two wounded and the 741st just one man slightly wounded during the first two weeks of September. The closer they got to the border, however, the higher casualties mounted. Losses were expected, but not so many. With the war now clearly being won and victory expected soon, a decision was taken to close down tank training schools in the United States.

By August the European theatre was desperate for trained American tankers. That month the black-recruited 761st Independent Tank Battalion, held back over D-Day, was summoned and departed New York for England. By 10 October they were in France and were personally addressed by General Patton at the end of the month. E.G. McConnell, who had enlisted in 1942, realised he was finally about to go to war. He recalled watching the brisk Patton step up dramatically on to a half-track and gaze at the assembled battalion from left to right. He announced:

> I sent for this battalion because I heard you were good. I have nothing but the best in my outfit, and I want you to go up there and kill them goddam Krauts. I want you to give them a licking. I don't care about what colour you are as long as you go up and kill those Kraut Sons of Bitches!

As he came to the end of his speech Patton fixed McConnell with steel grey eyes and repeated himself. 'Listen boy, I want you to go up there and shoot up every goddamn thing you see: haystacks, church steeples, graveyards, old ladies, children – any damn thing that you see. This is war.'

On their first day in action their white commanding officer Lieutenant-Colonel Paul Bates was severely wounded. E.G. McConnell was also wounded when he was knocked out in the lead tank with shrapnel lodged in his skull. Ironically he was saved by a white sergeant from the 'Yankee' 26th Division – who was chopped in half by machine-gun fire while pushing him to safety across an embankment. Another white soldier cared for him until he was moved back to a field hospital in France. He was the only black soldier in the ward. Here he learned that while the fighting and dying was integrated, all the rest was segregated.

A two-star general visited his ward solicitously enquiring, 'Good morning Corporal, how do you feel today? What unit are you?' When he approached McConnell, whose head was swathed in bandages, he hesitated and asked, 'What's wrong with you, boy, you got the claps?' McConnell was devastated. Next to him was a white patient encased in plaster from neck to feet. 'Hey, General,' he retorted, 'he got it from your mother; now send me back to the front you SOB!' There was little chance of that, McConnell recalled, because his friend 'was so broken up', but he was grateful for the moral support, reflecting:

> This hurt this guy but nothing like the hurt I got that day. Later on the same bum came back walking through the ward giving out Purple Hearts [a medal awarded to US personnel wounded in action]. I had a comic book up to my face as he went through the ceremony. I didn't even reach for it. He just put it down on the bed.

## TANK MEN IN VICTORY AND DEFEAT

The war was not over by Christmas, but there was every expectation from the tank men that this would be the last one of the war. Trooper Robert Whitehead of 44 RTR recalled being at the forefront of fighting continually since the D-Day landings in June, noting 'everybody was feeling the strain. The news that we would be withdrawn for Christmas came to us as great relief and joy.' Because of this 'I suppose many of us started to duck and weave more than usual as the day for relief approached', a tendency observable throughout all the armies.

Corporal Jack Clegg, aged twenty-one, a blond, fresh-faced tank gunner with the 1st Fife and Forfar Yeomanry, represented the typical

British tank crewman fighting at this late stage of the war. Jack's sister described him as 'very bright, and he had a great job in cotton waste working for Swiss firm' before joining the army. Like many such men he felt guilty occupying a 'safe' job and decided, with the war likely coming to a successful conclusion, that he should volunteer to serve abroad before the end. There was also a woman in his life. His sister explained the break with his girlfriend: 'She had wanted to get married straight away but Jack wanted to wait until after the war.' Jack went through the same domestic tensions as countless other serving crews. 'My parents did feel he needn't have gone,' his sister commented. Jack Clegg felt the need to participate in the war and lived a full life. 'He loved listening to Glenn Miller and the big bands,' she reflected.

By October 1944 Jack was in Holland. Although not a prolific letter-writer he did write to his father to wish him a happy birthday. 'You'd be surprised if you knew where I was writing this letter,' he wrote, 'all I can say is that I'm in a dug-out in a field.' Conditions in Holland with the winter drawing in were relatively static, and the weather was cold, wet and rainy. Crews could not afford to be complacent; the front may have been stationary, but it was dirty and dangerous. 'Tomorrow is Saturday and I wish I was going to some football match,' mused Jack. He felt the need to relate the familiar to his bizarre wartime surroundings, and to communicate with his dad. 'I think this is my first letter to you since joining the army,' he guiltily admitted, 'but I'm no letter-writer as you know, but I think you know my feelings just the same.' Jack Clegg's letters were like everyone else's: voicing thanks for gifts, describing films they may have jointly seen and football news. 'There is quite a lot of things I'd like to write about but the censor won't allow it,' he wrote. Soldiers could actually be grateful to the censor who provided a ready excuse to cut short letters and avoid discussing the real issues.

By November primitive living conditions and tensions took their toll. 'Dear Mum, I'm sorry if this letter is dirty, but writing in this dug-out is no picnic. Mud is everywhere and we've had no bath for three weeks, you'll have a good idea what we look like.' Jack reminded his mum about the popular wartime song 'We're going to hang out the washing on the Siegfried Line' – he loved popular music. He felt an urgent filial need to divulge feelings to his mother, despite irregular mail. 'Up to now I've always refrained from writing up at the front,' he admitted, 'but the other day I got shook up and just feel like writing you.'

Emotional watering-holes existed in the form of Rest and Recuperation Centres set up for the British in Brussels and as far back as Paris for the Americans, for those lucky enough to be selected for leave. 'Brussels is just like pre-war Blighty now,' recalled a tank gunner with 1 RTR. There was a limitless number of things to buy, English films were shown and English newspapers printed. All troops travelled the trams for free. At the Montgomery Club, 'which is a super effort, you can go in, have a bath, get your suit pressed, boots polished, hair cut, shaved, in just over an hour, and have a slap-up meal all for 25 francs' (about 22–23 pence). Trooper Ernie Cox with 141 RAC had not had a haircut since leaving Britain and recalled that it was 'tucked up under my beret'. Haircuts were rarely the primary objective. 'Before we knew it each had a girl on our laps,' he declared in a bar called The Star. 'You buy me drink?' was the normal stilted English greeting from the opposite sex. 'One thing led to another,' Cox admitted, 'and I said a few weeks ago they were doing the same thing for the Germans, only the colour of the uniform had changed.' This did not endear them to the girls, and Cox and his entourage were soon spending a 'busy night causing trouble and evading bouncers'.

Trooper Robert Whitehead of 44 RTR followed a similar course.

> We, of course, patronised the bars, which turned out to be brothels, to our amusement. Some succumbed to the blandishments of the girls, but I stuck to my guns despite blandishments and coaxing from the girls, showing they had no knickers, and breasts almost touching your face.

Crews lived for the moment. There was always the possibility this might be their last. 'It was all good clean fun, but it cost the boys who fell for it, I preferred to spend my money on booze,' Whitehead claimed. There was music, dancing, dog races and even the wax museum. Ernie Cox visited the medical exhibition. 'What took our eyes was the section on sexual diseases, what a turn-off that was. I was glad I didn't, while the others wished they hadn't,' he gleefully remarked. 'All the lectures we had from the MO, when all he had to do was show us this.'

They were having fun. Dangers might lie ahead but they were enjoying themselves, secure in the knowledge the front was far away and the war as good as won. 'Christmas was rapidly approaching, and so forage parties were sent out far and wide to bring the things needed to bring good cheer to everyone,' remembered Robert Whitehead. 'We also made endeavours to promote our own stocks of goodies.' Christmas occupied a cherished place in the emotional consciousness of soldiers even at this grim stage of the war.

Heinz Kauthold, a Panther commander with the 12th SS Panzer Division, believed they were assembling to build up a second defensive line when he saw the masses of men and vehicles on the move. 'That our higher commanders had planned an attack,' he mused, 'that was too much, that was unthinkable.' On unexpectedly receiving the order to move they conducted two night marches which brought them to the Eiffel, the rocky, tree-covered Ardennes region. 'We have to attack,' they were informed by the regimental commander. The *Hitlerjugend* was to be on the offensive yet again. 'One of the last trials,' the teenagers were assured, 'but we must do our best.'

Under cover of darkness and overcast weather the panzer divisions moved into their assembly areas. SS Lieutenant Hans Baumann was intrigued to see what looked like American soldiers driving past Panzer Brigade 150 in jeeps. 'They sat in a jeep,' he recalled 'and had American cigarettes and English or American newspapers.' 'What are you up to?' the panzer crews asked, but they kept their distance. 'They were not forthcoming and a little reserved,' Baumann remarked. After a while they drove on into the freezing mist and fog out of sight.

They were the vanguard of the panzer advance, designed to sow fear and uncertainty in the American rear areas. 'It started as a rumour,' remembered tank platoon leader Demetri 'Dee' Paris of the 9th US Armoured Division in one of their targeted areas, 'then we heard that the Germans were dressed in American uniform.' Disguised soldiers directed units in the wrong direction, sabotaged installations and assassinated unsuspecting American pickets. 'I can tell you we were scared spitless,' declared Paris, 'the fear of the thing – not knowing who it might be.' Everyone was stopped and challenged.

At 0535 hours on 16 December German artillery deluged the forward American line with fire on the weakly held sector in front of the Eiffel Mountains and Ardennes Forest. Eight newly equipped panzer divisions and a panzer-grenadier division spearheaded the 6th SS Panzer and 5th Panzer Army assaults on a segment of front held by four tired and inexperienced US Divisions. The objective was to cross the River Meuse and reach Antwerp 100 miles away. British and Canadian armies in the north would be separated from their American counter-parts in the south. Profiting from the mayhem and time gained, Hitler intended switching the armoured reserves east and then mounting a similar spoiling attack to forestall the Soviet advance on Berlin.

It was a virtual repeat of what occurred in 1940 and accomplished across the same terrain. Panzer traffic jams began to occur behind the front and this time bad weather kept the Allied air forces at bay. 'Ultra', the Allied secret code intercept, failed to detect any sources, owing to strictly enforced German radio silence. As in 1940, nobody envisaged heavy fighting in this difficult and remote region, and the assumption was that, if it did happen, air power could quickly attack the stacked-up vehicles. An 80km salient was created amid freezing fog and snow, with no chance of air interdiction.

Having assumed the war was won, the Americans gradually appre-ciated they were staring a potential disaster in the face. 'We had no concept that there was going to be a German attack,' recalled Lieu-tenant 'Dee' Paris, 'so when it came you thought this was some kind of little minor attack, a diversionary thing, something to irritate us, that was all.' It was much more. Henry Stairs, an American soldier, witnessed the confusion reigning in the rear areas. Someone who looked like an American suddenly appeared and called 'Hey – do you want some hot coffee?' 'Sure,' responded his friend, who was abruptly shot by the approaching German wearing an American uniform. 'That did not go down too well,' commented Stairs. Any that were subse-quently captured were routinely shot as spies.

No one knew where the enemy was in this highly charged fluid situation, except that he was advancing. 'A definite change in the mood of the men was evident,' reported Lieutenant Belton Cooper of the 3rd

US Armoured Division. Morale was sound but 'there was a great deal of anxiety because this was our first experience of a major retreat.' American press correspondent John Hall wrote: 'It was a curious experience to be with the Americans these last ten days and to see, when they realised what had happened, the stunned "it could never happen to us" look on their faces'; something the German soldier had endured from Normandy to the Siegfried Line. As Belton Cooper reflected, 'The main difference here was that instead of advancing most of the time, we were going backward. That's one hell of a difference.'

German panzer crews were fully aware. Victory in defeat was an emotion they had bitterly savoured on a number of occasions. It invariably translated into stubbornness, which was what resistance increasingly became. Heinz Kauthold of the SS *Hitlerjugend* called it 'the stubbornness of somebody who could not *believe* he could be attacked – you bloody idiots – we will stand here'. The build-up and initial assaults on 16 and 17 December were great morale boosters for the panzer crews, but their officers knew this offensive was going nowhere. 'Basically the Americans saw they had won the war at that time,' Kauthold reflected, 'and that we could launch such a big attack – that stung them.'

Bastogne became the focus of an American counter-attack from the south on 22 December. SS *Kampfgruppen*, or battle groups, led by Joachim Peiper of the SS *Liebstandarte*, shot dead seventy Americans at Malmedy, probably because prisoners would have impeded his advance. They did not secure vital US fuel supplies identified at Stavelot, which were blown to prevent capture. At no stage during the offensive did the panzers run on full fuel, and many were abandoned for lack of petrol. Atrocities hardened resistance still further. 'I think the situation at Malmedy stiffened everyone up,' admitted US tank platoon commander Dee Paris. 'I'm going to be a little tougher from now on.' he resolved, 'give no quarter.' The 2nd Armoured Division halted the German advance at Celles on 26 December, and Patton breached the ring around Bastogne the same day. Then the weather cleared.

'We were looking to the skies and would say: where the hell are they?' recalled Lieutenant Paris. 'They didn't fly, it was cloudy.' Few aircraft could operate in the freezing conditions. 'I can't say we felt kindly . . . when we first saw them, it was about Christmas Day.' The whole weight of the Allied air forces now fell upon the vulnerable

German columns, road bound or hemmed in by forest rides. 'They made movement impossible,' declared Fritz Langanke, a Panther commander with the 2nd SS Panzer Division. 'Things suddenly changed when about 25/26 December the air suddenly cleared up and the aircraft came down,' remembered Heinz Kauthold. A break-through was now out of the question.

The Battle of the Bulge was an unexpected and unwelcome experience for Allied tank crews who, unlike their opponents, had never been subjected to intense armoured operations in freezing weather. Montgomery's 21st Army Group counter-attacked from the north of the salient on 3 January, and by the 7th the US VII Corps had squeezed German routes into the Bulge to one single road. 'Man it was one cold blast up there,' declared Trooper E.G. McConnell with the black 761st Tank Battalion. 'Beautiful country, but you couldn't really appreciate the beauty. Every tree, snow-bank, we knew it could be really deadly.' Tank crews scanned Christmas card-like landscapes; 'the tracks were really quiet because of the snow,' he remembered. 'You couldn't touch the tanks in it or your hands stuck to the metal.' 'The weather was freezing and those tanks were cold, cold,' declared Sherman driver J. Ted Hartman, who was moving up to the Ardennes with the 11th US Armoured Division.

Hartman's 11th Armoured Division was diverted to meet the new threat. 'This change unnerved all of us, as a move to the western battlefront sounded much more ominous than did the previous orders to the south-west of France.'

'The tanks were difficult to start in the cold weather,' recalled Trooper A.J. King with the East Riding Yeomanry. Being powered by an aero engine they had to be crank started with 123 turns of a handle. As King acknowledged, it was one way of getting warm. 'When you were caught in the open by the enemy the unfortunate man turning the handle got to 123 turns very quickly.' Previously sodden ground was now frozen rock-hard, so digging under tanks was not an option. Crews were constrained to living inside tanks, now like mobile refrigerators. 'Being a steel box it never warmed up in winter,' King explained, because when the engine ran, the fan sucked inside a rush of cold air. 'The fact that we were still wearing the same issue of clothing in which we landed in June did not help matters.' Tanks were more vulnerable to anti-tank guns as they slithered and spun on ice-coated roads. 'As we entered Belgium, we found the fields covered with snow and the roads coated with ice,' reported Ted Hartman. 'Vehicles with metal tracks do not manoeuvre well on ice, so we were sliding in all directions.'

This was Hartman's first battle, and as a 'rookie' driver he relearned old lessons, coming to terms with claustrophobic confinement and closing hatches, relying on the periscope so that the 75mm could freely traverse. Hartman was now dependent on the commander to give frequent guidance, while he likewise directed the firing of the turret gun. 'Never did I imagine that at age nineteen I would be driving a tank in battle,' he reflected. As they moved forward he was unsettled by the presence of the division medical bivouac site as they drove past. 'An almost uncontrollable feeling of nausea swept over me as I saw all of those ambulances with red crosses on them.' It was with such foreboding that he learned his company commander was killed within hours of entering their first battle. He had just scrambled inside the sanctuary of the tank interior he saw the explosion that engulfed the two men he had been speaking to. 'With great force, it lifted him off the ground in a standing position and then laid him down on the ground on his back, lifeless,' he recalled. 'What a frightening sight.'

Hartman's fighting carried on through Bastogne and beyond, to Foy and Noville. He had also to combat the cold, 'with frost forming over the interior of the thick steel walls', and suffered trench-foot and frostbite in alternating freeze and thaw conditions. Above all it was a struggle to maintain mental equilibrium while viewing visceral scenes through his tank's tiny vision block. 'One soldier had gotten part way out of the half-track when he was caught' during an anti-tank ambush near Noville. 'He lay there burning. I almost lost faith in humanity,' he admitted, 'that was the most appalling sight I had ever seen.'

Jack Clegg, the Corporal tank gunner with the 1st Fife and Forfar Yeomanry, wrote to his mum on Christmas night sitting in an empty house the crew had taken over. 'We're sat here writing home,' he told her, 'also we've got one of the tank wirelesses with a loud speaker and at the present moment Glenn Miller is on, so I did get one Christmas present,' he announced. 'As we rode along this morning,' he wrote, 'I thought of you at home and wondered what you were doing. Well, next year,' he hopefully announced, 'I might be at home and then we'll make up for lost time.' Clegg kept a wary eye on signs of preparation for coming battle and appreciated the likelihood of involvement in the Bulge salient fighting. 'Also other things are happening,' he wrote, 'but I guess the censor wouldn't pass.' They were moving up to battle.

Hitler's final major offensive of the war was broken at the cost of 100,000 German casualties and 600 tanks, many of whom simply ran out of fuel. The Allies lost 76,000 men. 'Wacht am Rhein' was a total failure, delaying the Allied drive into Germany by six weeks. On 16 January 1945 the front line was back to its original start point. The following day the Russians decisively broke through on a 300-mile front around Warsaw and advanced 300 miles in two weeks. On 3 February the 1st Byelorussian Front armies had established bridgeheads across the Oder River, the last major river obstacle 40 miles outside Berlin.

Swarms of T-34 tanks laden with infantry formed 'flying columns' abruptly emerging from the snow storms sweeping through East Prussia in what was the worst winter for years. Careering through scattered Wehrmacht units and refugee columns alike, staying 25 to 55 miles ahead of the main Russian forces, they constantly kept the retreating German units off balance. This was part of the Soviet 'Deep Battle' tank philosophy, accelerating and maintaining the rate of advance. Tank driver Andre Gez glanced at the huge poster they passed as they swept across the East Prussian border in a swirling cloud of snow spray and exhaust. *Damned Germany Begins Here!* it read. Russian crews savoured the moment, driven on by 'Kill or you will be killed' slogans. They had reached the stalking wolf's den. 'We had to swear an oath,' Gez recalled. 'German men and women should remember the arrival of Soviet tanks on East Prussian soil for hundreds of years.' This was to be fulfilled in many respects, he felt; there would be revenge for the German crimes on Soviet soil. Alexandr Sacharow, another T-34 tank commander, also reached the border, declaring 'Now we must prosecute the victory to the end!' He claimed they were cordially received by some of the East Prussian population, but there were soldiers who 'harboured vengeful feelings against the Germans, but they were only a few, and we punished them severely ourselves'. This was not a view shared by the German defenders or fleeing civilians. Third and Fourth Tank Armies made the deepest penetrations but slowed down as they ran out of fuel again, 400 miles beyond their supply depots. Germany was now being engulfed by attackers from both east and west.

*Feldwebel* Hermann Eckardt unit Panzer Abteilung 8 was caught up in the Russian Oder offensive in early 1945. Manned by veteran ex-Panzer III and IV crews, the new Abteilung 8 had long since proved its worth. The low-silhouette 75mm gun on the improved Panzer III chassis was a lethal tank killer. Eckhardt was knocked out six times in the desert, but although hit frequently on the front glacis plate, he was never completely taken out of action in Russia. Eckhardt was as familiar with the exigencies of working tanks in sub-zero conditions and cranking frozen engines by hand under fire as Sherman tank crews in the Bulge. His experiences in the snowy expanse of Poland and East Prussia encapsulated the lot of the eastern front panzer crews during the dying months of the war. Odds were five to one against, yet the bizarre improvisations cobbled together to equalise them amazed even the phlegmatic Eckhardt. Bicycle *panzerfaust* units were formed under young officers obliged to operate 'in the slippery frost and deep snow conditions of January 1945 – with only ten metres effective range!' he exclaimed. Winter conditions froze logistic support to a precious few rounds per barrel with only 28 per cent of the 1944 fuel allocation per vehicle, an amount that had been declared insufficient even then.

Eckhardt's crew was caught up in the heavy fighting for the Polish pocket, where his assault gun barrel was struck by an enemy round. They had to pull back, towing another *Sturmgeschütz*, whose gun worked, but not the engine. Strung together, they trundled along a 100-kilometre marathon to reach their own lines through a snowy landscape punctuated by columns of oily smoke marking the gradual annihilation of their parent unit and its victims.

Cloaked by the blizzards and poor weather, their odyssey took them across an area traversed by seven Russian tank corps. They reached the German airfield outside the pocket at Jarocin, where they were able to refuel, ramming the gates of a Wehrmacht supply depot in an old brewery to liberate supplies his crews desperately needed. As the first Soviet shells began to crash into the town, food was thrown to the hungry German soldiers. Eckhardt managed to get the two damaged assault guns aboard a train to Sorau that steamed across the Oder River bridge as German engineers prepared it for demolition. Both vehicles took four days to repair and were soon in action again, this time supporting an assault engineer battalion. They were the last two assault guns from Panzer Abteilung 8 to get out of Poland. Only survivors on foot managed to get back.

Panzer crews fought on even though the war was clearly lost in both the east and the west. This incensed Allied troops. 'What makes me really angry,' declared Lieutenant Peter Balfour of the 3rd Battalion Scots Guards, 'is the way they fight like hell till you get up to them.' Damage and casualties lay more heavily on the infantry. 'Every time I see an infantry battalion I know well,' recalled Balfour, 'I am appalled at the number of new faces, but we have remained substantially un-changed from the beginning.' This became increasingly clear to both sides. 'There is no doubt it is much safer in a tank,' Balfour concluded, 'even though at times you think everything in the world is firing at you.'

It became more unsafe in American tanks. Very few Pershings were now trickling forward. Colonel G. MacLeod-Ross, a British officer staffing tank development in the United States, recalled the Chief Provision Officer, Brigadier-General Jack Christmas, remarking to him, 'We shall win the war with the Sherman.' These piled up in Europe despite the unrealised potential of the 90mm Pershing. Ful-filling the mass-versus-technology imperative was having shocking human consequences. 'The "best" flouted the "good",' remarked MacLeod-Ross, and Christmas's comment was followed through as 'we fought [the Sherman] in Europe to the bitter end'. By October 1944 it was disclosed that the United States had lost 1,400 tanks completely destroyed, of which 90 per cent were burned out. 'Tank battalions of fifty-five tanks are down to ten,' reported MacLeod-Ross. Shermans were being officially described as 'death traps' and the malaise attracted press attention. 'A demand now almost two years old, for a better tank than the Sherman, has at last been satisfied,' wrote the *New York Times* in January 1945, but the arrival of the Pershing was 'too little and too late'.

The human implications of earlier design priority decisions were now very apparent. Mass production of tanks was even outstripping the ability of crew training centres to fill them. At the time of the Rhine crossings there were 7,620 in theatre stocks awaiting delivery to units. Rash decisions were taken at the front to remedy shortfalls. Crews reduced from five to three were now obliged to confront superior German panzers manned by five men. Lieutenant Belton Cooper described the tragic outcome for one unit, the 33rd Armoured Regiment at Werbomont in January 1945, at the end of the Battle of the Bulge. 'They brought down about three truck-loads of raw infantry replacements,' he remembered. 'These kids had just gotten off the boat at Antwerp and they had only had basic training.' Of the thirty-four men 'most had never been in a tank or even close to one'. Cooper, an ordnance officer, was responsible for allocating a mix of seventeen new and repaired tanks that had just been brought forward for issue in the line. The new arrivals were formed into seventeen three-man crews including the driver. An Artificer Sergeant was summoned 'to teach them how to fire the main gun, and each man got to fire that gun three times, and that was all the training they had done,' Cooper recalled. He watched them move out to the smouldering front at about 1500 hours.

Cooper soon discovered what happened, as his job also involved recovery. 'We went down there at about seven o'clock that night, and of those seventeen tanks fifteen of them were knocked out on the side of the road.' Cooper had resigned himself to witnessing a tragedy before he even set off. 'I don't know whether any of those men survived or not,' he said.

German resistance in the east was perhaps more easily rationalised than that in the west. An East Prussian village at Nemmersdorf was briefly captured by the Russians in November 1944. Press cameras accompanied the counter-attack to recover it and the German *Wo-chenschau* newsreel broadcast rape and atrocity stories in cinemas, with on-the-spot audio accounts by shocked civilians. It was alleged that a naked German girl had been crucified to a barn door. True or not, the stories were believed. There was no recourse but to fight the 'bestial' Soviet invader, reaping the whirlwind sown by the Wehrmacht in Russia.

Though German resistance could be equally fanatical in the west, it was to be more patchy. Many panzer veterans viewed resistance to Hitler, for example, as a distraction from the main war effort. 'Unfortunately, the men who were executed after 20 July, 1944 didn't obtain anything for their people,' commented Leutnant Otto Carius with Heavy Tiger Battalion 502, referring to the attempt on Hitler's life. He acknowledged they were men who acted with conviction. 'In no way, however, have they earned more recognition and respect than any soldier who died faithfully and silently at the front for his homeland.' Many veterans react negatively to suggestions of a German 'Resistance' phenomenon. 'The dead of the resistance groups did not risk or lose any less, but also not any more than those who perished in battle,' Carius insisted. Ludwig Bauer recalled that at the time of the assassination attempt 'all the officers were gathered and informed and the regiment were told to get ten panzers and armoured personnel carriers together to deal with any trouble at home'. Bauer did not approve of the plot. 'Why didn't Stauffenberg and the others not shoot Hitler instead of blowing up the innocents with him?' he asked. The prevailing view in panzer units was that 'they did not like to hear conversations about the war likely to be over amid all the fighting,' Bauer commented. 'They had to keep going; otherwise it is hard to psychologically focus the mind on further resistance.'

In February 1945 only three weak Army Groups remained in the west. General Student was holding Holland and the northern Rhine; Model defended the Ruhr and Blaskowitz southern Germany. They were all under-strength, with hardly any tanks. Eisenhower deployed eighty-five full-strength divisions of which twenty-three were armoured and five airborne, all supported by overwhelming air power. The Rhine was crossed in late March and the drive into Germany began. 'It was not going to be a romp through friendly territory as the advance through France and Belgium had been,' declared Tom Heald of the 2nd Fife and Forfar Yeomanry. 'It would be a fighting advance all the way through Germany.'

Twenty-six German divisions offered patchy resistance in the west with the remaining panzer and motorised divisions fighting fanatically to hold in the east. The Ruhr was encircled by the 1st US and 9th Armies and surrendered on 18 April. Field Marshal Model committed suicide. Meanwhile the other Allied armies advanced up to fifty miles per day toward the agreed occupation zone borders. On 16 April the Russians began to fight their way through the five defence lines the Germans had established in the Oder-Neisse defence zone. Urban sprawl and numerous rivers and canals made Berlin a particularly tough nut to crack.

## REQUIEM

'Sorry for not writing before this,' wrote Corporal Jack Clegg of the 1st Fife and Forfar Yeomanry, 'but the last ten days have been the worst we've yet had on the continent.' Watch out for the photographs in the press, Clegg advised his mother. 'I'm keeping well and fit, but I'm a bit browned off. Three times I've had my best kit ready for Brussels, and each time I've had it stopped to go into action.' Jack Clegg did not write much and he apologised. 'I hope you haven't worried too much because of the lack of letters, but during the past six nights I've had one night in bed.' He complained about the deep snow and that 'it's deadly cold in the tanks'. Ominously he wrote that 'tonight we move into the rough spots at 10 p.m.', but ended his letter cheerily: 'Keep smiling, love to all, Your son Jack.'

'My mother never recovered from Jack's death,' his sister Bernice admitted after the war. 'She was devastated. My father was very quiet about it.'

'Johnny was wounded in the face,' wrote Keith Dawson to Mrs Clegg nineteen days after she received Jack's last letter. It happened about two miles outside the town of Simmerath in Germany, he told her, after a 'successful flaming of the pillboxes in the initial stages'. Jack, called 'Johnny' by his crew, was probably shot by a sniper in the opening battles for the Ruhr dams. 'We missed his cheerful smile and cheery word and his famous saying each morning that it was "one day nearer the end of the war".'

The war was now spluttering through such final actions. Berlin was under siege by 27 April, left with a strip of final resistance measuring ten miles long by three and a half miles wide. The British Army crossed the Weser on 5 April and reached the Elbe River on 24 April, establishing contact with the Russians on the next day. One issue only now dominated the minds of tank men. Who was to live and see the light of day at the end of the war?

Nothing was allowed to compromise this consideration. The victors could be as brutal in achieving this as their German conquerors had been before. Ted Hartman of the US 41st Tank Battalion overheard his commander relaying Combat Command B's instructions following the death of a popular company commander a week before the end of the war. 'These six checkpoints [villages] ahead will be burned to the ground by nightfall. Those people have got to learn that resisting is useless,' he radioed. The 70th Independent Tank Battalion history admitted:

Tanks swept across open fields from village to village, blasting relentlessly at every sign of resistance. Any town or city that tried to delay the advance soon became a raging inferno. The German landscape was dotted with burning villages. More white flags began to appear.

Remorse was a rapidly diminishing emotion at this stage of the war, especially when the concentration camps were liberated. Lieutenant Demetri Paris of the 9th US Armoured division explained his attitude to killing the enemy:

The feeling you got was not sorrow for him. You didn't think whether he had a family or children or anything. The guy started a war; his country has taken me from my home. My country brought me thousands of miles over here and – it's the satisfaction I had stopped one of them. The stronger feeling was always this buddy feeling: I've got him, he's not going to kill one of my buddies. It was that kind of satisfaction, not sorrow, not pain – no remorse'.

Panzer crews regarded American tanks as easy prey and likewise felt little remorse in dispatching them. 'Five Russians were more dangerous than thirty Americans,' declared Leutnant Otto Carius, fighting in the Siegen area with his Jagdtiger unit. He bemoaned their own falling standards, referring to his unit as men with 'a good attitude, but they had neither experience with heavy vehicles or enough training'. He remarked that all his old comrades, long dead, 'would have enjoyed firing up these Yanks "on parade".' Another panzer veteran, choosing his words carefully, claimed that the Americans were not particularly 'resilient'. 'If you had run out of armour-piercing, even an HE round would get them out of the turret.' By contrast there was 'enormous respect for Russian crews, not so much for their technical and tactical capabilities – which were good – but for their tenacity'. Carius regarded the Americans as weak. 'No real combat soldier found it in his heart, however, to allow himself to be captured prematurely by these "half-steppers", while at the same time our comrades on the Eastern Front were still bravely defending against the Russians.' If it meant saving lives American soldiers employed firepower indiscriminately, as did the British, if they had the resources.

War engenders hate and bitterness, and it is not always easy, even long after events, for veterans to be balanced in describing them. Carius, in no way an atypical panzer officer, was embittered at the prospect of approaching total and non-negotiable defeat. 'Everything had already gone completely crazy,' he commented. The infantry battalion he was supporting lived according to a deplorable motto along the lines: 'Enjoy the war! The peace will be terrible!' This, he said, 'was deeply repugnant to me'.

Ernest Hamilton of the 15/19 Hussars recalled the advance through many small towns and villages. 'The names of them were of no interest to the average soldier, other than would we have to fight for it?' The average American allegedly did not understand Europeans, but the British were equally prepared to do anything to finish the war and get home quickly. On capturing prisoners 'we would ask them were there any military in the next town?' Hamilton remembered. 'If they said no, we would put them at the front of the tank and advance to our objective.' In so doing the enemy ahead 'would think again about firing when they saw German field-grey on the tank'.

'In Megcheln they even continued to fight from houses that we had set on fire with the Crocodile flame-throwers,' reported Major John Stirling of the 4/7 RDG. 'Fanatical and misguided, yes, but brave and well disciplined, also yes,' he claimed of the German paratroopers, who 'fought with a grim, hopeless bravery that no man could fail to admire'.

Leutnant Ludwig Bauer, fighting with the remnants of Panzer Regiment 33, declared, 'We were *völlig hass-frei* [completely free of hate], but that changed for me when we saw what the US low-level fighters were doing to the civilians in the Cologne and Eiffel areas.' He saw 'American low-level fighters apparently chasing and shooting up farmers on horses – as if for sport!' It was the same emotional draining of remorse, as seemingly aimless casualties occurred with a victorious solution in sight. Bauer claimed resistance was motivated by three factors:

> We had heard about the call for unconditional surrender, we could not even imagine a situation where Churchill, Stalin and Roosevelt would carve up Germany. Secondly, the Americans knew the war was over in March yet continued to reduce German cities to ash and rubble. We further knew what the Russians were doing with all the rape and terror and felt we had to get our people out of the way.

The people had certainly had enough. Leutnant Otto Carius, fighting the final days with his Jagdtiger unit, realised that elements of the civilian population were co-operating with the enemy. 'I didn't have any problem understanding that the people were apathetic and tired of war, but that they would betray their own countrymen to the enemy I didn't want to believe at first.' After setting up a command post in a factory air raid shelter he began to appreciate the coincidence of civilians moving between the lines and precise American fire on his hidden assault guns 'even though they couldn't see the targets at all'. He sealed off the main battle lines. Discipline was creaking in the face of total enemy air superiority. Carius detected a 'strange attitude' that was expressed as 'Do anything but shoot! The pilots could discover our position!' There were even heated debates among isolated crew detachments about whether or not to open fire. Carius could see the end of hostilities approaching. 'Everyone had to decide for themselves,' he reflected, 'whether they wanted to experience the end decently or as a louse.' Many of the troops from other arms and services had opted for the latter; they were 'lying about in the woods by the hundreds and waiting for the end'.

Cynicism permeated many of the final panzer engagements. Karl Drescher of Reconnaissance Battalion 116 was always wary of groups of American aircraft seeking tell-tale indications of radio antennae. They occasionally put up speculative anti-aircraft fire 'to keep them from getting cheeky'. This prompted the unwelcome attention on one occasion of the local mayor who scolded them for attracting likely retribution. 'That tore it for me,' he recalled. 'I told him he'd better disappear or I'd shoot him. Up to now we had had to fight a war *he* started, not I!' At Aachen he was drawn into a similar exchange by an official who suggested he move his armoured vehicles to Oberhausen, which had already burned. 'I told him to get lost; we were fine where we were.' When the complaints intensified they lined up their vehicles in front of the official's residence and kept the engines running. 'When the planes came, we drove off quickly, but not before that house was destroyed,' he laughingly concluded.

Drescher recalled that at Hamm in the Ruhr he and his crew were obliged to search for food 'like robbers' while the civilians sat it out in air-raid shelters. Foraging for food from 'some officious rear-echelon paper pusher from the Wehrmacht who told us we had not asked and therefore would not receive anything' was peremptorily resolved. 'I told him to watch out, we had hand grenades and we would definitely get what we wanted. Then we took our stuff.' 'They all wanted to surrender, to allow the front line to roll over them,' complained Drescher. '*We* – we wanted to continue the war.' The fabric of German society was coming apart.

'Where before there had been tanks and anti-tank guns galore, they were now rarities,' claimed Major John Stirling of the 4/7 RDG. In the game of chance played by Allied tank crews anticipating an end to the war, odds were stacked against the lead tank. Progress was hindered by demolitions and road blocks, 'but it was no longer an army that was opposing us,' claimed Stirling. Hiding in ditches and hedges were old men and young boys armed with *panzerfausts* often prepared to blow themselves up if they could take a tank with them. Trooper 'John' of 1 RTR wrote to his family from hospital on 1 April 1945 explaining how 'one of those beggars lay in a ditch and waited until our tank was almost on top of him, then he stood up and let us have it with a *panzerfaust*'. It was 'small wonder that you acquire a fatalistic outlook' because the tank next to his was also hit and the gunner killed inside. The war had about a month to run. 'He had only just come over on a draft,' he remarked, 'and it was his first action.'

Lieutenant Tom Heald's 2nd Fife and Forfar Yeomanry were equipped with new Comet tanks, which had a far better gun than the Sherman and were mechanically reliable. It was the precursor to the future Centurion tank. 'A Comet would easily do 30mph,' he recalled, so the tactic adopted to overcome the panzerfaust was to drive past at speed.

> The leading tank would have its machine-guns firing at the hedge-rows in front of it and either side. The second tank would proceed about a hundred yards behind the first one, with its machine-guns also firing, not at the tank in front, but in the hedgerows behind it.

A third tank might do the same. 'Bazookered, Driver Speed Up!' was the reaction to a contact. The final fatality in the unit was Corporal Bush, killed in mid April as he tried to bail out of a bazookered tank. He was the last remaining tank commander from those who had commanded a tank in Normandy ten months before. Such was the chance of war. *Feldwebel* Eric Franzen's Tiger with the Kampfgruppe Schulz was destroyed by a Comet from 3 RTR at Fallingbostal the same month. What impressed him was that the Comet that had knocked him out 'allowed the crew to escape without trying to make things worse – a really noble action,' he remarked, 'in spite of total war'.

Leutnant Ludwig Bauer had been engaged in this nerve-racking game of chance since July 1941. At the end of March he was commanding a Sturmgeschütz IV (an SP mounted on a Panzer IV chassis) on a steep winding bend at Eiserfeld, near Siegen. Thus far he had survived being knocked out seven times, losing friends killed and injured each time. After destroying two Shermans approaching from below he was hit by another, an accurate first-round hit at 800 metres, making this the eighth time. Both his driver and gunner were killed. Bauer was positioned on the edge of a steep bend with precipitous sides. As life drained from the driver's legs the assault gun rolled backwards. Bauer, oblivious to the danger and unaware that the top half of his driver's head had been sliced off, called out directions. 'Left track, right track down,' he shouted as the panzer gathered momentum until it inexorably slid over the side of the road. It somersaulted three times before it reached the bottom.

Bauer had known his driver from the days he had been an NCO himself. 'He was an excellent driver and one of the original company' who regarded himself somewhat as a talisman, he fondly recalled. 'Stay with me,' he would assure Bauer, 'and you will survive.' He did but at a nightmarish cost. His injuries were relatively minor considering the spectacular demise of the assault gun: a chest wound and a damaged shoulder. Medics strapped him up and he carried on, but he was to be afflicted by dreams of decapitation for a considerable time. After the war he spent months searching for the grave before finally locating it and passing the sad details to the driver's parents in Austria. Eight of Bauer's proverbial nine lives had been extinguished.

Premonitions of death are cited too often by veterans to be completely dismissed as coincidental. Crews took extra care with the end so close. Ground was painstakingly examined with binoculars before being traversed. Every feature was methodically catalogued and considered, broken down into fore-ground, middle-ground and far distance to eliminate potential threats. Skylines were avoided and the immediate reaction to a shot from an 88mm was to bail out. All it took was fine adjustment and the time to reload – they never missed the second time. Rarely could the victim tank identify the correct range and line of fire to return a shot. Leave the fight to accompanying tanks, who had a better chance to see, was the firm advice. 'That's the way it happens' was the proverbial veteran explanation. The precursor to advancing across unknown ground was knee-trembling agitation: this may be for the last time. Some might scoff at premonition, but tank crewman Peter Elstob described the feeling: 'It was like coming to the end of anything – there was nothing you could do about it except wish it hadn't gone so fast.'

Sergeant George 'Stimo' Stimpson was one of Sergeant Jake War-drop's closest friends in 5 RTR and had known him since pre-war days on Perham Down. They were drinking in the tank leaguer the night before the advance on Rethem in April. For much of the war Wardrop had been at the 'sharp end' from Flanders in 1940, through the whole of North Africa and Italy, then Normandy, across north-west Europe and into Germany. He had been knocked out ten times in the desert, losing one or more friends each time, often having to climb into a replacement tank. His Colonel 'Paddy Doyle' recognised him as an enigmatic soldier, 'at his best in action', and who, like so many rugged soldiers, could 'cause more trouble in five minutes than the Military Police could clear up in a month'. As a consequence he see-sawed from trooper to sergeant and back again. Wardrop encapsulated the epic nature of the British tank man.

'We talked of the many friends who were no longer with us,' Stimpson recalled of that night in the leaguer. 'In retrospect I feel that Jake had a premonition of what the next day would bring, but we still managed to knock back a bottle of liberated German brandy.'

The following morning they advanced two troops abreast through a large wooded area about five miles south of Rethem. Wardrop's troop was ahead and slowed at a cross-track junction to check the map, sparking off a furious ambush. Only two tanks got back; two others including Jake's Firefly remained in the area of the junction, where a terrific fight continued to rage. Stimpson reached the area again the following day. 'I found Jake's body at the side of his tank, which was in the middle of the cross-tracks,' he recalled. They had been knocked out by a panzerfaust, and 'he had been killed by machine-gun fire'.

After experiencing the horror of liberating the Belsen concentration camp, Major Bill Close of 3 RTR overran a prisoner of war camp in the vicinity of Lüneburg. Inside, 'to my great surprise', he said, were several 3 RTR men who had been captured at Calais, from which he had escaped in 1940. Among them was a particular pal, Sergeant Socker Heath, who clambered aboard his tank and said with great emotion, 'I always knew the 3rd would come back for me.' This meeting captured the 'social levelling' process that had occurred among British tank men since the beginning of the war. Bill Close had been a troop sergeant when he last saw his friend in 1940; he liberated him five years later as a major and squadron commander. He had been shot out of eleven tanks during the interim. His experience was exceptional, but the commissioning of thousands of NCOs because of the war created the changed hierarchy that made it achievable.

Although a 'them' and 'us' relationship remained between officers and men, it had intangibly matured into something different. Social differences are meaningless within the cramped confines of a tank and this led to a tempering of attitudes. Perhaps this shared hardship was the beginning of attitudes that would one day underpin and inspire the National Health Service and the Welfare State.

On 10 April 1945 Ludwig Bauer's was commanding a Panther at Erndtebrook. He and his crew were exhausted after operating inside the tank for weeks and were surprised, caught out sleeping in an abandoned village house when American infantry unexpectedly walked in. Left behind in the rush to escape, Bauer found himself cut off and alone, hiding in the house for hours, minus his boots, which he had taken off to sleep. Eventually he crept into the driver's compartment of his Panther, which the Americans had assumed was abandoned, and sped off. He drove alone out of the village, leaving mayhem in his wake and bazooka rounds striking the rear. In one of those supreme ironies of war the Panther was shot in flames by a suspicious German self-propelled gun lurking on the outskirts of the village. Bauer barely escaped, clawing his way out through a blazing camouflage net that impeded the hatch. His comrades who had been obliged to abandon him when the village was overrun failed to recognise the blazing driver they put out as being in fact their commander. His face was unrecognisable and his uniform was glued to his back in a melted mass. Evacuated to a hospital at Olpe, he left within a day to evade capture. With his head and hands completely embalmed in bandages he managed to locate his battalion and remained with it until its surrender. Nine totally destroyed tanks meant that Ludwig Bauer had expended all his 'nine lives'. He had no right to be alive.

Fifteen days later the Soviet Army had surrounded Berlin and began to pound it to rubble with artillery. On the 26 April half a million Russian troops broke into the city centre, reaching the Reichstag on the 28th. Hitler committed suicide two days later and Berlin surrendered on 2 May. Hamburg was captured by the British 2nd Army on the May 3, and the following day the American 3rd Army entered Austria and Czechoslovakia. The war was virtually at an end.

On 2 May Sherman flail tanks belonging to the 22nd Dragoons crawled along the long, straight, ditch-lined road at Glinde, near Bremervorde, north of Bremen. They were supporting the 5th Cameronian Highlanders clearing the Baltic area. A stream of old *Volkstürm* (Home Guard) men and young boys was shambling past. 'It seemed as though every German soldier we took prisoner was no more than a schoolboy,' recalled Trooper Whitehead on similar clearance operations, but every one carried a panzerfaust 'which was very deadly to our existence'. On checking an area sprayed by their machine-guns after such an attack, they found eight young boys, all dead except one. 'He could not stop crying because of his friends' deaths. He was also very frightened and had messed his trousers, which is not surprising'. Dejected refugees and Wehrmacht soldiers bent on surrender shuffled apprehensively past the flail tanks as they raked woods and hedges with machine-gun fire, seeking enemy pockets.

Sergeant Jock Stirling in the lead tank ordered his gunner Jim Taylor to fire into a German self-propelled gun which had probably been abandoned, as it was teetering at an angle on the ditch-lined road edge, 'to make sure'. It soon began to burn with the 'crackle and spit' of burning ammunition. 'If it wasn't dead, it's dead now,' recalled Alan Walkden, the radio operator and loader. As they drove past and then beyond the burning armoured vehicle the road began to rise 'very straight, in unnatural quiet', remembered Walkden.

The troop commander Lieutenant Ian Hamilton moved to the left and behind. 'We were told that the end of hostilities was in sight and to proceed without taking any risks.' They monitored the advance of the infantry on their flanks and Hamilton had a Bren gun carrier immediately behind him. 'Jock Stirling, our tank commander, stares with sharpened concentration up the oddly deserted road.' Alan Walkden inside the tank could see his commander in the open turret but little else. 'A jarring metallic impact makes the whole tank shudder.' 'What the hell was that, Jock?' said Walkden. But his commander was leaning as if with resignation against the cupola, unable to respond. 'Where his head used to be, there's something out of a slaughterhouse,' Walkden recalled: 'bloody; shapeless; obscene.'

Ignoring call-sign procedure he shouted into his radio 'Help! Help! We've been hit! The commander's had it.' Hamilton, the troop commander, was already calling for smoke and his main gun was firing rapidly and blindly to distract their unseen assailant. As he reversed he started to push the Bren gun carrier along the road.

Basil Carlick, the driver of the stricken flail tank, shouted that the main gun was stuck over his hatch and he couldn't get out. The electrical traverse did not work but Taylor shifted the gun by traversing manually, and as the gun swung aside the hatch flipped open and the driver dived into the ditch. All this occurred within fractions of seconds as both Jim Taylor and Alan Walkden tried to tug at the 'inertly indifferent, horrendously butchered corpse' of their commander.

A second armour-piercing round clanged through the turret and out again going straight through the gunner. 'Now death looks certain,' surmised Walkden, 'I accepted it in a dazed calm. Two poor guys have died, up by that cupola. My turn next.' He struggled and wrestled with the gory corpses at the exit and managed 'God knows how' to get out. It would only be a matter of seconds before yet another projectile would come smashing through the tank, which because it was not yet burning, would merit further consideration from the enemy. Walkden's pistol lanyard snagged on the jagged, shell-damaged flap of the cupola and then he was free. On the hull he cringed at the prospect of machine-gun fire, but it did not come and he shoved off to drop into the ditch next to the only other surviving crew member.

Lieutenant Ian Hamilton's tank, grinding aside the Bren gun carrier, managed to turn off the dyke road into a farm entrance. Yet another crack and rush of air from the farewell shot of the German self-propelled gun clipped off the top of the telegraph pole beside them, showering the tank with timber and loose wires. Alan Walkden, bathed from head to foot in gore, made his uncertain way with the driver towards the Scottish infantry. 'Ma Gaud!' the first breathed: 'Whit the hell happened tae you?' 'Baz and I,' Walkden recalled, stood 'dumbly staring in a kind of stupidity at the Scot'. 'You laddies've juist aboot had enough,' he said comfortingly. 'Cm on in the hoose an' lets hae a wee drenk o' tea!'

Hamilton recalled that the two survivors were taken back to base by truck. Only forty-eight hours of hostilities remained. They were immediately sent on leave to Brussels, where they became embroiled in the madly enthusiastic VE Day celebrations.

Right up to the cessation of hostilities German dispatch riders and courier cars were delivering medals and awards across the war-torn Reich. *Feldwebel* Hermann Eckhardt received the Knight's Cross in hospital during March for fighting a heroic rearguard defence on the River Neisse approach to Berlin. He had knocked out twenty-five

British tanks in the desert and seventy-eight Russian tanks in the final eighteen months of the war. Ludwig Bauer received his Knight's Cross on 29 April with days to go before the end. Dispatch riders sought him out despite the haphazard nature of the actions he was involved in and a constantly shifting front. 'Madness,' he later reflected, 'to allow men to risk their lives in this way.'

Lieutenant Stuart Hills recalled the sun streaming through his window on 5 May after wild partying the night before. He was morose and reflective, having recently lost an old school friend, to whom he was very close. His thoughts echoed pervading veteran accounts of war's end. One could now consider a future of sorts. 'No more death, no more shooting, no more burning tanks or loud explosions.' Things were different. 'I could rise from my bed and go to breakfast,' he reflected, 'without worrying whether I would be blown to bits that day.' All restrictions had been raised in an instant. 'It was time for me to get on with my life.'

'On VE Day in Camberley I put a fistful of notes on the counter of the pub for everyone to drink to those who weren't coming back,' remembered Peter Roach of 1 RTR. There was not the number of takers he had anticipated. 'With a general lack of understanding and a catch in my throat it was not a success.' Tommy Atkins, as the Kipling poem suggested, would soon outlive his usefulness.

Back in Germany, Lieutenant Andrew Wilson's tanks with 141 Regiment RAC were called forward into Barracks. The RSM was ready to receive them. Tanks had to be lined up in immaculate rows. 'That'll do, sir. We'll get a white line drawn tomorrow.' Peace was breaking out and they were unprepared. Crews were unable to refrain from caching 'goodies', all the useful things one required on campaign, in special places inside their tanks, like so many squirrels. 'You never know; we may still need it,' he reflected. Now all these things were to be stored in foot-lockers and cupboards. This was unnatural. They did not need a lot of it because they would now be fed from the cookhouse.

Wilson felt distinctly uncomfortable gazing around their peacetime barracks, grim blocks still painted over with Nazi slogans.' It was so 'un-tactical', he kept thinking, despite the fact the war was over. 'What'll happen if there's an attack? They'll never get out.'

# POSTSCRIPT – VETERANS TODAY

An American friend operating with me in the desert during the final planning process for the coming Gulf offensive in February 1991 was unexpectedly appointed second-in-command of a tank battalion. As we exchanged glances on departure it was clear he would be in the thick of the approaching fighting. My experience as parachute infantry assured me it was not a bad option. Unlike me, he was going to enjoy a lot of armoured protection.

At the end of the war I had witnessed the immediate empathy my commander General Franks shared with a tank crew newly out of action, on cease-fire day. After speaking with a number of distinguished tank men about their experiences while writing this book I feel I know what passed between them. TV war dramatisations are apt to bog themselves down in the tension of the moment to the exclusion of reality. War is 98 per cent boredom and 2 per cent action. Dramatisations assume that soldiers are either frightened to distraction or psychopathic. If not, they are barely in control and held together by a few 'hard hands'. But it is human compassion which cements military cohesion – this shone through all the veteran accounts. They get over their fears, rarely displaying melodramatic emotion, because they, by necessity, are immersed in functional tasks like driving, controlling and operating guns. I have attempted to describe a little of the 98 per cent in order to explain the intensity of the 2 per cent.

My Gulf War was a spectacle, and I observed tanks at war from a distance. Ugliness was only apparent afterwards. My previously fixed view that armoured protection made it easier changed with an appreciation of what advanced technology can inflict on the loser when unmatched. The human implications of technical inequalities in tank fighting have been a consistent underlying theme of this book.

With their quietly understated tales, one perspective the veterans brought was an image of a world that has long passed them by. They projected a turret-eye view of the Second World War and vivid recollections of what it is like to be at the high or low end of the tank design technical plateau. In the Gulf we were at the high end, whereas British tank men between 1939 and 1945 were invariably at the lower end of the spectrum. I am grateful for their generosity in baring their souls to a total stranger.

Common to the veterans I interviewed was the realisation that they had lived through the best and worst that life can offer. As a consequence they have *lived* their lives to the full since.

James Carson, a subaltern with the Welsh Guards armoured battalion, summed up his feelings. Reflecting on his tank experiences, he spoke of 'relief that one survived it all, the solidarity and loyalty of comradeship and the sadness of those we lost'. So heartfelt were the losses that they had left 'a temporary loneliness and emptiness, a feeling of having grown up too fast and a vacuum at the end of *what now?*'

The main compulsion to describe what happened to them was the desire to relate their stories before it was too late. All of the veterans are in their eighties – or older – and in varying degrees of health. Some required bolstering from doctors before talking to me. One old panzer veteran in his eighties rejected the kid-gloves treatment and took me out for evening drinks, insisting on driving. Motivated by a desire to offer glimpses of experiences they believed no future generation should see, even the most guarded felt the need to open up after exploratory chats.

Many returned to problems and had to readjust when hostilities ceased. As Jim Carson succinctly put it: 'What now?' Eric Allsop, who had served with 8 RTR throughout the war, went to live with his 'maiden aunts' when he returned from the conflict, in which he had been constantly 'F'ing and blinding'. But once back, he declared, 'I never got it wrong.'

The spectre of nightmare images – mainly of burning and claustrophobia – was a common understated emotion. Heightened perceptions of comradeship and loyalty are less recognisable to the young living in the democratic west today. With no prompting all the veterans at some juncture remarked on their perception of declining moral standards, as they see it today. They have remained true to a different age, which understood patriotism more clearly, as well as to each other.

The intent of the stories they shared was largely to leave some sort of milestone to commemorate friends, and to pass on truths and images to their families before it was too late. Some even shared correspondence sent to the widows of newly deceased veterans, disclosing events their husbands would never have mentioned. These were generously handed across, giving remarkably candid, and poignant, snapshots of a past world.

In imparting the knowledge they also sought closure with regard to certain events and incidents. Not in anticipation of a response, but to assuage an underlying uneasiness that their story might otherwise never be told. Urgency was governed not so much by the fear of death, but rather the realisation that their mental faculties might suddenly be impaired.

Tape recorders are not always welcome at these sessions, and in any case they inhibit responses because of a restricted ability to monitor information disclosure. Quite often the best method was to share modern military experience against their own by drawing parallels and suggesting what had changed. This produced good results. The most honest and evocative stories frequently arose in the middle of a meal or when driving and had speedily to be committed to paper at the first available opportunity.

Many veterans had a rakish sparkle to the eye and knew how to enjoy life. With panzer veteran Hermann Eckhardt lunch was the highlight of his day, whereas the interview was mine. Love of food had clearly been a driving force in his military life, because his remembrance of operations with Panzer Regiment 8 against the British in the desert was as much about looting British rations from disabled tanks as knocking them out.

A sense of restrained guilt at having survived, when their friends did not, underlay many a conversation. 'So that others may live' was a truism governing why they fought. Their loyalties were first to each other in combat and secondly to their families. Gratitude at surviving undoubtedly sustained them in the years that followed the war, when every day lived was a bonus. Interestingly, all the veterans I interviewed were largely economically successful after the war. They appreciated the privilege of leading full lives. All their memories of the departed are of young men, a constant reminder of their own lost youths.

Polite and very generous with information, the veterans were too courteous to remark upon the extent to which their memories can be plundered by unscrupulous TV producers, scriptwriters or authors who 'cherry-pick' experiences to promote pre-composed versions of events. Entertainment as history is an easy snare to fall into. If acted upon, perception does, in fact, become truth. The difficulty is to disentangle conflicting threads that emerge in interviews and balance them as objectively as possible.

British, Russian and American veterans are treated with tremendous respect by their societies, who sense their sacrifice and compassionately appreciate the extraordinary pressures they were subjected to. They were the victors. It is not the same for panzer veterans, labouring beneath a collective guilt that intense treatment by German historians of the Holocaust and atrocities in occupied territories has occasioned. Films and exhibitions deservedly portray these events in a serious manner, but many panzer veterans confided to me how their national patriotism was often misconstrued as Nazi sympathy. Panzer veteran Ludwig Bauer remarked ironically on the reluctance of the post-war Bundeswehr to draw upon his active wartime experience for training when he was serving as a reserve officer in the 1950s.

German veteran experience is not dissimilar to Russian but in a different sense. The demise of the Communist Party in Russia resulted in a similar lack of clarity in terms of patriotic identification with the state in which they live. The Soviet wartime experience was very much influenced by T-34 commander Vladimir Alexeev's remark that 'we were never asked'. Soviet veterans are highly respected but, like their Wehrmacht counterparts, are coming to terms with a different state regime. This happened to the Germans in 1945 and for the Russians after 1991. It was interesting to see how Russian interviewees lamented the delay of the anticipated Allied Second Front. In the same way that British tank crews and veterans gently tease US tank men for arriving 'late' for the war, the Russians were visibly affected by the fighting and dying they had to endure before the Allies landed in Normandy.

The Russian veterans whom I interviewed were ostensibly guarded initially but, after scratching the surface, emerged as rich, passionate and humorous men, full of humanity and a pleasure to meet.

The veterans watch out for each other and give their all in much the same way that they conducted their war. I hope *Tank Men* has honestly reflected their experiences, because as they well appreciate, time is running out sixty years after the event. Eric Allsop succinctly expressed it:

'I know the names of my tank crew to this day – I forget a lot else!'

# ACKNOWLEDGEMENTS

I am particularly indebted to Mr David Willey, the Curator of Bovington Tank Museum (BTM), Stuart Wheeler, his assistant, and his staff for the wealth of interviews, letters and diary accounts that are included in this book. David is a committed enthusiast with a wealth of knowledge and advice that he readily shares, and he enabled me to crawl into, out of and over virtually every tank mentioned in this book as well as providing live rides on running models. Simon Braithwaite and the staff of the Second World War Experience Centre at Leeds (LEC) were likewise generous with their knowledge, guidance and documents, in particular a wealth of vivid interviews conducted by Peter Liddle.

I had outstanding support from British tank veterans who were totally supportive and generous, often sharing sensitive memories without inhibition. I am especially grateful to Eric Allsop, John Mallard, Jim Carson, Michael Trasenster and the tank designer Bert Foord for their unique glimpses into an age now long gone. Considerable help was forthcoming from panzer veterans including Willy Wothe, Albert Schick and Klaus Voss. Christophe Nehring very kindly passed on useful extracts from his father's papers covering the early years. Ludwig Bauer played a pivotal role with articulate and vivid glimpses of a very distinguished service, as did his companion Hermann Eckardt. They provided a true insight into the German tank men's experience. Russian support was forthcoming through Evgeny Kulichenko, who conducted me around the Stalingrad battlefields, and his wife Galina, and Elena Korovina, who likewise guided me at Kursk in the company of tank veterans Vladimir Alexeev and Anatoly Kotzov, who succinctly and convincingly offered the vital Russian perspective I needed to cover.

Every effort has been made to trace the source and copyright of quotations and photographs in the text, and these are acknowledged where appropriate. My thanks to those publishers who have permitted quotations and extracts from their books; sources are annotated in the notes that follow the text and the bibliography at the end. My apologies are offered in advance to those with whom, for any reason, I was unable to establish contact.

Special thanks go to my agent Charlie Viney for his advice and unerring instinct over what constitutes wheat relative to chaff, and to my wife Lynn for her loving support and patience while her husband became bound up in yet another wayward project as he left the army.

# SOURCES

## PUBLISHED SOURCES

Bähr, H.W.: *Die Stimme Des Menschen*, Piper and Co. Verlag, 1961.

Bartov, O.: *The Eastern Front 1941–5*, Macmillan, 1985.

Bealle, P.: *Death by Design*, Sutton, 1998.

Buckley, J.: *British Armour in the Normandy Campaign*, Frank Cass, 2004.

Carell, P.: *The Foxes of the Desert*, Macdonald, 1960.

Cooper, A.: *Cairo in the War 1939–45*, Hamish Hamilton, 1989.

Costello, J.: *Love Sex and War*, Guild, 1985.

Deighton, L.: *Blitzkrieg*. Jonathan Cape, 1979.

Delaforce, P.: *Marching to the Sound of Gunfire*, Chancellor Press, 2000.

Dinter, E.: *Hero or Coward – Pressures Facing the Soldier in Battle*, Frank Cass., 1985.

Dyer, G.: *War*, Guild Pub, 1986.

Fletcher, D., Ed,: *Tiger! The Tiger Tank: A British View*, HMSO, 1986.

Forty, G.: *Afrika Korps At War*, (2 Vols), Ian Allan, 1998.

– *US Tanks of World War II*, Blandford, 1983.

– *The Royal Tank Regiment*, Guild, 1989.

– *Desert Rats at War*, Purnell, 1975.

Frieser, K.H.: *Blitzkrieg Legende*, Oldenbourg, Verlag, 1996.

– *Das Deutsche Reich Und Der Zweite WeltKrieg*, Vol. 8. *Die Ostfront 1943/44*, Munchen, 2007. (Manuscript copy)

Foley, J.: *The Boilerplate War*, Frederick Muller Ltd, 1963.

Grossmann, D.: *On Killing: The Psychological Cost of Learning to Kill in War and Society,* Little Brown, 1995.

Hackett, J.: *Warfare in the Ancient World*, Sidgwick and Jackson 1989.

Harris, J.P.: *Men, Ideas and Tanks*, Manchester Univ Press, 1995.

Heckman, W.: *Rommel's War in Africa*, Granada 1982.

Icks, R.J.: *Famous Tank Battles*, Profile, 1972.

Jewell, D. ed.: *Alamein and the Desert War*, Sphere, 1967.

Kellet, A.: *Combat Motivation*, Kluwer-Nijhoff, 1982.

Kershaw, R.: *War Without Garlands*, Ian Allan.

 – *D-Day*, Ian Allan, 1993.

Kleine, E/Kuhn, V.: *Tiger – The History of a Legendary Weapon*, Fedorowicz, 1989.

Knopp, G.: *Hitler's Children*, Sutton Pub, 2000.

 – *The SS: A Warning From History*, Sutton Pub, 2002.

 – *Der Jahrhundert Krieg – Der Wustenkrieg*, Ullstein 2003.

Lewin, R. ed: *Freedom's Battle – The War on Land*, Arrow, 1969.

Liddle-Hart, B.: *The Other Side of the Hill*, Pan, 1978.

 – ed. *The Rommel Papers*, Hamlyn, 1953.

Macksey, K.: *Tank versus Tank*, Magna Books, 1991.

MacLeod-Ross, G.: *The Business of Tanks*, Arthur Stockwell, 1976.

Mellenthin, F.: *Panzer Battles* Univ of Oklahoma Press, 1956.

Merridale, C.: *Ivan's War*. Faber, 2005.

McGuirk, D.: *Rommel's Army in North Africa*, Stanley Paul, 1987.

Muir, K.: *Arms And The Woman*. Coronet, 1993.

Nipe, G.: *Decision in the Ukraine Summer 1943*, Ferdorowicz, 1996.

Pallud, JP.: *Then and Now: Blitzkrieg in the West*. After the Battle, 1991.

Piekalkiewicz, J.: *Tank War 1939–45*. Guild, 1986.

Pryce-Jones, D.: *Paris in the Third Reich* Collins, 1981.

Reese, R.: *The Soviet Military Experience*, Routledge, 2000.

Remy, M.: *Mythos Rommel*. Ullstein, 2004.

Simpkin, R.: *Human Factors in Mechanised Warfare*, Brassey's, 1983.

Sithers, A.J.: *A New Excalibur*, Guild, 1986.

Walker, I.: *Iron Hulls Iron Hearts*, Crowood Press, 2003.

Warry, J.: *Warfare in the Ancient World*, Salamander, 1980.

Wessel, W.: *Mit Rommel in der Wüste*, Bildgut-Verlag, 1943.

Williams, A.: *D-Day to Berlin*, Hodder, 2004.

Williamson, G.: *The Panzer Crewman 1939–45*, Osprey, 2002.

Zaloga, S.: *US army Tank Crewman*, Osprey, 2004.

 – *US Armoured Divisions ETO 1944–45*. Osprey, 2004.

 – *Sherman Medium Tank 1942–45,* Osprey, 1993.

## MEMOIRES AND PERSONAL ACCOUNTS

Becker, H.: *Devil on My Shoulder* Jarrolds, 1955.

Boscawen, R.: *Armoured Guardsmen*, Leo Cooper, 2001.

Böttiger, A.: *Im Panzer – Ich Kam Durch*, Flechsig, 2005.

Carius, O: *Tigers In the Mud*, Stackpole, 2003.

Christophé, CC.: *Wir Stossen Mit dem Panzern zum Meer*, Steiniger, 1940.

Close, W.: *A View From the Turret*, Dell and Bredon, 1998.

Crisp, R.: *Brazen Chariots* Frederick Muller, 1959.

Cooper, B.: *Death Traps*, Ballantine, 1998.

Douglas, K.: *Alamain to Zem-Zem* Faber, 1966.

Drabkin, A and Sherenet O.: *T-34 In Action*, Pen and Sword, 2006.

Dyson, S.: *Tank Twins*, Leo Cooper, 1994.

Elstob, P.: *Warriors For the Working Day*, Four square, 1960.

De la Falaise,.: *Through Hell to Dunkirk* 7/12 Lancers Museum, 1988.

Fuchs, K.: *Sieg Heil!* Archon Books, 1987.

Goddard, F.: *Battlefields of Life*, Finial Pub, 2004.

Guderian, H.: *Panzer Leader*, Michael Joseph, 1952.

Halder, F.: *The Halder War Diary 1939–42*, Presidio, 1988.

Halstead, M.: *Shots in the Sand*, Gooday, 1990.

Hamilton, S.: *Armoured Odyssey*, Tom Donovan, 1995.

Hammerton, I.: *Achtung Minen!*, Book Guild, 1991.

Hartman, JT.: *Tank Driver*, Indiana Univ Press, 2003.

Hennessey, P.: *Young Man in a Tank*, Private Pub. BTM.

Hills, S.: *By Tank Into Normandy*, Cassel, 2003.

Holbrook, D.: *Flesh Wounds*, Buchan and Enright, 1987.

Joly, C.: *Take These Men*, Penguin, 1956.

De Lee, N.: *Voices From the Battle of the Bulge*, David and Charles, 2004.

Lewis, B.: *Four Men Went to War*, Leo Cooper, 1987.

Luck, Hans von: *Panzer Commander*, Dell, 1989.

Metelmann, H.: *Through Hell For Hitler*, Patrick Stephens, 1990.

Meyer, K.: *Grenadiers*. Stackpole 2005.

Pope, M.: *Fighting for Freedom and Fun* Tiger and Tyger Ltd, 1999.

Roach, P.: *The 8.15 To War*, Leo Cooper, 1982.

Stahlberg, A.: *Bounden Duty*, Brassey's, 1990.

Wehrmacht, Bance A. trans.: *Mit Den Panzern In Ost und West. Blitzkrieg In Their Own Words*, Zenith Press, 2005.

Wardrop, J/Ed G Forty *Tanks Across the Desert*. Sutton, 2003.

Wilson, A.: *Flame Thrower*, William Kimber, 1984.

XYZ Private: *I Joined The Army*, May Fact, 1937.

## FILM AND TV

*Befreiung*, German Version of First Part *Der Feuerbogen* [Ognennaja duga], Director J. Oserow 1970.

*Die Befreiung*, G. Knopp, ZDF Ger TV, 2004.

*British Tanks At War*, Imperial War Museum DVD, 2006.

*Desert – The War in North Africa*, ITV *World at War* series.

*Die Deutschen Im Zweiten Weltkrieg*, Hess and Wuermelung, SWF Ger TV 1989.

*Die SS*, C. Frey/G. Knopp, ZDF Ger TV, 2002.

*The Desert Rats*, Dir M. Milne, 3BM TV, 1999.

*Fields of Armour – The Gentleman's War*, P. McKelvy, Discovery Channel TV.

– *Tommy Cookers* 1993.

– *A Wave of Terror* 1993.

*Hitler's Children,* P. Hartl/G. Knopp, ZDF Ger TV.

*Liberators – Fighting on Two Fronts in World War II*, W Miles and N. Rosenblum. US prod for Ch 4 TV.

*Mother of All Battles. Kursk 1943*, D. Richards and L Reece, *Timewatch* BBC.

*The Other Side of Dunkirk*, A. Laurence, BBC TV, 2004.

*Saving The Tiger. The Story of Tiger 131*, Hudson/da Costa, Bovington Tank Museum DVD.

*Tanks! Tank Crew*, Cromwell Productions, 1998.

*Tanks – Wonder Weapon of World War I.* H Bettinson. *Timewatch* BBC.

*The Great War:* BBC TV, part 13: *The Devil is Coming*, Aug 1964.

*Weapons at War – Tanks*, R. Kirk. History Channel TV, 1991.

*The Valor and the Horror*, B. McKenna,Gala Films, CBC TV, 1992.

*Der Verdammte Krieg*, G. Knopp, ZDF Ger TV, 1995.

## UNIT ACCOUNTS

Beale, P.: *Tank Tracks – 9 RTR at War 1940–45*, Budding Books, 1995.

Delaforce, P.: *Taming the Panzers – 3 RTR at War* Sutton, 2003.

Hartmann, B.: *Geschichte Des Panzer Regiments 5 1935–43 und der Panzer Abteilung 5 1943–45*, (2 Vols) Selbstverlag, 2002.

Jentz, T.: *Die Deutsche Panzertruppe 1933–42/42–45*, (2 Vols). Podzun-Pallas 1998.

Hinze, R.: *Hitze, Frost und Pulverdampf*, H Pöppinghaus, 1981.

Mace, P.: *Forrad: The Story of the East Riding Yeomanry*, Leo Cooper, 2001.

Meyer, H.: *The 12th SS* (2 Vols). Stackpole, 1994.

Perkins, N. Rogers, M.: *Roll Again Second Armoured*, Kristall Pub, 1988.

RHQ Irish Guards: *The Armoured Micks 1941–45*, Manuscript.

Tiemann, R.: *Chronicle of the 7th Kompanie 1st SS Panzer Division Leibstandarte*, Schiffer, 1998.

Yeide, H.: *Steel Victory*, Presidio Press, 2003.

## PERODICALS

Albrecht, M.: 'Das Panzer Regiment 6 und der Spanische Burgerkrieg 1936–39', *Kameraden Magazine* Dec 2006.

Erskine, D.: 'No Truce With Time' *Tank* Journal Vol 72, May 1990.

Hoehne, K.: 'With Rommel in the Desert', *MHQ* Vol 17, No 2, Pp. 74–9.

Lawrence, R.: 'A Little Death, A Little Life', *MHQ*, Vol 6, No 4, pp.38–9.

Meistrich, I.: 'War's Cradle', *MHQ*, Spring 2005. Vol 17. No 3. Pp 84–93.

Mulcahy, R.: 'Blitzkrieg's Beginnings'. Rolf Hertenstein interview. *World War II* magazine, Mar 2006. 'Remembering Barbarossa', *World War II* magazine, April 2006, pp. 34–40.

O'Connell, R.: 'The Insolent Chariot', *MHQ*, Spring 1990, Vol 2 No 3, pp 80–81.

Price, A.: 'Rocket Firing Typhoons in Normandy'. RAF Air Power Review. Vol 8 No 1, Spring 2005.

Rice, K.: 'A Day in the Gothic Line'. *Tank* Journal May 94 Vol 76.

Tucker-Jones A; 'Hitler's Great Panzer Heist',. *Military Illustrated*. Mar 2006.

## UNPUBLISHED ACCOUNTS AND MEMOIRES

| | |
|---|---|
| Balfour, Peter | Letters.Various 23 Jul 44–22 Feb 45, LEC. Interview, P. Liddle. Dec 1999. LEC. |
| Bauer, Ludwig | Pz Regt 33. Private letters, papers and correspondence with author, 2006. |
| Bright, T.A. Tpr | 7 Leeds Rifles RTR, Jan 97, BTM. |
| Brown, Sgt. | 10th Hussars and 8th Hussars, BTM. |
| Boast, Leslie Tpr | 7 RTR, BTM. |
| Boguslawski, Andrzej | 1939 Polish Cavalry account, LEC |
| Boyes, Robin A. Tpr | Northants Yeomanry, interview BTM. |
| Carson, James Lt | Welsh Guards Tank Bn, letters to author. |
| Carr-Gomm, Richard Lt | 4th Bn Guards Tank Bde. Accounts and notes. LEC. |
| Clark, James D'Arcy Lt | QOYD Letters Nov 42–Feb 43. LEC |
| Clegg, Jack Cpl | 1st Fife and Fofar Yeomanry. Letters Oct 44 – 21Feb 45, LEC. |
| Close, William Maj | Interview, P. Liddle, May 2002 LEC. |
| Cox, Ernie Tpr | 141 RAC The Buffs. Documents and accounts, LEC. |
| Dixon, John Lt | East Riding Yeomanry. Diary 1940. LEC. |
| Drescher, Karl | Aufkl Abt 116, joint interview transcript with Walter Zittats 1944–45, LEC. |
| Eckardt, Hermann | Pz Regt 8. Biographical notes passed to author 2006. |
| Flatow, AF Maj | 45 RTR. *A Personal Narrative of El Alamein*. BTM. |
| Hamilton, Ernest Tpr | 15/19 Hussars. Account Aug 97 BTM. |
| Heald, Tom Lt | 2nd Fife and Fofar Yeomanry. Account. BTM. |

| | |
|---|---|
| Howes, John Tpr | 141 RAC account. Mar 97. BTM. |
| Huggins, Ron Sgt | *The Tenth Hussars in France 1940.* BTM. |
| 'John' Anon, Tpr | Diary with 1 RTR 17 Aug 44–4 Aug 45. BTM. |
| Keller, Lt Col | CO 3RTR Reports on Calais Operations 1940. BTM<br>Reports by members of 3RTR on Calais 1940. BTM |
| Kent, Charles. Major | 6 AARR. Correspondence. BTM. |
| King, A.J. Tpr | East Riding Yeomanry. *Normandy* Through a Periscope. BTM. |
| Knight, Bob Tpr | 1st East Riding Yeomanry. Letter Account Nov 91. BTM. |
| Langabeer, Tpr | 6 RTR. Mar 98. BTM. |
| Langdon, JF Maj | 3 RTR *Aller Bridgehead 11–14 Apr 45.* Dec 96 Account. BTM. |
| Ling, David Capt | 44 RTR diary and papers of the Desert war, 2000. BTM |
| McGinlay, Jock Lt | 7 RTR in the desert. Aug 2001. |
| Nehring, Walther Gen | Papers passed by C. Nehring in correspondence with the author 2006. |
| Parramore, J.V. Sgt | 1st Lothian and Border Yeomanry. Sep 98. BTM. |
| Reeves, W. Maj | *Tanks in Calais 1940.* May 98. BTM. |
| Rendell, Bert Sgt | 1 RTR Desert Account. 1995. BTM. |
| Rollins, Paul Tpr | 40 RTR. Interview by Stuart Wheeler and Lisa Hill. Jun 2006. BTM. |
| Rollinson, Jack. | RAC. An account of his Experiences in the Desert War. BTM. |
| Sackville-West, Hugh | 7 RTR in WW2. BTM. |
| Schoeneker, Josef | SS Viking Division. BTM audio tape interview. |
| Stevenson, K. | Effects of Sleep Deprivation on Battlefield Performance. UK Army Staff Course Paper 84. |
| Strickland, E.V. | *Battle of Arras 1940.* Personal Account. BTM. |

Sprigg, Fred                6th Guards Tank Bde Normandy Account. BTM.

Sprot, A. LT Col            Royal Scots Greys. Interview by P Liddle May 2004. LEC.

Stiller, Gerhard Lt(SS)     Notes of conversation Normandy. LEC.

Sutton, Brian Tpr           With the 4/7 RDG in Normandy. LEC.

Tarrant, W.F. Tpr           1st Northants Yeomanry. *The Sherman Tank*. Letter Mar 98. BTM.

Toppe, A Maj Gen            *Desert Warfare: German Experiences in World War II*. Combined Arms research Library. Leavenworth Kansas.

Tout, Ken Tpr               1st Northamptonshire Yeomanry and Kings Dragoon Guards. Talk 'Lessons of War:The Tank Crew in Battle'. MOD DRAC Briefing Day 27 Nov 1986.

Trasenster, Michael Lt      Copies of correspondence to the author relating to experiences with the 4/7 RDG in Normandy 1944.

Vaux, Peter Lt              *Escape from Arras 1940*. Apr 96. BTM.

War Office UK               Notes From Theatres Of War: 1. *Cyrenaica Nov 41*. 10.: *Cyrenaica and Western Desert Jan–Jun 42*. 13. : *North Africa – Algeria and Tunisia Nov 42–Mar 43*. 14. : *Western Desert and Cyrenaica Aug–Dec 42. Survey of Tank Casualties*. Battle Study No 62. 1947.

Walden, Alan Tpr            *An Account of the Final Action of a Flail Tank Crew 2 May 45*. LEC.

Watson, Peter Cpl           'A Corporal's Story'. 2RTR BTM.

Wardrop, Jake Sgt           5 RTR. Part ms Account of *The Red and The Blue*. BTM.

Webb, Harry Tpr.            43 RTR Account. BTM.

Webster, Herbert Sgt.       *Joining the 58th at Bovington*. Apr 98. BTM.

Whitehead, Robert Tpr       Excerpts from the life of a trooper. 44 RTR. Aug 98. BTM.

Williams, R.W.S.            Tpr HMT Grimsby D Sqn 7RTR BEF 1940.

| | |
|---|---|
| Wollaston, Alan WOII | 3 RTR Desert account and interview. Feb 96. BTM. |
| Wothe, Willy | Pz Gren 3 Pz Div. Correspondence with author relating to Pz Regt 6 2006. |
| Voss, Klaus | Pz Comd Pz Regt 11. Correspondence with author 2006. |
| Young, Dennis Tpr | A Normandy Veteran. 153 RAC. BTM. |

## INTERVIEWS

| | |
|---|---|
| Allsop, Eric Lt. | Tank Commander 8 RTR. 6 Dec 06. |
| Alexeev, Vladimir Lt. | Soviet Tank Commander. 5th Guards Tank Army. 29/31 Jul 06. |
| Bauer, Ludwig Lt. | Panzer Commander. Pz Regt 33. 10/11/12 Jul 06 |
| Carson, James Lt. | Tank Commander Welsh Guards. 28 Sep 06. |
| Eckardt, Herman Fw. | Panzer Commander. Pz Regt 8. 11 Jul 06. |
| Foord, Herbert Mr. | Tank designer. 23 May 06 |
| Kozlov, Anatoly. Lt. | Soviet 5th Guards Tank Army. 30 Jul/1 Aug 06 |
| Mallard,l John Lt-Capt. | 44 RTR. Tank Commander. 4 Oct 06. |
| Trasenster, Michael Lt. | Tank Commander. 4/7 RDG. 25 Sep 06. |

# NOTES

## CHAPTER 1: GENESIS

(*BTM*: Bovington Tank Museum Document. *LEC*: Leeds Second World War Experience Centre Document.)

### 'Mother' Tank

p. 5 Casualties quoted p. 113 and 116 *Great Battles of the British Army*, ed. D.G. Chaundler and p. 156 *Great Battlefields of the World*, J. Macdonald.

Soldier interview, *The Great War*, BBC TV, Part 13 *The Devil is Coming*, August 1964.

Robbie Burns and Norman Dillon from *Britain's Last Tommies*, Richard van Emden, p. 192 and p. 189.

6 Bert Chaney quoted *How it Happened. World War I*. Ed J.E. Lewis p. 232.

Archie Richards,Van Emden p. 190.

7 Otto Schulz, quoted J. Foley *The Boilerplate War*, p. 15.

Chaney, Lewis, p. 232.

Schulz, Foley, p. 15–16, 23–4.

German Infantryman quoted G. Dyer, *War*, p. 87.

8 Vic Huffam, Foley, p. 18.

Richards,Van Emden, p. 192.

9 Tank casualty figures, J.P. Harris *Men, Ideas and Tanks*, p. 65 and A.J. Smithers, *A New Excalibur,* p. 75.

Press Reports, Foley p. 26.

Richards,Van Emden. p. 192.

Chaney, Lewis, p. 233.

10 Short Note quoted in *The Tank Story,* K. Macksey, Purnell's *History of World War I.* Vol 4. p. 1638.

11 Swinton, quoted *The Royal Tank Regiment,* G. Forty. p. 13.

12 Tank name, ibid. p. 16.

Lloyd George quote. Smithers p. 55.

Huffam, Foley p. 19.

13 Doc, quote Forty p. 17–18.

Edward Wakefield, interview *Timewatch* BBC TV, *Tanks – Wonder Weapon of World War I.*

14 Tank commander, Macksey, Purnell, p. 1644.

15 Allnatt, G. Forty, p. 41–2.

16 German officer quoted by D. Chaundler, *Cambrai – The British Onslaught,* Purnell, Vol 6, p. 2420.

Bacon, J.Foley p. 129.

## The View Through the Chain Mail Mask

16 Richardson, J. Foley, p. 82.

17 Potten, Interview, *Timewatch* BBC TV.

Simpson, J. Foley, p. 10–11.

18 Simpson, J. Foley, p. 11.

Richards, Van Emden, p. 192 and 194.

19 Tank commander quote G. Forty, p. 52.

Tankodrome film, BBC *Timewatch.*

Scrutton, G. Forty, p. 42.

20 Lloyd George quoted AJ Smithers, p. 56.

Richardson, J. Foley, p. 94

21 Simpson, J. Foley, p. 160.

## Crew Ergonomics and Tank versus Tank

22 Interview Roche, from *Weapons of War – Tanks,* History TV Channel 1991, Director R. Kirk.

23 Roche, ibid. History Channel.

Lytle, J. Foley, p. 181.

24/27 Engagement at Villers Brettoneux based on quotes taken from Volckheim: *Wehrmacht* Magazine. *Die deutsche Panzertruppe im Weltkriege*, Nr 22 Nov 1938, p. 24–27.
Mitchell, J. Foley, p. 181–184 and K. Macksey, *Tank Versus Tank*, p. 34–36.

27 Tank state figures from J.P. Harris, *Men, Ideas and Tanks*, p. 185.

28 Report quote taken from 5th Tank Bde Report on *Operations with the Australian Corps. 8 Aug – 15 Aug 1918* in answer to a Tank Corps questionaire, ibid. p. 185.

## CHAPTER 2 - NEW MACHINES

29 Old-school officer quoted, *Royal Tank Corps* G Forty. p. 73.
Jackson quote *Men, Ideas and Tanks*, Harris, p. 159.

30 Tank loss figures, L. Deighton *Blitzkrieg*, p. 31.
*Strategy of the Indirect Approach,* pub 1941.

31 *I Joined the Army*, Private XYZ p. 40.

32 Fuller RUSI essay 1919, *The Application of Recent Developments in Mechanics and the Scientific Knowledge to Prepare and Train for Future War on Land.*
Tank driver Pte XYZ p. 41 and 42–3.

33 Montgomery-Massingberd, Harris p. 220.
Müller from *Geschichte des Panzer Regiments 5 1935–43*, B Hartmann, p. 14.

34 Guderian, *Panzer Leader*, p. 20.

35 Müller, Hartmann, p. 12–14.

36 Nehring, Hartmann, p. 11.

37 Homer *The Iliad*, Trans. EV Rieu, p. 189. Folio pub.

## New Men

39 Wollaston, BTM interview tape.
Goddard, *Battlefields of Life*. p. 26, 29 and 31.
Webb, 1999 BTM tape recording.
Rollins, BTM interview Jun 06.

40 Heald, BTM tape recording.

Bright, BTM doc 1997.

Becker (pen name), *The Devil on my Shoulder*. p. 16–17.

Fuchs, *Sieg Heil!* p. 42.

Eckardt, author interview, 11 Jul 06.

Carius, *Tigers in the Mud*, p. 3.

41 Metelmann, *Through Hell for Hitler*. p. 19–20.

42 Zheleznov quoted *T-34 in Action* by A. Drabkin and O. Sheremet (D&S) p. 2.

Bodnor, Ibid p. 5–6.

43 Guderian *Panzer Leader*. p. 28–29.

Webb, BTM account.

44 Webster, BTM doc Apr 98.

Goddard, *Battlefields of Life*, p. 32.

Subaltern quoted Forty, *Royal Tank Corps*, p. 105.

Recruit Pte XYZ p. 11–12.

Close, Liddle interview May 02 LEC.

Pte XYZ p. 13.

45 Rendell, BTM tape recording 1995.

Boyes, BTM interview Sep 97.

Fuchs, *Sieg Heil!* Letter 3 Aug 40 p. 72–3.

46 Bauer author interview 10 Jul 06.

Webster, BTM doc Apr 98.

Pope, *Fighting for Freedom and Fun*, p. 21.

Close, *A View from the Turret*, p. 2.

Goddard, *Battlefields of Life*, p. 34.

47 Recruit Pte XYZ, p. 15–16.

Webster, doc BTM Apr 98.

Rollins, BTM interview Jun 06.

48 Metelmann *Through Hell for Hitler* p. 19.

Köppen interview, ZDF German TV *Hitler's Children*, Dir P. Hartl and G. Knopp.

Nehring article, *Panzer und Motor im Heer* from Nehring papers: *Die deutsche Kraftfahrkampftruppe* p. 68.

Kiemig interview *Mein Krieg* German WDR TV H Eder and T Kufus 1991.

49 Becker, *Devil on my Shoulder*, p. 16–17.

Hrt-Reger interview, *Mein Krieg*.

Metelmann, p. 19.

Bauer, author interview, 10 Jul 06.

Recruit Pte XYZ p. 19.

Munns, G. Forty *Royal Tank Regiment*, p. 108–110.

50 Webster, BTM tape recording Jun 97.

Recruit, G. Forty, p. 108.

51 Training: *Tagesdienstplan 6Kp/II Abt/Pz Regt 5 25–30 Nov 1938* shown in Hartmann p. 58–59.

## CHAPTER 3 – PREPARING FOR WAR

### Designer's War

53 Mörner story from *Das Pz Regt 6 und der Spanische Bürger Krieg 1936–39*, taken from M Albrecht *Kameraden* Magazine. Dec 06. p. 8.

54 Von Thoma from *The Other Side of the Hill*. B.H. Liddle-Hart, p. 122.

German casualty figures from *Spearhead – Condor Division*, I. Westwell, p. 51. Komosol Albrecht p. 9.

Von Thoma. Liddell-Hart,, p. 123.

55 Madrid fighting, Albrecht, p. 9.

56 Mitchell, *With the British MPs who Visited Franco's Forces. Illustrated London News*. Winter/Spring 1937, taken from *Marching To War*. M. Gilbert.

*L'Intrasigent* quoted T. Jentz. Die deustche Panzertruppe 1933–42, Bd 1, p. 46.

Spanish veteran experiences Albrecht, p. 10.

57 Official German Report, Jentz, p. 46–7.

58 *Illustrated London News*. Summer 1937. M. Gilbert., p. 127.

Rendell BTM tape rec 1995.

59 Chamberlain from J.P. Harris *Men, Ideas and Tanks*, p. 252–3.

Foord, author interview, 23 May 06.

60 MacLeod-Ross, *The Business of Tanks*, pp. 45,47 and 38.

Tank design figures, J.P. Harris, p. 274.

Foord, ibid. Author interview.

61  Sec of War quoted from P. Beale, *Death by Design.*, p. 115.
    Ironside, ibid, pp. 115–16.

## Manoeuvre versus Horse War

62  Ritgen, *The 6th Panzer Division 1937–45*, p. 8.
    Guderian, *Panzer Leader,* pp. 50–51.
63  Guderian, p. 54 and 58.
    Ritgen, p. 9, 93.
    Mellenthin, *Panzer Battles*, p. xix.
    Becker, p. 18.
64  Guderian, p. 64.
65  1923 Cavalry Journal quoted M. Halstead *Shots in the Sand*. Introd.
    Howard-Vyse. *Freedom's Battle. The War on Land.*, p. 26.
66  Hobart, *Notes Reviewing Progress of Tank Brigade. 10 Nov 1933*,
    from J.H. Harris, p. 245
    Brown, BTM letter, 1995.
    Goddard, *Battlefields of Life*, p. 38.
    Pope, *Fighting for Freedom and Fun*, p. 20.
    Sprot, Liddle interview May 04, LEC.
67  Goddard, p. 44.
68  Hammerton, *Achtung Minen!*, p. 21.
    Verney, *A Dinner of Herbs, Freedoms Battle, The War on Land*, pp.
    24–5., p. 118.
    Mallard, Author interview, 4 Oct 06.
69  Mace, *Forrard: The Story of the East Riding Yeomanry.*, p. 6
    Wade, from Mace, p. 4.
    Adam, J.P. Harris, pp. 301–02.
70  The 't' i.e. 35(t) for Czech tanks denotes 'tscheshich' or 'Czech' in
    German.
71  Tank figures from W. Haupt, *Die 8. Panzer Division im 2.
    Weltkrieg.*, p. 28–9 and T. Jentz. *Die deutsche Panzertruppe 1933–
    42.* Bd 1., p. 88, and Hartmann, *Geschichte des Pz Regts 5 1939–43.*
    Bd 1., p. 80.
    Guderian. *Panzer Leader.*, p. 28.
    Carius. *Tigers in the Mud.*, p. 25. .
72  Haupt. 8.Pz. Div., p. 30.

## War

Esebeck, quoted from *Blitzkrieg In Their Own Words*, trans A. Bance (hereafter *Blitzkrieg*), pp. 17 and 18.

72 Unteroffizier, Haupt, 8 Div. p. 32.
Hertenstein, Interview, *World War II* Magazine Article *Blitzkrieg*. Mar 06. Stahlberg, *Bounden Duty*, pp. 115–16.
Rundstedt. C Carr *Poland 1939. MHQ. Vol 12. No. 1 1989.* Von Esebeck. *Blitzkrieg.*, p. 16.

73 *Halder Diary*, 31 Aug 39, p. 44.
Behr, *Blitzkrieg*, p. 12.

74 Grafenwöhr Ex from K.H. Frieser, *Blitzkrieg Legende*, p. 22.
Lossen, *Blitzkrieg*, p. 19.
Von Esebeck, Ibid, p. 16.

## CHAPTER 4 – A DIFFERENT WAR

### A Baptism of Fire

75 Mitchell, G. Forty, *Royal Tank Regiment*, p. 117.

76 Webster, BTM, Apr 98.
Bright, BTM, 1997.
Hammerton, *Achtung Minen!*, p. 17.
Balfour, Liddle interview, Dec 99, LEC.
Foord, Author interview, 23 May 06.

78 Palmer, *The War Years: 1939*, Purnell's *Eyewitness History of World War II*, pp. 28–9.
Hamilton, BTM, Letter 1997.

79 Sprot, Liddle interview, May 04. LEC.
Halstead, *Shots in the Sand,* p. 22.
Mallard, author, ibid.

80 Goddard. *Battlefields of Life*, p. 47.
Hertenstein, Interview, *World War II* Magazine. Mar 06.
Meyer, *Grenadiers*, p. 2.
Von Esebeck, *Blitzkrieg*, p. 17.

81 Behr, ibid., p. 13.

82 Report 1830 hrs. Mlawa, T. Jentz, *Die deutsche Panzertruppe.*
   *1933–42* Bd 1. p. 92.

82 Hertenstein, *World War II* Mag, Mar 06.
   Behr, *Blitzkrieg*, pp. 13–14.

84 Bünau, ibid, p. 34.
   Von Esebeck, ibid, pp. 40–41.

85 Soldier Interview, Dieter F., *Die deutschen im Zweiten Weltkrieg.*
   SWF Ger TV. *Hess & Wuermeling.* 1989., p. 1.
   Mellenthin, *Panzer Battles*, p. 7.
   Lossen, *Blitzkrieg*, p. 23.

86 Mellenthin, p. 7.
   Pries, *Blitzkrieg*, p. 26.
   Guderian, *Panzer Leader*, p. 73.

87 Meyer, *Grenadiers*, p. 5.
   Von Esebeck, *Blitzkrieg*, p. 18.
   Warsaw fighting. Jentz. *Die deutsche Panzertruppe*, p. 93–96.

## Lance Against Tank

88 Dziewanowski, Article *MHQ*, Vol 2 No.1, Autumn 89.
   Meyer, p. 2.

89 Guderian, p. 72.
   Bruno. Interview. *Die deutschen im Zweiten Weltkrieg, Der Marsch in*
   *den Krieg.*

90 Reibel from *Tank War*, J Piekalkiewicz, p. 24.
   Lossen, *Blitzkrieg*, p. 24.

91 Jastrzebski, *The War Years: 1939*, Purnell., p. 17
   Boguslawski, Personal account, LEC.

92 Col. G.I. Antonov, *Purnell's History of the Second World War*, Vol 1,
   p. 83.
   Bielenberg, interview, *Der Marsch in den Krieg, Die deuschen im*
   *Zweiten Weltkrieg*, SWF TV 1989.
   Tank figures, Jentz, p. 104 and Hartmann *Pz Regt 5*, p. 89–90.
   Mellenthin, *Panzer Battles*, p. 5.
   Becker. *Devil on my Shoulder*, p. 18–19.

### The West - No Walkover

98. *Time* Magazine article, 25 Sep 1939.

96. Halder, *War Diary*, 29 Sep 39, p. 67.

94 Von Sodenstern, K.H. Frieser, *Blitzkrieg Legende*, p. 23.

95 Hitler, *Blitzkrieg Legende*, p. 19.

79 Veh figures Ibid, p. 26–7.

80 Von Luck. *Panzer Commander*, p. 37.

96 Tank strengths, K.H. Friesler, pp. 35 & 43–44.
Rendell, interview rec, BTM 1995.
Blankley, G. Forty, *Royal Tank Regiment*, p. 118.

97 Bright, BTM, Jan 97.
Rollins, BTM, interview, 12 Jun 06.
Close, Liddle interview, May 02. LEC.
Parnaby from *Forrard: The Story of the East Riding Yeomanry*, Mace, pp. 7 & 10.

98 De la Falaise, *Through Hell to Dunkirk*, p. 3.
Moor, Mace, pp. 11–12.

99 *Daily Telegraph* Gallup Poll: 38% believed the war would last one year, 25% two years and only 37% that it would last longer than two years. More than half polled believed it would be over within three years. *Daily Telegraph* article: *Countdown to War*. 2 Sep 1999.

### CHAPTER 5 - BLITZKRIEG IN FRANCE

### Stop-start War

100 Williams, *HMT Grimsby*, Ms BTM, May 96.
Close, *A View from the Turret*, p. 5.
De la Falais, *Through Hell to Dunkirk*, p. 11.

101 Carganico, *Blitzkrieg*, p. 70.
Movement details, KH Frieser, *Blitzkrieg Legende*, pp 130 & 135.

102 Möllmann, *Blitzkrieg*, p. 76.
Stahlberg, *Bounden Duty*, p. 132.
Kielmansegg, Frieser, p. 135.

Aircraft figures, Frieser, *Kraftevergleich* chart, pp. 65 & 57–58.
De la Falaise, pp 61 & 74.

103 Charlie Brown, BBC interview above.
Dixon, from P. Mace, *Forrard. The Story of the East Riding Yeomanry*, p. 28.
Brown, interviewing BBC, ibid.
Gillison, Mace, pp. 18–19.
Novak, *Inferno* from *Mit den Panzern*, quoted Frieser, p. 196.

104 Ruby and Michard, from Frieser, pp. 193 & 196–97.

105 Joke, P. Mace, p. 6.
Dixon, diary ms LEC.

106 Möllman, *Blitzkrieg*, p. 77.
Williams, BTM ms May 96.
Eldridge, 10th Hussars account, Ron Huggins, BTM.

107 De la Falaise, p. 21.
Becker, BBC Interview, *The Other Side of Dunkirk*.

108 Le Bel, *Then and Now: Blitzkrieg in the West*, J.P. Pallud, p. 161.

## Clash of Armour

109 Becker, *Devil on my Shoulder*, p. 18.
Panzer Training Manual, *D645 – Weisung für die Gefechtsausbildung der leichten und mittleren Panzer Kompanie für das Jahr 1939*.
Becker, ibid, p. 19.
De la Falaise, p. 18.

110 Hillion, J.P. Pallud, p. 161.
German after-action reports, Pz Regt 35, Pz Regt 1, from Jentz, pp. 117–18, 122–23.
Hillion. Pallud, p. 161–62.

111 Hits on Char-B, Frieser, p. 47.
Hertenstein. *World War II: Magazine. Blitzkrieg's Beginnings*, Mar 06.

112 After-action report, 7 Kp Pz Regt 1, from Jentz, p. 129 and Frieser on radio training, p. 426.

113 Becker, Interview, BBC TV, *The Other Side of Dunkirk*.

## Where are the British?

114 Williams, BTM 96.
115 War Reporter, Christophé, p. 41.
Steinbrecher, ibid. pp. 156–59.
De la Falaise, pp. 21–2 & 46.
116–7 Ibid. pp. 93–5 & 102.
118 Von Luck, Panzer Commander, p. 40.
119 Andow. *Images of War 1939–45*, Marshall Cavendish, 1989, p. 17.
Strickland, BTM ms Dec 96.
120 'Help' request, Frieser, p. 346.
Rommel, *Rommel Papers*, ed Liddell-Hart, pp. 32–3.
121 Vaux, *War on Land*, p. 70–1.
122 Williams, BTM 96.

## CHAPTER 6 – TANK ACTION FRANCE

### Arriving

124 Close, Liddle interview, LEC May 2002.
Reeves, *Tanks in Calais 1940*, BTM May 98.
Wollastan interview. BTM. Feb 96.
125 Scott *Tank Journal* ms, *10th Hussars* by R. Huggins pp. 131 & 144.
BTM
Keller, *Third Report of Calais Operation*.
126 Reeves, ibid.
Keller, Two secret papers: *First* (p. 2) and *Third* (p. 3–4),
*Report on the Calais Operation from 3 RTR's View, 21–26
May 1940*.

### Crossing the Start Line

127–8 Dunk, Huggins, *10th Hussars* account, BTM
128 Von Luck, *Panzer Commander*, p. 56.
129–30 Krawzek and Klay, *Blitzkrieg*, pp. 143 & 155.
130 Palmer, *The War Years, 1940*, Marshall Cavendish 1990, p. 49.

## Battle and Aftermath

131 Behr, *Blitzkrieg*, p. 144–45.

132 Krawzek, p. 150–51.

133 Huggins, ibid.
Keller, *Third Calais Report*, p. 6. BTM.

136 Close, Liddle interview LEC and *A View from the Turret*, p. 19.
Dixon, diary ms, LEC.
Close, ibid, p. 20.

## CHAPTER 7 – WESTERN DESERT SEE-SAW

### 'Fox Killed in the Open'

138 Bradshaw interview, *The Desert Rats*, Marian Milne 3BM TV production

139 Colacicchi, interview *The World at War*, Thames TV

140 Rommel, quoted F.W. Mellenthin, *Panzer Battles*, p. 53.
Walter McIntyre interview, *The Desert Rats*.
Roach, *The 0815 to War*, p. 42.

141 Colacicchi interview, *The World At War*.
Belchem, quoted from *Iron Hulls Iron Hearts*, Ian W Walker, p. 42.

142 Davies interview, *The Desert Rats*.
O'Connor interview, *The World at War*.

143 Moorehead, *African Trilogy*, quoted *Freedom's Battle – The War on Land*, p. 78–9.
Chadwick, *Tank* Magazine, Vol 48. Mar 41, p. 206.
Brown account, quoted from *Desert Rats at War*, Forty, p. 68–70.

144 Joly, *Take These Men*, p. 37 and 6.
Chadwick, ibid.

146 Brown, Forty, ibid, p. 69–70.
Palmer, *The War Years*, Purnell, p. 67.
Emanuell, *Images of War 1939–45*, Purnell, p. 101.

Figures, *The Second World War*, J. Keegan, p. 148 and *Freedom's Battle*, p. 87.

Bradshaw interview, ibid.

Palmer, The War Years, p. 68.


## The Pendulum War

147 Ringler, diary entry, 20 Jul 42.

148 Forty, *Afrika Korps at War*, p. 29.

Wardrop, *Tanks Across the Desert*, p. 17.

Susenberger, Forty, p. 28.

148–9 Bradshaw and Davies interviews, *The Desert Rats*.

150 Watson, BTM.

O'Connor interview, *The World at War*.

Hauber, quoted G. Knopp, *Der Wustenkrieg*, p. 129.

Publications, *Militargeographische Beschreibung von Nord Afrika, 1940*.

151 Behr, Knopp, p. 122.

Eckardt, Author interview, 11 Jul 2006.

Mechanical failures, report, taken from Jentz, p. 159–60.

*Bartholomew Committee Final Report*, (undated) likely 1940, Part 2, Sect 4. *Defence Against Tanks*. (b)-(d).

152 Behr, Knopp, p. 134.

Moorehead, *Freedom's Battle: The War on Land*, p. 79.

5 RTR, quoted Wardrop, *Tanks Across the Desert*, p. 14 and 32.

Crisp, *Brazen Chariots*, p. 15 and 41.

Rollinson, BTM, p. 4.

153 Eckardt, author interview, 11 Jul 2006.

Dale, quoted *Taming the Panzers*. Delaforce, p. 97.

Maint, Sgt from *Roll Again Second Armoured*, Perkins and Rogers, p. 87.

154 Rollinson, BTM

Wardrop, p. 24

Crisps, pp. 16 & 17

Joly, p. 22

155 Figures, *Tank Versus Tank*, K. Macksey and *Armour in Battle Series:*

*Part 5. North Africa, 1941–2.*
Panzer kills, Jentz, p. 182.
Joly, p. 150.
Eckardt, author interview, 11 Jul 2006.
156  Witheridge, Delaforce, p. 98–9.
157  Roach, p. 26.
158  Bradshaw and Volker interviews, *The Desert Rats.*
Ling, BTM Docs, 40 pages unmarked.
Rollinson, BTM.
159  Rendell, BTM.
Figures, Macksey and *Armour in Battle*. ibid.
160  Wardrop, p. 49.
160–1  Volker interview, *The Desert Rats.*

## CHAPTER 8 – DESERT TANK BATTLE

### Reveille and Moving Off

162  Crisp, *Brazen Chariots*, p. 31.
*Notes from Theatres of War, Cyrenaica and Western Desert*, No. 10,
Jan–Jun 1942. War Office, Oct 1942, p. 2. Henceforth referred to
as *Theatre Note*.
163  *The Effects of Sleep Deprivation on Battlefield Performance*, UK Army
Staff Course Project Paper, UK Army TDRC.
Gulf War, author's experience.
Overfield, quoted *Desert Rats at War*, Forty, pp. 49–50.
*Theatre Note*, ibid, p. 16.
Everth, *Afrika Korps at War*, p. 117.
Joly, *Take These Men*, p. 69 and 147.
Schorm, diary account 30 Apr–1 May 41, *Die Deutsche Panzer-
truppe 1933–42*, quoted Jentz.
164  Crisp, p. 163.
Roach, *The 0815 to War*, p. 54.
Crimp, *World War II*, J.E. Lewis.
*Desert Warfare: German Experiences in World War II*, Sect 8 and
38.

165 Roach, p. 59.
   Joly, p. 23 and 18.


### Finding and Locating the Enemy

166 *Theatre Note.*
   Watson, p. 16, BTM.
167 Crisp, p. 20.
   Klaue, *Foxes of the Desert*, quoted Carell, p. 9.
   Quaatz, *Der Wustenkrieg*, from G. Knopp, p. 124.
   Luck, *Memoires*, p. 95.
168 Hill, *The Desert Rats at War*, Forty, p. 86.
   Wessel, *Mit Rommel in Der Wuste*, p. 41.
   Roach, p. 60
169 Rollinson, BTM, p. 1 and 4.
   Two soldier interviews, *World at War*.
   Dale, Delaforce, p. 96.
   Overfield, Forty, p. 50.
170 Close, Delaforce, p. 100.
   *German Experiences* Chapt III/*Special Factors* 11: *Heat*.
   Joly, pp. 144 and 129.
   Crisp, p. 55.
171 Close, TV interview, Discovery TV, *Fields of Armour War – The Gentleman's War*.


### Advance to Contact

171 Wardrop, diary, *Tanks Across the Desert*, p. 32.
172 Hoehne, article, *With Rommel in the Desert*, MHQ, Vol 17. No 2, p. 74–5.
   Joly, p. 272.
   Lawrence, article, *A Little Death A Little life*, MHQ, Vol 6. No 4, pp. 38–9.
173 Hoehne, Knopp, p. 144.
174 Ling, BTM Docs and *Tank Magazine, (The Journal of the RTR)*, Feb 1981, p. 34.

## Tank on Tank

175 Wollaston, BTM, p. 6.
   Reay, Delaforce, p. 94.
   *Theatre Note*, p. 16.
   Jones, *Desert Rats at War*, Forty, p. 61.
   Bradshaw, interview, *The Desert Rats*.
176 RAF report quoted Wardrop, p. 30.
   Wardrop, p. 34.
   Rendell, BTM.
177 Figures, *Cairo in the War 1939–45*, Artemis Cooper, p. 112.
178 Eckardt, author interview, 11 Jul 2006.
179 Crisp, p. 56–7.
   Schorm, diary account, *Afrika Corps at War*, Forty, p. 113 and 111.
   Joly, p. 63.
180 Ling, *Tank* Magazine, Feb 81, p. 34.
   Davies. Interview, *Desert Rats*. Roach.p. 72.
181 Joly, p. 132.
182 Watson, BTM, p. 4.

## Disengagement and the Wounded

183 *Theatre Note*, p. 17.
   Joly, p. 169.
   *Theatre Note*, ibid.
184 Bradshaw interview, *The Desert War*.
   Coglitore, quoted from *Iron hulls Iron Hearts*. I. Walker, p. 115.
185 *Theatre Note*, Ibid.
   Piscicelli-Taeggi, Walker, p. 84.
186 Schorm, Forty, p. 113.
   *Theatre Note*, p. 16.
   Joly, 198 and 201.
   Schorm, diary 1 May 41, Forty, p 113.
187 Rendell, BTM, pp. 16–17, 25.
188 Buck Kite, Delaforce, p. 105.
189 Watson, BTM, p. 3.
   Joly, p. 201.

Ling, BTM Docs.

190 Rendell, BTM, p. 26.

191 Wessel, *Mit Rommel in der Wuste*, p. 45.
Roach, p. 49.
Joly, pp. 136 and 192.
Watson, BTM, p. 4.
Vaux. Interview, *Gentleman's War*.


## CHAPTER 9 – THE RUSSIAN CRUCIBLE


### Invasion

193 Figures, *War Without Garlands* (referred to now as '*Garlands*'), R.J. Kershaw pp 24–6.
Fuchs, *Sieg Heil!*, diary 9 Apr 40, p. 57, 9 Apr 41, p. 96.
Carius, *Tigers in the Mud*, (referred to now as '*Tigers*').

194 Bauer, author interview, Jul 06.
Fadin, *T–34 in Action*, Drabkin and Shermet. (referred to now as '*T–34*'), p. 77.

195 Matveev, ibid, p. 3.
Fuchs, 20 May 41, p. 103.

196 Grimm, German *Signal* Magazine, Heft 16. 2 Aug 41.

197 Maryevski, *T–34*, p. 151.

198 Blitzkrieg petered out, *Garlands*, Kershaw, p. 98.
Fuchs. 25 Jun 41, p. 114, 17 Jul, pp. 118–119.
Infantry officer. *Die 7. Panzer Division im Zweiten Weltkrieg*. 1986, HE Manteuffel, pp. 167–8.


### The Failure of Blitzkriegs

199 KV-1 tank account, *Garlands*, Kershaw, pp 68–9.
Halder, *Diary*, 24 Jun 41, pp. 418 and 420.

200 Hertenstein, *World War II Magazine*. Mar 06.
Carius, *Tigers*. pp. 3 and 10.

201 Fuchs, 28 Jun, 41, pp 115–16.
Golikow, Kershaw, p. 108.

202 Bryukhov, *T–34*, p. 128.
203 Fuchs, 20 Oct 41, p. 145 letter to wife, 11 Jul, p. 117 and 15 Aug, p. 125.
Carius, *Tigers*, p. 67.
204 Carius, ibid, p. 7–8.
Comd 18 Pz Div. *The Eastern Front 1941–5. German Troops and the Barbarisation of Warfare*, O. Bartov, p. 20.
205 Fuchs, 15 Oct 41, p. 143.
7 Pz Div Diary, 22 Feb 42, Manteuffel, p. 273.
206 Pz Div Bartov, pp. 20, 23 and 26.
Pz details, *Die Deutsche Panzertruppe 1933–42*, T. Jentz, pp. 208–9.
Hertenstein interview *World War II* Magazine, Apr 06. 20th Pz Soldier from *Hitze, Frost und Pulverdampf*, 20th Panzer Div History, R. Hinze, p. 101.
Pz Regt 25, Manteuffel, p. 249.
Bauer author interview 10 Jul 06.
Fuchs, 11 Nov 41, 12 Nov and 2 Dec, pp. 156–8.

### Crucible of Experience – Machines and Men

208 Ritgen, *Garlands*, Kershaw, p. 70.
T-34, taken from *T34/76 Medium Tank 1941–45*, S. Zaloga and P. Sarson, p. 6.
209 Casualty figs, Zaloga/Sarson, p. 17.
210 Hertenstein interview, *World War II* Magazine, Apr 06.
Langermann from Jentz, pp 205 and 208.
Carius, *Tigers*, p. 16.
German infantryman, *In Their Shallow Graves*, B. Zeiser, 1956, p. 67.
211 Aders, *Tiger – The History of a Legendary Weapon 1942–45*, E. Klein and V. Kühn, p. 6–7.
Report, ibid, Fletcher.
212 Pz 5 figures from *Geschichte des Panzer Regiments 5*, B. Hartmann. Charts pp. 89–90 and 118–19.
213 Bauer, author interview, 11 Jul 06.
Alexeev, author interview, 1 Aug 06.
Carius, *Tigers*, p. 54.

214 Carius, ibid, p. 13.
215 Carius, ibid, p. 25.


## CHAPTER 10 – DESERT COMEBACK


### New Men

216 Allsop, author interview, 6 Dec 06.
    Williams, BTM, May 96.
    Bright, BTM, Jan 97.
217 Douglas, *Alamein to Zem–Zem*, p. 12.
    Kuhn, Hartmann, p. 170.
    Böttiger, *Im Panzer – Ich Kam Durch*, p. 27.
    Roach, *The 0815 to War.*, p. 39.
218 Brothel sign, *Love, Sex and War*, J. Costello, 1985, p. 300.
    Goddard, *Battlefields of Life*, p. 74.
219 Rollins, BTM interview, 12 Jan 06.
    Flatow, *A Personal Narrative of Alamein*, BTM, p. 8.
    Allsop author interview, 6 Dec 06.
220 Allsop author interview.
    Close, interview with P. Liddle, LEC.
    Selmayr, Hartmann, pp. 207 and 205.
221 Allsop, author interview.
    Flatow, BTM narrative, pp. 17 and 45–6.


### New Battle – El Alamein

221 Hamilton, *Armoured Odyssey*, p. 3.
223 Flatow, narrative, p. 8.
    Foord author interview.
    'Michael' story, *US Tanks of World War II*, Forty, p. 98.
224 Eckardt, author interview.
    Flatow, p. 10.
    Close, *A View from the Turret*, p. 81.
    Allsop, author interview.
225 Selmayr, Hartmann, p. 245.

226 Bright, BTM. Jan 97.

Flatow. pp. 19 and 23.

227 Eckardt, author interview.

Heimberg and Volker interviews from *The Desert Rats*, 3BM. TV 1999, M. Milne.

228–30 Flatow, pp. 26, 28–9 and 33–4.

230 Selmayr, Harmann, p. 257–8.

231 Flatow, pp. 38 and 42.

232 Müller and Kohl, interview from *Fields of Armour:The Gentleman's War*, Discovery TV, P. McKelvry.

Watt, *The Sky Lit Up*, personal account of Alamein, BTM.


## New Terrain and the Americans

232 Wardrop, *Tanks Across the Desert*, pp. 64 and 66.

233 Close, *A View from the Turret*, p. 99.

Roach, *The 0815 to War*, p. 77.

234 Wardrop, p. 68.

75mm gun decision from P. Beale, *Death by Design*, p. 96–7.

Tiger spy reports, *Tiger!*, ed. D. Fletcher, reports pp. 4 and 6–7.

235 Tigers to N Africa, *Tiger The History of a Legendary Weapon*, Kleine and Kühne, pp. 9 and 29.

Gudgin interview from, *Saving the Tiger: The Story of Tiger 131*, BTM produced DVD 2004.

236 Wardrop, p. 78–9.

Cooper, *Death Traps*, p. 4.

237 Perkins, *Roll Again 2nd Armoured*, N Perkins/M Rogers, p. 31.

238 US exercises, ibid, pp. 36, 43, 74–5.

Training facts, *Steel Victory.*, H. Yeide, p. 9–11.

Scott, *What Do we Think of the British?*, From *Yank* magazine 30 Jul 43, reproduced *Yank*, ed. S. Kluger, 1991, p. 73.

239 Patton, Perkins/Rogers, p. 41.

240 Pope, *Fighting for Freedom and Fun*.P40.

241 D'Arcy Clark, letter to parents, 15 Feb 43, LEC.

Myers, Kluger's *Yank*, p. 349..

Rohr, Hartmann, p. 283.

242 Coley, *US Tanks of World War II*, Forty, p. 103.

O'Steen, ibid, p. 105.

Rohr, Hartmann, p. 283.

Coley, Forty, p. 107–08.

243 Perkins, Perkins/Rogers, p. 122.

Casualty figures, *Famous Tank battles*, RJ Icks, p. 156.

Rollins, interview, BTM 12 Jun 06.

244 Close, *A View from the Turret*, p. 100.

Wardrop, p. 86.


CHAPTER 11 – TANK ACTION EASTERN FRONT

Assembly Area – Waiting

246 Krivov, *T–34*, p. 11.

Force numbers, *Die Schlacht um den Kursker Bogen*, K.H. Frieser from *Die Deutsche Reich und der Zweite Weltkrieg*, vol 8 ms copy, p. 3 (Hereafter Frieser).

Sacharow. Interview *Der Verdammte Krieg*. ZDF Ger TV, G. Knopp/H. Schott taken from *Bis Zum Bitteren Ende, 1. Der Feurstürm*. (Hereafter *Verdammte Krieg*).

247 Bauer letter to author.

Schmükle, interview *Timewatch*, BBC TV, *Mother of All Battles: Kursk 1943*. Prod. D. Richards/L. Rees (Hereafter *Timewatch*.)

248 Bauer author interview 11 Jul 06.

Fuchs letter, 2 Dec 41, *Sieg Heil!*, p. 157.

249 Petluk, interview *Timewatch*.

Fadin, *T–34*, p. 19.

Anon female accounts from S. Saywell, *Women in War*, 1988, p. 145.

250 Sacharow interview, *Verdammte Krieg*.

251 Kozlov, author interview 1 Aug 06.

252 Stahlberg, *Bounden Duty*, p. 161–2.

Carius, *Tigers*, pp. 7 and 114–15.

Bauer, letter to author and interview, 10 Jul 06.

254 Belov, 13 Jun 43, *Ivan's War*, C. Merridale, 2005.

NOTES

## Operational Move

255 Bauer, letter to author.
256 Carius, *Tigers*, pp. 140–41.
    Kozlov and Alexeev, author interviews, 31 Jul 06.
257 March statistics, Frieser, p. 35.
    Petluk, *Timewatch* interview.
    Zheleznov, *T–34*, p. 18.
    Bodnar, p. 56,
258 Kirichenko, p. 116.
    Fadin, ibid, p. 18.
    Roes, *Timewatch* interview.
    Bauer, author interview 10 Jul 06.
259 Kozlov and Alexeev author interviews.
    Roes, *Timewatch* interview.

## Advance to Contact

260 Tank figures, Frieser, p. 26.
    Bauer, author interview.
    Sametreiter interview, *Die SS*. Deike, Heyde and Sherer, ZDF Ger TV 2002.
261 Alexeev, ibid, 29 Jul 06.
    Steiner, B. Lewis, p. 151.
    Sagun, *Timewatch* interview.
262 Zheleznov, *T-34*, p. 159.
    Carius, *Tigers*, p. 117–19.
263 Vishnevsky, *Timewatch* interview.
    Bauer, letter to author.
264 Carius, *Tigers*, p. 118.
    Roes, *Verdammte Krieg* interview.
    Schmükle, *Timewatch* interview.

## Meeting Engagement

265 Alexeev, author interview, 29 Jul 06.
    Ger tank figures, Frieser, p. 70.

Zheleznov, *T-34*, p. 160.
266 Roes, *Timewatch* interview.
Sagun, ibid.
267 Niemann, *Tiger: The History of a Legendary Weapon 1942–45*, E. Kleine/V. Kühn, p. 55, 58 and 40.
Bauer, author interview.
Alexeev, author interview.
268 Von Ribbentrop, *Decision in the Ukraine: II SS and III SS Panzerkorps*, G. M. Nipe, 1996, p. 40.
Tank no.s Prokhorovka, Frieser, p. 36 and map.
Bryukhov *T–34*, pp. 130–1.
Shkurdalov, *Timewatch* interview.
269 Roes, *Timewatch* interview.
Steiner, Lewis, p. 157.
270 Bryukhov, *T–34*, p. 130.
271 Fadin, *T–34*, p. 89.
Bauer, letter to author.
Burning, *Ivan's War*, Merridale, p. 188.
Alexeev, author interview.
Zheleznov, *T–34*, p. 160, 168–9.
272 Hertenstein interview, *World War II* Magazine, Apr 2006.
Bryukhov, *T-34*, p. 135.
273 Sacharow, *Verdammte Krieg* interview.
Borisenko, *Timewatch* interview.
Schmükle, ibid.

**Aftermath**

274 Alexeev, author interview during pilgrimage to Prokhorovka, 31 Jul 06.
275 Becker, *Devil on My Shoulder*, pp. 28–9.
Sacharow, *Verdammte Krieg* interview.
Bryukhov, *T-34*, p. 142.
Sacharow, *Verdammte Krieg* interview.
Roes, ibid.
276 Bauer, author interview.
Steiner, Lewis, p. 165.

277 Vishnevskaya, *Arms and the Woman*, K. Muir, pp. 94–5.
Carius, *Tigers*, p. 50.
Bauer, author interview.

278 Bozhek, K. Muir, p. 94.
Borisenko, *Timewatch* interview.

278–9 Tiemann and Ehrhardt, *Chronicle of the 7.Pz Kp 1 SS Pz Div. Leibstandarte*, R. Tiemann. pp. 55, 58 and 62.

279 Gratz, *Garlands*, Kershaw, p. 175.
SS Secret reports, *Meldungen Aus Dem Reich. Die geheimen Lagerberichte des Sicherheitsdienste der SS*, Band 8, Nr 231, 23 Oct 41, p. 2914–16.

280 Hoth, *Kursk 1943*, M. Healy, p. 90.
Eight for one, K.H. Frieser, p. 100.
Alexeev, author interview 31 Jul 06.

## CHAPTER 12 – MASS VERSUS TECHNOLOGY

### Preparing Mass

281 Hamilton, *Armoured Odyssey*, p. 80.
Roach, *The 0815 to War*, p. 118.
Allsop, author interview, 6 Dec 06.

282 Rollins, BTM interview 12 Jun 06.
Allsop, ibid.

283 Hamilton, p. 80.
Roach, pp. 124 and 127.
Close, *A View from the Turret*, p. 105.

284 Jilted soldier, *From the City, From the Plough*, A. Baron, p. 11.
Whitehead, *Excerpts from the life of a Trooper*, BTM ms Aug 98, p. 17.
Wardrop, *Homecoming with all its Shocks*, BTM ms.

285 Erskine, *Desert Rats at War*, Forty, p. 228.
Roach.p. 124.
Coldstream Guards MO, *The Armoured Micks 1941–45,* ms, p. 34.
Rice, 'A Day in the Gothic Line', *Tank* Journal, May 94.

287 Close, p. 107.

Allsop, author interview, 6 Dec 06.

Douglas, *Alamain to Zem–Zem*, pp. 167 and 157.

288 Hills, *By Tank into Normandy*, p. 64.

Balfour, LEC interview P Liddle Dec 99.

Dyson Tank Twins. Preface.

Hennessey. *Young Man in a Tank*, p. 28.

Tout, lecture to MOD audience 27 Nov 86.

289 Hamilton, BTM Aug 97.

Veteran, *Warriors for the Working Day*, P. Elstob, p. 49.

Trasenster, author interview, 25 Sep 06.

Sprigg, BTM doc.

290 Hammerton, *Achtung Minen!*, p. 38.

Cox, LEC account.

Holbrook, *Flesh Wounds*, p. 114.

291 HJ Div details, *Grenadiers*, K Meyer, p. 210.

Adrien interview, *Hitler's Children*, G Knopp, ZDF Ger TV Dir.
P. Harte.

292 Damaske interview, ibid.

Müller, *Hitler's Children*, G Knopp, p. 171.

Kunze, ibid, p. 198.

293 Samtrieter interview, *Die SS*, ZDF Ger TV 02. Dir. C. Frey/G.
Knopp.

Bauer, author interview, 11 Jul 06.

Köttilitz, *Hitler's Children*, p. 218.

Meyer, *Grenadier*, p. 212.

Training details, *The 12$^{th}$ SS*, H Meyer, p. 18.

294 Heisig interview, *Die SS*.

Bastion *Hitler's Children*, G Knopp, p. 219.

Girgensöhn interview *Die SS*.

Schoeneker audio interview, BTM.

295 Girgensöhn and Stiller interviews, *Die SS*.

296 Meyer, *Grenadiers,* p. 212–14.

Boscowen, *Armoured Guardsman*, p. 4.

Carr-Gomm, 1979 LEC doc.

Films, *British Tanks At War*, Imperial War Museum DVD, 2006.

297 German training film *Nachbekämpfung Russische Panzer über die
H.D.V. Heeresfilmstelle*, 469/4.

# NOTES

Tout lecture, 27 Nov 86.
Wardrop, BTM ms.

## Mass Version Technology

298 Roach, p. 129.
Carson, author interview, 28 Sep 06.
Wardrop, BTM ms.
Captured Sherman, *Die Geschichte des Pz Regts 5 1935–43*, Hartmann, Vol 2, p. 218.

299 Gudgin, interview *Saving the Tiger: The Story of Tiger 131*, BTM DVD.
Close, p. 104.
Trasenster, author interview, 25 Sep 06.
Boscowen, p. 9.

300 Wardrop, BTM ms.
Beale, *Death By Design*, p. vii.
Montgomery and Fireflys, Beale, p. 122.
Foord, author interview 23 May 06.

302 Kursk figures, *Die Deutsche Reich und der Zweite Weltkrieg*, KH Frieser, ms copy.

303 Roach, p. 129.
Carson, author interview.
Wardrop, BTM ms.

304 Wilson, *Flame Thrower*, p. 54.

## Beliefs and Concerns

304 US figures from *Sweet Invasion*, Marshall Cavendish, *Images of War*, p. 723.
Evans interview, *Weapons at War: Tanks*, Dir. R. Kirk, History Channel TV 1991.

305 Hartman, *Tank Driver*, pp. 3, 35 and 42.
Trg figures *US Army Tank Crewmen 1941–45*, S Zaloga, pp. 14–15.
Stephens, McConnell and Holmes interviews, *Liberators: Fighting on Two Fronts in World War II*. US TV documentary, W. Miles/N

441

Rosenblum, Ch 4 TV.

307 Hennessey, p. 52.

Dyson, p. 29.

Hahn, H. Meyer, *The 12<sup>th</sup> SS*, p. 28.

308 Rommel, *D–Day*, Kershaw, p. 32.

Freiberg, *Chronicle of the 7<sup>th</sup> Pz Kp 1<sup>st</sup> SS Pz Div LAH*, R. Tiemann, p. 17.

Carius, *Tigers*, p. 20.

309 Paris observer, Janet Flanner, *New Yorker* Magazine, quoted from Time-Life, *Liberation*, p. 138.

Illegitimate children figure from Paris Immigration Services Oct 43, quoted D. Pryce–Jones, *Paris in the Third Reich*, p. 160.

310 Dyson, p. 15.

Cartland, *Love, Sex and War*, T Costello, p. 19.

Woman, Costello, p. 23.

Illegitimate births, *Images of War*, p. 728.

Weddings, Costello, p. 322.

Whitehead, BTM Aug 98.

311 Dyson, pp. 16 and 21.

'Debauchery', *The Times* newspaper quote from issue commenting on release of docs, 1 Nov 2005.

Dyson, pp. 30 and 33.

Boscowen, p. 10.

### Technological Surprise – the Funnies

312 Langanke interview, *Fields of Armour: 'Tommy Cookers'* Discovery TV 1993.

313 Hills, p. 60.

Hammerton, pp. 69 and 53.

314 Wilson, p. 38–9.

315 Hills, p. 62.

Trasenster, correspondence with author.

Hennessey, p. 56–7.

Thornton, *Steel Victory*, H Yeide, p. 47.

Omaha, *D-Day*, Kershaw, p. 114.

316 Hennessey, pp. 57–8.

Tank driver, 'The Second Front', Botting, *Time-Life*, p. 174.
Hammerton interview, *Fields of Armour*.

317 Dyson, p. 28.
Boscowen, p. 11.


## CHAPTER 13 – NORMANDY TANK FIGHTING

### Unreality to Invincibilty

318 Balfour, LEC interview, Liddle, Dec 99.
Trasenster, author interview, 25 Sep 06.

319 Marchand and Swank, *Combat Neurosis: Development of Combat Exhaustion*, *Archives of Neurology and Psychiatry*. Vol 55. 1956.
Hamilton, *Armoured Odyssey*, p. 79.
'Battle' of D–Day, *D–Day*, R Kershaw, p. 225.
Morrison, *D–Day to Berlin*, A. Willliams, p. 61.

320 Trasenster, author interview.
Tank Bn losses, *Steel Victory*, H Yeide, pp. 17–18.
Cooper, *Death Traps*, p. 31.
Balfour LEC interview and letter to father 9 Sep 44.

321 Cooper, p. 83.

322 Wilson, *Flame Thrower*, p. 60.
Trasenster, author interview.
Tout interview, *Tommy Cookers*.
Cox, BTM doc.

323 Cooper, p. 158 and interview, *Weapons at War: Tanks*. Dir. R. Kirk. History Channel 91. (Henceforth *Tanks*.)
Panther exploit, Bauer author interview, 12 Jul 06.
Balfour LEC interview.
Trasenster, author interview.
Radley-Walters interview, *The Valor and the Horror*. CBC TV 1992, Dir. B. McKenna. (Henceforth *Valor*.)

324 Sprigg, BTM doc.

325 Comd, Bn 737, Yeide, pp. 83–84.
Hamilton, pp. 79–80.

326 Heisig, Vico and Filor interviews, *Hitler's Children*, ZDF Ger TV, Dir. P. Harte.

327 Sprig, BTM doc.
Trasenster, author interview.
Kauthold and Hennessey interviews, *Tommy Cookers*.
Barrie, Canadian 3$^{rd}$ Inf Div officer, *The SS – A Warning from History*, G. Knopp, p. 268.

328 Trasenster, author interview.
Heisig, *Hitler's Children*, p. 224.
Himmler, ibid, p. 223.

329 Heisig, ibid, p. 224.
Tout, Ambridge and Hennessey interviews, *Tommy Cookers*.
Dyson, p. 59.
Wilson, p. 55.

330 Balfour, letter to father, 9 Sep 44, LEC.

331 Cloudsley-Thompson, *D–Day to Berlin*, Williams, p. 102.
Wittmann article from *Signal 1944/45* Band 5. Jahr Verlag, 1977.

332 Background to tank/air ace figures from D Grossman, *On Killing: The Psychological Cost of Learning to Kill in War and Society*, pp. 181–82 and G Dyer's *War*, p. 119.
Wittmann background material includes interview D. Taylor, author of *Villers–Bocage Tanks!* Cromwell TV Productions 1998. Dir. B. Carruthers. Roach, p. 141.

334 Holbrook, *Flesh Wounds*, pp. 167–8.
Knight, BTM letter, 30 Nov 91.

### Caution to Fear

334 Hamilton, p. 80.

335 Swank and Marchand, *Combat Neurosis* article, 1946.
Trasenster author interview.
Hills, p. 114.
Cox, LEC doc letter.
Trooper Anon, BTM doc ms, Jan 97.
Parramore, BTM, Sep 98.
Trasenster taped audio conversation with Willets passed to author.

336 Bauer and Trasenster author interview.

Balfour interview, LEC.

Holbrook, p. 139.

337 Howes, BTM ac, Mar 97.

Hamilton, BTM letter, Aug 97.

Cox, LEC letter.

Skinner, *By Tank into Normandy*, Hills, p. 90.

338 Radley-Walters interview *Valor*

Stiller, LEC ac.

Landser jargon, according to K Voss 6 Pz Div, letter to author.

339 Pock, *The 12th SS*, H. Meyer, p. 192–3.

Cooper, p. 21 and 283.

340 Balfour, letter to mother 8 Aug 44, LEC.

341 Close, p. 130.

Carson, author interview, 28 Sep 06.

342 Guderian's Situation Report to Hitler, 20 Jun 44 from T. Jentz
*Die Deutsch Panzertruppe 1943–45,* Band II, p. 177.

Air attack figs, *D–Day*, Kershaw, p. 200.

343 Pock, ibid, pp. 194 and 196.

Hartdegen, ibid, p. 197 and Pz crew, p. 196–7.

Hartdegen, ibid, p. 199.

Drescher, LEC doc.

344 Holbrook, p. 148.

Sackville-West, BTM doc.

345 Voss, letter to author.

Roach, p. 136.

Tout, MOD audience lecture, 27 Nov 86.

Combat stress figs, *Psychiatry in the British Army in the Second World War*, R.H. Ahrenfeldt, p. 165–66.

346 Trasenster, letter to author.

Survey quote, *Combat Motivation* A Kellet, 1982, p. 274.

347 Wilson, p. 74.

Bauer, author interview.

Tout lecture.

Trasenster, letter to author.

348 Holbrook, pp. 177–8 and 130.

349 Tout lecture.

350 Hennessey, p. 82.

Close, LEC interview.

Radley–Walters interview, *Valor*.

### Fear to Shell-Shock

351 Hamilton, p. 80.
Wilson, p. 77.
Wardrop, BTM ms, pp. 6, 14 and 17.
352 Hamilton, BTM doc Aug 97.
353 Hills, p. 130.
Guardsman, *The Armoured Micks 1941–45*, p. 69.
354 Waddel, BTM doc.
354–5 Close and Balfour, LEC interviews.
Balfour, letter to father, 9 Sep 44 LEC.
Carr-Gomm, LEC doc.
Cooper, p. 34.
Trasenster, author interview.
356 Religious study figs, Combat Motivation, A Kellet, p. 195.
Allsop, author interview.
Dyson, p. 61.
357 Dietrich, *The 12$^{th}$ SS*, H Meyer, p. 199.
Müller, T. Jentz, pp. 190–193.
358 Cox correspondence, LEC.
359 Young, BTM doc.
360 Balfour, LEC interview.
361 Battle Exhaustion Centres, *British Armour in the Normandy Campaign 1944*, J. Buckley, p. 194.
Young, BTM doc.

### CHAPTER 14 – TANK MEN

### The Marriage of Men and Machines

363 Stirling, *Marching to the Sound of Gunfire*, P. Delaforce, p. 111.
Cooper, p. 81.
Stirling, ibid.

364 Hills, *By Tank Into Normandy*, pp. 148–9.

365 R Simpkin, *Human Factors in Mechanised Warfare*, Brasseys 1983.

366 K. Voss, author's correspondence.
Perkins, *Roll Again Second Armoured!*, p. 104.

367 Alexeev, author interview 31 Jul 06.
Tank casualty survey, *Military Operational Research, Battle Study No 6, A Survey of Tank Casualties*, Maj. B. Wright RAMC, Mar 47. Produced by the Department of the Scientific Advisor to the Army Council.

368 Bauer, author interview, 12 Jul 06.
Josupeit and 2nd SS Bn Comd 'The Rocket–Firing Typhoons in Normandy: Two Major Actions'. Dr A. Price, *RAF Air Power Review* Vol 18. No. 1 Spring 2005. pp. 79–88.
Damage surveys, ibid.

371 Isaev, *T-34*, p. 44.
Burtsev, ibid, p. 120.
Aria, ibid, p. 58.

372 Kozlov, author interview, 1 Aug 06.

373 US Tank Bn losses *Steel Victory*, H. Yeide, pp. 101 and 116.
Abatto interview, *Tanks*, History Channel TV, 1991.
3rd and 2nd Div losses, Cooper, pp. 168–9.
Evans interview, *Tanks*, ibid.

374 McConnell interview, *The Liberators*, Miles and Rosenblum TV doc.

### Tank Men in Victory and Defeat

375 Whitehead, BTM, Aug 98.
Clegg, Oct Letters and marked Fri 22 Nov 44, LEC.

377 Brussels Trooper 'John', 1 RTR, BTM.
Gunner/Operator Cox, LEC papers.
Whitehead, BTM Aug 98.

378 Kauthold and Paris interviews *Fields of Armour: A Wave of Terror*, P. McKelvy, Discovery TV 1993. (Henceforth *Terror*).
Baumann interview, *Die Befreiung*, G. Knopp, ZDF TV 2004.
Paris interview, *Terror*.

379 Stairs interview, *Die Befreiung* ZDF TV.
Cooper, p. 182.

380  Hall, *Stars and Stripes* newspaper quoted *Voices From the Battle of the Bulge*, N de Lee, p. 260.
    Kauthold interview, *Terror*.
381  Langanke interview, *Terror*.
    McConnell interview, *The Liberators*.
    Hartman, *Tank Driver*, pp. 47, 54 and 58.
382  Hartman, pp. 61–2.
    Clegg letter, 'Christmas Night', 44 LEC.
383  Gez and Sacharow interviews, *Der Verdammte Krieg: Das Ende 1945*, G. Knopp, pp. 125 and 123.
384  Eckardt, author interview and personal correspondence.
385  Balfour, letter 6 Nov 44.
    McLeod-Ross, *The Business of Tanks*, pp. 265 and 268.
    *New York Times*, ibid, p. 274–5.
386  Cooper interview, *Tanks* and *Death Traps*, pp. 210–11.
    Carius, *Tigers*, p. 193.
    Bauer, author interview, 12 Jul 06.
    Heald, BTM doc.


## Requiem

388  Clegg, sister's letter 1999 and last letter 29 Jan 45, LEC.
    Dawson letter, 21 Feb 45.
389  Hartman, p. 107.
    70^th Bn, Yeide, p. 250–1.
    Paris interview, *Terror*.
    Carius, *Tigers*, pp. 211, 220 and 205.
390  Panzer veteran, anon author interview.
    Hamilton, BTM Aug 97.
    Stirling, Delaforce, p. 199.
    Bauer, author interview.
391  Carius, p. 213, 208 and 210–11.
392  Drescher, LEC account.
    Stirling. Delaforce, p. 199.
    Trooper 'John', Anon diary, BTM.
393  Heald and Franzen, taken from, BTM doc *The Aller Bridgehead 3 RTR*, Dec 96.

394 Elstob, *Warriors For the Working Day*, p. 280.
   Stimpson, p. 130–2.
395 Heath, Close, p. 161.
396 Bauer, author interview, 12 Jul 06.
397 Whitehead, 44 RTR, BTM Aug 98.
   Walkden, *An Account of the Final Action of a Flail Tank Crew*, LEC.
398 Walkden, ibid.
   Hamilton, *Achtung Minen!*, p. 157.
399 Roach, p. 183.
   Wilson, p. 202.

# Picture Acknowledgements

Photographs are from the author's collection and additional sources as follows: Austrian Archives/Corbis, 13 top. Ludwig Bauer, 12 middle. Otto Carius *Tigers in the Mud, The Combat Career of German Panzer Commander Otto Carius*, 1992 J. J. Fedorowicz Publishing Inc, 12 top. Bill Close *A View from the Turret, A History of the 3rd Royal Tank Regiment in the Second World War*, 1998 Dell & Bredon, 2 top. Hermann Eckardt, 5 bottom, 7. Karl Fuchs *Sieg Heil! War Letters of Tank Gunner Karl Fuchs 1937–41*, 1987 Archon Books, Shoe String Press Inc, 12 bottom. Major Stuart Hamilton *Armoured Odyssey, 8th Royal Tank Regiment in the Western Desert, 1941-42, Palestine, Syria, Egypt, 1943–44, Italy, 1944–45*, 1995 Tom Donovan Publishing Ltd, 4 bottom left, 9 top. Imperial War Museum, London, 1 top left (Q6284) bottom (Q37344), 4 bottom right (E17966), 8 bottom (E18405), 11 top (E6864), 16 bottom (BU2919). *Kriegsende in Köln* 1945/US Army, 15. *Picture Post*/Hulton Archive/Getty Images, 2 bottom, 14 bottom. popperfoto.com, 1 top right. *Signal*, 1941, 4 top left, 6 top.

Every reasonable effort has been made to contact the copyright holders, but if there are any errors or omissions, Hodder & Stoughton will be pleased to insert the appropriate acknowledgement in any subsequent printing of this publication.

# Index

Italy, war in 281–3, 285–6, 295, 319

Jagdpanther tank 367
Jagdtiger tank xvii, 367, 370, 389, 391
Joly, Lt-Maj., then Bde Major Cyril xiii, 144, 145, 154, 163, 165, 167, 170, 172, 179–83, 186, 189–90, 191
'Joseph Stalin' tank 367
JU 52 transport planes 148

Kaiser's Imperial Army 48
Kampfgruppe Schulz 393
Kasserine Pass, battle of (1943) 243, 244, 304
Kazan, Russia 35, 41, 45, 370
Keil 'spearhead' formation 172, 196, 243, 260, 265
Kharkov, Ukraine 209, 214
Kiev 202
King's Own Royal Regiment (Lancaster) 356
Kitchener, Lord 12
Kleintracktor 35
Komsomol Communist Youth Organisation 249
Kozlov, Lt. Anatoly xvi, 251, 256–7, 259, 372
Krakow 80
Krefeld, Germany 99
Krupp 35, 40, 47, 48, 172, 211
Kummersdorf army ordnance testing ground 346
Kursk xvi, 213, 247, 254, 256, 263, 264, 266, 267, 270, 273, 278–9, 280, 281, 292, 295, 302, 303, 370
KV-1 (Klim Voroshilov) tank 200, 208, 209, 276, 365

Lancers
  7/12 xii
  9th 128
  12th 98
Landships Committee 10
Leeds Rifles see under Royal Tank Regiment
Lend-Lease vehicles xvi, 372
Lenin, Vladimir 41
Leningrad 36, 202, 235
Liddell-Hart, Captain B.H. 30, 32, 33, 34, 60, 134
Ling, Capt/Maj. David xiii, 158, 165, 173–4, 180, 188, 190
Little Mother (prototype tank) 14
Little Willie (prototype tank) 11, 21

Liverpool Scottish infantry 15
Lloyd George, David 12, 20
London
  V1 Flying Bombs attack 307
  British and foreign troops in 311
London Territorial Battalion, 7th 6, 7, 9
Lothian and Border Yeomanry, 1st 335
Luck, Lt-Oberst. Hans von xviii, 66, 94, 118, 128, 167, 243, 244
Ludendorff, General Erich von 27
Ludendorff Spring Offensive (1918) 23
Luftwaffe xii, 34, 48, 71, 262, 369
Luftwaffe 88mm Flak Comd. xvii
Luftwaffe
  invasion of Poland 80, 82, 84, 86, 90, 94
  Blitzkrieg 102, 103–4, 107, 122, 138
  and invasion of Russia 197, 303
Luftflotte 1 73
Luftflotte 4 73

M-26 Pershing tanks 301–2, 313, 366, 385
M3 Grant tanks 160, 223–4
M3 Stuart Honey tank 153, 155, 168, 175, 178, 179
M11 tanks 175
M11/39 tanks 139–40, 141
M13 tanks 144, 145, 175, 184
M13/40 tanks 144
M23/40 tanks 139–40
Maginot Line 96
Mallard, Lt-Capt. John xiii, 68–9, 70, 79
Malmedy massacre (1944) xviii, 380
MAN 211
Manstein, General von 96, 245, 280, 281
Mareth Line, Tunisia 233, 234, 240, 244
Mark I infantry machine-gun tank 67, 70
Mark I Mother prototype 15, 17
Mark II tank 95
Mark IV tank 15, 22, 25, 40
Mark V tank 27, 40
Mark VI light tank 95, 108, 119, 155
Mark VIB tank 66, 67
Martel, General Sir Giffard Le Quesne 34, 60–61, 118, 223
Marval, Somme 7
Matilda tanks 106, 107, 116, 118, 120, 121, 122, 126, 142, 153, 155, 158, 216, 222, 371
  Mark I 95, 96
  Mark II 100, 135–6, 141
    Grimsby 100, 114, 122
Medium Whippet tanks 32
  A 22–3, 26
  C 29

9th 269
10th 241
12th xvi, 275
13th Motorised 63, 200, 209, 272
15th 150, 225, 228, 230
18th 204–5, 205
20th 195, 206
21st xviii, 148, 150, 156, 163, 167, 225, 230, 233, 241, 317
116 357
*Kempf* 82
*Lehr* Divisions 308, 317, 323, 342, 343
Panzer Group Kleist 96, 101, 112
Panzer Heavy Tank Battalion (Schwere Panzer-Abteilung)
501 235
502 387
503 267, 322
504 235
Panzer Mark I tank 35, 43, 45, 53, 54, 55, 62, 70, 71, 87, 95, 212, 302
Panzer Mark II tank 70, 71, 87, 186
Panzer Mark III tank 57, 58, 71, 82, 92, 112, 151, 152, 153, 155, 175, 179, 180, 181, 186, 209, 210, 220, 222, 230, 234, 263, 276, 293, 294, 384
Panzer Mark IV tank 57–8, 71, 72, 73, 81, 83, 92, 111, 113, 120, 131, 152, 153, 155, 181, 205, 210, 211, 220, 221, 230, 234, 258, 261, 264, 265, 269, 275, 279, 289, 293, 328, 338, 343, 384, 393
Panzer Mark V *Panther* 212, 213, 265, 298, 302, 303, 321, 323, 324, 330, 338, 357–8, 367, 396
Panzer Mark VI *Tiger* xvii, 211–12, 213, 215, 234–6, 241, 243, 252, 264, 265–6, 271, 278, 298–9, 300, 302, 304, 308, 322, 323, 332, 333, 344, 367, 393
Panzer Regiment 4 72, 80, 82, 205
Panzer Regiment 5 xviii, 44, 51, 53, 61, 84, 85, 93, 148–51, 163, 212, 217, 220, 230, 298
6th Company 179
8th Company 167
I *Abteilung* 241, 242
II *Abteilung* 225
Panzer Regiment 6 53, 55, 74, 85, 86, 90
Panzer Regiment 7 82
Panzer Regiment 8 xvii, 149, 153, 155, 178, 223, 231, 384, 385, 402
Panzer Regiment 11 366
Panzer Regiment 21 210
Panzer Regiment 25 120, 196, 273

Panzer Regiment 29 252
Panzer Regiment 33 xvi, 46, 206, 213, 248, 252, 255, 293, 323, 347, 368, 390
Panzer Regiment 35 84
Panzer Regiment 36 45
Panzer Regiment 130 343
Panzergrenadier Regiment 104 147–8
*Panzergruppen* 193, 202
*Panzerjäger Abteilung* 42 120
Panzerwaffe 57, 193, 194, 220, 245, 331
number of tanks 34
Guderian becomes Chief of Staff 36
recruitment and training 40–41, 44–5, 48–9, 71
and the *Anschluss* 62
supply services 62–3
features in mass displays 64
firing 172–3
use of *Keil* formation in Russia 260
increasing reliance on technology 280
success in tank design race 302
philosophy of 365
Paris 308–9, 377
liberation of 364
Passchendaele, battle of (1917) 15
Patton, General George S. 239–40, 302, 363, 374, 380
Pearl Harbor (1941) 236
Perham Down, Wiltshire 58, 394
'Phoney War' (*Sitzkrieg*) 99, 125
*plavainschchiva* tanks 41
Poland
invasion of (1939) 71–4, 79–94, 104, 131, 135–6
revolt against the German garrison 362
Polish air force 90
Polish Army
1st Polish Lancers 91
OMS mechanised brigade 73
Pomorska Cavalry Brigade 89
Suwalki Cavalry Brigade 88, 89
Polish Corridor 79, 86
Porsche, Professor 211, 212
Porsche AG 211
Posen, Poland 87, 93
Prague, occupation of (1938) 64
Prokhorovka 257, 259, 265, 268–9, 273, 276, 277, 278

Queen's Bays (2nd Dragoon Guards) 39, 128, 282
Queen's Own Cameron Highlanders: 5th Battalion 396
Queen's Own Yorkshire Dragoons 240